BUSINESS
FINANCE
FOR
MANAGERS

3RD EDITION

BUSINESS
FINANCE
FOR
MANAGERS

AN ESSENTIAL GUIDE TO
PLANNING, CONTROL & DECISION MAKING

RAY FITZGERALD

KOGAN
PAGE

First published as *Practical Finance* in 1987 by The Irish Management Institute, Dublin

First published in Great Britain in 1990 by Kogan Page
Second edition published in 1992
Third edition published as *Business Finance for Managers* in 2002

Kogan Page Limited
120 Pentonville Road
London N1 9JN
United Kingdom
www.kogan-page.co.uk

British Library Cataloguing in Publication Data

A CIP record for this book is available from the British Library.

ISBN 0 7494 3850 9

Typeset by JS Typesetting Ltd, Wellingborough, Northants
Printed and bound in Great Britain by Biddles Ltd, Guildford and King's Lynn
www.biddles.co.uk

Contents

Part IV. Finance techniques for developing the organization

Preface

Have you ever wondered what is the most inappropriate job title used in business? In the era when shareholder value has belatedly been recognized as the key financial objective of business, I think it is 'financial controller'. Everybody who has the authority to spend money on behalf of his or her business is a real financial controller. This does not mean that to be an effective manager you need an accounting qualification. It does mean that you need to be tuned in to the financial consequences of the decisions you make. The big decisions are made by the board or by the management committee. These decisions often have a major effect on future profitability and financial stability. Are you properly equipped to participate in the vote on major actions that will impact on shareholder value? If not, then I believe this book is ideal for you. It will help you to understand financial statements and analyses. It will allow you to be comfortable with financial jargon and performance measurement.

I have often noticed managers or directors from non-accounting backgrounds switching off when financial matters are being discussed at meetings. This is not acceptable when the wrong decision can damage future performance and even put the very survival of an organization at risk. The startling reality is that even highly skilled chief executives and finance directors can sometimes put forward inappropriate proposals. As a voter on the decisions you need to be armed to ask the questions that will reveal any errors in assumptions about proposals that are on the agenda. If you don't and a major decision goes really sour, then the business may collapse. The investors may recover nothing from the liquidation. They will rightly blame each member of the committee who voted on the fatal decision. In this environment every director and manager must have the skill to look behind the figures and ask the questions that may reveal defects in the underlying assumptions. To develop this skill requires that you accumulate knowledge and practice in financial analysis and decision making. The knowledge part of this skill acquisition is at the core of this book. In more than 30 years of training non-accounting managers in financial decision making I have accumulated the knowledge to show you how to assess complicated proposals and identify potential pitfalls. The skill you will acquire through diligent study of this book will equip you to be a valuable contributor to company meetings. Through reading the book you will:

- become comfortable with the language of finance;
- learn how to read and interpret management accounts and audited accounts correctly;
- become skilled at identifying strengths and weaknesses in financial statements and budgets;
- realize that cash is the lifeblood of a business and that bad decisions lead to dire shortages of it;
- recognize the fact that profit is not always accompanied by extra cash and that in most businesses a high growth rate will dramatically consume cash;
- recognize your role in taking action when unfavourable variances are revealed in management accounts and in identifying whether such variances are one-offs or ongoing;
- realize that not all your products or services are profitable and that faulty analysis of product costs can lead to an inappropriate sales and marketing strategy;
- learn that operating in world markets leads to exposure to exchange rate losses and how to minimize the risk of such losses;
- realize that capital investment proposals and mergers and acquisitions can change the financial profile of your organization dramatically and not always for the good;
- realize that a defective strategy can destroy shareholder value and understand how such value is estimated.

All these gems will help you to become a more rounded manager, director or both. This is what you must become if you want to be a valued contributor to financial decision making.

In the book I have tried to steer a middle course between being too technical and too superficial. I think I succeeded in covering all the important and topical issues. In some cases I have suggested alternative sources of information for those who wish to examine a particular topic in greater detail now that the foundations are solidly laid.

I hope that you will approve of my aspirations and the way that I have tried to meet them. I recommend that you read the book in short bursts, as it will require excellent concentration if you are to learn how to respond effectively to the things you will learn. You will probably need to read some sections several times and to keep notes if you are to get full value from the text. When you have finished I recommend that you keep it on your office bookshelf. It is intended as a practical guide to financial decision making. You may need to refer to it when you find major issues with a financial dimension in board papers. I hope the book will be a constant ally in years to come. This is particularly true if your business is too small to justify the full-time employment of a skilled financial manager. Good reading and financial decision making.

Acknowledgements

It took a great deal of help, tolerance and understanding on the part of a variety of people and organizations to bring this book to market. I would particularly single out my wife and three sons who strongly supported my endeavours and accepted some inattention to family duties during the various stages, and the specialists who assessed the text for technical accuracy and appropriateness of illustrations.

I would also like to thank my publishers, printers and literary agent who helped me through the various complications involved in getting the book into the market place.

To all the above and the many colleagues and businesses whose ideas and practice I adopted in the text I wish to express my warmest appreciation for their help and support along the way.

Abbreviations

ABC	activity-based costing
diluted EPS	the earnings that would have been generated for shareholders had all options to buy shares been exercised
EPS	earnings per share: the earnings generated for shareholders
EVA	economic value analysis: the application of a shareholder value test to capital investment proposals
FASs	financial accounting standards: the rules that apply when recording and reporting complex transactions in the United States
FIFO	first in first out: a logical system for the rotation and valuation of stock
FRA	forward rate agreement: a financial instrument designed to guarantee the proceeds of a foreign currency sale to be collected at a future date or the cost of a foreign currency purchase to be settled at a future date
free cash flow	the cash generated that is not required for day-to-day operations, and can be used to develop the business or to pay dividends
FRSs	Financial Reporting Standards: the rules created by the Accounting Standards Board for the reporting of complex accounting transactions in the British Isles

GAAP	generally accepted accounting principles: the framework around which accounting standards are designed to record and report complex transactions
IASs	international accounting standards: the international rules on how complex transactions should be recorded and reported. In some cases there are significant differences between the treatment required by FRSs and SSAPs. At the moment FRSs override IASs but there are substantial moves towards harmonization
IRR	internal rate of return: the maximum rate of interest that a capital investment project could afford to pay and still be able to repay the capital and interest to the funds provider
LIFO	last in first out: a system of stock valuation popular in the United States
MIRR	modified internal rate of return: a recent improvement to capital investment appraisal techniques that caters for a fundamental flaw in IRR
NPV	net present value: a technique designed to convert future cash inflows and cash outflows to their value at the point of appraisal
PAT	profit after tax
PBIT	profit before interest and tax (often referred to as operating profit)
PBITDA	profit before interest, tax, depreciation and amortization: a relatively new measure of profit that is designed to approximate to free cash flow
PBT	profit before tax
PE	price earnings ratio: the current share price of a business divided by the latest earnings per share (EPS)
PEG	the relationship between the growth in sales of a business and its PE. Any business in which sales are expected to grow faster than the PE is worth considering as an investment opportunity
ROE	return on equity: a test of profitability that relates the profit before or after tax to the shareholders' investment
ROI	return on investment: a test of profitability that relates the operating profit (PBIT) to the total assets owned by a business
SSAPs	Statements of Standard Accounting Practice: rules for accounting for complex transactions issued by the

Accounting Standards Committee (the predecessor of the Accounting Standards Board) that still apply in the British Isles

SV   shareholder value: the modern approach to assessing the value that will be created or destroyed by the strategy of a business

WACC   weighted average cost of capital: the service cost of the basket of funds raised by a business to pay for development initiatives

1

Introduction

Many books on finance for non-accounting managers are available in the UK. Most focus on rules and concepts. The balance tends to be 70 per cent concepts and 30 per cent examples/applications. This book is different: its emphasis is on application. The principles that affect each topic area are developed, then illustrations and advice are used to ensure that the reader will be able to apply the ideas as they are learnt.

Financial management is not difficult. The key rule is to make sure enough cash is coming in to cover your outgoings and put a bit by for a rainy day. What makes it seem difficult is the use of jargon developed by experts to make it appear so. My major objective in writing this book is to help non-experts to understand the financial jargon, the techniques that the jargon describes and the opportunities such techniques offer to improve financial performance.

The book is designed for people from non-accounting backgrounds who recognize that financial decision making is not the sole province of accountants. It is a task in which everyone responsible for creating or spending significant amounts of cash must participate. The book was written for those from non-accounting backgrounds who wish to make a worthwhile contribution to financial decision making. It will be particularly relevant to managers in organizations that:

- Do not make enough sales to justify the cost of a professional finance manager. A non-expert must try to fit the accounting obligations into a diverse schedule in which other priorities may seem to be regarded as more important.
- Like to make fast creative financial decisions and are disenchanted with their conservative finance manager. When one or two attractive opportunities have been missed, due to agonizing over proposals, a company may be tempted to by-pass the accounting function in making important corporate finance decisions.
- Have a finance manager who views his or her role as to keep the books accurately and is not sufficiently active in the development of the organization's financial capability.

In these cases senior managers, responsible for significant movements of cash, must have the knowledge and skill to ensure that decisions with a financial dimension will improve the profitability and stability of the business.

CRUCIAL ERRORS IN FINANCE

A number of major errors can leave an organization exposed to the danger of receivership or liquidation. The following brief summary of these errors should inspire you to study the causes and the ways of avoiding the consequences as explained in detail in subsequent chapters:

- Borrowing too much.
- Borrowing from expensive sources when cheaper ones are available. Small companies often pay high interest rates, which their present and future profit potential cannot adequately service. It is sad but true that borrowing is cheaper and easier to arrange in large, established, profitable businesses and dearer and more difficult to arrange in recently established, smaller or less profitable businesses. Many of the most attractive funding forms are totally closed to small business borrowers.
- Committing a business to repay borrowings more quickly than the future cash will permit. (Would you raise a £1 million overdraft to acquire an apartment on the London docks?)
- Spending too lavishly. This can include:
  - making or buying products or services that your customers do not want;
  - palatial offices, equipment, vehicles, etc that the business cannot afford. This is often a smokescreen used by businesses in trouble.

Shrewd bankers see through it. Management would be wiser to aim for a modest survival than a lavish route into liquidation;
- inattention to cost control. Examples include: poor productivity, excessive waste, pilferage, breakage, rework etc, and clichés such as, 'that's the way we always did it' or 'if we spend only 5 per cent more than last year we will be doing well!'
- Not keeping the product range and manufacturing technology up to date.
- Failing to ensure an adequate contribution from the owners towards the cost of identifying and launching new products or services. Owners contribute in two ways. They can be asked: a) not to withdraw all of the profits – some must be retained to contribute towards funding expansion or modernization; and b) to give more capital to the business – this is called a rights issue. Shareholders are given the right to buy new shares in proportion to their existing holdings. These requests may fall on deaf ears if the past profits (the only justification for their existing investment) were disappointing, or the future prospects are discouraging.
- Overdependence on one customer. You can be squeezed for excessive credit or discounts. If the customer collapses the consequent bad debt may wipe you out.
- Poor control of high-risk business development. Examples include inappropriate take-overs, currency or commodity speculation, and ill-conceived capital investments.

These faults are easy to list. They are not easily identified in a business. If they *are* identified, a strategy must be developed to eliminate or mitigate them. The correct way to formulate such a strategy will emerge as you work your way through the book.

THE CONTENT AND SEQUENCE OF THE BOOK

Part I, Chapters 2 to 5, is designed to give readers a thorough understanding of the purpose and content of financial statements and the ways of putting correct monetary values on the items in the statements.

Part II, Chapters 6 and 7, deals with testing financial statements for strengths and weaknesses and developing plans to build on the strengths and minimize the impact of the weaknesses. It is akin to a medical that helps a manager to write a prescription for financial health.

Part III, Chapters 8 to 11, examines how to plan and control the finances of a business, while Part IV, Chapters 12 to 16, deals with corporate finance techniques designed to develop the organization.

Matters not included in the book

Detailed analysis of the methodology of bookkeeping is not covered. Most businesspeople don't need to understand and involve themselves in recording transactions. Those who wish to do the bookkeeping will find that there are many suitable textbooks and courses available. We start with the output from bookkeeping. This is when senior managers become involved in financial planning, control and decision making.

Conceptual frameworks that are part of some academic treatments of finance but are rarely used in practice are not included. I concentrate on methodologies that are tried and tested and extensively used in UK industry.

The book does not deal with financial manipulation aimed at prolonging the life of a dying business and fraudulent treatment of lenders and customers. Nor does it cover financial statements other than those of limited companies and public liability companies. Business promoters are advised to seek the protection of limited liability where permitted.

Using the book

The book is designed to provide a comprehensive understanding of practical finance. Three major points about using the book effectively are:

1. You can't expect to retain all relevant information from a quick reading. Deep concentration is required to derive full value from the content. Short reading sessions spread over several weeks are recommended. Many chapters will provide additional insights at a second reading.
2. It is unlikely that you can remember and apply all the concepts as you work through the book. I hope you will find a space for the book on your office bookshelf and revisit it frequently, to remind yourself of the relevant practice as important issues arise.
3. To get the best out of the book a reader must trace his or her way through the illustrations very carefully, not simply read them like a novel. If an illustration is difficult to understand or apply in your company, ask a friend or colleague, with a sound financial knowledge, for a little help.

The world of corporate finance is changing rapidly. Since the first edition of this book was published in 1987 significant changes have taken place. These include:

●   the introduction of the Financial Reporting Standards (FRSs) the framework for accounting;

- changes in VAT and corporation tax rates;
- economic and currency volatility that make financial planning and control very difficult;
- improved approaches to product, service and customer profitability analysis;
- the era of the mega-merger;
- 'unbundling';
- acceptance of shareholder value as the financial imperative.

I predict many further changes. Predictions that hardly require a crystal ball include:

- changes in taxation as part of EU harmonization;
- movement towards international accounting rules and statement formats – there are substantial differences between the standards and formats in different parts of the world (see below);
- inclusion of the UK in the euro currency;
- more mega-mergers;
- an increasing demand that accountants should help to make accounts more meaningful and to provide clearer insights into what is really happening in the business that is being reported.

The list is terrifying. Some vital issues of the 21st century will inevitably not have been addressed. Some illustrations will become dated. We can't afford to wait until the situation stabilizes; it never will. In spite of inevitable changes I predict that 90 per cent of the content of this book will be as relevant in five years' time as it is now. The effective manager will understand and apply this 90 per cent. He or she will also monitor changes in business thinking and legislation that affect planning, control and decision making as they emerge.

I wish you good reading and good fortune in applying the ideas. I hope the book will help you to survive and thrive in the battleground of business.

GENERALLY ACCEPTED ACCOUNTING PRINCIPLES

Generally accepted accounting principles (GAAPs) are the overall framework within which the treatment of complex transactions are recorded and reported. It may horrify you to learn that GAAPs and the accounting standards that implement them are not the same in all parts of the world. As a consequence, an accountant in the United States could arrive at very different results from his or her counterpart in the UK even if both were recording and reporting exactly the same transactions. Many UK businesses have significant ownership of their shares by US investors. Such businesses often choose to present the results as they were computed using US GAAPs and financial accounting standards (FASs) in the notes to the accounts. The results can be materially different from the UK version because of variations in principles and applications. For example, in a recent set of results the UK accounts for Imperial Tobacco Group plc showed a profit after tax of £347 million. The comparable figure when US GAAPs were applied was £323 million. The differences resulted from additional amortization of £17 million and additional provision for deferred tax of £7 million required under US rules.

Major moves towards harmonization of principles and standards are taking place as I write. The most notable trend is that standard setters in most countries have accepted that principles and application of standards should be the same regardless of the country in which they are applied. The implication of this in the British Isles is that when new standards are being created or existing standards revised, a great deal of attention is given to ensuring that the rules comply with emerging international approaches. These transnational approaches are found in international accounting standards (IASs). World-wide consensus on the way that complex transactions should be recorded and reported is still some distance away. Nevertheless, substantial progress is being made, notably in the treatment of a) pension fund assets and obligations; b) deferred tax; and c) goodwill amortization. I forecast that the majority of complex transactions will be recorded and reported in the same way, regardless of the country in which they are computed, within the next five years.

Part I

The purpose and content of financial statements

2

The profit and loss account

There are three major financial statements:

1. The profit and loss account.
2. The balance sheet.
3. The cash flow statement.

Directors, shareholders and managers need to understand the purpose of and conventions used in such reports. The business media place a huge emphasis on earnings when dissecting the financial results of plcs. For this reason we start with the profit and loss account.

THE PROFIT AND LOSS ACCOUNT

The profit and loss account reports the sales achieved and costs incurred over a period of time. It can be prepared in two significantly different formats.

First, there are management accounts. These often contain substantial detail about income and expenditure. Results are normally compared against the budget so as to measure progress. These accounts are prepared after each accounting period. They are valuable to managers and to directors in that they promote a culture of analysis, feedback and corrective action. Second, there are financial accounts. These are prepared for shareholders and contain comparatively little detail. Progress is measured by comparison with the previous year.

A simple example of the difference between the volume of information contained in management accounts as compared to financial accounts is the presentation of sales data. In financial accounts a single figure is normally disclosed unless segmental analysis is required, as described at the end of the chapter. In management accounts the sales figure may be reported by representative, geographic area and product or product group.

THE MEASUREMENT OF PROFIT OR LOSS

The concept of profit or loss is straightforward. If sales and other income exceed operating costs then a profit is earned. If sales and other income fall short of operating costs a loss is incurred. Company law lays down the format in which the profit and loss account is presented. Our first example is shown in Table 2.1.

Table 2.1 *The format for a profit and loss account*

£'000	Last year	This year
Sales	2,086	2,389
Cost of sales	1,235	1,358
Gross profit	851	1,031
Overheads	598	695
Profit before interest and tax	253	336
Interest	139	149
Profit before tax	114	187
Corporation tax	21	26
Profit after tax	93	161
Proposed dividend	36	45
Retained earnings	57	116

The collection of figures for entry in the profit and loss account is based on a series of conventions. Readers need to understand these conventions if they are to interpret a profit and loss account correctly. The conventions are summarized below. The computations involved are explained in a series of illustrations through the chapter.

Accounting conventions on which the preparation of a profit and loss account is based

A profit and loss account is not a cash document. It is prepared using a) sales that may be greater or less than collections from customers; b) purchases that may be greater or less than supplier payments; c) the actual costs for the accounting period whether paid for or not. Accruals and prepayments must be made in arriving at and reporting these costs; d) depreciation charges designed to reflect the loss of value that is incurred by using such items as machinery and vehicles in the business. The costs are reported in two categories. First, the costs incurred in acquiring or creating the product or service for sale are aggregated and reported as cost of sales. Second, the support costs such as marketing, distribution and administration are aggregated and reported as overheads. When these costs have been deducted from the sales the residue is the profit before interest and tax. This is often called the operating profit. Later in the book I will frequently use the abbreviation PBIT to describe this level of profit.

If a company has borrowings, the resultant interest cost must be reported. Calculation of the interest cost is straightforward in the case of overdrafts and term loans but can be quite complex in the case of hire purchase. Any interest receivable is deducted from the interest payable and the net amount is reported. After deduction of the net interest we arrive at the next level of profit called profit before tax, referred to later using the abbreviation PBT.

If a company makes a profit then this profit is exposed to corporation tax. The standard rate is currently 25 per cent with a small company rate of 20 per cent. The corporation tax bill must be provided for when preparing financial accounts even though it will not become due for payment for some time after the end of the financial year. The estimated corporation tax bill is deducted from the PBIT to leave the profit after tax, referred to later using the abbreviation PAT.

When a company makes a profit after tax, the directors must decide what level of dividend, if any, will be paid. The dividend decision is influenced by whether the business is growing or not. Growing businesses need to retain some profits to contribute to the funding of growth. In the profit and loss account provision is made for the proposed dividend even though it will not be paid until approved by shareholders at the AGM. After providing for the proposed dividend the balance remaining is the retained earnings. These are really an additional investment by the owners of the business.

A variety of pieces of supporting information must be provided and these are usually reported in the notes that accompany the profit and loss account.

THE NINE MAJOR TYPES OF INCOME

The nine major types of income are as follows:

1. Sales of products or services.
2. Rent charged to tenants/users of our assets.
3. Income from investments.
4. Earnings of related companies.
5. Interest earned on deposits.
6. Commissions.
7. Royalties.
8. Gains derived from favourable currency movements.
9. Settlement discounts from suppliers.

Each type of income is examined below.

Sales of products or services

The majority of the income earned by most organizations is from sales of their products or services. To understand sales income we need to resolve seven questions.

1. If we charge VAT when making a sale should this be included in our income? *Answer:* it should not. VAT is simply an add-on to the charge to customers, which the government obliges business to make. It will be paid to the tax authorities after deducting VAT on chargeable inputs. A business must make its profit from the sales net of VAT. This is one of the major rules of accounting that we will encounter at various stages in the book. These rules are contained in Statements of Standard Accounting Practice (SSAPs) and more recently Financial Reporting Standards (FRSs). The rule for accounting for VAT is in Paragraph 8 of SSAP 5. Turnover shown in the profit and loss account should exclude VAT on taxable outputs. If it is desired to show the gross turnover, the VAT relevant to that turnover should be shown as a deduction in arriving at the turnover exclusive of VAT.

2. If we pay excise duties and include these duties in the price charged to our customers, is the proportion of the sales price, which represents the

duties, included in income? *Answer:* surprisingly, yes. While VAT charged to or by us is excluded from income and expenditure, excise duties are not.

3. If we sold goods on credit and have not been paid for them by the end of the accounting period, will the value of these items be included in the profit and loss account? *Answer:* they should be. In spite of the propaganda used to stimulate cash collection that 'a sale is not a sale until it is paid for', credit sales not yet collected are treated as income.

4. If we sell goods subject to a retention of title clause until settlement is received, can these sales be regarded as income? *Answer:* yes. Sales covered by a retention of title clause are income.

5. If we sold goods that have not been paid for by the end of the accounting period, and we believe there are grounds for thinking the debt is not collectable, should these sales be included in income? *Answer:* yes. The sale is bona fide. If the debt is doubtful or uncollectable, allowance should be made in computing our expenditure and in determining the balance sheet value.

6. If we sold goods that are the subject of a dispute about quality, and we expect they will have to be taken back for full credit, should these sales be included in our income? *Answer:* no. It would be unwise to include them as income. The facts seem to indicate that the profit element will not be realized. Indeed, if we are liable for the cost of carrying the goods back to our stores, we should allow for this in computing our expenditure.

7. If we sold goods subject to a trade discount of 15 per cent and a settlement discount of 2 per cent for prompt payment, is our sales income a) 100 per cent, b) 85 per cent, or c) 83.3 per cent? *Answer:* 85 per cent. The trade discount reflects the true price we charged our customer and should be deducted in reporting the sales figure. At point of sale we do not know whether the customer will avail themself of the settlement discount or not. If we subsequently find that the customer takes the cash discount then this discount will be recorded as a cost.

So, a comprehensive definition of income is: *the value of goods or services sold to customers:*

- whether paid for or not;
- excluding VAT but including excise duties;
- after allowing for probable returns but ignoring potential bad debts;
- after deducting trade discounts but not settlement discounts.

Self-test: Income calculation

The following is the price structure of a small business:

Bought-in materials	20
Conversion costs	12
Total cost	32
Add profit margin	8
	40
Add VAT (17.5%)	7
Selling price	47

The following information relates to sales for a week:

20 items were sold.

A trade discount of 10 per cent was allowed on two of them. These have not yet been paid for.

Eleven items sold at full price have been paid for. Five customers took the 2 per cent cash discount offered for prompt settlement.

One item sold at full price is defective and will be returned to us for full credit.

One item sold at full price is now regarded as uncollectable.

You are asked to calculate:

a. The income for the week.
b. The debtors at the end of the week.
c. The VAT liability.
d. Expenditure that must be recorded as a result of the above information.

When you have answered the four questions you should check your figures with the solution in the Appendix at the back of the book.

Rent charged to tenants/users of our assets

Rental income is illustrated as follows.

We are preparing a profit and loss account for the year ended 30 June 2002. Our tenant rents a room from us on a calendar year basis and has paid £500 rent for the calendar year 2001 on 3 January 2001, and £600 rent for the calendar year 2002 on 5 January 2002. Rental income is:

	£
1 July to 31 December 2001	250
1 January to 30 June 2002	300
Total rent earned	550

Half of the rent for 2001 had been received in advance at 30 June in that year. This would have to be carried in the balance sheet at that date as unearned income. It will be earned in the financial year to 30 June 2002. Similarly, half of the 2002 rent has not yet been earned as at 30 June in that year. It will be carried as unearned income in the balance sheet at 30 June 2002. If the rent for 2002 had not yet been received it would still be recorded as income unless it was felt to be uncollectable.

Income from investments

Investments in other businesses are classified in three categories. There are those that confer control, significant influence, or neither control nor significant influence.

When a company controls another business all the sales, costs, profits or losses are included in the group profit and loss account. This is easy to do when all the shares are owned by the investing group and more difficult when some shares are owned by third parties; see Table 2.2 (p 16). In this case 25 per cent of the profit of the subsidiary was earned on behalf of non-group shareholders. Their share of the profit after tax, called a minority interest, is deducted in computing the profit earned for group shareholders.

Where an investment confers significant influence the investor must prepare group accounts. In the case of such investments the appropriate share of that company's profit or loss is brought into the profit and loss account.

Earnings of related companies

Earnings of related companies in group accounts are now illustrated. Tree Ltd holds 40 per cent of the shares of Branch Ltd. The group accounts are shown in Table 2.3 (p 16).

The income earned from investments that confer neither control nor significant influence is easiest to calculate. Only dividends received are taken into the profit and loss account as income. Dividends proposed but not yet paid are ignored until the year in which they are received. This is because the AGM of that company could cancel or reduce the dividend.

Table 2.2 *Differences in income according to shareholding*

Income earned from a 100% shareholding in another business

£'000	Parent	Subsidiary	Group
Operating profit	600	240	840
Corporation tax	150	60	210
Profit after tax	450	180	630

Income earned from a 75% shareholding in another business

£'000	Parent	Subsidiary	Group
Operating profit	600	240	840
Corporation tax	150	60	210
Profit after tax	450	180	630
Minority interest			45
Profit for ordinary shareholders			585

Table 2.3 *Profit and loss account, Tree group*

£'000	Tree plc	Branch Ltd	Group
Sales	10,000	4,000	10,000
Operating profit	1,000	615	1,000
Income of associate			246[1]
			1,246
Corporation tax	240	150	300[2]
Profit retained	760	465	946

Notes:

[1] £615,000 × 40%.

[2] £240,000 + (£150,000 × 40%).

£186,000 will be added to the value of the investment and to the reserves in the group balance sheet. Only the group figures are published. I gave you the figures for the individual companies to show you how the group figures are derived. Note that if the associate had made a loss then this loss would have to be deducted in preparing the group accounts.

16

Interest earned on deposits

Interest income is computed as follows:

1. establish the interest received in the year;
2. deduct any proportion of this earned in previous years. It has already been brought into income;
3. add interest earned but not received at the end of the year.

To illustrate this I will assume that the financial year of Surplus Ltd ended on 30 September 2001. It had £50,000 on deposit at 10 per cent pa from 1 October 2000 to 30 June 2001. From 1 July 2001 to 31 March 2002 it had £50,000 on deposit at 8 per cent pa. The interest is calculated quarterly and paid half yearly at 31 December and 30 June. Surplus Ltd is calculating the interest for the year ended 30 September 2001:

	£
Interest received on 31 December 2000	1,250
Interest received at 30 June 2001	2,500
Interest receivable at 30 September 2001	1,000
	4,750

Where the amount on deposit or the interest rate fluctuates, the depositor will seek a certificate of interest receivable for inclusion in its income.

Commissions

Commission is the main source of income for some businesses, eg auctioneers, stockbrokers and insurance brokers. Commission received and receivable is included in income. The amounts not yet collected (excluding possible bad debts) are debtors and will be recorded in the balance sheet.

Royalties

Royalties can be an important source of income for businesses that license or franchise their technology. A typical licence agreement could include a payment of 5 per cent of the income earned as the licensee sells the product. The royalties are brought into income whether received or receivable. Amounts not collected are included in debtors in the balance sheet.

Gains derived from favourable currency movements

There are three ways in which a UK company can earn income from currency movements:

1. Sale of goods on credit followed by local currency weakness before settlement.
2. Purchase of goods on credit followed by local currency strength before settlement.
3. Assets and liabilities of subsidiaries and associates denominated in foreign currencies.

We will discuss these separately as the accounting treatment is not always the same.

Sale of goods on credit followed by local currency weakness before settlement

A UK company sold goods to a US customer denominated in dollars. Sterling weakens before the customer pays. The amount collected converts into a higher amount of sterling than was expected at the point of sale. The gain arising from the foreign currency movement is extra income. When the accounting year end intervenes between date of sale and settlement, it is necessary to establish the loss or gain in two sections. The following example illustrates this.

A Scottish company sells goods to a US customer on 3 July for $377,146 payable on 3 October. The financial year of the Scottish company ends on 31 August. Relevant rates of exchange are: 3 July £ = $1.58; 31 August £ = $1.54; 3 October £ = $1.55. Recognition of income at 3 July is $377,146/1.58 = £238,700. This is recorded as the sale and as a debtor.

At 31 August the amount still outstanding converts to $377,146/1.54 = £244,900. Because the dollar has strengthened we now expect to make an extra profit of £6,200 from the sale (£244,900 − £238,700). This is brought in as extra income receivable at 31 August.

At 3 October, $377,146/1.55 = £243,320. Because sterling strengthened we will not now earn £1,580 of the extra income anticipated at 31 August. This will be brought into account as an exchange loss in the next financial year.

Purchase of goods on credit followed by local currency strength before settlement

A Welsh company bought goods priced in euros from a Spanish supplier. Sterling strengthened between the date of purchase and the date of settlement. It will cost less sterling than expected to buy the euros at settlement. The decline in cost is an exchange gain. As with the sale situation, the end of a financial year coming between purchase and settlement can give rise to two separate recognitions of profit or loss.

On 3 July a Welsh company bought goods at a cost of €309,400. The financial year of the Welsh company ends on 31 July and settlement of the bill takes place on 3 September. Relevant rates of exchange were: 3 July £ = €0.65; 31 July £ = €0.70; 3 September £ = €0.68.

The purchase cost, creditor at year end and settlement cost are recorded at 3 July as €309,400/0.65 = £476,000. This is recorded as the purchase cost and as a trade creditor.

At 31 July €309,400/0.70 = £442,000. The strength of sterling has reduced the cost and the outstanding debt. An exchange gain of £34,000 will be reported.

At 3 September €309,400/0.68 = £455,000. Sterling weakness has lost back £13,000 of the gain recorded at 31 July. An exchange loss will be reported.

Assets and liabilities of subsidiaries and associates denominated in foreign currencies

A third area for creating currency gains arises where a UK company has an overseas subsidiary. This item will be dealt with in Chapter 14.

Settlement discounts from suppliers

Suppliers sometimes give discounts for prompt payment. Such settlement discounts are treated as income rather than as deductions from the relevant expenditure. Only discounts actually taken should be treated as income. Some businesses try to take discounts even when paying late. If these are misrepresented as income, problems can arise when auditors obtain supplier statements, which have disallowed the discount and thus do not correspond with the customer records. Trade discounts are treated differently: they lower the cost of buying goods and services.

EXPENDITURE

Many problems arise in computing the expenditure to be reported in the profit and loss account. Among the major ones are:

- How do you compute the material, labour and overhead cost of sales?
- How do you cope with unpaid and prepaid expenses?
- What impact (if any) does depreciation have on profitability?
- What happens when depreciating assets are grant aided?
- Are bank loan repayments and owners' drawings appropriately charged as expenditure?
- How should extraordinary items be treated?

Cost of sales

The calculation of the cost of sales is often the most complex computation in the profit and loss account. Once you understand the correct treatment of purchases and stock in trade it is usually straightforward in a trading business. In a manufacturing business the computation is more complicated. All the costs relating to the creation of the products that are sold must be taken into account. In management accounts a variety of production expenses such as factory wages, maintenance, factory rent and rates, and many other types of factory expenditure must be reported. In published financial accounts these are all reported under the heading 'cost of sales'.

Cost of sales. Example 1

A company bought 2,000 items for resale. They cost £11.75 each including VAT. During the accounting period it sold 1,500 items at £14.10 each including VAT. If there were no other expenses, did it make a profit or a loss?

The real cost per item is £10 net of the VAT. The balance of £1.75 per item will be netted against the VAT charged to customers in computing the VAT liability. The real selling price is £12 excluding £2.10 VAT. Based on these net prices you might expect that the business lost £2,000 computed as follows:

Sales (1,500 × £12)	18,000
Cost of sales (2,000 × £10)	20,000
Loss	2,000

This conclusion is faulty. Common sense suggests that if the company made a profit of £2 on each of the 1,500 items that it sold then the answer should be a profit of £3,000. In answering this question accounting must take into account the value of the 500 items that have not yet been sold. The accounting convention is that the value of unsold stock is transferred from the period in which it was purchased to the period in which it is sold. As a consequence the term 'cost of sales' must be interpreted literally as the cost of the items sold. When valuing the unsold items you follow the general principles of accounting that require that you a) do not recognize profits until they are earned, and b) make provision for all known losses. SSAP 9 deals specifically with the valuation of stock. Paragraph 26 of this standard requires that 'The amount at which stocks are stated in periodic financial statements should be the total of the lower of cost and net realizable value of the separate items of stock or of groups of similar items.'

We will now consider four situations that could apply to the unsold stock:

a. they all remain in stock in first-class saleable quality;
b. they all remain in stock but because of deterioration are believed to have a reduced saleable value of £8 each;
c. 150 items are missing or unsaleable;
d. 500 are in stock but will be sold at £9 each and in addition £2.50 per unit will have to be spent on delivery and commission.

The profit and loss account will be different in each case, as shown in Table 2.4 (p 22).

Cost of sales. Example 2

Example 1 showed the results in the first month of trading. We will now examine the results for the second month. In this case we will assume that there are no problems with deterioration, theft or falling prices. In the second month of trading the company bought 2,000 items at £10 each and sold 1,200 items at £12 each. Did they make a profit or a loss? Decide on the result before reading on.

The common-sense answer is a profit of £2,400. Since there are no quantity or valuation complications the accounting answer must be the same; see Table 2.5 (p 22).

The key to understanding this accounting treatment is to remember that the 500 items that were unsold in month 1 were not treated as a cost in that period. So, these must be brought back into account in calculating the result in month 2. The heading 'cost of potential sales' is not usually found in financial statements. It is a very descriptive title that I developed to help non-experts to understand how cost of sales is computed.

Table 2.4 *Unsold stock*

		Situation 1		Situation 2
Sales		18,000		18,000
Purchases	20,000		20,000	
Less stock	5,000[a]		4,000[b]	
Cost of sales		15,000		16,000
Profit		3,000		2,000
		Situation 3		**Situation 4**
Sales		18,000		18,000
Purchases	20,000		20,000	
Less stock	3,500[c]		3,250[d]	
Cost of sales		16,500		16,750
Profit		1,500		1,250

Notes:

[a] 500 items valued at £10 each are deducted in calculating the cost of sales. They are an asset and will be carried in the balance sheet at £5,000. Note that the profit in situation 1 is the £3,000 that common sense indicated. It is only when the circumstances in situations 2–4 indicate that the stock is not worth £5,000 that the profit changes.

[b] A prudent valuation is £8 each, making the stock worth £4,000. The decrease in the value of the stock pushes up the cost of sales and depresses the profit by £1,000.

[c] 350 items valued at £10 each are deducted in calculating the cost of sales. This recognizes the loss caused by theft or deterioration and leads to a profit of only £1,500.

[d] The net realizable value of the stock is £6.50 (£9 – £2.50). This is lower than cost. The stock value is £3,250 and this reduces the profit to £1,250.

Table 2.5 *Profit and loss account, example 2*

		£
Sales (1,200 × £12)		14,400
Opening stock (500 × £10)	5,000	
Purchases	20,000	
Cost of potential sales	25,000	
Closing stock (1,300 × £10)	13,000	
Cost of sales		12,000
Profit		2,400

Cost of sales. Example 3

A further problem arises when stock is purchased at different prices. We will again assume that there are no problems such as deterioration as described in Example 1.

The data in Table 2.6 have been extracted from the stock control records of a business.

Table 2.6   *Cost of sales, example 3*

	Units in	Units out	Units balance	Cost per unit
Stock 1 January			900	£5
Sales 1 January		120	780	
2 January		80	700	
3 January		100	600	
Delivery 3 January (close of business)	1,000		1,600	£6
Sales 4 January		140	1,460	
5 January		170	1,290	
7 January		130	1,160	

We will now value the stock at 7 January for inclusion in the cost of sales for that week. There are four basic approaches to the valuation of this stock (Table 2.7, p 24):

a. First in first out (FIFO) following what ought to be the physical movement.
b. Base stock. A conservative method of valuing stock when prices are rising. The stock is valued at the price of the first order. In this example we will use £5 as the cost of the opening stock. In practice the base stock could have been purchased many years ago at a much lower price.
c. Last in first out (LIFO). A variation on base stock also aimed at conservative stock valuation when prices are rising. The stock is judged to theoretically move in reverse of FIFO, even though sensible stock rotation should ensure that the oldest units are the first ones supplied to customers.
d. Weighted average. When a new delivery arrives at a different price from the current stock a new average price is computed.

Table 2.7 *How stock valuation methods affect the cost of sales*

	FIFO	Base stock	LIFO	Weighted average
Opening stock[a]	4,500	4,500	4,500	4,500
Purchases	6,000	6,000	6,000	6,000
Cost of potential sales[b]	10,500	10,500	10,500	10,500
Closing stock	6,800[c]	5,800[d]	6,360[e]	6,525[f]
Cost of sales	3,700	4,700	4,140	3,975

Notes:

[a] This stock was not included in cost of sales for the previous accounting period. It must be brought back into account in this period. The value is 900 at £5 each.

[b] The accumulation of what we started with and what we bought.

[c] FIFO valuation: 160 old stock at £5 plus 1,000 new stock at £6 equals £6,800.

[d] Base stock valuation: Base stock 1,160 at £5 each = £5,800. Even though the new stock cost £6 each, it is valued at £5. The lower stock valuation compared with FIFO increases the cost of sales and leaves a smaller profit.

[e] LIFO valuation: 560 new stock at £6 plus 600 old stock at £5 equals £6,360. The value lies between the extremes of FIFO and base stock. 300 of the original stock were sold prior to the new delivery. That left 600 in stock. 440 of the new delivery were sold. That left 560 in stock.

[f] Weighted average.

	Units	Per unit £	Value £
Opening stock	900	5	4,500
Cost of sales pre-delivery	300	5	1,500[h]
Stock at delivery	600	5	3,000
Delivery	1,000	6	6,000
Stock after delivery	1,600	5.625[g]	9,000
Cost of sales post-delivery	440	5.625	2,475[h]
Closing stock	1,160	5.625	6,525

[g] Stock value is £9,000/1,600 units = £5.625. [h] Cost of sales is £1,500 + £2,475 = £3,975.

None of these valuations offend the broad concept of cost.

The key issues in stock valuation

The basis of stock valuation should be consistent from year to year. It would be undesirable for a company to shift from one method to another so as to show the period results in the most favourable light. If a change in the valuation method is made, the auditors' report should contain a commentary such as 'If the stock valuation method had not been changed, the company would have reported a stock value £x (higher or lower) and a profit before tax of £x.' The accounting policy on stock valuation must be stated (SSAP 2).

Most UK businesses use FIFO to value trading stocks, because it corresponds with their physical movement, and the Inland Revenue does not normally accept base stock or LIFO.

Maintenance stocks are frequently valued at weighted average. It is often the most suitable method in the case of slow moving parts. Consider the following. A part for a machine was purchased in 1997 at a cost of £50,000. It has not been used. In January 2002 a similar part was purchased for £84,000. There are now two in stock. In April 2002 one of them was issued. In assessing the cost of the repair should you charge out £50,000 (FIFO) or £84,000 (replacement cost)? It is generally felt that with a large variety of spares that are only occasionally needed, £67,000 (weighted average) is the most appropriate stock valuation and charge-out rate.

If the parent company is a foreign multinational and we are preparing accounts for the UK subsidiary, we may use LIFO or base stock valuation methods so as to comply with group accounting policies. In this case the Inland Revenue will require a restatement of profits for corporation tax purposes.

Valuation of work in progress

Valuation of work in progress is more difficult. In addition to the raw material content it is necessary to consider the value added by completing part of the manufacturing process. The following is a simple example. A company starts to manufacture a product on a Monday. The product takes two days to complete and the company operates a five-day week. During the first week of operations, two items are fully completed and one item is half-way through the process. The costs were:

	£
Materials (3 items)	300
Labour	55
Power	35
Cost of production	390

The costs of the business each day are charged to that day's manufacturing activity. The work in progress is valued as follows:

	£
Material	100
Labour* (55/5)	11
Power* (35/5)	7
	118

*Divide by 5. Only on Friday (one-fifth of the week) was work done on the third product.

This is a simple example with one stock unit half-processed. In a normal factory there may be work at various stages making it necessary to examine job cards to establish the labour and overhead content.

Valuation of finished stock

In valuing finished stock we must also consider value added in production. If the item finished on Thursday had not been sold it would be valued as follows:

	£
Material	100
Labour (2 days)	22
Power (2 days)	14
	136

In most factories the valuation of work in progress and finished stock is difficult. We will leave it to the accountants to sort out the valuation.

We will now consider the manufacturing and trading account for our factory assuming that: a) one item was sold for £200; b) one item was in the finished store; and c) one item was half-way through production. Before you examine the manufacturing and trading account you should consider why the profit must be £64:

	£	£
Material	300	
Labour	55	
Power	35	
Cost of production		390
Deduct work in progress	118	
Finished stock	136	254
Cost of sales		136
Sales		200
Profit		64

Unpaid and prepaid expenses

One of the problems in computing profitability is that you must charge the expenditure that is relevant to the accounting period whether paid for in the previous period, in the current period, or remains unpaid at the end of the current period. The following areas must be considered.

The suppliers of some goods and services charge for them in arrears. For example, British Telecom charges corporate clients for calls in the month following. Nevertheless, BT customers should recognize the cost of such calls and charge them in the profit and loss account in the month in which they are made. To do so the accountant estimates the bill and includes it in the profit and loss account. The estimate is called an accrual. Accruals need to be made for electricity, bank interest and many other areas where the customer is billed in arrears. The estimated amounts outstanding are very real liabilities and as such must be included in the balance sheet. We will examine this in Chapter 3.

Providers charge for items such as rent and insurance in advance. Consider an all-risks insurance policy costing £1,300. This amount is paid at the start of the year. It must be allocated to the profit and loss account at the rate of £25 per week. The unexpired balance is not treated as an expense but is included as a prepayment in the balance sheet. We will see this in Chapter 3.

Depreciation and profitability

Items such as delivery vehicles and factory machines decline in value as they are used. This loss of value is a very real cost of running a business and must be provided for in the profit and loss account. The charge is called depreciation. To calculate the depreciation that needs to be provided for, the board must set appropriate depreciation policies. For example, consider a vehicle that cost £20,000. Let us suppose that the vehicle will be driven for three years and then sold for £8,000. The loss of value over its operating life in the business will then be £12,000. The board should decide to depreciate it at the rate of £4,000 per year. This is a straight-line depreciation charge of 20 per cent of the cost of the vehicle. By including the depreciation charge in the profit and loss account the company aims to recognize the true cost of using the vehicle in the business and ensure that the funds that will be needed to replace the vehicle three years later are retained in the business.

Depreciation and saving for replacement

The need for a business to save money to pay for the replacement of assets is best illustrated by examining the way that a small business might be mismanaged if depreciation were not taken into account.

Consider a person who uses his £20,000 of redundancy money to set up a taxi business. In a typical week he drives passengers about 3,000 miles and makes a good living. Nevertheless, his business and family outgoings are large and he has very little saved after three years. At this point his taxi has more than 450,000 miles on the clock and maintenance has become very expensive. Ideally it is time to buy a new vehicle but he does not have enough money to pay for the purchase. The driver has made an error by spending virtually all of his takings. He has really consumed most of the capital with which he started his business. Ideally, he should have saved about £6,000 each year towards the cost of a replacement vehicle. The inclusion of a depreciation charge in his profit and loss account is designed to help him to do this. An operational imperative for any business is to save money for replacement of assets. The taxi driver should restrict his spending to the profits he makes and place the depreciation funds in an asset replacement deposit account. After three years the deposit account and the trade-in should provide sufficient funds for replacement.

This approach is less easy to apply in a more complicated business. The basic problem is caused by two facts: most businesses run on a bank over-draft, and banks charge a higher rate of interest on borrowings than they credit on savings. To operate efficiently in this environment most businesses leave the depreciation charges in their current account. If they do so it is vital that over the life of fixed assets the size of the overdraft is systematically reduced to a level from which it will be permitted to increase to pay for a replacement.

It is important to realize that the Inland Revenue does not recognize depreciation as a deductible expense in computing corporation tax liability. It allows a writing down allowance instead.

Impairment

Occasionally the application of a depreciation policy can lead to understating the loss of value experienced through use in the business. This situation usually arises when something happens to the assets or to the economic environment in which they operate. The foot and mouth disease in 2001 is a typical example. The damage it caused to agribusiness was such that the future operations of many farms are in doubt. Consequently, the value of land, buildings and equipment that would be reported in their balance sheet using normal depreciation policies could be overstated. FRS 11 requires an impairment review in this type of circumstance. Any additional loss of value revealed by the impairment review must be included as a cost in the profit and loss account.

Grant-aided assets

Where a capital grant has been received towards the cost of a fixed asset the loss of value recorded in the profit and loss account should be restricted. This is done by depreciating the grant and crediting this to the profit and loss account. The process is described in Chapter 3.

Bank loan repayments

The repayment of bank loans is not a cost of running a business. Consequently, the repayments cannot be reported as expenditure in the profit and loss account. Loan repayments are simply a reduction in the bank debt shown in the balance sheet.

Dividends and drawings

A successful company usually rewards its shareholders with dividends. Sole traders and partnerships simply withdraw part of the profits. Such withdrawals are called 'drawings'. Dividends and drawings must not be taken into account in determining the pre-tax profit of a business. They are appropriations of profit rather than a cost that must be taken into account in determining profit.

Extraordinary items

Until 1993 the extraordinary item was a much-abused accounting concept. The most frequent abuses were the treatment of the cost of rationalization and of losses on disposal of parts of a business. The cost of such business restructuring must be recognized and provided for in the profit and loss account. SSAP 6 permitted the extraordinary items to be shown after the results of normal activities. SSAP 3 allowed them to be ignored in computing earnings per share (EPS). EPS is widely used in the investment community to examine progress over time. It is computed by dividing the profit for ordinary shareholders by the weighted average number of shares in issue during the year. (The calculation and interpretation is discussed in detail in Chapter 6.) The classification of items as 'extraordinary' made it possible to paint an unwarranted picture of growth in EPS. In many businesses rationalization and restructuring could fairly be described as normal rather than extraordinary. Consequently, many commentators, me included, regarded it as misleading to exclude such items in computing the profit from normal activities and the EPS.

The introduction of FRS 3 in 1993 put a stop to such abuses. The overall thrust of FRS 3 is that it is in the nature of major businesses to expand and contract by buying and selling businesses and that such items should be taken into account in measuring profits and computing EPS. The standard does not stop reporting entities from showing such items separately so as to help readers to recognize structural changes in the business when trying to predict future profits. It also permits reporting entities to present other calculations of EPS. It does require that such costs and losses be included in calculating profits or losses on ordinary activities and in the calculation of 'headline' EPS.

FRS 3 also requires that the profit and loss account be broken down so as to show:

- the results of continuing existing operations and acquisitions;
- the results of discontinued operations;
- profits or losses on disposal of discontinued operations.

An example profit and loss account FRS 3 format is shown in Table 2.8.

STATEMENT OF TOTAL RECOGNIZED GAINS AND LOSSES

Some gains and losses of a business are not included in the profit and loss account. The most notable example is the paper profit or loss on translation of foreign currency assets and liabilities. For the present it will be sufficient if you understand that an asset held in a foreign currency will on paper become more valuable if your local currency weakens and less valuable if

Table 2.8 *Example FRS 3 format*

	Continuing operations Acquisitions		Discontinued operations	Total
Sales	500	200	190	890
Cost of sales	380	85	155	620
Gross profit	120	115	35	270
Net operating costs	37	36	42	115
Operating profit	83	79	(7)	155
Loss on disposal			(53)	(53)
Operating profit	83	79	(60)	102
Interest payable				(36)
Profit on ordinary activities before tax				66
Tax on profit on ordinary activities				(22)
Profit on ordinary activities after tax				44
Dividends				10
Retained profit for the financial year				34
Earnings per share				3.4p

your local currency strengthens. For example, if your company has a US subsidiary with assets of $2.1 million at the start and end of year they will have to be translated into sterling for inclusion in the group accounts. Suppose that during the year sterling weakens from £ = $1.50 to £ = $1.40. The sterling value of the assets on translation rises from £1.4 to £1.5 million. An unrealized profit of £100,000 is shown in the statement of total recognized gains and losses.

Equally, the sterling value of a liability such as a bank loan denominated in a foreign currency will decrease as the local currency strengthens during a year and increase as the local currency weakens. The profits (increase in local currency translated assets or decrease in local currency liabilities) or losses (decrease in local currency translated assets or increase in local currency liabilities) are not included in the profit and loss account. They are reported in the statement of total recognized gains and losses that follows the profit and loss account; see Figure 2.1 (p 32).

Local currency

	Strengthens	Weakens
Foreign Currency Assets	Value decreases Paper loss	Value increases Paper profit
Foreign Currency Liabilities	Value decreases Paper profit	Value increases Paper loss

Figure 2.1 *Table of currency translation gains and losses*

Prior year adjustments dealt with through the profit and loss account

These arise from corrections and adjustments, which are the natural result of estimates inherent in accounting and more particularly in the periodic preparation of financial statements. Estimating future events will require reappraisal as new events occur, more experience is acquired, or new information is obtained. Care must be taken to ascertain that the change is a reappraisal rather than a change in accounting policy.

Prior year adjustments not included in the profit and loss account

These fall into two categories. First, restatements of previous years are regarded as the most appropriate method for dealing with changes in accounting policies. (The most likely source of such changes arises when a new FRS makes figures for previous years unreliable as a basis for comparison with the revised accounting approach used in the current year.) Second, accounts containing significant errors, which would have been withdrawn if the errors had been discovered in sufficient time, are most appropriately treated by restating the prior year's, resulting in the opening balance of retained profits being adjusted.

Profit and loss account supporting information

Schedule 4 of the Companies Act 1985 requires that additional information must be presented to shareholders. These data are usually added by way of notes accompanying the financial accounts. The additional data are of two major types: details of costs and segmental information.

Details of costs

These include:

- Staff costs, distinguishing between wages and salaries, company proportion of social security and other pension costs.
- Average number of people employed by the company in the financial year.
- Depreciation and diminution in the value of tangible and intangible fixed assets.
- Auditors' remuneration (including expenses).
- Directors' remuneration:
  - emoluments, which includes fees, salaries, bonuses, commissions, taxable expense allowances, benefits in kind and company superannuation contributions;
  - directors' or past directors' pensions;
  - compensation to directors or past directors in respect of loss of office;
  - emoluments of the chairperson;
  - emoluments of the highest paid director, if he or she was not the chairperson;
  - the number of directors whose emoluments lie between nil and £5,000 and in each band of £5,000 above this;
  - the number of directors who have waived emoluments and the aggregate value of such emoluments waived.
- The number of employees whose emoluments exceed £30,000 in bands of £5,000 above this amount (excluding employees who worked wholly or mainly outside the UK).
- Payments for hire of plant and machinery.

Segmental information

SSAP 25 is designed to provide the information required by paragraph 55(1) of the Companies Act 1985. It requires disclosure of information to help users of financial statements to interpret performance and assess future prospects where an entity operates in several business areas and/or geographic markets. It requires analysis of sales, assets and profits by class of business and geographical market. SSAP 25 follows the principles of the EC Fourth Directive. All entities are encouraged to provide segmental information. However, where, in the opinion of the directors, disclosure would be seriously prejudicial to the interests of the reporting entity, segmental information need not be disclosed but the fact that it has not been disclosed must be stated. The key segmental information is defined in paragraph 8 as follows:

- Significant classes of business which:
  - earn a return on investment that is out of line with the remainder of the business; or
  - are subject to different degrees of risk; or
  - have experienced different rates of growth; or
  - have different potentials for future development.

Significance is defined in paragraph 9 as:

- third party turnover in excess of 10 per cent of total; or
- profit or loss in excess of combined profit or loss for all segments; or
- net assets in excess of 10 per cent of total net assets of the entity.

Table 2.9 *SSAP 25 segmental report*

Classes of Business	Industry A £'000	Industry B £'000	Other industries £'000	Total £'000
Turnover				
Total sales	33,865	42,867	19,343	96,075
Inter-segment sales	(1,265)	–	(1,963)	(3,228)
Sales to third parties	32,600	42,867	17,380	92,847
Profit before tax				
Segment profit	1,263	1,567	875	3,705
Common costs				(1,862)
Segment profit				1,843
Net interest paid				(207)
Profit before tax				1,636
Net assets				
Segment net assets	9,869	13,438	9,632	32,939
Assets not allocated				831
Total net assets				33,770

An illustration of a segmental report required by SSAP 25 is given in Table 2.9. The geographic analysis is similar. The turnover, pre-tax profits and net assets are broken down by major markets.

Small and medium-sized company exemptions

A small company, as defined in the Companies Act 1985, is not required to file a profit and loss account. A medium-sized company, as defined in the Companies Act 1985, may begin its profit and loss account with gross profit.

3

The balance sheet

The second major financial statement that we will examine is the balance sheet. The main purpose of a balance sheet is to pinpoint financial stability or instability. It paints a picture of a business at a point in time. The picture shows what the business owns (the assets) and how the ownership of the assets is financed (liabilities and shareholders' funds). The key indicator of stability is the amount of indebtedness as compared with the value of assets. The title 'balance sheet' is appropriate: the assets must always be matched by an equal amount of funding (provided by the owners and various kinds of lenders).

MISCONCEPTIONS ABOUT THE BALANCE SHEET

The balance sheet framework needs to be clearly understood. There are two serious misconceptions. First, in a balance sheet the assets are valued on a *going concern basis.* It does not attempt to show their disposal value. For example, John Bermingham recently started a small manufacturing business. He bought a machine for £55,000. John expects the machine to produce goods for profitable sale over the next five years. In preparing his balance sheet after one year in business, John might value the machine at £44,000. He would argue that four-fifths of its useful life (and ongoing value to the business) remained. The fact that if the machine were sold it might realize, say, £20,000 is not relevant. John has no intention of selling it. The value he puts on it is called 'the value in use'. This value is only appropriate if it is clear that John's business can survive. If the business were in serious financial difficulties John could not justify this value. The machine would probably have to be sold to repay a secured lender. A going concern value would not be appropriate. A receiver or liquidator would be controlling the business and would prepare a Statement of Affairs instead. This would show the estimated break-up value of the assets.

Second, the value of some of the assets rises and falls during the year, particularly in a seasonal business. When the amount invested in assets is high, the organization will need substantial borrowings to support them. When the assets decline as the season ends, the borrowings can be repaid. Stock in trade is the most important example of an asset whose value can vary substantially during a year. Consider a business the major asset of which is a crop that when harvested in September yields 12,000 tonnes costing £100 per tonne. This crop is expected to be sold at the rate of 1,000 tonnes per month. The balance sheet at various times in the following year is presented in Table 3.1.

Table 3.1 *The balance sheet of a seasonal business at different times in the year*

£'000	30 Sept	31 Dec	31 Mar	30 June
Stock	1,200	900	600	300
Financed by:				
Owner's funds	300	300	300	300
Bank overdraft	900	600	300	–
	1,200	900	600	300

If the business published its balance sheet as at 30 June it would show a low stock investment and no bank overdraft. If it published the figures as at 30 September it would show four times as great a stock figure and a large bank overdraft (three times as much as the owners' funds).

A company in this type of business would be unwise to publish its balance sheet as at 30 September. Bank borrowings will be at their peak. A seasonal business should set its year to end at the point where the combined investment in stocks and debtors is at its lowest and consequently bank loans have been repaid. For example, if an Easter egg maker presented its balance sheet as at 31 March, the assets and borrowings would be at their peak. This company would be wiser to report as at 31 May or 30 June, by which time hopefully all the stock would have been sold and most of the cash collected from customers. On examining this balance sheet a superficial analyst might classify the business as very safe. A prudent investor on examining the balance sheet would be wise to pose the question 'How typical is the picture of assets and borrowings disclosed?' An analyst who understood the seasonal pattern should conclude that the stock and the trade debtors would have been much higher before Easter and that large bank borrowings would then have been required to finance it. This could be partly verified by checking the interest charge shown in the profit and loss account. The significant interest charge would confirm that there were substantial bank borrowings earlier in the season. This is a simple and very logical example of the need for a thoughtful approach when assessing financial statements. The management and the balance sheet will not draw attention to the size of high-season borrowings.

KEY ITEMS IN THE BALANCE SHEET

Now that you are aware of the going concern and seasonal issues we can examine the key items that you will find in the balance sheet of a typical business. These are summarized in Table 3.2.

Table 3.2 *The assets and finances of a typical business*

Types of assets	Sources of finance
Land	The owners
Buildings	The bankers
Plant and machinery	The creditors
Vehicles	The state
Fixtures and fittings	
Stocks	
Trade debtors	
Prepayments	
Cash	

When an accountant is preparing a balance sheet he or she follows the general accounting principle that assets should be reported at cost unless they are worth less than they cost. In applying this principle the assets must be divided into two groups: fixed assets and current assets. How is it decided whether an item is a fixed asset or a current asset? The Companies Act 1985 Schedule 4 Paragraph 75 provides the answer: 'Assets of a company shall be taken to be fixed assets if they are intended for use on a continuing basis in the company's activities. Any assets not intended for such use shall be taken to be current assets.' The meaning of the term 'continuing' in this context is not as obvious as it sounds. A manufacturing business will continually have both machinery and stock. The machinery will be kept and used in the business for a long time (ie continuing use) whereas the stock will be sold as quickly as possible and is a current asset, even though the business will always have some stock.

Categories of fixed assets

The fixed assets of a business are reported in three categories:

1. tangible fixed assets;
2. financial fixed assets;
3. intangible fixed assets.

The first five types of assets in Table 3.2 are tangible fixed assets while the last four are current assets. Most tangible fixed assets tend to decline in value as they age. In Chapter 2 we saw how this loss of value was reported as an operating cost in the profit and loss account. This loss of value also affects the balance sheet. The depreciation is deducted from the cost of the fixed asset, which is then reported at its value in use, often called 'book value'.

We will now start to assemble the balance sheet of John Bermingham as he starts in business and buys a machine for £55,000. In order to set an appropriate depreciation policy for this type of fixed asset John should ask himself three questions:

1. What is the operating life of the asset?
2. Will it become obsolete and uncompetitive before the end of its operating life?
3. What, if anything, will I get when I scrap it?

Let's say that the machine has an expected operating life of 10 years but that John believes technological advances will make it uncompetitive in five years.

John also predicts a disposal value of £3,000. John is now in a position to set his depreciation policy and predict the balance sheet value of the machine at various points in its life. The depreciation calculation is:

$$\frac{\text{Cost} - \text{disposal value}}{\text{Working life}} \quad \frac{£55,000 - £3,000}{5 \text{ years}} = £10,400$$

The balance sheet on the date of purchase and in subsequent years is presented in Table 3.3.

Table 3.3 *The book value of John's machine at various points in its life*

£'000	Day 1	Year 1	Year 2	Year 3	Year 4	Year 5
Machine at cost	55.0	55.0	55.0	55.0	55.0	55.0
Aggregate depreciation	–	10.4	20.8	31.2	41.6	52.0
Book value	55.0	44.6	34.2	23.8	13.4	3.0

The deduction of depreciation is designed to show the machine at its 'value in use'. Readers are warned that this value is not what it would realize if put up for sale. If a depreciation policy were not formulated and applied to fixed assets then the report would be very misleading. In the absence of a depreciation policy the machine might be reported in the balance sheet at cost. This valuation would be unduly optimistic. Furthermore, the absence of a depreciation charge would mean that a) profits would be overstated or the losses understated, and b) the directors might be tempted to pay money out of the business as dividends that should be retained to pay for a replacement asset when it wears out or becomes obsolete.

Alternatively, the machine might be charged in full as a cost in the profit and loss account. Such an approach would mean a) that the reported costs would be excessive in years when fixed assets were purchased and inadequate in years when none were bought, and b) that owners and lenders would be kept in the dark in relation to the ongoing value of the fixed assets.

The charging of depreciation is an appropriate compromise between these two extremes.

Depreciation and inter-firm comparison

A key task for the directors of a new business is to formulate an appropriate depreciation policy. The useful lives attributed to assets and the disposal values are matters of judgement. It is certainly true that the boards of some companies apply optimistic lives to assets while the boards of others apply pessimistic lives, which makes interpretation of the balance sheet difficult and can make inter-firm comparison misleading. For example, consider the machine bought by Bill Glasgow, a competitor of John's, also for £55,000. He predicts a life of six years and a disposal value of £1,000. The depreciation charge and balance sheet consequences are:

$$\frac{\text{Cost} - \text{disposal value}}{\text{Working life}} \quad \frac{£55,000 - £1,000}{6 \text{ years}} = £9,000$$

The balance sheet on the date of purchase and in subsequent years is presented in Table 3.4, which shows that Bill reports his asset to be worth £10,000 after five years whereas John reports his at £3,000.

Table 3.4 *The book value of Bill's machine at various points in its life*

£'000	Day 1	Year 1	Year 2	Year 3	Year 4	Year 5	Year 6
Machine at cost	55	55	55	55	55	55	55
Aggregate depreciation	–	9	18	27	36	45	54
Book value	55	46	37	28	19	10	1

Neither valuation is incorrect: it is simply that they used different judgements about the life and disposal value. Nevertheless, Bill's business will appear stronger (higher asset value) and more profitable (lower depreciation charge). This leads me for the first time to warn you that the rule of *caveat emptor* applies to financial statements. In this case readers are advised to examine the notes accompanying the accounts to establish the depreciation policy. This helps to put the valuation of the fixed assets in a proper context. Typical lives for fixed assets are shown in Table 3.5 (p 42).

Impairment

In Chapter 2, I briefly mentioned the issue of impairment. It can have a very significant impact on the value of tangible fixed assets. Accounting for impairment is dealt with in FRS 11. This FRS defines impairment as 'a reduction in the recoverable amount of a fixed asset or goodwill below its

Table 3.5 *Typical lives for fixed assets*

Asset type	Life	Depreciation range
Land[1]	Indefinite	None
Freehold buildings[2]	25–100 years	1% to 4% Straight line
Leasehold buildings	Period of lease	Decided by lease period
High-tech plant	3–5 years	20% to 33% Straight line
Other plant	5–20 years	5% to 20% Straight line
Vehicles	3–5 years	20% to 33% Straight line
Office furniture	5–10 years	10% to 20% Straight line
Purchased goodwill	5–20 years	5% to 20% Straight line

Notes:

[1] The exception is land that contains minerals that are being extracted. The land declines in value as mining takes place.

[2] Many people argue that buildings appreciate in value and should not be depreciated. Nevertheless, the rules of accounting require that buildings be depreciated but leave the option to revalue them, as we will see later in the chapter.

carrying amount'. The standard defines recoverable amount as 'the higher of net realizable value and value in use'. Paragraphs 8 to 10 of the standard describe the key indications of impairment as follows:

8 A review for impairment of a fixed asset or goodwill should be carried out if events or changes in circumstances indicate that the carrying amount of the fixed asset or goodwill may not be recoverable.

9 Impairment occurs because something has happened either to the fixed assets themselves or to the economic environment in which the fixed assets are operated. It is possible, therefore, to rely on the use of indicators of impairment to determine when a review for impairment is needed.

10 Examples of events and changes in circumstances that indicate an impairment may have occurred include:

a current period operating loss in the business in which the fixed asset or goodwill is involved or net cash outflow from the operating activities of that business, combined with either past operating losses or net cash outflows from such operating activities or an expectation of continuing operating losses or net cash outflows from such operating activities a significant decline in a fixed asset's market value during the period evidence of obsolescence or physical damage to the fixed asset a significant adverse change in:

- either the business or the market in which the fixed asset or goodwill is involved, such as the entrance of a major competitor
- the statutory or other regulatory environment in which the business operates
- any 'indicator of value' (for example turnover) used to measure the fair value of a fixed asset on acquisition
  a commitment by management to undertake a significant reorganization
  a major loss of key employees
  a significant increase in market interest rates or other market rates of return that are likely to affect materially the fixed asset's recoverable amount.

Paragraph 21 is the key rule in implementing the standard:

21 When an impairment loss on a fixed asset or goodwill is recognized, the remaining useful economic life and residual value should be reviewed and revised if necessary. The revised carrying amount should be depreciated over the revised estimate of the remaining useful economic life.

FRS 11 is very technical, as it needs to be, to guide those preparing financial statements. Nevertheless, it is important for directors and managers to recognize that impairment can occur and must be taken into account in valuing fixed assets.

Discussion of other fixed assets (intangible and financial) is covered later in the chapter.

The assets of John Bermingham

We will now consider the assets that John Bermingham may wish to own in his fledgling business.

Asset type	Investment decision
Tangible fixed	
Land and buildings	I will rent as I cannot assemble enough funds to buy.
Plant and machinery	I will use some of my capital to buy it. I will also arrange a government grant and a term loan.
Fixtures and fittings	I will lease it as I cannot assemble enough funds to buy it.
Motor vehicles	I will buy using part of my capital and my term loan.

Current

Stock in trade	I will use some of my capital to pay for it. Fortunately, I will get some credit from suppliers. This will ease the pressure on my limited capital.
Trade debtors	My customers will require a period of trade credit. I will have to pay my running costs during this credit period and will try to arrange a bank overdraft to cover them.
Prepayments	An all-risks insurance policy will cost me £1,300. The bank overdraft will also be required to pay for this.
Petty cash	There are always some small cash expenses to pay. I will need a float and will get it by drawing down part of my overdraft facility.

Any prospective new business promoter should prepare a list like the one above. It should include the amounts to be invested and the funds to be raised to pay for them. The full list after 10 weeks in business is presented later in the chapter. This list shows only the types of assets and funds that a small and uncomplicated business will have. More complex assets and funds will be examined later in the book.

Current assets

Current assets are the engine room of any business. They provide the source for profitable sales. The starting point is cash. This cash is spent to buy or create the product or service that the business sells and to pay for the overheads. The major current assets are:

- material stocks;
- work in progress;
- finished stocks;
- trade debtors;
- prepayments;
- cash balances;
- bank balances; and
- short-term investments.

In order to estimate the amount he will need to invest in current assets, John will need to predict the purchases, production and sales for his business. To save this analysis from becoming too cumbersome we will confine it to the first 10 weeks of John's business. If you are considering the start-up of your own business I must warn you that the forecast should be made for three years. This is particularly important when sales are expected to grow rapidly. The problem with such growth is that the business has to pay for additional purchases and production long before increased collections from credit customers start to arrive. This problem, called 'over-trading', is discussed in detail in Chapter 7.

We will now look at the operating plan for the first 10 weeks in the life of John's business (see Table 3.6). This will help John to pinpoint the investment in current assets that he will have to make.

Table 3.6 *Operating plan for the first 10 weeks of John's business*

1. Cost and price structure

Material cost per unit	£10
Production cost per unit	£2
Selling price per unit	£16

2. Purchase, production and sales volumes in units:

Week	Purchases	Production	WIP	Sales
1	1,000	60	20	40
2	100	80	20	40
3	100	110	20	55
4	100	110	20	55
5	100	110	20	55
6	100	110	20	55
7	120	120	20	90
8	120	120	20	90
9	120	120	20	90
10	120	120	20	90

Where items are in process at the end of a week, £1 per unit of the production cost will have been spent. A further £1 per unit will be spent in the following week to complete them. Customers are expected to pay seven weeks after sale. John commenced business with £20,000 available to fund his current asset investment; we will look at the position after the first five weeks (see Table 3.7, pp 46–47). This shows the frightening pace at which John's cash is consumed. The main reason is that he has to pay for his materials and his production expenses while he will not yet have collected anything from his customers. If the business continues to grow, John could soon run out of cash.

Table 3.7 *The position after the first five weeks in John's business*

	£
Raw material stock (910 not yet issued to production)[1]	9,100
Work in progress (20 in production)[2]	220
Finished stock (225 produced but not yet sold)[3]	2,700
Trade debtors (245 sold but not yet paid for)[4]	3,920
Cash (starting position £20,000 less £14,960 paid)[5]	5,040
	20,980

Notes: [1] Material stock

Week	Units purchased	Units issued	Closing material	Unit cost £	Stock value £
1	1,000	80[a]	920	10	9,200
2	100	80	940	10	9,400
3	100	110	930	10	9,300
4	100	110	920	10	9,200
5	100	110	910	10	9,100
	1,400	490			

[a] Sixty were produced and work in progress was 20 units. The issues must have been 80 units in week 1.
[2] Work in progress
Twenty items valued at the full material cost £10 plus half the production cost £1 = £11 per unit.
[3] Finished stock

Week	Units produced	Units sold	Closing units	Unit cost £	Stock value £
1	60	40	20	12	240
2	80	40	60	12	720
3	110	55	115	12	1,380
4	110	55	170	12	2,040
5	110	55	225	12	2,700
	470	245			

Table 3.7 *(continued)*

(4) Sales and trade debtors

Week	Units sold	Unit price £	Sales revenue £	Trade debtors £
1	40	16	640	640
2	40	16	640	1,280
3	55	16	880	2,160
4	55	16	880	3,040
5	55	16	880	3,920
	245		3,920	

(5) Cash

Week	Opening Cash	payments Suppliers	Production	Closing Cash
1	20,000	(10,000)	(140)	9,860
2	9,860	(1,000)	(160)	8,700
3	8,700	(1,000)	(220)	7,480
4	7,480	(1,000)	(220)	6,260
5	6,260	(1,000)	(220)	5,040

John Bermingham's current assets

You should now prepare similar tables for weeks 6–10 and John's current asset investment after 10 weeks. This will help you to understand the effect of these key items on the balance sheet of a business. The results are given in the Appendix at the back of the book.

If you prepared the schedules for weeks 6–10 correctly you will have found that the cash balance will fall to £1,100. John will have experienced substantial further pressure on his cash resources. To compound the cash problem, he needs to buy the machine and a delivery vehicle to achieve his production and sales targets, and to pay an insurance premium of £1,300 for one year in advance. In his profit and loss account this prepayment will be charged against profits at the rate of £25 per week. The unexpired balance is treated as a further current asset. These assets will require more than the capital of £30,000 that John will be able to inject into the business. He will need to obtain additional finance if he wants to survive and develop his business.

Valuation of assets

As a general principle, the assets of a business are valued at cost, unless they are worth less than this. We will now explore the valuation of various types of assets:

- Land. Usually valued at cost. It is good practice to revalue land at least every five years. Only land where the purchase price reflected some mineral wealth that is being extracted should be depreciated. As explained earlier, the asset should be reviewed for impairment.
- Freehold buildings. Usually valued at cost less depreciation. This can understate their real value. It is good practice to revalue at least once every five years and to include the revised figure instead of cost. Freehold buildings are regarded as having a defined life. Depreciation must be provided. As explained earlier, the asset should be reviewed for impairment.
- Leasehold buildings. Usually valued at cost less depreciation. They may also appreciate and can be revalued. Depreciation must be provided over the period of the lease. As explained earlier, the value may have to be reduced as a result of an impairment review.
- Plant, vehicles, fixtures and fittings. These items are valued at cost less depreciation. Do not forget the impairment review.
- Stock. SSAP 9 requires that stock be valued at the lower of cost or net realizable value. Some problems arise in the interpretation and application of this rule. Stock valuation was explained in Chapter 2.
- Trade debtors. The records of the company should show all amounts owed to the business. Amounts that are deemed to be unrecoverable should not be included. Such amounts should be charged as bad debts in the profit and loss account.
- Prepayments. In Chapter 2 we saw that an all-risks insurance policy costing £1,300 was paid in advance and would be charged into the profit and loss account at the rate of £25 per week. John Bermingham bought this policy, which further depressed his bank balance. In his profit and loss account for the first 10 weeks in business he will show a cost of £250. In the current assets in his balance sheet after 10 weeks he will show a prepayment of £1,050.
- Cash. The easiest to value. You count it.
- Bank. Not quite as easy as it sounds. A bank statement shows the amount due to or collectable from its client. This reflects all lodgements that have been credited to the account and all cheques that have been cashed. The company view of the account is often different. This is because some of the cheques they have written have not yet been presented and some of

the lodgements they have made have not yet been credited. The company view of the bank position is shown in the balance sheet. In order to explain the difference between the balance per the company records and the balance per the bank records, a wise company will carry out a regular reconciliation.

FINANCING THE ASSETS

At the start of this chapter we learnt that funds that enabled a business to own assets were raised from four major sources:

1. the owners;
2. the bankers;
3. the creditors;
4. the state.

We will now examine these sources of funds.

The owners

We will consider the funds subscribed by the owners only in a limited company or plc context. Bankers and creditors favour this type of structure and form of capital injection because it is difficult to withdraw. The capital subscribed will, along with other forms of owners' investment, be reported in the section of the balance sheet called 'shareholders' funds'.

There are six main divisions of shareholders' funds:

- ordinary share capital;
- preference shares;
- revenue reserve;
- share premium;
- revaluation reserve;
- capital redemption reserve.

These are now examined.

Ordinary share capital

When a company is formed it normally commences life with shares that have a nominal value of £1 each. The promoter(s) subscribe for shares at this price.

49

The shares are valued in the balance sheet at this price regardless of whether the company prospers and the value increases or is not very successful and the value declines. Sometimes a successful business subdivides its shares to a nominal value of 50p, 20p, 5p or even 1p to make them more attractive to potential investors. For example, if shares with a nominal value of £1 each were trading on the stock market at £20 each, then a buyer could only acquire 500 shares for a £10,000 investment. If the shares were subdivided so that existing holders were given 20 shares with a nominal value of 5p each in exchange for one share with a nominal value of £1 then the share price could be expected to fall to about £1. An investor could buy 10,000 shares for £10,000. This sounds more substantial even though the real worth is the same.

The balance sheet or supporting notes will disclose both the authorized share capital, defined in the memorandum of association (the rule book of the company) and the issued share capital. A decision to subdivide the shares simply changes the denomination, but not the amount of funds in the business. A decision to consolidate the shares (for example, to give one share of £1 in exchange for 10 shares of 10p) also simply changes the denomination. A subsequent issue of shares would change the quantity of shares but not their nominal value.

Preference shares

Preference shares are a kind of half-way house between lending money to a business and providing ordinary share capital to it. They confer on the holders preferential rights, a) to a dividend before the ordinary shareholders, which is useful if there are only sufficient profits to justify the payment of a preference dividend; and b) priority repayment in a liquidation (this is attractive where some funds are available for shareholders but not enough for all).

In order to obtain these advantages preference shareholders sacrifice the opportunity to be paid a higher dividend if the profits of the business grow. Preference shares have not been popular in recent years as investors focus their attention on capital appreciation and dividend growth. Nevertheless, the balance sheets of many companies contain such shares issued in the past. Types of preference share include:

- Cumulative preference shares. If in any year the profits are insufficient to pay the dividend, then the dividend obligation is carried forward to the following year when it will become payable if profits are adequate to cover the arrears.
- Redeemable preference shares. The company can buy them back at defined future date(s).

- Participating preference shares. As well as providing a preferential fixed dividend such shares entitle the holders to additional payment when the dividends on ordinary shares exceed a defined percentage.
- Convertible preference shares. These can be converted into ordinary shares on defined future dates at specified exchange rates. They can be attractive to both the company and the shareholders, where the funds are invested long term and profits from the investment are likely to grow significantly.

Several of the above features can be combined, eg cumulative redeemable preference shares.

Revenue reserve

In order to grow, a business will have to invest in additional assets. Funds are needed to pay for this expansion. Some of these funds should be invested by shareholders or the borrowings will become excessive. A relatively painless way of subscribing additional funds is to leave some of the profits in the business. This is the most tax-efficient way of increasing investment because if these profits were paid out as dividends they would be liable to income tax in the hands of the recipients. The revenue reserve shows the aggregate of profits retained since the commencement of operations. Note that if a business makes a loss then this is deducted from the revenue reserves.

There is a further reason why new businesses need to retain some of their profits. The majority of new businesses start life with an inadequate capital base. To get started, the promoters try to arrange large borrowings to finance the assets. Excessive borrowings place the fledgling organization at risk. In such cases lenders usually seek a freeze on dividends and a limitation on proprietors' salaries in order to help ensure that the shareholders' stake is improved. Retained profits can then be used to pay off some of the excessive debt. Such action can quickly bring the shareholders' funds to an acceptable level. Revenue reserves are often converted into share capital. This is done through a bonus issue (free shares).

The effect of a bonus issue is twofold. First, it reduces the share price, but not the value of the underlying investment. This makes the shares more marketable. Many people would be happy to ask their broker to buy 5,000 shares at £1 each, but would be reluctant to order 250 shares at £20 each, even though both orders would cost £5,000 plus expenses. Second, conversion of revenue reserves into share capital increases lenders' confidence in their security. Lenders are wary of large revenue reserves. If they are used to pay dividends, their security declines. They rightly regard share capital as more permanent and secure.

Share premium

When a successful business wants to embark on an expansion it often invites shareholders to subscribe for additional shares. The new shares are offered to shareholders in proportion to their existing holdings. The offer, called a 'rights issue', invites existing shareholders to subscribe at a price that is usually higher than the nominal value. The share premium is the excess over the nominal value that shareholders pay to exercise their rights. For example, a company started life with 1 million shares of £1 each. Later it wished to raise further capital for expansion. The company broker advised it to offer shareholders the right to buy one new share at £1.60 for each share held. If all the shareholders accept the offer then the company will raise £1.6 million; £1 million of this is the nominal value of the new shares. The remaining £0.6 million is the share premium. The cost of the issue, £160,000, must be deducted from the share premium so the company raises a net sum of £1.44 million.

In a rights issue shares are usually offered at below the current market price. This is because the share price could fall during the offer period, making it more attractive to buy existing shares rather than those offered in the rights issue. This discounted price leads to an inevitable fall in the stock market price of the shares in the short term. For example, suppose that the share price was £1.80 immediately prior to the announcement of the rights issue. Table 3.8 shows how the market estimates the price subsequent to the rights issue, called the 'ex-rights price'.

Table 3.8 *The ex-rights price*

	Number of shares	Estimated value
Existing shares	1,000,000	1,800,000
New shares	1,000,000	1,440,000[1]
	2,000,000	3,240,000

Notes:
The ex-rights price is estimated at £1.62. This is obtained by dividing the new estimated value by the number of shares now in issue.
[1] In the short term the additional value is based on the cash injected into the business, When extra profits are earned by using the proceeds the share price will be expected to rise.

Revaluation reserve

A company can make a 'paper' profit through holding appreciating assets such as land or buildings. Businesses are encouraged to revalue appreciating assets at least every five years so that the balance sheet will present a realistic statement of their value. If the assets are increased in value in line with the opinion of a property valuation, then in order to make the balance sheet balance and properly reflect the owners' investment in the business, the paper profit is included in revaluation reserve as part of the shareholders' funds. This recognizes the additional shareholder investment that is represented by the paper profit.

The rules relating to revaluation of assets are:

- The directors must determine for each category of fixed asset whether it is accounting policy to carry that class at cost or valuation.
- It is good practice to revalue fixed assets at least every five years.
- Any surplus recognized in the valuation must be credited to revaluation reserve.
- If an asset that has appreciated is sold the vendor becomes exposed to a capital gains tax liability. FRS 19, Accounting for deferred tax, says that when an asset that is not for sale is revalued no provision for deferred tax should be made.
- Where there is a permanent diminution in the value of a fixed asset, FRS 11 requires that it be recognized by reducing the balance sheet value of the asset and charging the shortfall in the profit and loss account for the period in which it occurs.

The following example shows how a revaluation is included in the balance sheet. Spread Ltd bought a property 10 years ago for £250,000. The depreciation policy was 2 per cent per annum straight line. The property was reported in the latest balance sheet at £200,000. Spread Ltd recently obtained an independent professional valuation of £500,000. It decided to include the new valuation in the next balance sheet. Table 3.9 (p 54) shows how the balance sheet would appear with and without the revaluation.

The £300,000 increase in the value of the property is added to the balance sheet value. Note that the depreciation charge will have to be increased from £5,000 to £12,500 per year. This is because the new valuation must now be amortized over the remaining 40 years of the 50-year depreciation period. The paper profit on revaluation is not available for distribution.

Capital redemption reserve

Where a public company buys back shares and does not replace their par value with the proceeds of a fresh issue, Section 170 of the Companies Act 1985 requires the transfer of an amount equivalent to their nominal value

Table 3.9 *Including a property revaluation in the balance sheet*

Balance sheet, Spread Ltd

	Without revaluation	With revaluation
Cost less depreciation	200,000	
Valuation		500,000
Represented by:		
Share capital	200,000	200,000
Revaluation reserve		300,000
	200,000	500,000

from the revenue reserves to a capital redemption reserve. This law is designed to protect other lenders against diminution of their security. In the case of redeemable preference shares it is wise to start providing for such transfer from the outset.

On 1 January 2002 Growth plc issued £1 million preference shares redeemable on 31 December 2007. The company should replace these shareholders' funds from revenue reserves at a rate of £200,000 per annum, unless it intends to redeem them from the proceeds of a subsequent issue. Each £200,000 is shown in the capital redemption reserve.

Other major sources of finance

Most of the other major sources of finance are borrowings of one kind or another. In reporting these borrowings a company is required to break them down into two categories.

The first is amounts due and payable in under one year. This category of funds used to be called 'current liabilities' and some published accounts still contain this title. The second is amounts due and payable in beyond one year. This breakdown is very important to readers of financial statements. The relative immediacy of the first category imposes substantial pressure on liquidity.

When a company is preparing its balance sheet, funds such as term loans are partly due and payable in under one year and partly due and payable in beyond one year. The ways to correctly break down such funds can be quite complex.

The bankers

Bankers provide money to corporate clients in a variety of ways. These include:

- Bank overdrafts. As overdrafts are repayable on demand, a prudent business will only use them to tide them over a temporary shortage of cash such as would be required by the Easter egg business we discussed earlier.
- Term loans. These are usually repayable over a period of years and the amount outstanding must be broken down into components that are due and payable in under and beyond one year. Term loans are frequently supported by security. Sometimes the lender is given the title deeds to company property and first claim on such property in the event of default. Such loans are similar to the mortgage of a homeowner.
- Hire purchase. The interest rate charged on hire purchase loans tends to be high and consequently organizations will prefer other forms of bank finance if they are available.
- Finance leases. These are similar to hire purchase loans except that the asset reverts to the lessor at the end of the lease period. Accounting for finance leases is examined in Chapter 16.

John has applied for and been granted a term loan of £40,000 and overdraft facilities of up to £10,000. In order to obtain these loans the bank requested the following:

- A presentation on John's business to persuade them that it is a good risk. This should cover the management, the technology, the competition, financial stability and profitability.
- Security to protect them against loss if the business fails. Security is normally sought by way of first claim on assets in liquidation and personal guarantees from the owners.
- A good indication of when the funding will no longer be required. Remember that bank overdrafts are repayable on demand. They are only suitable to pay for short-term investment. John will not be able to repay on demand, so he should seek a long-term loan.

The breakdown of term loan repayment obligations

A term loan commits an organization to periodic capital and interest payments. The capital element is a liability and must be shown in the balance sheet. Interest accrued but not yet paid is also a liability. The treatment is shown in the following illustration.

On 1 July 2001 Hungry Ltd arranged a term loan of £100,000 from its bankers. The loan was repayable in five equal annual instalments including interest at a fixed rate of 8 per cent pa. Compound interest tables (dealt with briefly in Chapter 12) will indicate a repayment of £25,046 per annum. Table 3.10 shows the breakdown of the repayments into amounts due and payable in under and beyond one year.

Table 3.10 *The breakdown of term loan repayment obligations*

Term loan repayment schedule, Hungry Ltd

	Opening loan	Interest	Loan and interest	Repaid	Closing loan
	A	$A \times 8\% = B$	$A + B = C$	D	$C - D = E$
1 July 2001	100,000	8,000	108,000	25,046	82,954
1 July 2002	82,954	6,636	89,590	25,046	64,544
1 July 2003	64,544	5,164	69,708	25,046	44,662
1 July 2004	44,662	3,574	48,236	25,046	23,190
1 July 2005	23,190	1,856	25,046	25,046	0

Division of annual repayments into capital and interest components

	Total repaid	Interest element	Capital element
30 June 2002	25,046	8,000	17,046
30 June 2003	25,046	6,636	18,410
30 June 2004	25,046	5,164	19,882
30 June 2005	25,046	3,574	21,472
30 June 2006	25,046	1,856	23,190
	125,230	25,230	100,000

Amounts due and payable in under and beyond one year

	Under 1 year	Beyond 1 year	Total
31 December 2001	17,046	82,954	100,000
31 December 2002	18,410	64,544	82,954
31 December 2003	19,882	44,662	64,544
31 December 2004	21,472	23,190	44,662
31 December 2005	23,190	0	23,190

In the balance sheet as at 31 December 2001, £17,046 will be recorded as due and payable in under one year and £82,954 will be recorded as due and payable in beyond one year. In addition, interest of £4,000 must be included in amounts due and payable in under one year and charged as an expense in the profit and loss account even though it may not be paid until 30 June 2002.

Hire purchase repayment obligations

If John decided to hire purchase his vehicle and it involved a 25 per cent deposit and 12 quarterly repayments (including interest at a flat rate of 12 per cent pa) and VAT at 17.5 per cent on the interest element, then the repayment obligations would be as shown in Table 3.11.

Table 3.11 *John's hire purchase of his vehicle*

Cost of vehicle		19,500.00
Less deposit		4,875.00
		14,625 00
Interest[a]	5,265.00	
VAT[b]	921.38	6,186.38
Total repayable		20,811.38

Quarterly repayment £20,811.38/12 = £1,734.28

Notes:
[a] £14,625 × 12% for 3 years = £5,265
[b] £5,265 × 17.5% = £921.38

The easiest way to compute the capital repayments is to use the Rule of 78. Using this rule, 12/78 of the total interest is allocated to the first quarter while the balance of this payment is the capital element. In the second quarter, 11/78 of the total interest is allocated, etc. Table 3.12 (p 58) shows the repayment obligations broken down into quarterly periods.

The creditors

A number of other liabilities are normally found in the amounts due and payable in the under one year section of the balance sheet. These include:

- trade creditors;
- accruals;

Table 3.12 *Hire purchase repayment obligations*

Quarter	Fraction	Gross interest A	Total repaid B	Capital repaid B–A	Total due	Under 1 year	Beyond 1 year
1	12/78	952[c]	1,734	782	13,843	3,923	9,920
2	11/78	872	1,734	862	12,981	4,240	8,741
3	10/78	793	1,734	941	12,040	4,557	7,483
4	9/78	714	1,735	1,021	11,019	4,874	6,145
5	8/78	635	1,734	1,099	9,920	5,192	4,728
6	7/78	555	1,734	1,179	8,741	5,509	3,232
7	6/78	476	1,734	1,258	7,483	5,826	1,657
8	5/78	397	1,735	1,338	6,145	6,145	–
9	4/78	317	1,734	1,417	4,728	4,728	–
10	3/78	238	1,734	1,496	3,232	3,232	–
11	2/78	159	1,734	1,575	1,657	1,657	–
12	1/78	78[d]	1,735	1,657	–	–	–
		6,186	20,811	14,625			

Note:
The capital repayments are included in the balance sheet as per the last two columns. The interest is charged as a cost in the profit and loss account (after deducting VAT, which will be offset against the amount charged to customers). The allocation of interest, using the rule of 78, is: [c] £6,186 × 12/78 = £952 [d] £6,186 × 1/78 = £78, etc.

- proposed dividends;
- customer advances.

Trade creditors

Trade creditors are suppliers that have not yet been paid. Most businesses relieve some of the pressure on cash by purchasing goods from suppliers on credit. If John Bermingham could arrange six weeks' credit it would slow down the cash decline. He would start by paying £10,000 to suppliers in week 7. At the end of 10 weeks he would not yet have paid for supplies bought in weeks 5–10. The improvement in the cash position is shown in Table 3.13.

Accruals

In Chapter 2 we saw that some services such as telephone and electricity are billed to an organization in arrears. Such costs must be estimated and accrued. This involves including them in the balance sheet as a liability and

Table 3.13 *The effect of supplier credit on the cash position*

Original closing cash			1,100
Unpaid amounts	Week	£	
	5	1,000	
	6	1,000	
	7	1,200	
	8	1,200	
	9	1,200	
	10	1,200	6,800
Revised closing cash			7,900

Note:
The £6,800 not yet paid will be shown in his balance sheet as trade creditors in the category amounts due and payable in under one year.

in the profit and loss account as a cost. The term loan example examined earlier requires an interest accrual.

Proposed dividends

A successful business usually pays a dividend to its shareholders. Normally the draft accounts are submitted to a board meeting charged with recommending an appropriate dividend. In Chapter 2 we saw how the directors made provision for the dividend in the profit and loss account. This dividend will not be paid until it is approved by shareholders at the AGM. In the meantime it is an amount due and payable in under one year.

Customer advances (unearned income)

Some organizations are in the fortunate position where customers pay in advance. For example, you pay for your package holiday some time before you travel. In the accounts of the travel agent the amount you have paid will not be earned until you travel. Consequently, while their cash box is enriched, their profit and loss account will not include the cash inflow, which is really a form of creditor. This must be included as unearned income in the amounts due and payable in under one year.

An interesting example of the difficulty that can be involved in estimating unearned income is the Royal Mail. It receives cash when you buy stamps but does not earn the income until you post the letter or parcel. It is difficult but necessary to estimate the amount and value of unused stamps so that these can be excluded from its profit and loss account and recognized as unearned income in its balance sheet.

The state

The state provides funds to business in three major ways:

- unpaid taxes;
- capital grants; and
- cost subventions. These are netted against the gross cost in the profit and loss account and do not affect the balance sheet.

Unpaid taxes

Any organization can quite legitimately obtain some credit from the tax authorities. VAT, National Insurance and PAYE are paid in arrears. Since the money has been charged to the customers or deducted from the employees, this credit eases the pressure on cash. The nice thing about it is that the funding is reasonably permanent. For example, a company has started a new cycle of VAT charges before it pays the VAT for the previous accounting period. Readers should note that the practice of not paying taxes when they become due is to be avoided. The penal interest charges make this a very expensive source of funds.

In Chapter 2 we saw that a profitable business must provide for corporation tax. The company and its auditors will calculate the liability. It will then be deducted from the profit before tax in the profit and loss account. The provision will be included in the amounts due and payable in under one year.

Capital grants

If John starts his business in a 'development area', he may obtain a grant towards the cost of his plant. SSAP 4 requires that in the balance sheet such grants are recorded as deferred income rather than as a reduction from the cost of the related asset. This is necessary to comply with paragraphs 17 and 26 of schedule 4 to the Companies Act 1985. The main requirements of SSAP 4 are:

a. Fixed assets should be shown at purchase price or production cost.
b. Depreciation based on this cost must be deducted to provide for replacement.
c. Grants, which contribute towards specific expenditure on fixed assets,

must be released to profit and loss over the expected lives of the related assets.

d. Deferred credits in respect of grants must be included under the heading 'Accruals and deferred income' and identified separately in a note to the balance sheet.

e. The amount credited to the profit and loss account in respect of grants must be disclosed in a note.

f. Potential liabilities to repay grants in specified circumstances should be disclosed in accordance with SSAP 18, Accounting for Contingencies.

Grant illustration

A company has just purchased a machine at a cost of £100,000. It obtained a capital grant of 15 per cent. The grant agreement specified that it would be repayable in full if the asset was disposed of within five years and that the amount repayable on disposal would decline at a rate of 20 per cent pa thereafter. The machine will have a 10-year life and zero disposal value; see Table 3.14.

Table 3.14 _Balance sheet disclosure_

Year	Plant at cost	Aggregate depreciation	Book value	Deferred credit	Contingent liability
0	100,000	–	100,000	15,000	15,000
1	100,000	10,000	90,000	13,500	15,000
2	100,000	20,000	80,000	12,000	15,000
3	100,000	30,000	70,000	10,500	15,000
4	100,000	40,000	60,000	9,000	15,000
5	100,000	50,000	50,000	7,500	15,000
6	100,000	60,000	40,000	6,000	12,000
7	100,000	70,000	30,000	4,500	9,000
8	100,000	80,000	20,000	3,000	6,000
9	100,000	90,000	10,000	1,500	3,000
10	100,000	100,000	–	–	–
Rule	A	B		D	F

The company provides £10,000 per annum for depreciation but offsets £1,500 of this by reducing the amount of deferred income each year. The contingent liability is shown in the notes to the accounts (rule F). The depreciated liability is shown as deferred income in the funding section of the balance sheet (rule D). This treatment would not be used if a 'going concern' approach could not be justified. The liability would be real rather than contingent.

The Companies Act 1985 permits two balance sheet layouts. We will now examine the balance sheet as John Birmingham expects it to look after 10 weeks in business; see Table 3.15.

Table 3.15 *Balance sheet, John Bermingham as at week 10*

Layout 1

	£	£
Fixed assets[1]		71,750
Current assets		
Stocks[2]	14,020	
Debtors	7,520	
Insurance prepaid[3]	1,050	22,590
		94,340
Financed by:		
Creditors amounts due in under one year		
Trade creditors	6,800	
Bank overdraft[4]	6,900	13,700
Creditor amount due beyond one year		
Term loan		40,000
Deferred income[5]		10,788
Shareholders' funds		
Share capital	30,000	
Less loss on operations[6]	148	29,852
		94,340

Notes:

[1]	Plant	Vehicle	Total
Cost	55,000	19,500	74,500
Depreciation	2,000	750	2,750
Book value	53,000	18,750	71,750

The plant is depreciated at the rate of £200 per week. After 10 weeks the book value will be £53,000. The vehicle, which will cost £19,500, is depreciated at the rate of £75 per week. After 10 weeks the book value will be £18,750

[2] Material £9,000 + WIP £220 + Finished £4,800 = £14,020

[3] 42 weeks' unexpired insurance.

[4] The closing overdraft is made up as follows:

Table 3.15 _(continued)_

Inflows		Outflows	
Capital introduced	30,000	Paid for materials[a]	13,000
Term loan introduced	40,000	Paid for conversion[b]	2,140
Grant received	11,000	Insurance	1,300
Collections from customers	3,040	Fixed assets	74,500
	84,040		90,940

With £90,940 to be paid out and £84,04 to be collected John will need an overdraft of £6,900.

[a] Purchases £19,800 less creditors £6,800 = £13,000
[b] Weeks 1–5 = £960. Weeks 6–10 = £1,180
[5] 510 weeks of the 10-year grant period remains deferred.
[6] The draft profit and loss account is:

Sales	10,560
Cost of sales	7,920
Gross profit	2,640
Depreciation	(2,750)
Insurance	(250)
Grant amortization	212
Loss for period	148

LAYOUT 2
Fixed assets

			71,750
Current assets			
Stocks	14,020		
Debtors	7,520		
Insurance prepaid	1,050	22,590	
Creditors due within one year			
Trade creditors	6,800		
Bank overdraft	6,900	13,700	8,890
			80,640
Financed by:			
Creditors due in beyond one year			
Term loan			40,000
Deferred income			10,788
Shareholders' funds			
Share capital	30,000		
Loss on operations	146		29,852
			80,640

Layout 1 shows the total assets and how they are financed. Layout 2 shows the net assets (after deducting short-term liabilities) and how they are financed. Most organizations use layout 2. I prefer layout 1: it highlights the total assets. This corresponds with disclosure in the United States.

Provisions for deferred tax and rationalization will be shown separately as is the deferred income such as government grants.

WHAT A BALANCE SHEET DOES NOT TELL YOU

At the start of the chapter I stressed that a balance sheet is normally prepared on a going concern basis. Consequently, it does not take into account potential liabilities, some of which may only mature in unexpected circumstances. Consider the contingent liability that should be provided where a customer is suing for product defect. SSAP 18 requires that contingent liabilities are disclosed in the notes to the accounts.

There used to be a more sinister way of excluding relevant information from the balance sheet. This is referred to as 'off-balance sheet finance'. It involves the creation of an artificial, but legal, structure designed to permit netting of assets and liabilities with a view to concealing debt. The most popular approach is to transfer legal title to a third party while the 'real' owner continues to bear the risks and enjoy the benefits related to such items. FRS 5, Reporting the substance of transactions, is designed to tackle cases where devices were used to obscure the presentation of a 'true and fair view'. The key principle is that the substance of a transaction takes precedence over its legal form. Before the introduction of this standard SSAP 21 had already enshrined this principle in accounting for finance leases. FRS 5 broadened the principle to apply to all attempts to make a balance sheet show less than a true and fair view. FRS 5 thus helps readers of financial statements to interpret them correctly. It proposes that where a complex transaction is entered into for the specific purpose of removing items from a balance sheet, such items should be restored with the intention of providing 'a true and fair view'.

Examples of devices with a specific intent to remove items from a balance sheet include:

- *Finance leases.* These were specifically reinstated in the balance sheet by SSAP 21.
- *Consignment stock.* This is stock to which legal title does not transfer at point of delivery. The vital issue is whether the balance sheet of the vendor or the purchaser should include this stock. The answer is: the

balance sheet of the entity that bears the risks and rewards consistent with ownership. In practice this is often the purchaser.

- _Sale and repurchase agreements._ For example, disposal of trading stock to a third party, accompanied by an option to repurchase it for the same amount plus interest. Is such a transaction a bona fide sale or has it the characteristics of a secured loan? The answer is frequently a secured loan that must be reinstated.
- _Debt factoring._ This involves the replacement of a group of debtors with one debtor the factor. A problem only arises where factoring results in a speed up of cash collection. The issue is whether the enhanced cash flow has the characteristics of a loan or of a reduction in trade debtors.
- _Quasi subsidiaries._ This usually involves the creation of an entity that has all the attributes of a subsidiary except legal form. Assets and liabilities are transferred from the originator to its quasi subsidiary. Prior to the introduction of the standard the transferred items could have been netted and shown as an investment in the group accounts. FRS 5 requires the asset and liability to be shown if the risks and rewards flow to the originator.
- _Loan transfers._ These arise where a borrower lends part or all of the loan to a third party. Only when onerous tests are satisfied can the asset be netted against the liability.

FRS 5 has had a stormy reception from the legal profession. Lawyers argue that objectivity is best served by sticking to the letter of the law rather than following the 'substance over form' rule. A major battle between the professions is ongoing. Table 3.16 (p 66) is an example of off-balance sheet transactions.

Prior to FRS 5 the result of these manoeuvres would have converted a company that was substantially in debt into a cash-positive one. FRS 5 ensures that a 'true and fair view' based on 'substance taking precedence over legal form' is reported.

SUMMARY

The balance sheet shows the assets and how they are financed, at a particular point in time, on a going concern basis. If prepared one week earlier or later, it could disclose a very different picture.

The content is broken into five major categories:

1. fixed assets;
2. current assets;

Table 3.16 *Illustration of off-balance sheet transactions: The Tricky plc balance sheet*

	Pre-manoeuvre	Pre-FRS5	Post-FRS5
Buildings	1,800,000	–	1,800,000[1]
Investment		200,000 [1]	–
Trading stock	500,000	–	500,000[2]
Short-term debt			(500,000)[2]
Cash		500,000[2]	500,000
	2,300,000	700,000	2,300,000
Financed by:			
Share capital	600,000	600,000	600,000
Reserves	300,000	100,000[1]	100,000
Minority interest			200,000[1]
Long-term debt	1,400,000	–	1,400,000[1]
	2,300,000	700,000	2,300,000

Notes:

[1] The building and term loan were transferred to a friendly company. Tricky plc holds 50% of the shares but does not control the composition of the board of directors. This is the legal position. In reality Tricky plc can buy back the building for £1.8m at any time and it must make the repayments on the term loan. Prior to FRS5 the book value of the building and the term loan obligations could have been removed from the balance sheet and replaced with an investment (50% of the net assets of the friendly company). Tricky plc has apparently given away 50% of the net assets (£200,000); this 'loss' is deducted from reserves. The building and term loan must be reinstated. A minority interest of £200,000 is included in the Tricky plc balance sheet.

[2] Tricky plc sold the trading stock to a third party. The stock remains on their premises and they will sell it. As sales are made, Tricky plc pays the cost plus interest to a finance house. Tricky carries the risk or reaps the reward. Prior to FRS5 the stock would have been replaced with cash. The stock is reinstated but matched by a loan of a similar amount.

3. amounts due and payable in under one year;
4. amounts due and payable in beyond one year;
5. shareholders' funds.

The balance sheet is not meant to disclose the disposal value of the assets.

Some complex issues encountered in balance sheets are covered in the final part of this chapter. If you are eager to push on with the basics of finance, you may choose to proceed to Chapter 4 and return to this when you encounter strange items in a balance sheet.

OTHER BALANCE SHEET ITEMS

Here we deal with complex items that may affect the balance sheet of a business: loan stocks; finance leases; operating leases; investments in other businesses; and intangible fixed assets.

Loan stocks

Loan stocks are long-term funding, with priority over preference and ordinary shares for payment of interest and return of capital. Variations are similar to preference shares:

- fixed interest (eg 10 per cent);
- variable interest (eg revised quarterly relative to London Interbank Offered Rate, for instance, LIBOR plus 2 per cent.);
- secured or unsecured;
- redeemable or irredeemable;
- convertible or non-convertible.

The various forms of loan stock are similar to those of preference shares described earlier in the chapter. In the United States, loan stocks are often referred to as 'junk bonds'.

Finance leases

The rules of accounting relating to finance leases are explained in Chapter 16 where two examples are also given. For the present it is sufficient to state that SSAP 21 regards any lease in which the repayment obligations, after netting out the interest charges, represents 90 per cent or more of the fair value of the leased asset, as really akin to bank borrowings. This was the first example of the principle that substance should take precedence over legal form. SSAP 21 requires that:

- Interest should be eliminated from the future lease obligations and the balance broken down and disclosed in amounts due and payable in under and beyond one year. The computation is similar to that illustrated in the term loan example earlier in the chapter.

- A leased fixed asset should be installed in the balance sheet (included in tangible fixed assets but shown separately) to match the indebtedness thus created.
- The lease instalments be divided into a depreciation element and a finance charge and reported in the profit and loss account.
- In the accounts of the lessor the leased asset should not be recorded as a tangible fixed asset as it would have been prior to the introduction of SSAP 21. Instead, the real underlying asset, a loan repayable by instalments, is reported.

Prior to the introduction of SSAP 21 the lease instalments were charged as an expense in the profit and loss account. This charge is now replaced by the depreciation and finance charges that such instalments are designed to recoup.

This is an excellent piece of accounting legislation. It recognizes that the lessee takes the risks and rewards consistent with ownership and presents the underlying asset and the bank debt that would have been concealed under the previous rules.

Operating leases

If, after netting out the finance charge, less than 90 per cent of the capital cost is repaid through the life of the lease, then it is an operating lease. A typical example is a three-year lease of an aircraft. The lessee in this case does not take the major risks and rewards consistent with ownership, as the asset reverts to the owner who depends on finding a new lease customer or selling the aircraft second-hand. The asset and debt are not included in the balance sheet and the expense to be charged against profits is the lease instalments for the accounting period. The repayment obligations must be disclosed in the notes to the accounts. The treatment of operating leases is explained in more detail in Chapter 16.

Investments in other businesses

Where a business has surplus funds it may decide to invest them in other businesses. The investments may be short term in nature and be classified as current assets, or strategic in nature and classified as fixed assets. There are some difficulties with the balance sheet valuation of investments in other businesses. Such investments arise in three situations:

1. investment in subsidiaries;
2. investment in related companies;
3. smaller investments.

Investment in a subsidiary

A subsidiary is defined by section 736 of the Companies Act 1985 as:

a) A company in which another body corporate either;
  i) Is a member and controls the composition of the board of directors, or
  ii) Holds more than half in nominal value of its equity share capital, or
b) A company, which is a subsidiary of a holding company's subsidiary.

Group accounts are required. The investment is replaced by the underlying assets in the group accounts. An example of how this is done is given in Chapter 16. Delicate issues arise in relation to goodwill, minority interests, third party transactions, etc.

Investment in a related company

A related company is defined in paragraphs 13–16 of SSAP 1:

13 A company not being a subsidiary of the investing group or company in which:

a) the interest of the investing group or company is effectively that of a partner in a joint venture or consortium and the investing group or company is in a position to exercise a significant influence over the company in which the investment is made; or
b) the interest of the investing group or company is for the long term and is substantial and, having regard to the disposition of the other shareholdings, the investing group or company is in a position to exercise a significant influence over the company in which the investment is made. Significant influence over a company essentially involves participation in the financial and operating policy decisions of that company (including dividend policy) but not necessarily control of those policies. Representation on the board of directors is indicative of such participation but will neither necessarily give conclusive evidence of it nor be the only method by which the investing company may participate in policy decisions.

14 Where the interest of the investing group or company is not effectively that of a partner in a joint venture or consortium but amounts to 20 per cent or more of the equity voting rights of a company, it should be presumed that the investing group or company has the ability to exercise significant influence over that company unless it can clearly be demonstrated otherwise. For example, there may exist one or more other large shareholdings that prevent the exercise of such influence.

15 Where the interest of the investing group or company is not effectively that of a partner in a joint venture or consortium and amounts to less than 20 per cent of the equity voting rights of a company, it should be presumed that the investing group or company does not have the ability to exercise significant influence unless it can clearly be demonstrated otherwise. Unless there are exceptional circumstances, this demonstration should include a statement from the company in which the investment is made that it accepts that the investing group or company is in a position to exercise significant influence over it.

16 Where different companies in a group hold shares in a company, the investment in that company should be taken as the aggregate of the holdings of the investing company together with the whole of those of its subsidiaries but excluding those of its associates in determining whether significant influence is presumed to exist.

Group accounts are again required. The investment is shown in these at cost plus appropriate proportion of the undistributed profits less losses since the shares were acquired.

Tree plc bought 40 per cent of the shares of Branch Ltd at par. In the year after the investment, Branch Ltd made a profit of £400,000 after tax. No dividends were declared or paid. Table 3.17 shows how the investment in Branch Ltd is reported in the group balance sheet.

Table 3.17 *The group accounts of Tree plc*

Balance sheets (£'000)	Tree plc	Group
Other net assets	5,000	5,000
Investment in Branch Ltd	1,600	1,760[1]
	6,600	6,760
Share capital	4,000	4,000
Reserves	2,600	2,760[1]
	6,600	6,760

Note:
[1] 40% of the profit after tax is added to the value of the investment and the revenue reserves.

If Branch Ltd had paid a dividend of £200,000 on its share capital then the group accounts would be as shown in Table 3.18.

Table 3.18   *The group accounts of Tree plc if a dividend had been received*

Balance sheets (£'000)	Tree plc	Group
Other net assets	5,080	5,080[1]
Investment in Branch Ltd	1,600	1,680[2]
	6,680	6,760
Share capital	4,000	4,000
Reserves	2,680[1]	2,760[1]
	6,680	6,760

Notes:

[1] A dividend of £80,000 was received. This increased the net assets and reserves of Tree.

[2] 40% of the profit retained is added to the value of the investment and the revenue reserves.

Investments that do not confer subsidiary or related status

The treatment of smaller investments depends on whether the shares are quoted on the stock exchange or not. In the case of quoted shares that at the balance sheet date are worth more than they cost, the valuation is usually the cost supported by a note in the accounts that shows the market value. Sometimes the shareholding company decides to revalue the shares to reflect the capital gain. In line with the general principle that provision should be made for all known losses and the rules of impairment, the value shown in the balance sheet should be reduced to reflect the capital loss. The market value is normally the mid-market price at the close of business on the balance sheet date.

In the case of unquoted shares they are usually shown at cost unless they are worth less than they cost. The directors of the investor company are responsible for carrying out the valuation. As a general guideline the shares of unquoted companies are usually deemed to be worth 20 per cent to 25 per cent less than quoted peers.

Intangible fixed assets

The term 'intangible assets' is derived from Latin and means you cannot touch (feel) them. Intangible assets generally reflect the potential to provide

71

future profits. The model layouts permitted by the Companies Act 1985 require the disclosure of intangible assets as a section of fixed assets.

Purchased goodwill

FRS 10 defines goodwill as the difference between the cost of an acquired entity and the aggregate of the fair values of that entity's identifiable assets and liabilities. (Fair value is defined in FRS 7 as the amount at which an asset or liability could be exchanged in an arm's length transaction between informed and willing parties, other than in a forced sale or liquidation.) Positive goodwill arises when the acquisition cost exceeds the fair value of the identifiable assets and liabilities. Negative goodwill arises when the aggregate fair values of the identifiable assets and liabilities of the entity exceed the acquisition cost. The best way to help you to understand goodwill is to give you an example of how it arises.

Acquisitive plc is interested in the take-over of a company the fair value of whose net assets is £10 million and has 5 million shares in issue. Acquisitive plc offers £2.50 cash per share, thereby valuing the company at £12.5 million. If this offer is accepted then the value of goodwill is £2.5 million. In this case the purchase consideration exceeds the fair value of the net assets acquired. Why might a company offer £12.5 million for the net assets of another business when that business has net assets of only £10 million? The reason is that the company may enjoy advantages that are not attributable to the identifiable assets and liabilities. Such advantages include:

- customer loyalty;
- reputation for quality;
- marketing and distribution skills;
- technical know-how;
- established business connections;
- management ability;
- level of workforce training, etc.

These factors could lead to increased economic benefits above those that would be expected using the same basket of identifiable assets and liabilities without these advantages. The existence of negative goodwill would imply disadvantages.

The major problem with goodwill is that it can only be known with reasonable certainty at the point when a business and its inherent goodwill is sold.

The key rules relating to goodwill are:

- Purchased goodwill only arises in the case of acquisition accounting. (The difference between an acquisition and a merger is examined in Chapter 15.)
- Paragraph 7 of FRS 10 requires that positive purchased goodwill should be capitalized and classified as an asset in the balance sheet. The previous approach used by many companies of cancelling the goodwill against reserves is no longer allowed. Paragraph 68 of the standard permits the reinstatement of goodwill previously written off but it is not mandatory to do so.
- Purchased goodwill is based on the difference between the fair value of the assets less liabilities acquired and the purchase consideration.
- No amount should be included for non-purchased goodwill. (It may exist but cannot be objectively valued).
- The amount attributed to purchased goodwill should not include any value for identifiable intangible fixed assets. Such value should be included under the appropriate intangible asset heading.
- FRS 10 requires that purchased goodwill should be amortized through the profit and loss account only to the extent that the carrying value is not supported by the current value of the goodwill within the acquired business. Systematic amortization is a practical means of recognizing the reduction in value of goodwill that has a limited useful economic life.
- The useful life should not exceed 20 years. A period of up to 40 years is permitted where it can be demonstrated to be more appropriate.
- Goodwill should be reviewed annually to determine whether the carrying value is excessive. Each acquisition should be reviewed separately. Any permanent diminution should be written down immediately through the profit and loss account. Purchased goodwill should not be revalued upwards.
- Negative goodwill should be credited systematically to the profit and loss account. The average life of the fixed assets acquired may provide a suitable period over which to take the credit.

Purchased goodwill illustration

To illustrate the approach to accounting for purchased goodwill we will assume that the offer of £2.50 per share made by Acquisitive plc was accepted by all shareholders. The assets and liabilities to be included in the group balance sheet are shown in Table 3.19 (p 74).

Table 3.19 *Calculating and reporting purchased goodwill*

£'000		Pre-acquisition	For consolidation
Goodwill			1,500[2]
Premises at cost	4,000		
Less depreciation	400		
		3,600	4,900[1]
Plant at cost	2,000		
Less depreciation	600		
		1,400	1,100[1]
Other assets		9,800	9,800
Liabilities		(4,800)	(4,800)
Net assets		10,000	12,500

Notes:

[1] The premises were valued at £4.9 million shortly after the acquisition. This fair value was included in the group balance sheet. The plant is three years old and was depreciated at a rate of 10% pa straight line. The Acquisitive plc depreciation policy is 15% pa straight line. The book value is adjusted to comply with the group accounting policy.

[2] The adjusted value of the net assets acquired is £11 million. Comparison with the purchase consideration of £12.5 million gives rise to a goodwill valuation of £1.5 million.

If Acquisitive plc decided to ascribe a life of 10 years to the purchased goodwill, the balance sheet value would be reduced by £150,000 per annum. This amount would be charged as a cost in the profit and loss account.

FRS 11 requires that an impairment review be carried out each year. If the review of goodwill relating to this acquisition three years later suggested that a life of six years was more appropriate, owing to a decline in the scale of advantages promising economic benefits, the value would be adjusted as shown in Table 3.20.

Table 3.20 *Adjusting for a decline in the value of goodwill*

£'000	Pre-review	Post-review
Goodwill at cost	1,500	1,500
Less depreciation	450	750
Balance sheet value	1,050	750

The effect of this would be to increase the amortization charge in the third year to £450,000. This charge is required because the impairment review revealed that there was a shortfall of £100,000 per annum in the amortization charge in the previous two years and a charge of £250,000 is required in the current year. The charge in subsequent years will be £250,000 pa unless a further impairment review leads to another change.

Brand names

As previously stated, the current rules of accounting do not permit the inclusion of a value for internally generated goodwill in the balance sheet. An internationally recognized brand is similar to internally generated goodwill and is allowed to be included in the balance sheet. A brand name such as Guinness or Coca-Cola is a very valuable asset of its owners. It leads to a reasonable expectation of customer loyalty and exceptional future profits. FRS 10 permits the inclusion of a value for brands in the intangible fixed assets of a business. Brand valuation is based on the present value of the future stream of earnings that are expected to be derived from them. The present value technique is described in Chapter 12. To permit a brand value to be included in a balance sheet its name must be capable of being sold separately from the underlying business. Multinational drinks companies tend to include brands in their balance sheets as the 'household' names indicate the possibility of sale of the name rather than the business.

The issue of branding first came to prominence with the take-over offer for Rowntree Macintosh by Nestlé. In the UK it was widely believed that the shareholders accepted an inadequate offer because the balance sheet failed to recognize the value of the company brands. It has now become popular to include major brands in the balance sheet as a defence against unwanted take-over bids at inadequate prices. Perhaps the best example was the inclusion of £678 million for brands in the balance sheet of Rank Hovis McDougall (representing more than 50 per cent of its stock market capitalization).

When a company includes brands in its balance sheet the value must be amortized and regular impairment reviews carried out. The previous example showing the impact of an impairment review of goodwill applies to brands in exactly the same way.

Patents

A patent is a legal protection against imitation by competitors. A business should try to protect itself against such imitation: competitors with better marketing or distribution might otherwise capture your profitable future business. Patents can be difficult to register and breaches of patent are notoriously difficult to prove. However, registration or purchase of a patent can protect profit potential. FRS 10 requires that patents be amortized over their useful economic life (generally not exceeding 20 years) and reviewed annually to determine whether the amortization period remains appropriate or whether impairment has occurred.

Trademarks

A trademark is a protection against imitation of a product name. A good product name offers an expectation of future profit. As with the previous intangible fixed assets, FRS 10 must be applied.

Licences and franchises

A company may not have the capability to manufacture and/or market a product that it has developed and patented. In this case, it may license or franchise other companies to manufacture or sell the product. A household name, eg Coca-Cola or McDonald's, would charge a substantial up-front fee for the licence or franchise. An acquirer is paying a premium in the hope of future profits. FRS 10 also applies to licences and franchises.

Research and development

The rules of accounting for research and development are defined in paragraphs 24–26 of SSAP 13:

24 Expenditure on pure and applied research should be written off in the year of expenditure through the profit and loss account.

25 Development expenditure should be written off in the year of expenditure except in the following circumstances when it may be deferred to future periods:

a) there is a clearly defined project,
b) the related expenditure is separately identifiable, and
c) the outcome of such a project has been assessed with reasonable certainty as to:
   i) Its technical feasibility, and
   ii) Its ultimate commercial viability considered in the light of factors such as likely market conditions (including competing products), public opinion, consumer and environmental legislation, and

d) the aggregate of the deferred development costs, any further development costs, and related production, selling and administration costs is reasonably expected to be exceeded by related future sales or other revenues, and

e) adequate resources exist, or are reasonably expected to be available, to enable the project to be completed and to provide any consequential increases in working capital.

26 In the foregoing circumstances development expenditure may be deferred to the extent that its recovery can reasonably be regarded as assured.

In these circumstances the development expenditure is reported as an intangible fixed asset.

Preliminary expenses

When a company is formed, certain legal expenses are incurred in developing an appropriate set of rules (the Memorandum and Articles of Association). Since the company will not have any income at this stage, there is no place to offset the preliminary expenses. They can be carried forward as an intangible asset. Preliminary expenses have no ongoing value to a business. They should be written off as soon as profits are earned.

Disclosure of intangibles in the balance sheet

The model layouts permitted by the Companies Act 1985 require the disclosure of intangible assets as a section of fixed assets.

4

The cash flow statement

It may seem strange, but the majority of businesses that become bankrupt are making a profit at the time they fail. They simply run out of cash. There are two major reasons. First, rapid growth in sales is usually accompanied by increased investment in stocks and debtors. This results in insufficient cash flowing into the business to pay suppliers, staff and other running costs. The faster the growth the greater will be the pressure on cash resources. Second, the management might imprudently use the cash needed to pay the day-to-day running costs, to buy fixed assets or to acquire another business. Such tragic liquidations need not happen. To avoid them management must recognize that it needs to have access to substantial cash resources.

Until 1991 the reporting of cash was presented in the less than informative Source and Application of Funds Statement. The spotlight was more firmly placed on cash with the introduction of FRS 1 in 1991, which was revised and updated in 1996. The primary role of FRS 1 is to provide readers of accounts with an understanding of whether the organization has experienced an increase or reduction in cash in the reporting period and the reasons why. By reviewing liquidity the cash flow statement, in my opinion, is a more important financial report than the profit and loss account or balance sheet. The liquidity review is carried out by:

- revealing the cash inflows and outflows during a reporting period;
- summarizing them to show the cash created or consumed in running the business from day to day;

- reconciling this cash creation or consumption with the net cash or net debt in the opening and closing balance sheet.

Paragraph 2 of the standard provides a very specific definition of the word 'cash':

A) Cash in hand
B) Deposits repayable on demand
C) Less overdrafts repayable on demand.

Deposits are deemed to be repayable on demand if they can be withdrawn at any time without notice and without penalty, or if a maturity period of not more than 24 hours has been agreed.

This three-part definition may seem surprising. However, it makes sense when deposits are readily accessible and carry no interest penalty for withdrawal and it is possible to have immediate access to further cash by drawing down the firm's overdraft facility.

The following example shows the primary reason why cash flow can be a major business problem. Deborah Derby is about to set up a new business. Extracts from her financial plan are presented in Tables 4.1 (below), 4.2 (p 80) and 4.3 (also p 80).

Table 4.1 _Key operating forecasts, Deborah Derby_

Month	Capital introduced	Sales[1]	Collections from customers	Supplier payments	Staff payments	Overhead payments
Jan	50,000	10,000	–	7,500	3,000	5,000
Feb		20,000	5,000	12,500	5,000	7,000
Mar		30,000	15,000	17,500	7,000	9,000
Apr		40,000	25,000	22,500	9,000	11,000
May		50,000	35,000	27,500	11,000	13,000
Jun		60,000	45,000	32,500	13,000	15,000

[1] Selling price £1 per unit

Deborah also arranged an overdraft facility of £40,000. Given her predicted cash flows this will not be enough to allow her to pay her bills over the first six months. Consider her cash forecast, shown in Table 4.3 (p 80).

If Deborah sticks to this plan she will be trying to sell more than her cash resources will permit. She is said to be 'over-trading'. The problem for Deborah is caused by two major factors. First, she expects to collect 50 per

Table 4.2 *Forecast profit and loss account, Deborah Derby*

	£'000	£'000
Sales		210
Purchases	120	
Payroll	48	
Overheads	60	
Less stock (30,000 at 90p each)	(27)	201
Profit		9

Table 4.3 *Cash forecast, Deborah Derby*

£'000	Jan	Feb	Mar	Apr	May	Jun	Total
Inflows							
Capital	50.0						50
Collections	–	5.0	15.0	25.0	35.0	45.0	125
	50.0	5.0	15.0	25.0	35.0	45.0	175
Outflows							
Suppliers	7.5	12.5	17.5	22.5	27.5	32.5	120
Staff	3.0	5.0	7.0	9.0	11.0	13.0	48
Overheads	5.0	7.0	9.0	11.0	13.0	15.0	60
	15.5	24.5	33.5	42.5	51.5	60.5	228
Month balance	34.5	(19.5)	(18.5)	(17.5)	(16.5)	(15.5)	(53)
Opening cash	–	34.5	15.0	(3.5)	(21.0)	(37.5)	
Closing cash	34.5	15.0	(3.5)	(21.0)	(37.5)	(53.0)	

cent of each month's sales in the following month and the remaining 50 per cent after a further month. Deborah will be making a major investment in trade debtors. Second, her production in each month will be 5,000 units greater than her sales. This will allow her to be sure to have product for sale at all times. Deborah will be making a major investment in stock.

Neither of these investments may be obvious to Deborah. They reflect the fact that she must pay her suppliers, staff and overheads a considerable time before she will collect from her customers. A cash flow statement would show the problem; see Table 4.4.

A footnote to her cash flow statement would explain the reason for the large outflow to operating activities. It can be presented in an indirect or direct method format, as shown in Table 4.5.

Table 4.4 *Cash flow statement, Deborah Derby*

	£'000
Net cash flow to operating activities	(103)
Financing activity	
Issue of shares for cash	50
Decrease in cash for period	53

Table 4.5 *Footnote to cash flow statement, indirect and direct methods, Deborah Derby*

Indirect method		Direct method		
Operating profit	9	Collections from customers		125
Less increase in stocks	(27)	Payments to suppliers	120	
increase in debtors	(85)	Payments to staff	48	
	(103)	Payment of overheads	60	228
				(103)

Both formats have advantages and disadvantages. The advantage of the indirect method is that it is easy to see how it is linked to the operating profit. The disadvantage is that the reason for some of the adjustments is difficult for non-experts to understand. The converse is true of the direct method. The advantage is that it is easy for non-experts to understand. The disadvantage is that it is not easy to see how it is linked to the operating profit.

The Accounting Standards Board (ASB) has allowed companies to use either format. Personally I prefer the direct method. It paints a clear picture of the underlying cash flows. Most companies have chosen to use the indirect method. Such a report may be more meaningful to accounting experts since it reconciles the operating profit (£9,000 in this case) with the cash flow to or from operating activities.

Deborah will need to recognize that through the second half of the year her cash problem will become even more serious. If her sales continue to grow by 10,000 units per month her cash outflows will continue to exceed her cash inflows, albeit at a declining rate. Deborah's cash forecast for the second half of the year is shown in Table 4.6 (p 82).

Table 4.6 *Cash forecast July to December, Deborah Derby*

£'000	Jul	Aug	Sep	Oct	Nov	Dec	Total
Inflows							
Collections	55.0	65.0	75.0	85.0	95.0	105.0	480
Outflows							
Suppliers	37.5	42.5	47.5	52.5	57.5	62.5	300
Staff	15.0	17.0	19.0	21.0	23.0	25.0	120
Overheads	17.0	19.0	21.0	23.0	25.0	27.0	132
	69.5	78.5	87.5	96.5	105.5	114.5	552
Month balance	(14.5)	(13.5)	(12.5)	(11.5)	(10.5)	(9.5)	(72)
Opening cash	(53.0)	(67.5)	(81.0)	(93.5)	(105.0)	(115.5)	(53)
Closing cash	(67.5)	(81.0)	(93.5)	(105.0)	(115.5)	(125.0)	(125)

Note:
Deborah will need a bank loan of £125,000 to cover her planned expenditure for the first year. Her business is predicted to be quite profitable but could run out of cash.

Profit and loss account January to December

£'000		
Sales		780
Purchases	420	
Staff costs	168	
Overhead costs	192	
	780	
Less stock (60,000 × 90p)	54	726
		54

Note:
In addition to her need for cash to pay operating costs Deborah will be faced with a tax bill of some £10,000 in the second year. She will need to try to borrow even more money to pay this tax.

The forecast cash flow statement shows why the bank debt will accelerate at a frightening pace if Deborah achieves her production and sales goals.

Budgeted cash flow statement £'000

Budgeted cash flow statement	£'000
Operating activities	(175)
Capital introduced	50
Decrease in cash	(125)

Indirect method			**Direct method**		
Operating profit	54		Collections from customers		605
Less increase in stocks	(54)		Payments to suppliers	420	
Increase in debtors	(175)		Payments to staff	168	
	(175)		Payment of overheads	192	780
					(175)

This example illustrates the horrifying drain on cash that can occur in a manufacturing industry that must hold stock and give credit to customers. If you operate in a service industry you might think that a similar problem could not occur. It certainly could. In many service industries staff costs and overheads have to be paid in advance of collections from customers.

Deborah could try to take some of the pressure off her cash resources. There are four possible options. She might arrange to:

1. operate with a lower level of stock;
2. collect from her customers more quickly;
3. obtain credit from her suppliers;
4. reject some orders. This is not a happy solution. It would ease her cash problem but at the expense of her profit potential.

Growth is causing the pressure on Deborah's cash position. In the first six months she hopes to sell 210,000 units. Now suppose that she could arrange to sell 35,000 units in each of the first six months. This would mean that only £52,500 would be invested in trade debtors as compared to £85,000 in her original plan. Let us also suppose that she will limit her stockholding to 10,000 units at any time. This would reduce her stock investment to £9,000 as compared to £27,000 in the original plan. She would still expect to earn a profit of £9,000. Her revised cash forecast and cash flow statement, based on these changes, are presented in Tables 4.7 (below) and 4.8 (p 84).

Table 4.7   *Cash forecast, Deborah Derby, version 2*

£'000	Jan	Feb	Mar	Apr	May	Jun	Total
Inflows							
Capital	50.0						50.0
Collections	–	17.5	35.0	35.0	35.0	35.0	157.5
	50.0	17.5	35.0	35.0	35.0	35.0	207.5
Outflows							
Suppliers	22.5	17.5	17.5	17.5	17.5	17.5	110.0
Staff	9.0	7.0	7.0	7.0	7.0	7.0	44.0
Overheads	11.0	9.0	9.0	9.0	9.0	9.0	56.0
	42.5	33.5	33.5	33.5	33.5	33.5	210.0
Month balance	7.5	(16.0)	1.5	1.5	1.5	1.5	(2.5)
Opening cash	–	7.5	(8.5)	(7.0)	(5.5)	(4.0)	
Closing cash	7.5	(8.5)	(7.0)	(5.5)	(4.0)	(2.5)	

If Deborah can organize production and sales in this way she will solve the initial over-trading problem.

Table 4.8 *Cash flow statement, Deborah Derby, version 2*

	£'000
Net cash flow to operating activities	(52.5)
Financing activity	
Issue of shares for cash	50.0
Decrease in cash for period	(2.5)

The footnote to her cash flow statement would now become:

Indirect method		**Direct method**		
Operating profit	9.0	Collections from customers		157.5
Less increase in stocks	(9.0)	Payments to suppliers	110	
increase in debtors	(52.5)	Payments to staff	44	
	(52.5)	Payment of overheads	56	210.0
				(52.5)

The maximum overdraft that Deborah would need is £8,500 in February. If it can be delivered, this is a much better plan.

Growth is not always accompanied by a net outflow to operating activities. For example, a well-run supermarket will create extra cash as it grows. This is because there should not be any trade debtors and the trade creditors should exceed the stocks.

A business can encounter complications in reconciling the operating profit to the net cash flow to or from operating activities. There are four potential problems.

1. The profit and loss account will include any profits or losses on the sale of fixed assets. Since the proceeds must be shown in the cash flow statement under the heading of capital expenditure and investment the charge or credit in the profit and loss account is a non-cash item. Consider two examples, shown in Table 4.9. In case 1 the profit, being a non-cash item, must be deducted from the operating profit when reconciling it to the cash flow to or from operating activities. In case 2 the loss, being a non-cash item, must be added to the operating profit when reconciling it to the cash flow to or from operating activities. These adjustments are only required in the indirect

Table 4.9 _Proceeds of the sale of fixed assets_

	Case 1	Case 2
Vehicle at cost	20,000	20,000
Aggregate depreciation	12,000	12,000
Book value	8,000	8,000
Sale proceeds	10,000	5,000
Profit (loss) on disposal	2,000	(3,000)

method format. In the direct method they are automatically excluded as only operating cash flows are shown.

2. Depreciation is a very real cost of running a business. In the indirect method report it must be added back as a non-cash cost. In the direct method it is ignored as only operating cash flows are shown.

3. When a business plans a rationalization programme it must make provision for the cost in its profit and loss account. At the end of the financial year some of the rationalization may not have been completed and paid for. The non-cash (unpaid) element must be added back in the indirect method format. Once again the issue is irrelevant in the direct method report.

4. Paragraph 39 of FRS 1 requires that collections from customers and payments to suppliers be shown net of Value Added Tax. The elimination of VAT only arises in the direct method format. The cash flows can be derived straight from the company receipts and payments records. It can also be deduced from relevant profit and loss account and balance sheet data, as illustrated in Table 4.10.

Table 4.10 _Computing the cash flows net of VAT_

Collections from customers			Payments to suppliers		
	Gross	Net of VAT		Gross	Net of VAT
Opening debtors	25,850	22,000	Opening creditors	10,575	9,000
Sales	103,400	88,000	Purchases	65,800	56,000
Collectable	129,250	110,000	Payable	76,375	65,000
Closing debtors	24,675	21,000	Closing creditors	14,100	12,000
Collected	104,575	89,000	Paid	62,275	53,000

The report would show £89,000 as collected from customers, and £53,000 would be reported as paid to suppliers. I strongly disapprove of this treatment of VAT. In paragraph 28 of Appendix 3 the ASB argues that 'normally

VAT is a short-term timing difference as far as the entity's overall cash flow is concerned and the inclusion of VAT in the cash flows may distort the allocation of the cash flows to standard headings'. In layperson's language we can illustrate this using the two transactions that took place in an accounting period of a business.

Dealer Ltd supplies goods to Customer Ltd and charges £10,000 plus VAT at 17.5 per cent. Customer Ltd then pays the full amount due: £11,750. The standard requires collections from Customer Ltd to be reported at £10,000 because the remainder of the proceeds will have to be paid to the Inland Revenue at a later date. For profit and loss account purposes it is certainly sensible to report the sales as £10,000. This is all that is left to cover the costs and hopefully make a profit. For cash flow purposes it is ludicrous to report collections as £10,000 when £11,750 was received.

Marking the recommended treatment of VAT out of 10, I will award the ASB 10 for conceptual excellence and 0 for realism. It is almost like a riddle. When is £11,750 only £10,000? Answer: when the ASB tells you how to report it. I believe the ASB has allowed itself to be ensnared by the similarity of the collections issue to that of providing for deferred tax where the taxable profit is out of synch with the accounting profit. In fairness the ASB does not regard non-experts as its primary audience. I think it should.

The complete range of cash outflows as summarized in the structure of FRS 1 are presented in diagrammatic form in Figure 4.1. Servicing all these categories places a heavy cash burden on any organization. The complete range of cash inflows as summarized in the structure of FRS 1 are presented in diagrammatic form in Figure 4.2.

THE EIGHT CATEGORIES OF CASH FLOWS

To make cash flows easy to read and understand, FRS 1 requires that they be shown in eight categories:

1. Operating activities.
2. Return on investments and servicing of finances.
3. Taxation.
4. Capital expenditure and financial investment.
5. Acquisitions and disposals.
6. Equity dividends paid.
7. Management of liquid resources.
8. Financing.

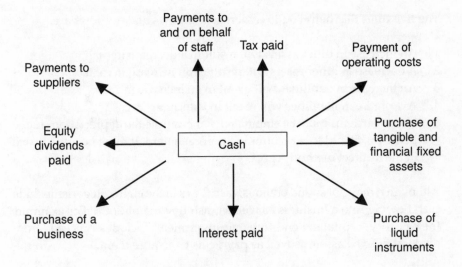

Figure 4.1 *The cash outflows*

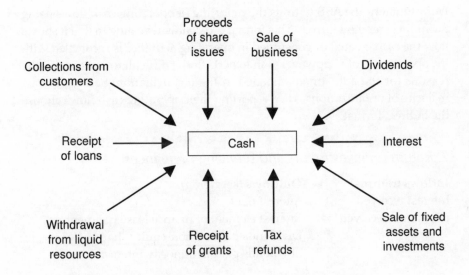

Figure 4.2 *The cash inflows*

The five rules that help you to understand inflows and outflows are:

1. An increase in other assets will result in a decrease in cash.
2. A decrease in other assets will result in an increase in cash.
3. An increase in liabilities will result in an increase in cash.
4. A decrease in liabilities will result in a decrease in cash.
5. Non-cash items must be eliminated. For example the depreciation charge in the profit and loss account is a non-cash item. It must be added back in the indirect method report.

Although it may not sound obvious, cash flows in the eight categories include cash flowing into a business as well as cash flowing out of it. For example, the category 'capital expenditure and investment' includes proceeds from disposal of fixed assets as well as payments to acquire them.

Commentary on the eight categories of cash flows

1. Operating activities

Unfortunately, the ASB permits the reporting of operating cash flows using the indirect method format. This format is certainly revealing in that it shows how the cash created or consumed in operating activities is reconciled with the operating profit. However, non-experts find it difficult to understand the reasons for the adjustments needed in the reconciliation. Sadly, the vast majority of organizations when reporting their operating cash flows choose the indirect format.

2. Return on investments and servicing of finances

Inflows (returns)	Outflows (servicing)
Interest received	Interest paid
Dividends received	Interest element of finance lease payments
	Dividends paid on non-equity shares
	Dividends paid to minority interests

3. Taxation

Inflow	Outflow
Tax refunded	Tax paid

4. Capital expenditure and financial investment

Inflows	**Outflows**
Purchase of tangible fixed assets	Sale of tangible fixed assets
Purchase of financial fixed assets	Sale of financial fixed assets

5. Acquisitions and disposals

Inflows
Proceeds from sales of:

Outflows
Payments to acquire:

- investments in subsidiaries
- investments in associates
- investments in joint ventures
  trades or businesses

In the case of acquisition and disposal of investments, any cash or overdraft bought or sold must be netted against the cash cost or sale proceeds.

6. Equity dividends paid

Outflow
Dividends paid to group shareholders net of corporation tax

7. Management of liquid resources

Inflows	**Outflows**
Withdrawal from short-term deposits	Placement of short-term deposits
Redeem investments in liquid resources	Investment in liquid resources

8. Financing

Inflows	**Outflows**
Proceeds of share issues	Repay borrowings other than overdrafts
Receipt of loans other than overdrafts	Capital element finance lease payments
Receipt of capital grants	Buy-in of own shares
	Expenses related to share issues

Some of these items relate to complex transactions. It is important that you understand why they are inflows or outflows as you may encounter them in a published cash flow statement. Unless you aspire to become the finance director you will not need to do the accounting for them.

Interest, tax and dividends

It is sometimes difficult to see how the cash flow data for these items relate to the profit and loss account and balance sheet. The examples in Table 4.11 show the relationships.

Table 4.11 *Relationship between cash flow data, profit and loss account, and balance sheet*

Interest paid		Corporation tax paid	
Accrued at start of year	100	Provision in previous year	32
Charge for year	450	Provision in current year	56
Interest payable	550	Tax payable	88
Accrued at end of year	125	Provision in current year	56
Interest paid	425	Corporation tax paid	32

Dividends paid	
Provision for final dividend last year (paid this year)	40
Interim dividend paid this year	30
Total paid	70

Note:
The final dividend for this year will not be paid until next year. It is provided for in the profit and loss account and appears as a liability in the balance sheet.

RECONCILIATIONS

In addition to the reconciliation between the operating profit and the cash flow to or from operating activities, FRS 1 requires reconciliation between the increase or decrease in cash during the period and the opening and closing net cash or net debt as shown in the balance sheets. Study of these reconciliations shows how the three primary financial statements interlock; see Table 4.12.

Your first impression might be that last year was a poor one with cash declining by £946,000. A more detailed examination shows that last year was

Table 4.12 _Cash flow statement, Avonmore Foods plc_

£'000	Last year	This year
Net cash inflow from operating activities[1]	29,479	31,253
Returns on investments and servicing of finance		
Interest paid	12,009	13.833
Interest received	1,363	1,727
	(10,646)	(12,106)
Corporation tax (paid) recovered	976	(1,495)
Free cash flow	19,809	17,652
Capital expenditure and financial investment		
Purchase of tangible fixed assets	(19,543)	(22,052)
Purchase of investments	(511)	(703)
Proceeds from the sale of tangible fixed assets	926	1,485
	(19,128)	(21,270)
Acquisitions and disposals	(5,268)	(38,652)
Equity dividend paid	(2,165)	(4,063)
Cash flow before use of liquid resources and financing	(6,752)	(46,333)
Management of liquid resources	(51,185)	50,135
Financing activities		
Term loan repayments	(1,061)	(4,656)
Grants received	6,102	2,306
Term loans received	21,428	–
Proceeds from share issues	30,522	75
	56,991	(2,275)
Increase (decrease) in cash for period[2]	(946)	1,527

[1] Reconciliation of PBIT to indirect method inflow from operating activities

	Last year	This year
Profit before interest and tax	26,714	36,509
Depreciation	10,999	13,019
Increase in debtors	(6,237)	(16,724)
Increase (decrease) in creditors	(2,055)	5,936
Decrease (increase) in stocks	368	(7,422)
Profit on sale of fixed assets	(310)	(65)
	29,479	31,253

Table 4.12 *(continued)*

[2] Reconciliation of change in cash to the balance sheet

	Cash	**Call deposits**	**Overdraft**	**Total**
Balance start last year	1,710	13,496	(3,345)	11,861
Translation adjustment[3]	105	383	(288)	200
Decrease during year	(193)	(1,336)	583	(946)
Balance end last year	1,622	12,543	(3,050)	11,115
Translation adjustment[3]	39	73	(20)	92
Increase during year	89	1,522	(84)	1,527
Balance end this year	1,750	14,138	(3.154)	12,734

[3] The rules of accounting require that assets and liabilities, denominated in foreign currencies, be translated at the rate ruling on the balance sheet date. The translation adjustments are needed to convert the opening cash balances to the closing rate.

excellent. The company raised a massive £56.991 million of financing in anticipation of the major development expenditure that it was to undertake in the following year. Since this cash was not required immediately, £51.185 million was placed on short-term deposit as reflected in the management of liquid resources. Readers of last year's cash flow statement might wonder why such a large fund-raising campaign was undertaken. They should suspect that a major development plan was being put in place to grow the business organically or by acquisition. The publication of the cash flow statement for the following year confirmed that this was the case. Notable in the cash flows for that year was the expenditure of £38.652 million on acquisitions. The company was following exactly the right approach to funding expansion.

There are two major principles involved. First, the funds should be put in place before the expansion commences. Second, the funds should be obtained from long-term sources. This is because the supplier of short-term funds can withdraw them and leave the borrower impossibly placed if such funds are invested long-term. Short-term funds are of two major types: creditors and bank loans. Long-term funds are of five types: surplus cash previously accumulated, proceeds of share issues, term loans, capital grants, free cash flow, and proceeds from sales of assets. This example, adapted from the published accounts of Avonmore Foods plc, is an excellent demonstration of how it arranged financing in advance of a major expansion.

STRATEGIC CASH FLOW PLANNING

The FRS 1 structure should be used for strategic cash planning. This approach is designed to make sure that funds will be available to finance increases in assets as a business grows. It is a three-step process:

1. Assess the amount of funds required to maintain and develop the business.
2. Predict the funds that will be available to spend.
3. Shrink the planned development expenditure if it exceeds the funds available.

The funds available and required to develop the business

Funds available	Funds required
Opening cash	Purchase fixed assets
Liquid resources	Acquisitions
Free cash flow	Loan repayments
Loan proceeds	Lease payments
Proceeds of share issues	Increase in stocks
Capital grants	Increase in debtors
Asset disposals	Decrease in creditors
Decrease in stocks	Dividend payments
Decrease in debtors	Closing cash
Increase in creditors	

The funds required are composed of three groups:

1. Those to be used to meet existing commitments. These include loan and lease repayments, replacement costs for worn out and obsolete fixed assets, and dividend payments.
2. Those to be used to support organic growth. This includes additional fixed assets and additional working capital (stocks plus trade debtors minus trade creditors).
3. The cash cost of acquisitions.

In order to use the funding and investment data correctly, the funds available and funds required must be divided into long-term and short-term elements. The resulting matrix can be used to test the appropriateness of development plans. We will now examine the Avonmore cash flow statement as if it were the strategic plan rather than the historic report. This will show you how you can use the FRS 1 format to plan your strategic cash flows correctly. The data for last year are presented in Table 4.13. The data for the current year are presented in Table 4.14.

Table 4.13   *The Avonmore strategic cash flow plan, year 1*

Funds available		Funds required	
Long term			
Opening cash	12,061	Purchase fixed assets	20,054
Free cash flow[1]	27,733	Acquisitions	5,268
Loan proceeds	21,428	Dividend payments	2,165
Proceeds share issues	30,522	Loan repayments	1,061
Capital grants	6,102		28,548
Asset disposals	926		
	98,772		
Short term			
Decrease in stocks	368	Increase in debtors	6,237
		Decrease in creditors	2,055
			8,292
	99,140		36,840

Notes:

Funds available exceed funds required by £62.3 million. Of this surplus, £51.185 million was placed on short-term deposit and the remaining £11.115 million was held in cash. Free cash flow is composed of the operating profit plus interest received minus interest paid and corporation tax.

[1] Make-up of free cash flow

Profit before interest and tax	26,714
Depreciation	10,999
Profit on sale of fixed assets	(310)
Net interest paid	(10,646)
Corporation tax recovered	976
	27,733

You might wonder why the company built up a huge store of cash (£11.861 million on hand plus £51.185 million on short-term deposit). It is only when we see that the company was anticipating and preparing for developments in year 2 that the cash mountain accumulated in year 1 makes sense.

Table 4.14   *The Avonmore strategic cash flow plan, year 2*

Funds available		Funds required	
Long term			
Opening cash	62,392	Purchase fixed assets	22,755
Free cash flow[1]	35,862	Acquisitions	38,652
Proceeds share issues	75	Dividends paid	4,063
Capital grants	2,306	Loan repayments	4,656
Asset disposals	1,485		70,126
	102,120		
Short term			
Increase in creditors	5,936	Increase in debtors	16,724
		Increase in stocks	7,422
			24,146
	108,056		94,272

Notes:
The matrix also shows an excellent strategic cash profile: £102.12 million of long-term funds will be available and £70.126 million of this will be invested long-term. After allowing for increased investment in stocks and debtors £13.784 million of cash will remain available for use in the following year.

[1] Make-up of free cash flow

Profit before interest and tax	36,509
Depreciation	13,019
Profit on sale of fixed assets	(65)
Net interest paid	(12,106)
Corporation tax paid	(1,495)
	35,862

Movements in working capital are shown separately for two reasons. First, cash can be released from the operating system through a move towards JIT, improved credit control, or increased supplier credit. Second, cash will be consumed in the operating system as stocks and debtors rise in response to growth in sales. The cash effect should be partially offset by an increase in supplier credit.

Financial institutions – an exception

There is one exception to the rule that using short-term cash inflows to fund long-term investment is dangerous. This approach is normal practice for banks and building societies. They accept call deposits and lend these funds to homeowners for periods of up to 25 years. Financial institutions can adjust interest rates to balance supply and demand. Provided there is public confidence in these institutions, they can continue to borrow short and lend long. The regulatory mechanism works by:

- Holding interest rates if supply and demand are in balance.
- Increasing interest rates to reduce demand and increase supply. (This was the major cause of the collapse of the UK property market in 1989).
- Reducing interest rates if funds available exceed loan applications.

The euro, with its transnational interest rates, will make this fund balancing more difficult.

COMPLICATIONS IN PREPARING CASH FLOW STATEMENTS

There are a number of technical problems associated with the preparation of a cash flow statement, which must be fully understood by those responsible for them. As a reader of such statements you should be aware of the problems:

- *The treatment of VAT.* Collections from customers and payments to suppliers must be shown net of VAT in the direct method, as explained earlier in this chapter.
- *Mergers and acquisitions.* The price paid for an acquisition must be adjusted to reflect holdings of cash. For example, suppose that you paid £10 million to buy a business and that you obtained £0.5 million of cash in the assets acquired. The acquisition cost would be shown as £9.5 million. Difficult issues arise with regard to the treatment of consolidation reserve, goodwill, minority interest, etc. Such intricacies are best left to accounting professionals.
- *Asset revaluations.* Asset revaluations have no impact on cash and must be disregarded.
- *Undistributed profits of related businesses.* These profits increase the carrying value of investments. They do not affect the liquidity of the investor company and must be excluded from the operating activities cash flow even though the investor company's share is included in the group profit or loss from ordinary activities.

● *Movements in working capital.* Where a group has acquired or disposed of another business the movements in stocks, debtors and creditors, disclosed in an indirect method cash flow statement, may be difficult to reconcile with the figures in the balance sheet. This is because part of the movement will be reflected in the cash flow relating to additions and disposals.

Is an increase in cash always good?

When interpreting accounts some readers go immediately to the bottom line. In the case of the cash flow statement they are looking for an increase in cash. If this has been achieved they may consider the picture complete and look no further. To do so is to totally ignore the factors that have led to the increase in cash. There are four situations in which an increase in cash could be concealing serious problems. The company could be:

1. Not investing enough in tangible fixed assets to keep the technology up to date and competitive. The capital expenditure and depreciation will help you to become aware of this type of problem. This questionable strategy is frequently used to disguise a business in decline.

2. Encountering a decline in sales. This often leads to a reduction in stocks and debtors. If demand recovers in the following year the additional stock and debtor investment could cause a collapse in cash. It is debatable whether a more permanent decline in sales or a collapse in cash is the worse of two evils.

3. Not paying its suppliers of goods and services on time. This strategy is not sustainable. It is particularly inappropriate where suppliers are in position to charge interest on the outstanding accounts or cut off supplies that cannot be sourced elsewhere. In Chapter 7 we will examine how to assess the supplier credit period. This will pinpoint inappropriate treatment of suppliers.

4. Using too much medium- and long-term bank debt while disclosing satisfactory liquidity. Many organizations, including 'household names', have excessive borrowings. It is only when the gearing, as described in Chapter 6, is calculated that it becomes clear that total bank debt is excessive.

Is a decrease in cash always bad?

A decrease in cash is usually a disturbing pointer to liquidity. There are two major situations in which a decrease in cash is not bad. First, the business may have put substantial liquid resources in place prior to embarking on a major expansion, such as we saw in Avonmore Foods. Second, the returns available for short-term deposits are currently very low. The effective organization should be running down its surplus cash so as to improve its asset management. Buying-in its own shares has become popular as a way for a company to run down excess liquidity. The effect of such a strategy only becomes clear when the capital expenditure and financial investment section of the cash flow statement is examined.

SUMMARY

Cash is the lifeblood of a business. The good company ensures that it will have adequate cash through the use of the strategic cash flow statement. The key to avoiding a collapse in cash is to follow the two major rules in funding expansion: first, put the funds required in place before starting an expansion programme, and second, borrow at least as much long-term as you expect to invest long-term. Failure to do this can lead to bankruptcy. It is a tragedy when a profitable business runs out of cash. The planning techniques outlined in this chapter and in Chapter 5 help to avoid such problems.

5

Cash forecasting

To be in control, any business needs to prepare a reliable forecast of cash inflows, cash outflows and the cash balance for at least six months into the future. Such forecasts are vital in that they provide an early warning of a shortage of cash. This warning gives a business the breathing space needed to negotiate additional bank loans. Cash forecasting is particularly important for businesses that are growing rapidly and have to give credit to customers. Such businesses have to pay for the increasing cost of creating products or services for sale before the collections from customers rise.

A cash forecast is best prepared on a spreadsheet. This is because the conversion of an accrual-based operating budget into cash flows is simplified by using some of the standard spreadsheet formulae. In addition, careful modelling helps to avoid calculation and totalling errors that can be difficult to locate when a cash forecast is prepared manually.

Avoid Complications Ltd has prepared its sales budget for the next six months and is now setting out to convert this into its predicted cash collections for the period. In preparing the cash budget the company predicted that the historic collection pattern would continue. The prediction is that 30 per cent of sales will be collected in the next month, with 45 per cent collected in the following month and 25 per cent in the month after that. The spreadsheet forecast is reproduced in Table 5.1 (p 100). An explanation of the formulae and control mechanism I used to ensure that the forecast has been correctly prepared is given in the notes to the table.

Table 5.1 *The cash collection budget of Avoid Complications Ltd*

Cells	A	B	C	D	E
		Collections budget			
	Month	**Sales**	**VAT 17.5%**	**Collectable**	**Collections**
2	October	26560	4648	31208	
3	November	27640	4837	32477	
4	December	49880	8729	58609	
5	January	20000	3500	23500	39999
6	February	21000	3675	24675	41543
7	March	22600	3955	26555	32630
8	April	21000	3675	24675	24945
9	May	24000	4200	28200	25521
10	June	22000	3850	25850	6203
		234680	41069	275749	190841
		Control total		190841	

Notes:

In cells B2, B3 and B4 I inputted the actual sales for the last three months of last year. In cells B5–B10 I inputted the budgeted sales for the next six months. In cell C2 I inputted the formula =B2*0.175. This calculated the VAT charged to customers. I then copied the formula in cell C2 to cells C3–C10. This computed the VAT for the other eight months. In cell D2 I inputted the formula =B2*1.175. This calculated the amount collectable from customers based on the October sales. The formula in cell D2 was then copied to cells D3–D10. This calculated the total amount collectable in each of the subsequent months. In cell E5 I inputted the formula =(D2*0.25)+(D3*0.45)+ (D4*0.3). When entered this showed that £39,999 was expected to be collected from customers in January. The formula modelled collection of 25% of the October collectable, 45% of the November collectable and 30% of the December collectable. The formula in cell E5 was then copied to cells E6–E10, thereby predicting the collections for the following five months. The final step was to design a test to ensure the calculations were done correctly. In cell D13 I entered the formula =(D2*0.25)+ (D3*0.7)+Sum(D4:D7)+(D8*0.75)+(D9*0.3). The result was a total collection forecast of £190,841. Since this equalled the total of the individual monthly collections, it proved that the logic had been correctly modelled. When preparing a spreadsheet table like this one you should always build in a control mechanism.

Any manager with spreadsheet skills should be able to prepare a cash budget even if lacking professional accounting skills.

A CASH FORECASTING EXAMPLE

Larry Leeds proposes to start a new business in January 2003. We will prepare his forecast in detail for one year; see Table 5.2. I must stress that if you are a budding entrepreneur you should develop a three-year cash forecast. Failure to do so could leave you unaware of your peak borrowing requirements, particularly if you intend to start a seasonal business, a business that takes several years to earn a profit, or a business that will grow rapidly.

Table 5.2 _Cash forecast, Larry Leeds_

Monthly sales volumes

January	250	July	2,500
February	500	August	2,750
March	750	September	2,000
April	1,000	October	2,000
May	1,500	November	2,000
June	2,000	December	2,500

Total units in the year 2003 will be 19,750. The product will sell at £20 per unit plus VAT at 17.5 per cent, a total price of £23.50. Sales in January and February 2004 are forecast at 2,000 units each month. Of each month's sales 60 per cent will be to UK customers. Larry is obliged to charge 17.5 per cent VAT on these items. The balance will be exported. The exports are zero-rated so Larry will not have to charge VAT. Ten per cent of sales will be collected in month of sale, 60 per cent will be collected in the month following sale, and 29 per cent of sales will be collected in the next month. The 1 per cent balance will be bad debts.

Purchasing will be arranged so that Larry will have one and a half months' future sales in stock at each month end, composed of raw material = one month and finished stock = one half month. Purchases will be 1 per cent higher than sales to allow for wastage and pilferage. The raw material cost will be £6 per unit. The price will fall to £5.20 from 1 April. Suppliers will give one month's credit. Suppliers will charge him VAT at 17.5 per cent.

Production staff can make 1,600 units without overtime at a cost of £6,400. Each unit produced in excess of 1,600 will cost £5. All payroll costs will be paid in the month in which they occur. Non-production pay costs will be £6,250 per month. The overhead costs and fixed assets are as shown in Table 5.3 (p 102).

Table 5.3 *Overhead costs and fixed assets, Larry Leeds*

Overhead	£	Payable
Power	1,800	Monthly
Light	840	Bi-monthly
Telephone	600	Quarterly
Insurance	10,800	At start of year
Rent	12,000	Quarterly in advance
Rates	7,000	Half-yearly in advance
Pensions	15% of annual payroll	At end of year
Bank interest rate	10%	Charged in March and Sept
Bank deposit rate	5%	Receivable in March and Sept
Lease charges	3,600	Monthly in advance
Post and packing	1,200	Monthly %

Jan 2% Feb 5% Mar 6% Apr8 % May 9% Jun.15%
Jul 12% Aug 11% Sep 8% Oct 8% Nov 8% Dec 8%

Advertising	1,500	Monthly %

Jan 10% Feb 10% Mar 15% Apr 15% May 10% Jun 10%
Jul 5% Aug 5% Sep 5% Oct 5% Nov 5% Dec 5%

Fixed assets will be bought and paid for in January 2003

Plant	£23,600
Truck	£12,000
Car	£8,400
	£44,000

Larry expects to receive a 30% grant towards the cost of the plant in April.

Larry and some friends will introduce £40,000 of share capital. The bank will provide a term loan of £40,000 carrying a two-year moratorium on capital and interest payments, and overdraft facilities of £30,000 provided that the overdraft is cleared for at least two months during 2003.

Larry prepared his cash budget on a Microsoft Excel spreadsheet. This forecast is presented in Table 5.4. This is followed by a series of support tables that show how the various items in the cash forecast were computed.

Table 5.4 *Cash budget, Larry Leeds*

						Cash forecast							
	Jan	Feb	Mar	Apr	May	Jun	Jul	Aug	Sep	Oct	Nov	Dec	Total
Cash inflows													
Capital introduced	40000												
Term loan	40000												
Collections home sales (1)	353	2820	6310	9800	13642	19599	26579	33206	36308	30985	27918	28623	236140
Collections export sales (1)	200	1600	3580	5560	7740	11120	15080	18840	20600	17580	15840	16240	133980
VAT refund (3)		668											668
Capital grant				7080									7080
	80553	5088	9890	22440	21382	30719	41659	52046	56908	48565	43758	44863	457868
Cash outflows													
Suppliers (2)		8011	6230	8901	10799	13885	16199	14656	12342	12342	13885	13885	131136
VAT (3)				371			3361			9366			13098
Payroll (4)	12650	12650	12650	12650	13400	15900	17775	16525	14650	14650	15900	15900	175300
Overhead (5)	14499	875	972	3986	783	4645	3744	872	846	3836	696	30781	66535
Plant	23600												23600
Vehicles	20400												20400
Total before interest	71149	21536	19852	25908	24982	34430	41079	32053	27838	40194	30481	60566	430069
Monthly balance	9404	-16448	-9963	-3469	-3601	-3711	579	19992	29069	8371	13277	-15703	27799
Cumulative monthly balance	9404	-7044	-17007	-20475	-24076	-27787	-27208	-7215	21854	30225	43502	27799	27799
Bank interest (6)		161							805				967
Monthly balance including interest	9404	-16448	-10124	-3469	-3601	-3711	579	19992	28264	8371	13277	-15703	
Opening cash	0	9404	-7044	-17168	-20636	-24237	-27948	-27369	-7377	20887	29258	42535	
Closing cash	9404	-7044	-17168	-20636	-24237	-27948	-27369	-7377	20887	29258	42535	26832	26832

Table 5.4 (continued)

Schedule 1 Sales and cash collectable

	Jan	Feb	Mar	Apr	May	Jun	Jul	Aug	Sep	Oct	Nov	Dec	Total
Total sales units	250	500	750	1000	1500	2000	2500	2750	2000	2000	2000	2500	19750
Home sales													
Volume	150	300	450	600	900	1200	1500	1650	1200	1200	1200	1500	11850
Price	20	20	20	20	20	20	20	20	20	20	20	20	20
Revenue	3000	6000	9000	12000	18000	24000	30000	33000	24000	24000	24000	30000	237000
VAT	525	1050	1575	2100	3150	4200	5250	5775	4200	4200	4200	5250	41475
Collectable	3525	7050	10575	14100	21150	28200	35250	38775	28200	28200	28200	35250	278475
Collection forecast	353	2820	6310	9800	13642	19599	26579	33206	36308	30985	27918	28623	236140
Export sales													
Volume	100	200	300	400	600	800	1000	1100	800	800	800	1000	7900
Price	20	20	20	20	20	20	20	20	20	20	20	20	20
Revenue collectable	2000	4000	6000	8000	12000	16000	20000	22000	16000	16000	16000	20000	158000
Collection forecast	200	1600	3580	5560	7740	11120	15080	18840	20600	17580	15840	16240	133980

Reconciliation of sales debtors and collections

Sales

	Home	Export
Collections per cash forecast	236140	133980
Debtors 89% December	31373	17800
Debtors 29% November	8178	4640
Bad debts 1% of collectable	2785	1580
Sales including VAT per schedule 1	278475	
Sales per schedule 1		158000

Bad debts

Home	2785
Export	1580
	4365

Trade debtors

	Home	Export	Total
November × 29%	8178	4640	12818
December × 89%	31373	17800	49173
	39551	22440	61991

Table 5.5 *Schedules 2 and 3, Larry Leeds*

Schedule 2 Analysis of purchases and supplier payments

	Jan	Feb	Mar	Apr	May	Jun	Jul	Aug	Sep	Oct	Nov	Dec	Total
Sales volume	250	500	750	1000	1500	2000	2500	2750	2000	2000	2000	2500	19750
Purchases units	1136	884	1263	1768	2273	2651	2399	2020	2020	2273	2273	2020	22978
Unit price	6	6	6	5.2	5.2	5.2	5.2	5.2	5.2	5.2	5.2	5.2	
Purchase cost	6818	5303	7575	9191	11817	13787	12474	10504	10504	11817	11817	10504	122109
VAT	1193	928	1326	1608	2068	2413	2183	1838	1838	2068	2068	1838	21369
Supplier payables	8011	6230	8901	10799	13885	16199	14656	12342	12342	13885	13885	12342	143478
Supplier payments		8011	6230	8901	10799	13885	16199	14656	12342	12342	13885	13885	131136

Reconciliation of purchases, supplier payments and sales

	Volume			
Sales units	19750		Purchase cost	143478
Stock year end	3000		Less trade creditors	12342
	22750		Payments	131136
Uplift for shortages	228			
Purchases schedule 2	22978			

Table 5.5 (continued)

Schedule 3 Analysis of VAT

	Jan	Feb	Mar	Apr	May	Jun	Jul	Aug	Sep	Oct	Nov	Dec	Total
Charged to customers	525	1050	1575	2100	3150	4200	5250	5775	4200	4200	4200	5250	41475
Charged by suppliers	-1193	-928	-1326	-1608	-2068	-2413	-2183	-1838	-1838	-2068	-2068	-1838	-21369
Net monthly position	-668	122	249	492	1082	1787	3067	3937	2362	2132	2132	3412	20106
Recovered and paid	0	668		-371			-3361			-9366			-12430
Balance outstanding	-668	122	371	492	1574	3361	3067	7004	9366	2132	4264	7676	38760

VAT reconciliation

Amount paid	12430	
VAT creditors		
Oct.	2132	
Nov.	2132	
Dec.	3412	7676
Net annual liability 3		20106

Table 5.6 *Schedule 4, Larry Leeds*

Schedule 4 Payroll

	Jan	Feb	Mar	Apr	May	Jun	Jul	Aug	Sep	Oct	Nov	Dec	Total
Production for sale (units)	250	250	375	500	750	1000	1250	1375	1000	1000	1000	1250	10000
Production for stock (units)	250	375	500	750	1000	1250	1375	1000	1000	1000	1250	1000	10750
Total production	500	625	875	1250	1750	2250	2625	2375	2000	2000	2250	2250	20750
Overtime units	0	0	0	0	150	650	1025	775	400	400	650	650	4700
Paid at normal time	6400	6400	6400	6400	6400	6400	6400	6400	6400	6400	6400	6400	76800
Paid at overtime	0	0	0	0	750	3250	5125	3875	2000	2000	3250	3250	23500
Other payroll	6250	6250	6250	6250	6250	6250	6250	6250	6250	6250	6250	6250	75000
Total payroll	12650	12650	12650	12650	13400	15900	17775	16525	14650	14650	15900	15900	175300

Table 5.7 *Schedule 5, Larry Leeds*

	Jan	Feb	Mar	Apr	May	Jun	Jul	Aug	Sep	Oct	Nov	Dec	Total
						Schedule 5 General overheads							
Power	150	150	150	150	150	150	150	150	150	150	150	150	1 800
Light		140		140		140		140		140		140	840
Phone			150			150			150			150	600
Insurance	10800												10800
Rent	3000			3000			3000			3000			12000
Rates						3500						3500	7000
Pensions												26295	26295
Leases	300	300	300	300	300	300	300	300	300	300	300	300	3600
Post and packing	24	60	72	96	108	180	144	132	96	96	96	96	1200
Advertising	150	150	225	225	150	150	75	75	75	75	75	75	1500
Other	75	75	75	75	75	75	75	75	75	75	75	75	900
Total overhead	14499	875	972	3986	783	4645	3744	872	846	3836	696	30781	66535

(6) Analysis of bank interest

	Jan	Feb	Mar	Apr	May	Jun	Jul	Aug	Sep	Oct	Nov	Dec	Total
Interest payable	0	59	142	172	202	233	228	61	0	0	0	0	1097
Interest receivable	39	0	0	0	0	0	0	0	91	122	177	112	541
Monthly net interest	39	−59	−142	−172	−202	−233	−228	−61	91	122	177	112	−556
Interest paid			161						805				

Table 5.8 *Schedules 6, 7 and 8, Larry Leeds*

Schedule 6, Bank interest

		£
(A)	January cash £9,404 × 5%/12 =	(39)
	February o/d £7,044 × 10%/12 =	59
	March o/d £17,007 × 10%/12 =	
	(Pre interest)[1]	141
		161

[1] £17,168 – £161 = £17,007

		£
(B)	April o/d £20,636 × 10%/12 =	172
	May o/d £24,237 × 10%/12 =	202
	June o/d £27,948 × 10%/12 =	233
	July o/d £27,369 × 10%/12 =	228
	August o/d £7,377 × 10%/12 =	61
	September cash £21,854 × 5%/12 =	
	(Pre interest) [2]	(91)
		805

[2] £20,887 – £805 = £21,854

		£
(C)	Interest accrued	
	October cash £29,258 × 5%/12 =	(122)
	November cash £42,535 × 5%/12 =	(177)
	December cash £26,832 × 5%/12 =	(112)
		(411)

			£
(D)	Term loan £40,000 × 10%		£4,000
	Total cost (a + b + c + d)		£4,656
	Accrued interest £4,000 – £411	=	£3,589

Note:
Larry used simple interest of 10% on overdrafts and term loans and 5% on surplus cash in computing his provisions and earnings. He assumes that the balance at month end is a fair representation of the position during the month. In practice the banks calculate overdraft interest on a daily basis.

Table 5.8 *(continued)*

Schedule 7, Profit and loss account 2003

Sales[1]		395,000
Purchases	122,109	
Less material stocks[2]	10,400	
Materials consumed	111,708	
Production payroll	100,300	
	212,008	
Less finished stocks[3]	9,200	
Cost of sales		202,808
Gross profit		192,192

Operating expenses

Power	1,800	
Light	840	
Telephone	600	
Insurance	10,800	
Rent and rates	19,000	
Pensions	26,295	
Lease charges	3,600	
Postage and packing	1,200	
Advertising	1,500	
Salaries and wages (non-production)	75,000	
Other	900	
Bad debts[4]	4,365	

Depreciation

Plant[5]	3,304	
Truck[6]	2,400	
Car[7]	2,100	153,704
Profit before interest and tax		38,488
Term loan interest	4,000	
Net bank interest	556	4,556
Profit before tax		33,932
Corporation tax[8]		6,521
Profit retained		27,411

Notes:

[1] 19,750 units at £20 each = £395,000

[2] Material stocks 2,000 items at £5.20 each. It is assumed that stock losses occur prior

Table 5.8 *(continued)*

to issue.

[3] Finished goods stock 1,000 items at £9.20 each. Larry plans to value the finished stock at material cost £5.20 plus 'normal' labour £4.00 = £9.20 per unit.

[4] Bad debts per schedule 1 (2,785 + 1,580) = £4,365

[5] The plant is depreciated over 5 years straight line.

	Cost	Grant
Plant	23,600	7,080
Depreciation	4,720	1,416
Balance sheet	18,880	5,664

[6] The truck is depreciated over 5 years straight line.

	Cost	
Truck	12,000	
Depreciation	2,400	(expense charge)
Balance sheet	9,600	

[7] The car is depreciated over 4 years straight line.

	Cost	
Car	8,400	
Depreciation	2,100	(expense charge)
Balance sheet	6,300	

[8] Corporation tax provision.

Profit forecast	33,932
Add depreciation	7,804
	41,736
Less WDA 25%[a]	9,130
Taxable	32,606
Tax at 20%[b]	6,521

[a] The writing down allowance is restricted as follows:

Plant net of grant	16,520
Van	12,000
Car (maximum allowed)	8,000
	36,520
Allowance at 25%	9,130

111

Table 5.8 *(continued)*

(b) Larry will be liable to corporation tax at 20%. This preferential rate applies to profits of under £250,000.

Schedule 8, Balance sheet as at 31 December 2003

Fixed assets	Cost	Depreciation	Book Value
Plant[5]	23,600	4,720	18,880
Truck[6]	12,000	2,400	9,600
Car[7]	8,400	2,100	6,300
	44,000	9,220	34,780
Current assets			
Stocks materials[2]	10,400		
Stocks finished goods[3]	9,200		
Trade debtors[9]	61,991		
Cash	26,832	108,423	
		143,203	
Payable in under one year			
Suppliers[10]	12,342		
VAT[11]	7,676		
Bank interest	3,589		
Corporation tax[8]	6,521	(30,128)	
Net assets		113,075	
Financed by:			
Share capital	40,000		
Revenue reserve	27,411	67,411	
Government grant[5]		5,664	
Bank term loan		40,000	
		113,075	

(9) Per schedule 1 £49,172 + £12,819 = £61,991.
(10) Per schedule 2. December purchases £12,342.
(11) Per schedule 3 £7,676.

Understanding the sales and cash collections schedule

Schedule 1 provides key information for the following budgets:

- Collections from customers are computed and transferred to the cash forecast.
- Sales (net of VAT) and bad debts are computed for inclusion in the profit and loss account.
- The trade debtors are computed for inclusion in the balance sheet.
- The sales determine the purchases that are computed in schedule 2.
- The VAT charged to customers is computed and transferred to schedule 3.

The data in schedule 1 are determined by the input of: a) the monthly forecasts for home (60 per cent) and export (40 per cent) sales; b) the projected selling price per unit of £20 per unit net of VAT; c) the VAT rate of 17.5 per cent charged on home sales; d) the forecast that 10 per cent of the amount due from customers would be collected in the month of sale with 60 per cent collected in the following month and 29 per cent in the month after that; and e) the expected bad debts of 1 per cent of amounts collectable. In order for you to understand the logic used in the model I recommend that you work out all the figures that relate to the month of March before reading on.

First, the 750 units to be sold are divided into 60 per cent home (450 units) and 40 per cent export (300 units). Application of the £20 selling price leads to home sales of £9,000 and export sales of £6,000. Inclusion of VAT at 17.5 per cent in the home sales leads to an amount collectable from home sales of £10,575. The collections from customers are shown in Table 5.9 (p 114).

Table 5.9 *Collections from customers, Larry Leeds*

	Home	Export
10% of March collectable	1,058	600
60% of February sales	4,230	2,400
29% of January sales	1,022	580
	6,310	3,580

The VAT obligations are transferred to schedule 3; see Table 5.5 (p 106).

Understanding the purchases and supplier payments schedule

The purchases and supplier payments in schedule 2 are determined by a) the sales forecasts; b) the supplier prices; c) the allowance for pilferage; d) the VAT charged by suppliers; and e) the stocking policy. For example, the purchases for January must cover all the sales in January and February and half the sales for March plus the pilferage allowance. The volume forecast is $((250 + 500 + 375) \times 1.01) = 1,136$ units. At a price of £6 each this gives purchases of £6,818 to which VAT at 17.5 per cent must be added, leading to creditors of £8,011 that will be paid in February. The VAT charged by suppliers is transferred to schedule 3. Once again I recommend that you check your understanding of the logic by computing the March creditors that will be paid in April.

As a result of the stocking policy the purchases in March will be one half of the April sales and one half of the May sales plus the pilferage allowance. This was computed as $((500 + 750) \times 1.01) = 1,263$ units at £6 each = £7,575 plus VAT of £1,326, giving creditors of £8,901 to be paid in April.

Understanding the VAT schedule

Larry expects to be charged £668 more VAT by suppliers than he will charge to customers in January. He plans to make a refund claim and expects to recover this amount in February. In all subsequent months the VAT that he charges to customers exceeds what he will be charged by suppliers. He computes his liability quarterly and pays it in the month following the quarter end. For example, in April he pays the net VAT of £122 for February and £249 for March, making a total of £371.

To simplify the illustration I assumed that VAT on purchases was the only deductible input. In practice, VAT paid on other items that add value to goods or services sold to third parties can be offset against VAT charged to customers. The inclusion of this would make the illustration more complicated and I deemed it undesirable because the amounts involved are small and a suitable bookkeeping system ensures they are handled correctly.

Understanding the payroll schedule

In schedule 4 (Table 5.6, p 107) Larry computes his payroll. First, in January he makes enough units to cover all of his January sales and one-half of his February sales. This pattern is followed in all the succeeding months. Larry has the capacity to produce 1,600 units per month during normal working hours. In the four months January to April he will suffer a serious idle capacity penalty as he produces far less than he could with normal-hours working. In subsequent months Larry will have to arrange a significant amount of overtime to comply with his stocking policy.

Larry also wrote a version of his plan in which he produced to capacity in the first four months and thereby eliminated most of the planned overtime. This plan would yield significantly improved profits but at the expense of a greater need for cash in the early months. Larry plans to discuss this alternative plan with his bankers if he feels that they trust him enough to provide him with the additional funds.

The normal time, overtime and other staff payments are added together and transferred to the cash forecast. For example, in May Larry expects to pay £13,400 as reported in schedule 4 and the cash forecast.

The general overheads/understanding the general overheads

This schedule (Table 5.7, p 108) simply breaks down the annual overheads into monthly components, summarizes them and transfers them to the cash forecast. January and December are much more expensive than the other months. In January Larry will have to pay a £10,800 insurance bill. In December he will have to pay a £26,295 pension contribution.

Comments on the forecast profit and loss account, balance sheet and cash

The forecast profit is based on what Larry believes is a conservative sales target and no production in excess of half the following months expected demand. This causes poor utilization of the labour force in early months.

Capacity is available to produce significantly more than is required at a production labour cost of £6,400 per month up to end April. It would be possible to meet the demand in peak months with little overtime by utilizing this surplus capacity. Much of the overtime budget could be eliminated in this way. In addition, 15 per cent of this sum, £3,112, would not have to be put into the pension fund. If Larry does this he will have to increase his purchases and supplier payments in the first four months. This would increase the overdraft he needs to above £41,898. Larry feels this would be asking too much.

Larry hopes to earn a higher profit than this in 2003. In 2004, using similar conservative volume forecasts, Larry anticipates significant profit growth. He intends to expand his production level by recruiting additional staff and acquiring a second machine. His cash forecast for 2003 shows that this could be achieved without further bank loans provided that he retains all of the profit earned in 2003.

PRESENTING CASH FORECASTS IN FUNDING NEGOTIATIONS

Negotiating bank loans can be difficult. One major reason is that bankers expect promoters' forecasts to be optimistic. They frequently adjust revenues downwards and costs upwards in assessing loan applications. The unfortunate consequences of this can be twofold. First, a project with great potential that is conservatively forecast can sometimes be rejected because the bank adjustments take out the substance rather than the excessive optimism. Good projects that fail to get off the ground are a tragic waste.

Second, sometimes promoters, anticipating downward adjustments, deliberately place some padding in the forecasts. Tactically there is a good deal to be said for this approach. It helps get the loan decision based on something similar to the position that is expected. However, bankers frequently review projects previously approved. Unfortunately, they tend to compare actual achievements with the promoter's forecasts, rather than their risk-adjusted versions. This reinforces their view that promoters are always too optimistic.

Qualities of a good funding application

The financial figures should generally cover a period of three years from the start of the loan. The first year should be presented in detail, with monthly (and sometimes even weekly) cash forecasts, and quarterly profit and loss account and balance sheet figures. The figures should be supported by the following data:

- A detailed description of the business history of the promoter(s).
- A well-argued justification of the size of the market and the share you expect to obtain.
- An explanation of the key assumptions implicit in the plan. These include:
  - stockholding period;
  - location of key customers;
  - customer collection period;
  - location of key suppliers;
  - supplier payment period;
  - availability of operative skills required;
  - productivity expectations;
  - quotations for fixed asset costs;
  - source(s) of capital introduced;
  - proposed salary and dividend restrictions;
  - guarantees and security available.

The forecasts and commentary should appear professional and credible. Never forget that at best forecasts are only well thought out paper. A big part of the lending decision is based on the credibility of the promoter. If a banker likes you, and is confident of your ability to cope with the inevitable business crises, it is possible to obtain loans for moderate projects. If you are disliked or distrusted, then you may not be able to finance the best project of the decade.

Larry Leeds made a presentation to his local bank. A member of the new business section of the Regional Development Agency accompanied him. The bank authorized overdraft facilities that were sufficient to allow a stock build-up that would overcome the mid-year overtime payments. All that Larry needed to do was to increase purchasing and production to 3,232 units in January and 1,616 in February and March, and production to 1,600 in each of these months. Since he had built his cash forecast on a computer spreadsheet he was able to adjust it quite easily. The revised cash forecast is presented in Table 5.10 (p 118).

Table 5.10 *Cash forecast, Larry Leeds, version 2*

	Jan	Feb	Mar	Apr	May	Jun	Jul	Aug	Sep	Oct	Nov	Dec	Total
						Cash forecast version 2							
Cash inflows													
Capital introduced	40000												
Term loan	40000												
Collections home sales (1)	353	2820	6310	9800	13642	19599	26579	33206	36308	30985	27918	28623	236140
Collections export sales (1)	200	1600	3580	5560	7740	11120	15080	18840	20600	17580	15840	16240	133980
VAT refund (3)		2869	647	122									3637
Capital grant				7080									7080
	80553	7289	10537	22561	21382	30719	41659	52046	56908	48565	43758	44863	460837
Cash outflows													
Suppliers (2)		22786	11393	11393	9874	9874	9874	9874	9874	9874	9874	13268	127955
VAT (3)							5038			10813			15852
Payroll (4)	12650	12650	12650	12650	12650	12650	12650	12650	12650	12650	12650	15400	154550
Overhead (5)	14499	875	972	3986	783	4645	3744	872	846	3836	696	27668	63423
Plant	23600												23600
Vehicles	20400												20400
Total before interest	71149	36311	25015	28029	23307	27169	31306	23396	23370	37173	23220	56336	405780
Monthly balance	9404	−29022	−14478	−5468	−1925	3550	10352	28650	33538	11392	20538	−11473	55057
Cumulative monthly balance	9404	−19619	−34097	−39564	−41489	−37939	−27587	1063	34601	45993	66531	55057	
Bank interest (6)			408						1088				1497
Monthly balance including interest	9404	−29022	−14887	−5468	−1925	3550	10352	28650	32450	11392	20538	−11473	
Opening cash	0	9404	−19619	−34505	−39973	−41898	−38347	−27995	655	33104	44496	65034	
Closing cash	9404	−19619	−34505	−39973	−41898	−38347	−27995	655	33104	44496	65034	53561	53561

Table 5.11 *Revised plan, Larry Leeds*

					Purchases and supplier payables version 2								
	Jan	Feb	Mar	Apr	May	Jun	Jul	Aug	Sep	Oct	Nov	Dec	Total
Opening stock units	0	2950	4050	4900	5500	5600	5200	4300	3150	2750	2350	2500	0
Purchases units	3232	1616	1616	1616	1616	1616	1616	1616	1616	1616	2172	2020	21968
Wastage and pilferage	-32	-16	-16	-16	-16	-16	-16	-16	-16	-16	-22	-20	-218
Sales units	-250	-500	-750	-1000	-1500	-2000	-2500	-2750	-2000	-2000	-2000	-2500	-19750
Closing stock units	2950	4050	4900	5500	5600	5200	4300	3150	2750	2350	2500	2000	
Unit price	6	6	6	5.2	5.2	5.2	5.2	5.2	5.2	5.2	5.2	5.2	
Purchase cost	19392	9696	9696	8403	8403	8403	8403	8403	8403	8403	11292	10504	119402
VAT	3394	1697	1697	1471	1471	1471	1471	1471	1471	1471	1976	1838	20895
Supplier payables	22786	11393	11393	9874	9874	9874	9874	9874	9874	9874	13268	12342	140298
Supplier payments	22786	11393	11393	11393	9874	9874	9874	9874	9874	9874	9874	13268	127955

Purchases supplier payments and sales

	Units
Sales units	19750
Stock year end	2000
	21750
Uplift for shortages	218
Purchases per schedule 2	21968

Purchase cost per schedule 2	140298
Less trade creditors	12342
Payments	127955

Table 5.11 (*continued*)

Schedule 3 Value added tax version 2

	Jan	Feb	Mar	Apr	May	Jun	Jul	Aug	Sep	Oct	Nov	Dec	Total
Charged to customers	525	1050	1575	2100	3150	4200	5250	5.775	4.200	4.200	4.200	5.250	41.475
Charged by suppliers	-3394	-1697	-1697	-1471	-1471	-1471	-1471	-1471	-1471	-1471	-1976	-1838	-20895
Net monthly position	-2869	-647	-122	629	1679	2729	3779	4304	2729	2729	2224	3412	20580
Recovered and paid	0	2869	647	122			-5038			-10813			-12214
Balance outstanding	-2869	-647	-122	629	2309	5038	3779	8084	10813	2729	4953	8365	43064

VAT reconciliation

Amount paid		12214
VAT creditors		
Oct.	2729	
Nov.	2224	
Dec.	3412	
Net liability per schedule 2		20580

Schedule 4 Payroll version 2

	Jan	Feb	Mar	Apr	May	Jun	Jul	Aug	Sep	Oct	Nov	Dec	Total
Production for sale (units)	250	500	750	1000	1500	2000	2500	2750	2000	2000	2000	2500	19750
Production for stock (units)	1350	1100	850	600	100	-400	-900	-1150	-400	-400	-400	-900	-550
Total production	1600	1600	1600	1600	1600	1600	1600	1600	1600	1600	1600	1600	19200
Overtime units												550	550
Cumulative finished stock	1350	2450	3300	3900	4000	3600	2700	1550	1150	750	350	1050	
Normal time units	1600	1600	1600	1600	1600	1600	1600	1600	1600	1600	1600	1600	19200
Overtime units	0	0	0	0	0	0	0	0	0	0	0	550	550

Paid at normal time / payroll	Jan	Feb	Mar	Apr	May	Jun	Jul	Aug	Sep	Oct	Nov	Dec	Total
Paid at normal time	6400	6400	6400	6400	6400	6400	6400	6400	6400	6400	6400	6400	76800
Paid at overtime	0	0	0	0	0	0	0	0	0	0	0	2750	2750
Other payroll	6250	6250	6250	6250	6250	6250	6250	6250	6250	6250	6250	6250	75000
Total payroll	12650	12650	12650	12650	12650	12650	12650	12650	12650	12650	12650	15400	154550

Schedule 5 General overheads version 2

	Jan	Feb	Mar	Apr	May	Jun	Jul	Aug	Sep	Oct	Nov	Dec	Total
Power	150	150	150	150	150	150	150	150	150	150	150	150	1800
Light		140		140		140		140		140		140	840
Phone			150			150			150			150	600
Insurance	10800												10800
Rent	3000			3000			3000			3000			12000
Rates						3500						3500	7000
Pensions												23183	23183
Leases	300	300	300	300	300	300	300	300	300	300	300	300	3600
Post and packing	24	60	72	96	108	180	144	132	96	96	96	96	1200
Advertising	150	150	225	225	150	150	75	75	75	75	75	75	1500
Other	75	75	75	75	75	75	75	75	75	75	75	75	900
Total overhead	14499	875	972	3986	783	4645	3744	872	846	3836	696	27669	63423

Schedule 6 Bank interest

	Jan	Feb	Mar	Apr	May	Jun	Jul	Aug	Sep	Oct	Nov	Dec	Total
Interest payable	0	163	284	333	349	320	233	0	0	0	0	0	1683
Interest receivable	39	0	0	0	0	0	0	3	144	185	271	223	866
Monthly net interest	39	−163	−284	−333	−349	−320	−233	3	144	185	271	223	−817
Interest paid			408						1088				

Table 5.11 *(continued)*

Schedule 7. Revised profit and loss account 2003		
Sales		395,000
Purchases	119,402	
Less material stocks	10,400	
Materials consumed	109,002	
Production payroll	79,550	
Cost of sales		188,552
Gross profit		206,448
Operating expenses		
Power	1,800	
Light	840	
Telephone	600	
Insurance	10,800	
Rent and rates	19,000	
Pensions	23,183	
Lease charges	3,600	
Postage and packing	1,200	
Advertising	1,500	
Salaries and wages (non-production)	75,000	
Other	900	
Bad debts	4,365	
Depreciation		
Plant	3,304	
Truck	2,400	
Car	2,100	150,592
Profit before interest and tax		55,856
Term loan interest	4,000	
Net bank interest	817	4,817
Profit before tax		51,039
Corporation tax[1]		9,943
Profit retained		41,096

[1] Corporation tax provision.	Profit forecast	51,039
	Add depreciation	7,804
		58,843
	Less WDA 25%	9,130
	Taxable	49,714
	Tax at 20%	9,943

Table 5.11 *(continued)*

Schedule 8. Revised balance sheet as at 31 December 2003

Fixed assets	Cost	Depreciation	Book value
Plant	23,600	4,720	18,880
Truck	12,000	2,400	9,600
Car	8,400	2,100	6,300
	44,000	9,220	34,780
Current assets			
Stocks materials	10,400		
Trade debtors	61,991		
Cash	53,561		125,952
			160,732
Payable in under one year			
Suppliers	12,342		
VAT	8,366		
Bank interest	3,321		
Corporation tax[1]	9,943		(33,972)
Net assets			127,670
Financed by:			
Share capital		40,000	
Revenue reserve		41,096	81,096
Government grant			5,664
Bank term loan			40,000
			127,670

Comments on the revised cash forecast

Larry recognized that there was a major defect concerning capacity utilization in his production plan. This was related to the fact that it was possible to produce 1,600 units each month at a cost of £4 per unit. In his original plan he intended to produce 500 items in January. These would cost £16.80 each. In addition to this substantial cost penalty, when sales from June onwards exceeded his normal time production capacity he would have to arrange overtime and this would add a further £1 per unit to his cost penalty. Both of these cost penalties could be largely eliminated if he decided to produce to his production capacity from the outset. In the early months this would lead to additional purchases, supplier payments, stock and an increase in overdraft requirements. However, a significant saving in overtime would compensate for this as he progressed through the year. The major differences between his original and revised plan are shown in Table 5.12 (p 124).

Table 5.12 *Original and revised plan, Larry Leeds*

	Original	Revised	Change
Production (units)	20,750	19,750	
Production pay (£)	100,300	79,550	20,750
Average cost per unit (£)	4.96		4.03
Material consumed (£)	111,808	109,002	2,706
Finished stock (£)	9,200	–	(9,200)
Pensions (£)	26,295	23,183	3,112
Net interest (£)	4,556	4,817	(261)
			17,107

In this second version of his plan Larry predicted that he would order 1,616 units per month to fill his need to produce to capacity up to November 2003. In November he would need 2,172 to service his planned sales in December. In December he would need 2,020 to service his planned sales in January. In the revised purchasing plan he would reduce his payments to suppliers by £3,181 over the year. Furthermore, in November he would use up all of his finished stock and would have to make for immediate sale, and in December he would have to arrange overtime for the first time to fill his predicted sales.

The major snag with this plan was that, mainly owing to increased purchases in the early months, his overdraft requirement would peak at £41,898 in May rather than the peak of £27,948 in June that his original plan predicted. Larry convinced the bank that the revised plan, which promised an additional profit before tax of £17,107 and a cash balance at the end of the year of £53,561, deserved its support. He was granted an overdraft facility of up to £50,000. This should be ample to cover his planned purchasing, production and sales and leave a little in reserve to cover the unexpected. Larry then set out to deliver on this second version of the plan. We will see how he performed in Chapter 9.

If you aspire to starting your own business you will need to be able to forecast the cash flow, profit and loss account and balance sheet based on your key assumptions. If you can use a spreadsheet it simplifies the task.

CONTROL AGAINST CASH FORECASTS

Cash forecasting depends on ability to accurately predict key variables. The major variables in Larry's proposal are:

- The ability to achieve the production and sales volumes at the unit prices he predicted.
- Obtaining the fixed assets at a price within the capital budget and the project grant.
- Collecting cash from customers at least as quickly as forecast, and paying suppliers at least as slowly as forecast.
- Non-deviation from the stockholding policy.

If some of these items prove to be wrong (and they invariably will) then it will be necessary to revise the forecasts. If Larry does not do this he will run the risk of exceeding his overdraft limit. Banks expect their customers to provide substantial advance notice when additional funds are required. If they do not get this notice, they charge an interest penalty and 'bounce' cheques. This would be very serious at a time when Larry is trying to establish his reputation with suppliers, customers and the bank. We will see how Larry approaches this in Chapter 9.

SUMMARY

Cash is the lifeblood of a business. In a large company the cash forecasting is done in the accounts department. In smaller companies that cannot afford an in-house accounting professional the cash forecast must still be prepared and regularly updated. In order to prepare a reliable forecast you need to predict:

- sales quantities and prices;
- customer credit period;
- purchase, production and stocking policies;
- supplier payment period;
- overhead and interest payments;
- VAT payments or recoveries;
- payments for fixed assets;
- corporation tax; and
- dividend payments.

The use of a computer spreadsheet to prepare the cash forecast is highly recommended. It confers two main benefits. First, it is easy to prepare formulae that convert items like sales into cash collections. Second, when the end of an accounting period is reached, the budget for that period should be replaced with the actual cash flows. For example, if the sales for the period exceed the budget then the collections from customers in subsequent periods will be updated automatically using the relevant formula.

A spreadsheet also helps by providing automatic cross tots and down tots which can be designed to ensure accurate data entry and processing. For example, when the monthly cash balances are completed they should give the same figure as the annualized cash flows. This type of reconciliation is time-consuming and exposed to error when the cash forecast is prepared manually.

The wise organization will always have a cash projection for at least six months ahead and will update this forecast every month by revising the future cash flows to reflect operating experience in the current month, and adding an extra month.

Part II

Testing financial statements

6

Ratio analysis

In the same way that a doctor can test the health of a patient, a skilled financial analyst can test the health of a business. The analyst uses ratios that test financial stability, management effectiveness and investment attractiveness. Ratios help to answer five major questions:

1. Is the business financially stable?
2. Is the profitability adequate?
3. How productive are the staff?
4. How good is the business development strategy?
5. Is it attractive to buy or hold shares in the business?

The various stakeholders may view financial health in different ways:

Stakeholder	Primary focus	Question
Owners	Investment attractiveness	5
Lenders	Financial stability	1
Management	Profitability	2

I regard financial stability as the most important of these questions. It is relevant to all stakeholders. Bankers will be concerned about the size of loans to corporate clients and the customers' ability to repay instalments and interest as they fall due. Equally, other creditors will be concerned with

129

financial stability, particularly as they are usually lower down the queue than bankers if a customer's business fails. Once a business is financially stable the focus turns to profitability. If the profitability is adequate then it helps to pinpoint whether buying or retaining shares is sensible. In a world that is changing so fast it is vital for any business to look to the future. It does so by focusing on the development of new products, the identification of new customers and keeping up to date in the technology race. The business development ratios provide this perspective. The effective management of working capital is a vital challenge to any business. It is so important that it is given a chapter to itself – Chapter 7.

A ratio is the relationship between two numbers. To be meaningful it needs to do two things. First, it needs to *measure progress*. You should compute and graph each ratio for a period of three to five years. The graphs will highlight whether the business has strengthened, remained stable or weakened during the period under review. Second, it needs to *benchmark*. Comparing the most recent result with appropriate, high-quality competitors can be very revealing. Finding a suitable benchmark can prove difficult owing to variations in scale, product mix and financial structure. For example, if you wished to benchmark ITV you might be tempted to choose the BBC. The comparison would prove unsatisfactory. Reasons include size, programme mix, the lack of advertising on BBC, and the lack of licence fees for ITV. A comparison between two ITV regional networks should be more meaningful even though you would still have problems with size and programme mix. While benchmarking can provide valuable insights, management should not overreact if the result is unfavourable.

I will illustrate how ratios are computed and interpreted using Construction Products plc. To begin, in Table 6.1 we look at the profit and loss accounts and balance sheets for the past four years.

FINANCIAL STABILITY RATIOS

One way of assessing financial stability is through the eyes of the company bankers. When lending to a business a bank will look for two forms of protection: operational security, judged by interest cover; and structural security, judged by gearing.

Operational security is based on the ability to create cash that can be used to repay loan instalments and interest. It is similar to the salary criterion used in mortgage lending. Structural stability is based on assets. The lender stakes a claim to the sale proceeds if the borrower's business fails. It is similar to the 80 per cent guideline in property loans.

Table 6.1 *Construction Products plc, profit and loss and balance sheet summaries*

| | Profit and loss summary, £ million | | | |
	1998	1999	2000	2001
Sales	4079.6	5034.3	6599.4	8701.8
Cost of sales	2843.4	3413.4	4511.3	5945.4
Gross margin	1236.2	1620.9	2088.1	2756.4
Operating expenses	892.7	1184.5	1372.3	1885.3
Operating profit	343.5	436.4	715.8	871.1
Earnings of associates	14.2	15.4	11.8	16.5
PBIT	357.7	451.8	727.6	887.6
Interest	36.2	42.9	92.7	190.9
PBT	321.5	408.9	634.9	696.7
Tax	75.7	99.9	177.7	193.7
PAT	245.8	309.0	457.2	503.0
Minority interest	2.2	3.3	3.1	4.6
Preference dividends	0.1	0.1	0.1	0.1
PFO	243.5	305.6	454.0	498.3
Ordinary dividends.	57.1	66.6	78.5	93.4
Retained	186.4	239.0	375.5	404.9
Support information				
Depreciation	129.1	164.6	255.4	351.7
Amortization		1.3	19.6	43.3
Number of employees	22708	27303	36665	42488
Average shares in issue	381.6	386.2	390.1	398.9
EPS	63.81	79.13	116.38	124.92
Closing shares in issue	364.876	387.86	391.469	414.475

Table 6.1 *(continued)*

	Balance sheet summaries, £ million			
	1998	**1999**	**2000**	**2001**
Fixed				
Tangible	1518.8	2287.6	3225.8	4550.9
Intangible	0	138.2	629.2	954.6
Financial	131.5	52.6	66.6	104.0
	1650.3	2478.4	3921.6	5609.5
Current				
Stocks	419.5	575.7	662.3	903.0
Trade debtors	662.5	761.4	931.0	1302.9
Other	114.5	144.2	151.5	232.8
Cash	1178.8	1314.2	972.2	1361.9
	2375.3	2795.5	2717.0	3800.6
Under 1 year				
Loans	131.8	188.9	260	1071.5
Trade creditors	383.9	483.0	548.2	782.3
Other	424.6	619.4	493.8	640.1
Corporation tax	34.4	24.5	39.7	34.5
Proposed dividends	40.2	46.8	55.2	66.7
	1014.9	1362.6	1396.9	2595.1
Net assets	3010.7	3911.3	5241.7	6815
Provisions	143.6	166.2	365	521.8
Capital grants	10.4	19.9	18.8	17.3
Minority interest	13.7	285.3	37.0	35.7
Beyond 1 year				
Loans	1512.2	1854.8	2381.5	2910.2
Other	21.2	31.1	237.7	254.9
	1533.4	1885.9	2619.2	3165.1
Shareholders' funds				
Ord Capital	126.8	128.0	133.1	140.9
Pref Capital	1.2	1.2	1.2	1.2
Revenue reserve	670.5	887.8	1496.4	1992.2
Share premium	501.2	527.1	561.1	930.9
Other	9.9	9.9	9.9	9.9
	1309.6	1554.0	2201.7	3075.1
	3010.7	3911.3	5241.7	6815

Note: The latest share price of Construction Products is £18.20.

Method 1. Interest cover

Interest cover focuses on the adequacy of profits to pay interest on loans and to repay loan instalments as they fall due. It also takes into account the other reasons why a business needs an operating profit. The ratio is calculated by comparing the PBIT with the net interest payable; see Figure 6.1.

	Interest cover				
	1998	**1999**	**2000**	**2001**	**Average**
PBIT	357.7	451.8	727.6	887.6	606.2
Interest	36.2	42.9	92.7	190.9	90.7
Ratio	9.88	10.53	7.85	4.65	6.69

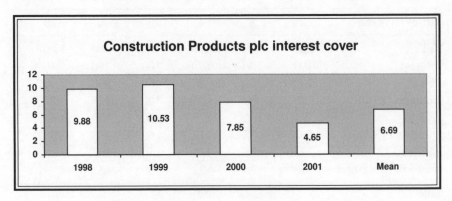

Figure 6.1 *Interest cover*

$$\frac{\text{profit before interest and tax (PBIT)}}{\text{net interest payable}}$$

The interest cover is very sound in all four years. However, it declined substantially in 1999 and 2000. This reflects a conscious decision by the board to carry a higher proportion of interest-bearing debt in their financial structure. The cover averaged 6.69 times for the four-year period. To calculate the four-year average I instructed my computer to a) add the profit before interest and tax for the four years together and divide by four; b) add the net interest payable for the four years together and divide by four; and c) calculate the average cover based on the average PBIT and the average net interest. This averaging methodology called the 'mean' is used, computed, reported and graphed in many of the ratios discussed in this chapter.

Bankers tend to look for an interest cover of at least 3. The logic for this is that £3 of operating profit is needed to service the constituencies required from the operating profit:

- £1 to pay the interest cost;
- about £1 to cover taxation and loan repayments;
- at least £1 to pay dividends and to contribute towards expansion.

If the cover is less than 3 a business has an unpleasant choice between reducing dividends and making too small an owners' contribution towards growth. If interest rates fall it becomes easier to service the constituencies. If interest rates rise it becomes more difficult. The higher the cover, the greater the potential to fund growth through reinvestment. This is illustrated in Table 6.2.

Table 6.2 *Impact of interest cover on funds for expansion*

Times covered	2	3	4	5	6	10
PBIT	200	300	400	500	600	1,000
Interest	100	100	100	100	100	100
PBT	100	200	300	400	500	900
Taxation (25%)	25	50	75	100	125	225
PAT	75	150	225	300	375	675
Dividend (50%)	37	75	112	150	188	337
Retained	38	75	113	150	187	338
% of PBIT retained	19	25	28	30	31	34

Note:
As profits increase, the corporation tax provision grows. Nevertheless, as interest cover improves, the proportion of profit available for dividends and reinvestment grows.

Method 2. PBITDA cover

Since the Accounting Standards Board now requires goodwill to be carried in the balance sheet as an intangible fixed asset and amortized through the profit and loss account, a variation on the interest cover calculation has become popular. This variation compares the profit before interest, tax, depreciation and amortization (PBITDA) with the net interest payable. This is a sensible revision since it recognizes that depreciation and amortization are valuation issues that do not result in cash outflows or damage the ability of a company to repay loan obligations and interest. PBITDA cover is shown in Figure 6.2.

A new guideline has stated that PBITDA cover should be at least 5. Once again Construction Products plc has allowed this ratio to run down towards the minimum as a result of using increased interest-bearing debt in the funding mix.

			PBITDA cover		
	1998	**1999**	**2000**	**2001**	**Average**
PBIT	357.7	451.8	727.6	887.6	606.2
Depreciation	129.1	164.6	255.4	351.7	225.2
Amortization	0	1.3	19.6	43.3	16.1
PBITDA	486.8	617.7	1002.6	1282.6	847.4
Interest	36.2	42.9	92.7	190.9	90.7
PBITDA cover	13.45	14.40	10.82	6.72	9.35

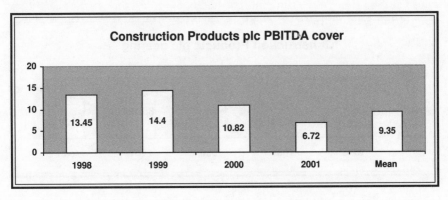

Figure 6.2 *PBITDA cover*

Method 3. Gearing

The second aspect of protection for bankers is the security provided by the net assets. This is measured using the gearing ratio. Gearing is the relationship between net bank borrowings and shareholders' funds:

$$\frac{\text{net bank borrowings}}{\text{shareholders' funds}}\ \%$$

Net bank borrowings are calculated by deducting the cash from the bank loans due and payable in under one year and those due and payable in beyond one year. The ratios are shown in Figure 6.3.

The gearing has been allowed to grow consistently over the four-year period. The peak of 85.19 per cent of shareholders' funds in 2001 is about as high as a prudent company will allow it to rise to. Many organizations starved of subscribed capital have a far higher gearing. Financial institutions regard a company with a gearing in excess of 90 per cent of shareholders' funds as over-borrowed. The logic for this is based on possible proceeds from a liquidation. As the owners are last in the queue for repayment in a liquidation it should be clear that the greater the shareholders' proportion of the

	1998	1999	Gearing 2000	2001	Average
Short term debt	131.8	188.9	260.0	1071.5	413.1
Long term debt	1512.2	1854.8	2381.5	2910.2	2164.7
Cash	−1178.8	−1314.2	−972.2	−1361.9	−1206.8
Net bank debt	465.2	729.5	1669.3	2619.8	1371.0
Equity	1309.6	1554.0	2201.7	3075.1	2035.1
Ratio	35.52	46.94	75.82	85.19	67.37

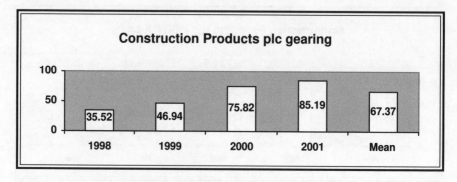

Figure 6.3 *Gearing*

funding, the better the bank is protected. When the gearing reveals excessive borrowings, bankers sometimes overreact by putting pressure on the client to dispose of assets in order to reduce it. Unfortunately, the most profitable assets are usually the most liquid and tend to be suggested by the bank as the ones to sell. While this resolves the excess gearing it does so at the expense of future profitability. Where the gearing exceeds 100 per cent – that is, more than £1 of net bank borrowings for each £1 of shareholders' funds – the bank manager tends to have sleepless nights thinking about the excessive exposure.

How can excessive gearing arise? The easiest way is through operating losses. For example, suppose that Construction Products plc were to make a loss of £100 million in 2002. The shareholders' funds would fall by this amount while the bank's borrowings would have to be increased by a similar amount as money is borrowed to fund assets no longer supported by shareholders' funds. As the borrowings rise, more interest becomes payable and the company gets sucked into a whirlpool of debt from which it is very difficult to escape.

Another way to undermine gearing is through inappropriately funded capital investment or cash acquisitions. Suppose that Construction Products plc were to use an additional £800 million of bank debt to pay for an acquisition during 2002, then the gearing would become unacceptable. In fact it set out to improve the gearing by arranging a rights issue early in 2002. This would reduce the gearing unless unprecedented levels of investment and cash acquisitions were carried out during that year.

Two imperatives can be deduced from the above comments. First, avoid losses: they double the negative impact on gearing. Second, fund expansion appropriately: the shareholders must make an adequate contribution to funding growth through a rights issue or retained earnings.

Method 4. Current ratio

A possible criticism of the gearing ratio is that it is totally focused on bank debt. Lenders such as trade creditors are interested in assessing how secure their loans are. Their security can be measured using the current and liquidity ratios. The current ratio is:

$$\frac{\text{current assets}}{\text{amounts due and payable in under one year}}$$

			Current ratio		
	1998	**1999**	**2000**	**2001**	**Average**
Current	2375.3	2795.5	2717.0	3800.6	2922.1
<1 year	1014.9	1362.6	1396.9	2595.1	1592.4
Ratio	2.34	2.05	1.95	1.46	1.84

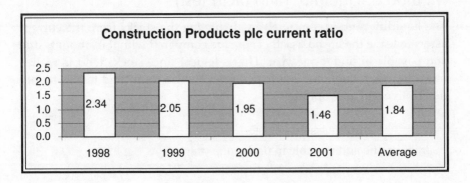

Figure 6.4 *Current ratio*

In common with the gearing ratio the current ratio has been allowed to run down significantly through the four-year period. The current ratio measures the surplus or deficit of current assets (which will turn into cash) over amounts due and payable in under one year (which will have to be paid out

137

in cash). It is a major test of liquidity. Textbooks often suggest the ratio should be at least 2. This is rather superficial. It fails to recognize the asset and liability structure of different industries. Consider the business types in Table 6.3.

Table 6.3 *Asset and liability structures of different industries*

	Construction	Manufacture	Wholesale	Retail
Material stock	Very high	Medium	None	None
Work in progress	Very high	Medium	None	None
Finished goods	Low	Medium	High	High
Trade debtors	Medium	High	High	None
Trade creditors	Medium	Medium	High	High
Recommended range	2–3	1.5–2	1–1.5	1–1.3

Construction Products plc is mainly involved in manufacturing and retailing construction components. Given this mix of core businesses, the 2001 current ratio of 1.46 is about the minimum acceptable. The rights issue in 2002 should again reinforce this ratio.

Method 5. Liquidity ratio (acid test)

The liquidity ratio is computed by deducting the stocks from the current assets to leave the liquid assets. These are compared with the amounts due and payable in under one year. This is logical since stocks tend to realize much less than they cost in a forced sale. The US term 'acid test' is highly descriptive and appropriate.

$$\frac{\text{current assets} - \text{stocks}}{\text{amount due and payable in under one year}}$$

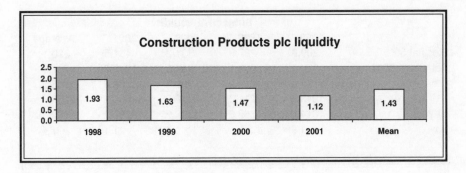

	Liquidity ratio				
	1998	**1999**	**2000**	**2001**	**Average**
Current	2375.3	2795.5	2717.0	3800.6	2922.1
Stock	419.5	575.7	662.3	903.0	640.1
Liquid assets	1955.8	2219.8	2054.7	2897.6	2282.0
<1 year	1014.9	1362.6	1396.9	2595.1	1592.4
Ratio	1.93	1.63	1.47	1.12	1.43

Figure 6.5   *Liquidity ratio*

In common with the other financial stability ratios our analysis shows that liquidity is being allowed to run down. The liquidity ratio is a rather crude instrument. Many debtor accounts would be hard to collect, in a cash crisis, whereas some stocks could be sold. The assumption is that what you gain on the swings (cash from stocks) you lose on the roundabouts (less cash from debtors). Successful businesses rarely show a ratio in excess of 1 in a manufacturing business or 0.8 in a trading business.

Method 6. Subjective liquidity ratio

If you need a better measure of liquidity you need to predict amounts that would be realized in a forced sale of the current assets. For example, suppose that you predict that the stock could be sold at 50 per cent of its stated value and debtors at 80 per cent of their stated value. What the liquidity ratio becomes is shown in Figure 6.6.

	Subjective liquidity				
	1998	**1999**	**2000**	**2001**	**Average**
Stock at 50%	209.8	287.9	331.2	451.5	320.1
Debtors at 80%	530.0	609.1	744.8	1042.3	731.6
Other	1178.8	1314.2	972.2	1361.9	1206.8
	1918.6	2211.2	2048.2	2855.7	2258.4
<1 year	1014.9	1362.6	1396.9	2595.1	1592.38
Ratio	1.89	1.62	1.47	1.10	1.42

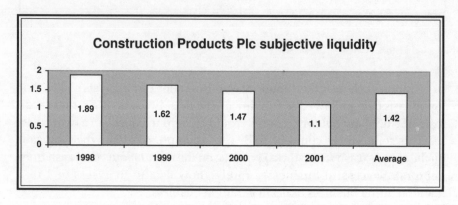

Note: This is a better indicator of liquidity. The trouble is that the realizable value of the stocks is at best an informed opinion. In computing subjective liquidity I look for a ratio in excess of 1

Figure 6.6 *Subjective liquidity*

PROFITABILITY RATIOS

The most popular measures of profitability are based on margin. Margin is profit expressed as a percentage of sales.

Margin can be expressed using four different levels of profit. None of these tells the whole story. For this reason profitability is best measured using Return on Investment (ROI) and Return on Equity (ROE).

Method 1. Gross margin

$$\frac{\text{gross profit}}{\text{sales}} \%$$

Gross margin as a percentage of sales					
	1998	1999	2000	2001	Average
Gross margin	1236.2	1620.9	2088.1	2756.4	1925.4
Sales	4079.6	5034.3	6599.4	8701.8	6103.8
Gross margin %	30.30	32.20	31.64	31.68	31.54

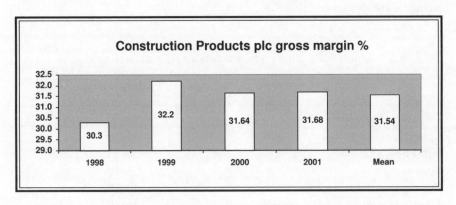

Figure 6.7 *Gross margin as a percentage of sales*

141

The gross margin measures the amount left over out of each £1 of sales when the cost of production has been paid. The gross margin has been remarkably consistent over the four-year period: it peaked at 32.2 per cent in 1999 and averaged 31.54 per cent. Gross margins are similar to product contributions; these are examined in detail in Chapter 11.

Gross margin can vary wildly from one business sector to another. Necessities tend to yield low margins, often supported by government price controls. Luxuries tend to yield higher margins. Businesses that must constantly adapt to fast-changing technology or customer taste require a high gross margin to help fund new product development. Pharmaceuticals and electronics are good examples.

Even within a business sector the gross margin can vary significantly. Some products in a range contribute high margins and others lower ones. For example, in the public house trade beers tend to offer lower margins than mixers. Consequently, a pub in a working class area will have a lower gross margin than one in the gin and tonic belt. Some products are sold direct to the consumer, while competitors buy-in products in a partly manufactured state. This can lead to large variations in margins. Approximate gross profit margins are shown in Table 6.4.

Table 6.4 *Approximate gross profit margins for different sectors*

	%
Department stores	44–50
Public houses	35–50
Food retailers	10–35
Pharmacies	25–40
Boutiques	40–60
High-technology manufacturing	30–60
Low-technology manufacturing	15–30

Method 2. Net margin

$\dfrac{\text{PBT}}{\text{sales}}$ %

	1998	**1999**	**2000**	**2001**	**Average**
			Net margin		
PBT	321.5	408.9	634.9	696.7	515.5
Sales	4079.6	5034.3	6599.4	8701.8	6103.8
Net margin %	7.88	8.12	9.62	8.01	8.45

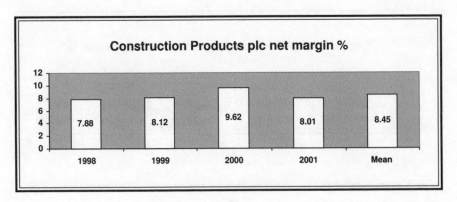

Figure 6.8   *Net margin*

This ratio shows the amount of profit before tax that is left out of each £ of sales. Part of the profit will be set aside to pay the corporation tax bill. The remainder will be proposed as a dividend or retained to help fund growth. The margin tightened significantly in 2001.

Large variations in margin can occur between business sectors. Some businesses require a large asset base to create their sales and profits. They must obtain a high profit margin. For example, a manufacturing business needs plant and machinery, material stocks, work in progress, finished stocks and trade debtors. Some businesses need a smaller asset base. For example, a supermarket would not need many of the assets required by a manufacturer. Consequently it needs a smaller pre-tax margin. This difference in asset base is properly dealt with by measuring Return on Investment (method 5, below).

Method 3. Profit after tax margin

$$\frac{\text{PAT}}{\text{sales}}\%$$

	1997	1998	1999	2000	Average
		Profit after tax margin			
Sales	4079.6	5034.3	6599.4	8701.8	6103.8
Profit after tax	245.8	309.0	457.2	503.0	378.8
After tax margin	6.03	6.14	6.93	5.78	6.21

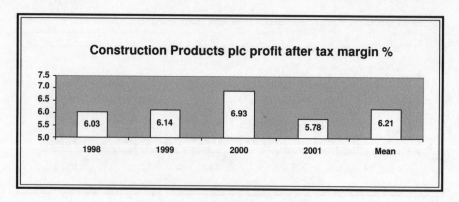

Figure 6.9 *Profit after tax margin*

The after-tax margin also declined significantly in 2001. Investors tend to be most interested in this margin as it reveals what is earned on their behalf. However, Earnings per Share (EPS), dealt with later, tends to provide a clearer insight into the trend.

Method 4. Operating (profit before interest and tax) margin

$$\frac{\text{PBIT}}{\text{sales}}\%$$

	Operating margin				
	1998	**1999**	**2000**	**2001**	**Average**
PBIT	343.5	436.4	715.8	871.1	591.7
Sales	4079.6	5034.3	6599.4	8701.8	6103.8
PBIT margin	8.42	8.67	10.85	10.01	9.69

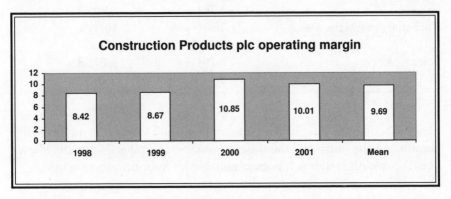

Figure 6.10 *Operating margin*

The margins before and after tax are affected by the financing policy of a business. Conservative businesses finance their assets mainly with shareholders' funds. Their interest charge is low. Aggressive businesses finance their assets mainly with interest-bearing debt. Their interest charge is high. Comparison between businesses with high and low amounts of interest-bearing debt can be misleading. If sales and other costs are equal, the conservative business appears to be more profitable. However, there is more share capital to be rewarded. Adding back interest and comparing the companies on a profit before interest basis removes the impact of financing styles. The PBIT margin is much more suitable for inter-firm comparison than the margin before or after tax. The PBIT margin declined in 2001 after three years of substantial growth. Nevertheless, it was very attractive at 10.01 per cent in 2001. This allowed Construction Products plc to take on substantial additional interest-bearing debt to pay for acquisitions during that year.

Consider a business similar in all respects to Construction Products plc except that it has an additional £500 million of share capital. Suppose that it saves £50 million of interest charges because the additional capital replaces borrowings. The PBT and PBIT margins for 2001 are shown in Table 6.5 (p 146).

Table 6.5 *Comparison of PBT and PBIT margins*

	CP	Similar
PBIT	871.1	871.1
Sales	8,701.8	8,701.8
PBIT margin (method 4)	10.01%	10.01%
PBT	696.7	746.7
Sales	8,701.8	8,701.8
PBT margin (method 2)	8.01%	8.58%

Method 2 suggests that Similar plc is more profitable whereas method 4, by eliminating the impact of the different financing strategy, correctly shows equal operating margins. It is more suitable for inter-firm comparison.

Method 5. Return on investment (ROI)

$$\frac{\text{PBIT}}{\text{total assets}}\%$$

	Return on investment %				
	1998	1999	2000	2001	Average
PBIT	343.5	436.4	715.8	871.1	591.7
Fixed assets	1650.3	2478.4	3921.6	5609.5	3415.0
Current assets	2375.3	2795.5	2717	3800.6	2922.1
Total assets	4025.6	5273.9	6638.6	9410.1	6337.1
ROI	8.53	8.27	10.78	9.26	9.34

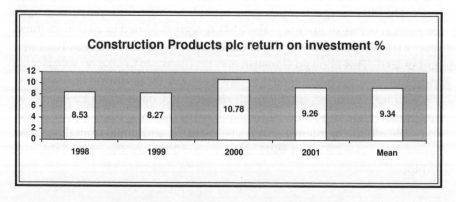

Figure 6.11 *Percentage return on investment*

ROI is the most powerful way of analysing profitability. It compares the operating profit with the total assets used in the business. This comparison helps to identify two major aspects of management effectiveness by asking: How good are they at squeezing profit out of sales? How good are they at squeezing sales out of assets?

To reveal the whole story we need to restate ROI as follows:

$$\frac{\text{PBIT per cent}}{\text{Sales}} \times \frac{\text{Sales}}{\text{Total assets}} = \text{ROI per cent}$$

Splitting the ratio answers these two questions. The first part is the operating margin that we saw in method 4, the second part is the asset turns. These are shown in Figure 6.12.

	Asset turns				
	1998	**1999**	**2000**	**2001**	**Average**
Sales	4079.6	5034.3	6599.4	8701.8	6103.8
Total assets	4025.6	5273.9	6638.6	9410.1	6337.1
Asset turns	1.01	0.95	0.99	0.92	0.96

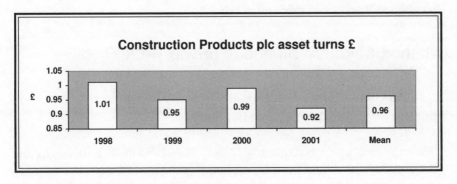

Figure 6.12 *Asset turns*

Construction Products plc has been very consistent in squeezing sales out of assets with a minimum turns ratio of £0.92 in 2001 and a maximum of £1.01 in 1998.

We will now examine the combination of the operating margin and the asset turns to confirm the ROI reported at the start of method 5; see Table 6.6. Reporting the ratio in this way shows the importance of squeezing at least £1 of sales out of each £1 of assets. In 1998 when this was done the ROI exceeded the operating margin. In subsequent years failure to do so diluted the ROI.

Table 6.6 *Return on investment*

	1998	1999	2000	2001	Average
	\multicolumn{5}{c}{Return on investment %}				
Operating margin	8.42	8.67	10.85	10.01	9.69
Asset turns	1.01	0.95	0.99	0.92	0.96
ROI %	8.53	8.27	10.78	9.26	9.34

Most businesses need to earn an ROI of at least 10 per cent. This provides a base to gear up the return to ordinary shareholders. The ROI will be over-stated if out-of-date asset values are used in the balance sheet. When calculating the ROI within the firm, up-to-date valuations of land and buildings should be used so that the report of asset turns is meaningful. External analysts, unable to access the latest valuation, may be misled into thinking that the asset turns are better than they really are, resulting in an overstatement of the ROI. Where an up-to-date valuation is not available indices of movements in values of land and buildings can be used to help calculate ROI and asset turns more reliably.

Method 6. Return on equity pre-tax (ROE)

$$\frac{\text{PBT net of preference dividends and minority interests}}{\text{ordinary shareholders' funds}}$$

This ratio measures the return to ordinary shareholders. It is driven by the ROI and the use of borrowed funds. Some of the borrowings such as trade credit and unpaid taxes provide cost-free funds provided that their credit limits are not exceeded. The use of these interest-free funds boosts the return to shareholders. The use of interest-bearing borrowings will also improve the return to shareholders provided that they cost less than the ROI. ROE is usually calculated before tax to highlight the impact of borrowings on the return.

	Return on equity (pre-tax)				
	1998	**1999**	**2000**	**2001**	**Average**
PBT	321.5	408.9	634.9	696.7	515.5
Minority and preference	2.3	3.4	3.2	4.7	3.4
Profit for ordinary pre-tax	319.2	405.5	631.7	692	512.1
Shareholders funds	1309.6	1554.0	2201.7	3075.1	2035.1
Preference	1.2	1.2	1.2	1.2	1.2
Ord. shareholders' funds	1308.4	1552.8	2200.5	3073.9	2033.9
ROE	24.40	26.11	28.71	22.51	25.18

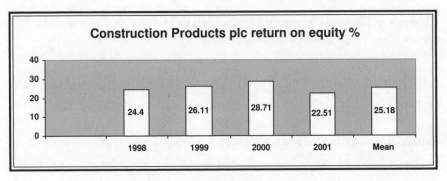

Figure 6.13   *Return on equity (pre-tax)*

The shareholders obtain a tremendous benefit because the average cost of borrowings is much lower than the ROI. The ROE peaked in 2000 but was excellent in all four years.

We will leave Construction Products plc temporarily, to examine how increases or decreases in ROI impact on ROE. The summarized funds of a business are shown in Table 6.7.

Table 6.7   *How changes in ROI impact on ROE*

Shareholders' funds			400		
Free borrowings			300		
Interest-bearing borrowings			300 (cost 10%)		
			1,000		
ROI and ROE comparison					
ROI %	**8**	**10**	**12.5**	**14**	**16**
PBIT	80	100	125	140	160
Interest	30	30	30	30	30
PBT	50	70	95	110	130
ROE %	**12.5**	**17.5**	**23.75**	**27.5**	**32.5**

The reason for the large increase in ROE as you move to the right of the table is that the average cost of borrowings is 5 per cent. It costs 30 of interest to service 600 of funds borrowed from all sources. For a business to thrive it needs an ROE of at least 16 per cent. Unless there is a high level of 'free' borrowings this will require an ROI of at least 10 per cent.

TRENDS IN THE FINANCIAL STRUCTURE

Changes in financial structure are not always obvious from financial statements. Percentages can be more revealing.

Method 1. Restating the balance sheet in percentage terms

Table 6.8 *Restating the balance sheet in percentage terms*

	2000	2001	Change
Fixed assets	59.1	59.6	0.5
Stock	10.0	9.6	−0.4
Debtors and prepayments	16.3	16.3	
Cash	14.6	14.5	−0.1
Total assets	100.0	100.0	
Shareholders' funds	33.2	32.7	−0.5
Bank borrowings	39.8	42.3	2.5
Trade creditors	8.8	8.3	−0.5
Other funding	18.2	16.7	−1.5
Total funds	100.0	100.0	

The most significant figure in this table is the increased level of bank borrowings in the funding mix. This confirms the comments I made when discussing the financial stability ratios.

Method 2. Restating the profit and loss account in percentage terms

Table 6.9 _Restating the profit and loss account in percentage terms_

	2000	2001	Change
Sales	100.0	100.0	
Cost of sales	68.4	68.3	−0.1
Gross profit	31.6	31.7	0.1
Overheads	20.6	21.5	0.9
PBIT	11.0	10.2	−0.8
Interest	1.4	2.2	0.8
PBT	9.6	8.0	−1.6
Corporation tax	2.7	2.2	−0.5
PAT	6.9	5.8	−1.1
Dividends	1.2	1.1	−0.1
Retained profits	5.7	4.7	−1.0

The main features of the profit and loss account are the significant increases in overheads and interest. These resulted in a 0.8 point drop in operating profit and a 1 point drop in retained earnings.

Method 3. Indexing figures from year to year

To measure growth or decline from year to year the previous year's figures are set at a base 100. Percentage changes in the profit and loss account are shown in Table 6.10.

Table 6.10 _Percentage changes in the profit and loss account_

	99/98	00/99	01/00
Profit and loss account			
Sales	23.4	31.1	31.9
Cost of sales	20.0	32.2	31.8
Gross margin	31.1	28.8	32.0
Operating expenses	32.7	15.9	37.4
Interest	18.5	116.1	105.9
PBT	27.2	55.3	9.7
Tax	32.0	77.9	9.0
PAT	25.7	48.0	10.0

Sales are the fulcrum against which growth is measured. In 1999 sales increased by £954.7 million or 23.4 per cent. The fact that the cost of sales rose by only 20 per cent resulted in a substantially improved gross margin. However, overheads rose substantially faster than sales. The 18.5 per cent increase in interest payable helped to increase the profit before tax faster than sales. The increase in corporation tax, which was greater than the profit before tax, led to an increase in the profit after tax of 25.7 per cent. Ideally, tighter control of the growth in overheads should have led to a significantly better increase in profit after tax.

The overhead situation was dramatically reversed in 2000. There we find that a growth in operating expenses of 15.9 per cent on the back of a sales increase of 31.1 per cent led to a 48 per cent increase in profit after tax in spite of a large increase in interest payable (116.1 per cent) and corporation tax (77.9 per cent).

In 2001 overheads and interest charges increased more quickly than sales. This led to an increase in profit after tax of only 10 per cent on the back of a 31.9 per cent increase in sales. Clearly, a top priority for 2002 must be to bring the overheads back into line.

Table 6.11   *Balance sheet trends*

Balance sheet	99/98	00/99	01/00
Stocks	37.2	15.0	36.3
Debtors	14.9	22.3	39.9
Creditors	25.8	13.5	42.7
Fixed assets	61.5	52.2	52.0
Net bank borrowings	56.8	128.8	56.9

With regard to the balance sheet trends in 1999, the fact that growth in stocks and fixed assets outpaced sales is a source of concern, while the debtors situation was excellent. In 2000 the stock trend was reversed and the debtors position was again satisfactory. However, the fixed asset growth continued to outpace the sales. In 2001 stocks and debtors both grew faster than sales while the fixed asset investment continued to outpace sales. These balance sheet trends were the key reason why the asset turns, discussed earlier in the chapter, disimproved. In all three years the growth in net bank borrowings greatly exceeded the increase in sales. As noted previously, this was clearly the result of a board decision to allow the gearing to increase.

PRODUCTIVITY RATIOS

The two major ratios that test productivity are sales per employee and profit per employee. Productivity ratios help to benchmark performance against comparable organizations. Problems can arise: a bigger business may be able to utilize staff more effectively, and most businesses have some diversifications from their core activity. Such diversifications make inter-firm comparison difficult.

Public houses illustrate these problems. Sales and profit per employee vary due to the balance of trade between bar and lounge (prices are higher in lounges and can vary significantly between houses), and the balance of sales between pints (lower gross margin line) and mixers (higher gross margin line). Food sales tend to be more labour-intensive than drink sales, and square footage of counter/customer space, eg 25 per cent more space should not require a comparable increase in staff.

Method 1. Sales per employee

	Sales per employee			
	1998	**1999**	**2000**	**2001**
Sales (£m)	4079.6	5034.3	6599.4	8701.8
Employees	22708	27303	36665	42488
Sales per employee £'000	179.65	184.39	179.99	204.81

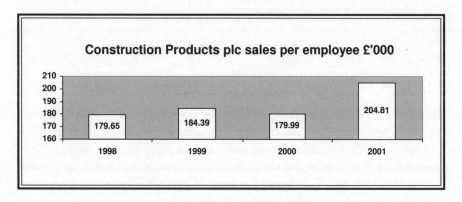

Figure 6.14 *Sales per employee*

The sales per employee have improved substantially despite a hiccup in 2000. Nevertheless, when inflation is considered, the growth in productivity is at best described as modest.

Method 2. Profit per employee

	Pre-tax profit per employee			
	1998	**1999**	**2000**	**2001**
PBT (£M)	321.5	408.9	634.9	696.7
Employees	22708	27303	36665	42488
Profit per employee £'000	14.158	14.976	17.316	16.398

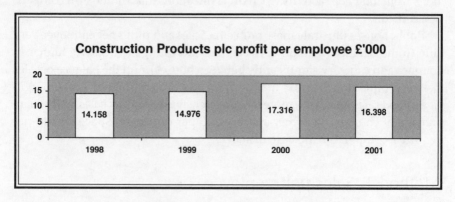

Figure 6.15   *Pre-tax profit per employee*

The growth in profit per employee was also modest when inflation is taken into account. The decline in 2001 confirms the need for attention to cost control in 2002, discussed previously.

COMPETITIVENESS RATIOS

Method 1. Average age of operating fixed assets

To assess this we compare the cost of the relevant fixed assets with their book values. The figures for Construction Products plc are taken from the published accounts for 2001. These were not included in the summarized accounts at the start of the chapter, as they would make the summaries excessively detailed. Following the normal process in published accounts these data were relegated to notes to the accounts.

Table 6.12 *Average age of tangible fixed assets*

	Plant	Transport
Cost or valuation	3170.4	364.7
Aggregate depreciation	1101.7	145.2
Book value	2068.7	219.5
Percentage written off	34.75	39.81
Depreciation rate	3–20%	20%

This analysis points to an average age of transport of two years (39.81 per cent/20 per cent). The average age of plant is difficult to judge because of the wide spread of depreciation rates used. Suffice it to say that the percentage written off is not big enough to point to a need for massive reinvestment. If the buildings (depreciated at 2.5 per cent pa) had been shown separate from the land, then I would have shown it in the average age analysis. Since Construction Products plc did not provide a breakdown the ratio is meaningless. Nevertheless, I recommend that you calculate the percentage written off property when analysing the accounts of your own company, a competitor or acquisition target.

Method 2. Reinvestment rate

$$\frac{\text{current year capital expenditure}}{\text{current year depreciation}}$$

Table 6.13 *Reinvestment rate*

	1998	1999	2000	2001
Capital investment	147.3	232.1	360.1	429.5
Depreciation	129.1	164.6	255.4	351.7
Reinvestment rate %	114.10	141.01	140.99	122.12

This ratio discloses the degree to which depreciation charges are sufficient to cover capital investment. At current inflation rates a business should be investing at least 1.4 times its annual depreciation charge. Construction Products plc fell below this guideline in 1998 and 2001.

155

Method 3. Business development statistics

To assess the amounts being used to protect and develop a business it is wise to calculate the following:

- Product development expenditure as a percentage of sales.
- Market development expenditure as a percentage of sales.
- Customer care as a percentage of sales.

Unfortunately, these data are not compulsory in published accounts. If analysing your own company you should calculate them and compare them with industry norms. We will see the importance of these ratios when we examine shareholder value later in the book.

The working capital ratio is also crucial to competitiveness. It earmarks the level of investment that needs to be made in stocks and debtors as sales grow. This ratio is dealt with in Chapter 7.

INVESTMENT RATIOS

There are 11 major ratios that can be used to evaluate whether shares should be bought, sold or retained. There is an immediacy about investment decisions. For this reason the emphasis is focused on two major questions. First and most important, the analyst is asking whether a share represents good value at the current market price. The relevant ratios are:

- Method 3. Dividend yield.
- Method 5. Price earnings and diluted price earnings.
- Method 7. PBITDA multiple.
- Method 9. Market to book.
- Method 10. Sales to capitalization.
- Method 11. Price earnings to growth.

These ratios report a single figure at a point in time. The ratio changes with every movement in the share price and should be recomputed when the price moves significantly. The best way to do this is to prepare the ratio analysis on a spreadsheet with the sales price in a single cell. In this way the ratios above will be recomputed when the value in that cell is changed. Second, the focus is placed on growth. In methods 1, 2, 4, 6 and 8 the development of the business is reported and graphed. Unlike the ratios computed previously, the mean is not computed. Far and away the most important statistic is the ratio for the latest year. Of secondary but significant importance is the progress towards the present ratio that has been achieved over the previous years. The mean is irrelevant when assessing the present position and the progress made to reach that position, and is not reported in these graphs.

Method 1. Earnings per share (EPS)

$$\frac{\text{profit attributable to ordinary shareholders}}{\text{weighted average number of ordinary shares in issue}}$$

	Earnings per share (pence)			
	1998	**1999**	**2000**	**2001**
Earnings for ordinary shareholders	243.5	305.6	454	498.3
Weighted average shares in issue	381.6	386.2	390.1	398.9
Absolute (p)	63.81	79.13	116.38	124.92
Growth year on year %		24.01	47.07	7.34
Growth absolute %	100	124.01	182.39	195.77

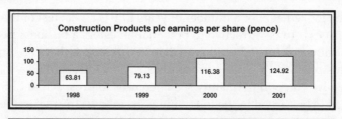

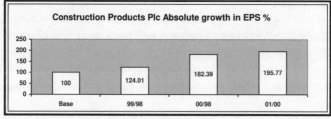

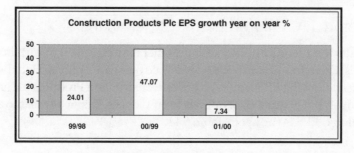

Figure 6.16 _Earnings per share_

Three graphs are presented to reflect the EPS data. First, the actual EPS is reported as a measure of progress. Second, the growth in earnings per share from year to year is reported. Third, the absolute growth over the four-year period is reported. To do this the earnings per share in each of the three years 1999, 2000 and 2001 is compared with the 1998 result.

The basic ratio shows the amount earned per ordinary share in issue. FRS 14 requires that the EPS be shown on the face of the profit and loss account. The major calculation of EPS must be made after allowing for extraordinary and exceptional items. It must also be based on the weighted average number of ordinary shares in issue during the year. For example, suppose that a company had 1 million ordinary shares in issue at the start of the year and issued a further 500,000 at mid-year. The weighted average number of ordinary shares is 1.25 million. This is because 500,000 for half a year is deemed to be equivalent to 250,000 for a full year. The logic for using weighted average is that the funds received from the sale of the additional shares should provide extra profits for the portion of the year when they are in place.

When looked at over a number of years EPS is a vital test of the progress of a business. To be attractive to potential investors a business needs to be able to paint a picture of rapid growth in EPS. A snag is that EPS is measured using historic results. Future prospects are a key influence on a share price. This is why you will frequently see references to prospective EPS (the EPS expected to be earned in the following year) in investment commentaries.

The earnings per share of Construction Products plc almost doubled through the four-year period. This level of growth is superb even though the growth slowed dramatically in 2001. Only the actual EPS tends to be shown in published accounts. The really important statistic occurs when the growth year-on-year is calculated. For example, when the 2000 EPS of 116.38p was compared with the 1999 results, an excellent growth of 47 per cent was revealed.

Method 1A. Diluted earnings per share

There are frequently additional shares that may be issued in certain circumstances. Often this occurs because of employee share options. Had these been exercised then the EPS would be lower. Construction Products plc has given a relatively small number of options to employees. Taking these into account, the diluted EPS is shown in Table 6.14.

Table 6.14   *Diluted earnings per share*

	1998	1999	2000	2001
Earnings for ordinary shareholders	243.5	305.6	454	498.3
Weighted average ordinary shares in issue	381.6	386.2	390.1	398.9
Add share options	2.0	2.7	5.3	6.3
	383.6	388.9	395.4	405.2
Diluted EPS (pence)	63.48	78.58	114.82	122.98

Method 2. Dividend per share

$$\frac{\text{ordinary dividends paid and proposed}}{\text{number of ordinary shares in issue}}$$

	Dividend per share (pence)			
	1998	1999	2000	2001
Absolute	14.86	17.14	20.00	22.80
Growth year on year %		15.34	16.69	14.00
Growth absolute %	100	115.34	134.59	153.43

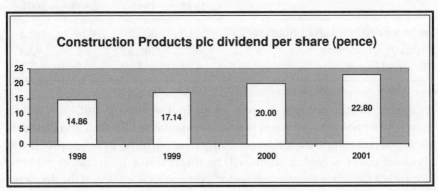

Figure 6.17   *Dividend per share*

The report of the dividend per share in the notes to published accounts is of limited benefit. Shares are unlikely to be trading at their nominal value. Nevertheless, the pattern of growth is highly informative. Over the four-year period the increase in dividends paid and proposed was an excellent 53.4 per cent, though this was far behind the growth in EPS.

Method 3. Dividend yield

$$\frac{\text{dividend per share}}{\text{current market price per share}} \quad \frac{22.8p}{£18.20} = 1.25\%$$

The dividend yield relates the latest annual dividends (interim plus final) to the current share price. At the time of writing the dividend yield of successful companies is very low. Investors are seeking substantial capital gains to compensate for low dividend yields.

Method 4. Dividend cover

This ratio shows the relationship between profit paid out as dividends and profit retained for growth.

$$\frac{\text{profit attributable to ordinary shareholders}}{\text{ordinary dividends paid and proposed}}$$

Table 6.15 *Dividend cover*

	1998	1999	2000	2001
Profit for ordinary shareholders	243.5	305.6	454	498.3
Ordinary dividends	57.1	66.6	78.5	93.4
Dividend cover	4.26	4.59	5.78	5.34

As a general rule companies pay about half of their profit after tax to shareholders and retain the rest to finance expansion. Construction Products plc has a consistently high cover compared with the average plc. If the dividend cover is high a share will be unattractive to investors seeking income but attractive to investors seeking capital appreciation. If the dividend cover is low a share will be unattractive to investors seeking capital appreciation but attractive to those whose priority is income. Dividend income is exposed to personal tax. Consequently, a decision to invest for dividends probably implies a low marginal tax rate, while one to invest for capital appreciation probably implies a high one.

Method 5. Price earnings ratio (PE)

$$\frac{\text{market price per share}}{\text{earnings per share}}$$

Table 6.16 _PE ratio_

Latest share price (£)	18.20
EPS (pence)	124.92
PE	14.57

At its current rate of earnings Construction Products plc would take nearly 15 years to earn its current share price. The PE ratio is a key to valuing a business. The multiple is highest in industries that the market believes will offer substantial growth in the future, and lowest in industries with discouraging prospects. At the time of writing, the average PE for all companies included in the _Financial Times_ index was about 12. Comparison with other companies in the sector may reveal a deviation.

The PE. What a difference eight months makes

When I drafted this chapter in June 2001 I took the PEs for a range of major UK businesses so as to show you the huge variations in multiples when you look at different industries. Before sending the final copy to the publisher I updated the PE data based on the closing prices on Monday 22 February 2002. Some of the changes are very substantial, as you can see in Table 6.17.

Table 6.17 _Changes in price earnings ratios_

Company	PE 8 June 2001	PE 22 Feb 2002
Barclays	14.7	12.6
Cadbury Schweppes	18.4	15.6
Diageo	20.2	25.0
Glaxo Smith Kline	37.0	33.4
Marks & Spencer	23.4	35.0
Prudential	27.0	28.6
Sainsbury's	27.1	23.7
Vodafone group	52.3	30.7

The biggest changes took place in Vodafone, down from 52.3 to 30.7 and Marks & Spencer up from 23.4 to 35.0. I feel the PE of Vodafone remains very high when you consider that the telecommunications industry worldwide is having a difficult time at the moment. Buyers at the current price are clearly anticipating a major reversal of fortunes. By contrast, the stock market in June 2001 was taking a pessimistic view of the product range being offered by Marks & Spencer, for many years a darling of the investment community. The current share price is anticipating a major recovery of profits since the M & S PE is well ahead of competitors.

The PE ratio for important quoted enterprises is shown in the *Financial Times* and other major newspapers every day. The PE shown is based on the share price at close of dealing on the previous day and the latest published results from the company. I suggest that you buy the *Financial Times* today and check the PEs for this selection of companies. It is likely that you will see further major movements as the market re-rates the prospects.

Where conversion rights attach to shares, or loan stock or options exist, a second version of the price earnings ratio will sometimes be quoted. This is the fully diluted PE. At 31 December 2001 employees of Construction Products plc had options to acquire 6.3 million shares. Had these options been exercised then there would have been a weighted average of 405.2 million shares in issue through 2001. The diluted PE becomes:

Latest share price (£)	18.20
Diluted EPS (p)	122.98
Diluted PE	14.80

Prudent investors use the PE to help them to decide whether to buy, hold or sell shares. Suppose that an investor thinks the growth prospects of Construction Products plc justifies a PE of 20. On the basis of this judgement the investor would buy the shares in the hope that the stock market would recognize that the shares were undervalued. If the market bid the price up to £25 per share then this would yield a handsome 37 per cent profit for the investor, who would then be well advised to sell the shares since they had reached the top price that the investor could expect. The fact that the construction industry is exposed to major swings from boom to gloom explains why the market is not prepared to trade up the price of Construction Products to a PE of 20. Unless the whole sector is re-rated by professional investors the target price of £25 per share is unlikely to be realized.

Method 6. PBITDA per share

In recent times stock markets have placed a much greater emphasis on corporate cash flows than was previously the case. Earlier in our discussion on financial stability we saw that PBITDA provided the basis for calculating the relationship between operating cash flow and interest. PBITDA also provides the basis for calculating cash flow per share and the relationship between this cash flow and the latest share price. The PBITDA per share is computed using the formula:

$$\frac{\text{profit before interest, tax, depreciation and amortization}}{\text{weighted average number of shares in issue}}$$

	PBITDA per share (pence)			
	1998	**1999**	**2000**	**2001**
PBIT	357.7	451.8	727.6	887.6
Depreciation	129.1	164.6	255.4	351.7
Amortization	0	1.3	19.6	43.3
PBITDA	486.8	617.7	1002.6	1282.6
Weighted average shares in issue	381.6	386.2	390.1	398.9
PBITDA per share (p)	127.57	159.94	257.01	321.53
Growth year on year %		25.38	60.69	25.11
Growth from base year %	100	125.38	201.47	252.05

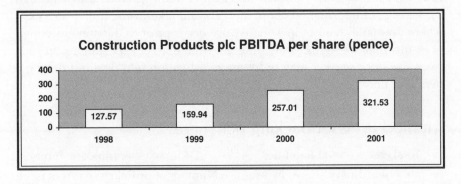

Figure 6.18 *PBITDA per share*

The PBITDA (cash flow) per share has grown by 152 per cent over the four-year period. This provided a very strong base from which to increase the dividend and to contribute towards growth.

Method 7. PBITDA multiple

Until recently the PE was the major basis for assessing buy, hold and sell decisions. The new emphasis on cash flow has led to the PBITDA becoming popular. It relates the PBITDA per share to the latest share price. The PBITDA multiple is:

$$\frac{\text{Latest share price}}{\text{PBITDA per share}} \quad \frac{£18.20}{321.53} = 5.66$$

The PBITDA multiple for an average company is currently about 5. Since Construction Products plc is achieving growth in sales that is much higher than average, a potential investor might reasonably take the view that the shares are worth more than their current PBITDA multiple. A multiple of 7 might be the investors' target. This would suggest a price of £22.50 per share and points to Construction Products plc as an interesting investment prospect.

Insider trading

This is an appropriate point to mention the thorny issue of insider trading. There is a vital difference in law between a person who invests or divests on the basis of a personal judgement and a person who does so on the basis of facts not available to other investors. A person who uses privileged information to deal in shares is guilty of insider trading. Such a person can be liable to a heavy fine or even a jail sentence. Insider trading mainly arises through the leakage of information about mergers and take-overs. It may also exist where dramatic changes in a share price occur prior to the announcement of results that are significantly different from market expectations. In such cases the stock market may order an investigation into dealings during a period of unexpected share price volatility.

Method 8. Asset backing per share

$$\frac{\text{Total assets – total liabilities}}{\text{Number of ordinary shares in issue}} \quad \text{or} \quad \frac{\text{Ordinary shareholders' funds}}{\text{Number of ordinary shares in issue}}$$

For a balance sheet to balance, the net assets must exactly equal the shareholders' funds. Consequently, we can use either of the above to calculate the asset backing. We use the number of shares in issue at the end of the year rather than the weighted average because shares have equal claims on the assets whether they have been held for a short or a long period.

	Net assets per share			
	1998	**1999**	**2000**	**2001**
Net assets	1309.6	1554	2201.7	3075.1
Ordinary shares	364.876	387.86	391.469	414.475
Net assets per share (£)	3.59	4.01	5.62	7.42

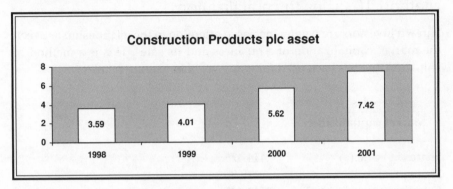

Figure 6.19   _Net assets per share_

Shares in Construction Products plc are trading at £18.20 whereas the net asset backing is £7.42. Clearly shareholders are basing their investment decisions on prospects for continued growth rather than the underlying security provided by the net assets. One way of looking at the difference between the asset backing and the share price is to recognize that the difference of £10.78 is the internally generated goodwill that cannot be carried in the balance sheet.

Asset backing provides a backstop for the share price in difficult economic conditions as investors turn their attention towards security. Some caution is indicated when the share price greatly exceeds the asset backing, as in this case.

Method 9. Market to book

$$\frac{\text{Latest share price}}{\text{Net assets per share}} \quad \frac{£18.20}{£7.42} = 2.45$$

This ratio is an indicator of the amount of goodwill, either positive or negative, that is built into the share price. The ratio is very important in the judgement of manufacturing businesses that need substantial assets to generate and support sales. It is not relevant in service industries where the net assets are often very small as compared to the sales. In common with most

165

shares in companies that are growing rapidly, the share price is substantially higher than the net assets per share. The difference represents the internally generated goodwill, as we noted earlier.

Method 10. Sales to capitalization

Shrewd investors are paying increased attention to the relationship between the market capitalization of a business and its sales. This is a method of valuation that has been used for many years in valuing retailers.

$$\frac{\text{Sales}}{\text{Market capitalization}}$$

Shares in issue (a)	414.475
Share price (b)	18.20
Capitalization (a × b)	7543.445
Sales	8701.8
Sales to capitalization	0.87

In computing this ratio the number of shares in issue at the end of last year is used, rather than the weighted average. The stock market currently values Construction Products plc at £7.54 billion. This valuation is less than 88 per cent of the sales and reflects concern about prospects for the construction industry. Some 'new economy' companies are still capitalized at immense multiples of sales despite the collapse in the share price of many high-tech businesses.

Method 11. Price earnings growth (PEG)

Many analysts rightly argue that a business whose sales growth is higher than its PE is an investment that is well worth considering. A business that has a PE of 10 can be expected to achieve growth in sales and earnings of less than 10 per cent. In spite of the unexciting prospects the PEG is greater than one. Many rapidly growing businesses have never achieved a profit but still trade on a PEG of greater than one. The PEG for Construction Products plc is a very interesting 0.46:

PE	14.57
Sales growth	31.86
PEG	2.19

It is reasonable to predict that if the growth in sales can be sustained then the share price will rise significantly.

TYPES OF INVESTMENT STRATEGY

Category 1. Investing for recovery

Shares in this category usually have a strong asset backing (occasionally well in excess of the share price) and a low PE due to recent losses or indifferent profits. Investments of this type promise substantial capital appreciation if profit recovery occurs. If not, the asset backing may underpin the share price unless serious losses are incurred. This type of investment is very attractive where the company is well managed and the industry may have reached the bottom of its cycle.

Category 2. Shares in a high-growth company

The difficulty with this type of investment is that forecasters tend to have excessive expectations for future profit potential. The dramatic rise and subsequent decline of the US-based Nasdaq index is a recent example. Investors bid up technology shares without regard to conventional valuation methods simply on the basis that growth prospects were enormous. Non-achievement of expected profit growth often results in a collapse in the share price. The change in the US outlook from boom to gloom saw such a collapse. Furthermore, in many of the so-called 'new economy' stocks there is insufficient attention to sound control procedures during a chase for growth. I dislike this type of investment because the downside risk is high. Management frequently has little experience in coping with a crisis. Nevertheless, large capital gains are available to early spotters of potential.

Category 3. Shares in highly speculative businesses

Exploration stocks are a good example. They are unsuitable for widows and orphans. Such shares can yield huge capital gains and losses. My view is that they should be left to the experts. You should not use money you will need later or bank overdraft facilities to finance this type of investment. It is like a big bet on an odds-on favourite at a very wet Royal Ascot.

Category 4. Shares in a highly profitable company

Typically, shares in this category have a high price earnings ratio and a share price far in excess of the asset backing. Investment of this type should normally be for the long term. It is wisest to have a portfolio to reduce the impact of a decline in a particular business sector. Unit trusts are the prudent way to acquire a portfolio, unless the investor has a large investment fund and either considerable time and analytical skills or a highly skilled and reputable adviser.

Some final words of advice on this subject are:

- Even non-professionals should analyse the ratios to inform their buy, sell and hold decisions.
- Never invest on gossip alone. You will lose in the long run.
- Do not use your holiday money or a bank overdraft. If you do, Murphy's Law says that anything that can go wrong will.

SUMMARY

In this chapter we examined a number of ratios. Some are crucial performance indicators. It is not always necessary to compute all the ratios. When a key ratio is unstable it becomes necessary to dig deeper. The favourites for initial diagnosis are:

- gearing;
- interest cover;
- ROI;
- ROE;
- gross margin.

The best way to prepare and interpret ratios is to build a picture of the last four years and the plan for the current year. This is best done using a spreadsheet to prepare and graph the calculations. This five-year analysis shows you the picture of strengths and weaknesses and the actual and planned development of the business.

In addition to preparing ratios covering a period of time, the wise analyst will identify a similar business and analyse its ratios to provide an appropriate benchmark. Ideally, any business should strive to be in the upper quartile when compared to its peers.

7

Working capital

Understanding and managing working capital is a top priority in any business that is growing. Unfortunately, many businesspeople do not understand what working capital is, never mind know how to manage it. The problem is exacerbated by the popular and misleading definition of working capital as net current assets (current assets minus amounts due and payable in under one year). Why is this definition misleading? Because it fails to recognize the two aspects of the working capital issue. First, the need to invest in stocks and in customer credit in order to fill orders from customers; the net cost of this investment can be reduced if the business can obtain credit from suppliers. The correct definition of working capital investment is *stock + trade debtors − trade creditors*. Second, the access to funds that will enable the business to pay for the working capital investment; the faulty definition of working capital as net current assets mixes up the funding and the investment issues.

The chapter is divided into four sections:

- *The real meaning of working capital.* This section explains why funding is required from the point where goods and services are bought, to collection from customers. In particular it focuses on the reasons why funding requirements change as volumes or costs rise and fall.
- *Over-trading.* This section deals with the situation that arises when a company tries to invest more money in stocks and debtors than its

funding permits. It also deals with the causes of the problem and the possible solutions to an over-trading crisis.

- *Working capital ratios.* This section describes and illustrates a selection of ratios designed to examine the effectiveness of working capital management.
- *Management of working capital.* This section examines the management of stocks and debtors. It describes the steps that can be taken to keep down investment without damaging profit potential. It also explains how to optimize credit from suppliers.

THE REAL MEANING OF WORKING CAPITAL

The need for working capital investment is determined by the operating cycle of a business. The level of investment is itself determined by stockholding policy, customer credit terms and settlement patterns and supplier credit. In Figure 7.1, I show the operating cycle that will operate in the business of Neil New.

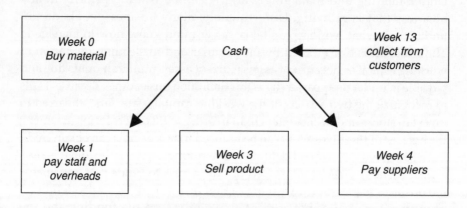

Figure 7.1 *Business operating cycle, Neil New*

Neil New is about to start in business. His key assumptions are as follows:

- He will buy 6,000 units at start-up. Thereafter he will buy 1,000 per week.
- Material will cost £10 per unit.
- Labour will cost £5 per unit.
- Overheads will cost £1 per unit.

- Material suppliers will be paid four weeks after purchase.
- Customers will pay 10 weeks after sale.
- Sales will be 1,000 units per week at £20 each, starting Week 3.
- He has arranged £220,000 of funds to cover working capital requirements.

Neil recognizes that he will be very exposed in the early weeks. He will be paying suppliers, staff and overheads but not collecting from customers. His cash forecast is shown in Table 7.1.

Table 7.1 _Cash forecast, Neil New_

Week	Units purchased	Cost of purchases	Supplier payments	Wage and o/h payments	Working capital
0	6,000	60,000			
1	1,000	10,000	–	6,000	6,000
2	1,000	10,000	–	6,000	12,000
3	1,000	10,000	–	6,000	18,000
4	1,000	10,000	60,000	6,000	84,000
5	1,000	10,000	10,000	6,000	100,000
6	1,000	10,000	10,000	6,000	116,000
	12,000	120,000	80,000	36,000	

By the end of week 6 Neil will have spent £116,000. No cash will have been collected from customers. The working capital invested is represented in the balance sheet as shown in Table 7.2.

Table 7.2 _The working capital investment of Neil New (version 1)_

Stock of raw materials	60,000 (six weeks at £10,000 per week)
Stock of finished goods	32,000 (two weeks at £16,000 per week)
Cost element of trade debtors	64,000 (four weeks at £16,000 per week)
	156,000
Less supplier credit	40,000 (four weeks at £10,000 per week)
Net working capital investment	116,000

The cash position will continue to deteriorate at a rate of £16,000 per week. By the end of week 12, £212,000 of working capital will be required. In week 13 the cash position will start to improve. He will continue to spend £16,000 per week but expects to collect £20,000 per week from customers. If Neil did not have at least £212,000 of funds arranged to cover his working capital needs he would not be able to achieve his plan. Neil would be said to be over-trading: trying to sell more than the finances available will permit.

OVER-TRADING

The causes of over-trading:

- Operating losses.
- Commencing operations with inadequate funds.
- Trying to grow too quickly.
- Incurring cost increases. The additional cash outflows will start long before the cash inflows increase when higher prices are charged to customers.
- Simultaneous growth in volume and price.

Losses and over-trading

Operating losses are one of the surest ways to damage the financial structure of a business. They are usually accompanied by an acute shortage of cash as the day-to-day outflows exceed collections from customers.

Commencing operations with inadequate funds

To start a business properly the promoter will need a significant amount of long-term funds. These are required to pay for fixed assets, working capital investment, and product and market development costs. If Neil had only £160,000 of funds he would run out of cash long before he started to collect from his customers. His promising business would probably die in its infancy since his bank would not cash cheques that would push him over his overdraft limit.

Trying to grow too quickly

When a business grows, the cash paid to suppliers, staff and overheads increases before the collections from customers. This exerts additional pressure on the cash resources. Suppose that in weeks three and four, Neil's sales were 1,200 units. Suppose that he now expects to sell this quantity every week. He revises his plan to increase purchasing and production accordingly. In week 5 he increases his purchase to 3,200 units to bring his stock into line with the new sales forecast. Thereafter he buys 1,200 units each week. Payments to staff and for overheads rise to £7,200 per week. The working capital needed is shown in Table 7.3.

Table 7.3 _The working capital investment of Neil New (version 2)_

Week	Units purchased	Cost of purchases	Supplier payments	Wage and o/h payments	Working capital
0	6,000	60,000			
1	1,000	10,000	–	6,000	6,000
2	1,000	10,000	–	6,000	12,000
3	1,000	10,000	–	6,000	18,000
4	1,000	10,000	60,000	6,000	84,000
5	3,200	32,000	10,000	12,000	106,000
6	1,200	12,000	10,000	7,200	123,200
7	1,200	12,000	10,000	7,200	140,400
8	1,200	12,000	10,000	7,200	157,600
9	1,200	12,000	32,000	7,200	196,800
10	1,200	12,000	12,000	7,200	216,000
11	1,200	12,000	12,000	7,200	235,200
12	1,200	12,000	12,000	7,200	254,400
	21,600	216,000	168,000	86,400	

Notes:
The funds required for working capital rise to £254,400 as a result of growth. The working capital investment at the end of week 12 is made up as follows:

Stock of raw materials	72,000 (six weeks at £12,000 per week)
Stock of finished goods	38,400 (two weeks at £19,200 per week)
Cost element of trade debtors	192,000 (ten weeks at £19,200 per week)
	302,400
Less supplier credit	48,000 (four weeks at £12,000 per week)
Net working capital investment	254,400

As Neil has access to only £220,000 of funds he will run out of cash in week 11.

Incurring cost increases

When suppliers implement price increases, the normal response from their customers is to also raise prices. Nevertheless, a shortage of cash can occur as supplier payments rise long before collections from customers. Suppose that just when the first order is being placed the supplier increases his price to £11 per unit. To recover this cost Neil decides to increase his selling price to £21 per unit. The effect of the price increase on the cash forecast is shown in Table 7.4.

Table 7.4 *The working capital investment of Neil New (version 3)*

Week	Units purchased	Cost of purchases	Supplier payments	Wage and o/h payments	Working capital
0	6,000	66,000			
1	1,000	11,000	–	6,000	6,000
2	1,000	11,000	–	6,000	12,000
3	1,000	11,000	–	6,000	18,000
4	1,000	11,000	66,000	6,000	90,000
5	1,000	11,000	11,000	6,000	107,000
6	1,000	11,000	11,000	6,000	124,000
7	1,000	11,000	11,000	6,000	141,000
8	1,000	11,000	11,000	6,000	158,000
9	1,000	11,000	11,000	6,000	175,000
10	1,000	11,000	11,000	6,000	192,000
11	1,000	11,000	11,000	6,000	209,000
12	1,000	11,000	11,000	6,000	226,000
	18,000	198,000	154,000	72,000	

Notes:

The funds required rise to £226,000 as a result of the increased cost. The working capital investment at the end of week twelve is made up as follows:

Stock of raw materials	66,000 (six weeks at £11,000 per week)
Stock of finished goods	34,000 (two weeks at £17,000 per week)
Cost element of trade debtors	170,000 (ten weeks at £17,000 per week)
	270,000
Less supplier credit	44,000 (four weeks at £11,000 per week)
Net working capital investment	226,000

Because of the cost increase Neil will now run out of cash in week 12.

Simultaneous growth in volume and price

The pressure on cash becomes more intense when both volume and costs are rising. To illustrate this we will assume that:

- production and sales are 1,200 units each week;
- the supplier charges £11 per unit;
- to recover the supplier increase Neil raises his selling price to £21 per unit.

The working capital now required is shown in Table 7.5.

Table 7.5   *The working capital investment of Neil New (version 4)*

Week	Units purchased	Cost of purchases	Supplier payments	Wage and o/h payments	Working capital
0	7,200	79,200			
1	1,200	13,200	–	7,200	7,200
2	1,200	13,200	–	7,200	14,400
3	1,200	13,200	–	7,200	21,600
4	1,200	13,200	79,200	7,200	108,000
5	1,200	13,200	13,200	7,200	128,400
6	1,200	13,200	13,200	7,200	148,800
7	1,200	13,200	13,200	7,200	169,200
8	1,200	13,200	13,200	7,200	189,600
9	1,200	13,200	13,200	7,200	210,000
10	1,200	13,200	13,200	7,200	230,400
11	1,200	13,200	13,200	7,200	250,800
12	1,200	13,200	13,200	7,200	271,200
	21,600	237,600	184,800	86,400	

Notes:
The funds required for working capital will now total £271,200 owing to the combination of increased volume and increased cost. The working capital at the end of week 12 is made up as follows:

Stock of raw materials	79,200 (six weeks at £13,200 per week)
Stock of finished goods	40,800 (two weeks at £20,400 per week)
Cost element of trade debtors	204,000 (ten weeks at £20,400 per week)
	324,000
Less supplier credit	52,800 (four weeks at £13,200 per week)
Net working capital investment	271,200

Neil expects to show a profit of £48,000 before interest in the first 12 weeks when the volume and cost increases are taken into account. His forecast profit and loss account and balance sheet are shown in Table 7.6.

Coping with over-trading

There are five major approaches to tackling an over-trading crisis:

1. Get the owners to invest more capital. This is certainly the best solution. Unfortunately, the extra capital is not available in many small businesses where the owners have invested all the funds that they can lay their hands on.
2. Attract a minority shareholder that will invest more capital in the business (and possibly as a result of the improved gearing facilitate additional bank borrowing). The owners of many small businesses are not prepared to exercise this option as it results in a dilution of control. In my opinion such a reaction is foolish. To own 75 per cent of a thriving business is more attractive than 100 per cent of an under-capitalized one.
3. Dispose of assets that are surplus to current requirements.
4. If a business is starved of funds to feed the never-ending working capital cycle and cannot quickly raise additional funds, it will be faced with three unpalatable options:
    - reduce the stockholding period: this could cause a stock-out and result in the loss of profitable sales;
    - put pressure on customers to pay more quickly: if the demands become unreasonable the customers might stop buying;
    - slow down supplier payments: if this goes too far, they will stop supplies and the production planning process can quickly become unmanageable.
5. Assess the working capital and profitability of each product group. This examination may lead to a decision to discontinue certain products that make a poor contribution to profits or require too great a working capital investment. Analysis of this type is difficult. It requires a detailed breakdown of stocks, debtors and creditors over the range of products. The work is justified if it explains why the working capital investment is unsustainably high. Such analysis is a crucial element of good financial management.

Table 7.6 _Forecast profit and loss account and balance sheet, Neil New_

Forecast profit and loss account, Neil New

Sales (12,000 at £21 each)		252,000
Purchases (21,600 at £11)	237,600	
Less material stock (7,200 at £11)	79,200	
Issues to production	158,400	
Staff and overheads	86,400	
	244,800	
Less finished stock (2,400 at £17)	40,800	
Cost of sales		204,000
Profit before interest		48,000
Interest payable		3,645
Profit before tax		44,355
Corporation tax		8,871
Profit retained		35,484

Forecast balance sheet, Neil New

Current assets		
Stock of raw materials	79,200	
Stock of finished goods	40,800	
Trade debtors (12,000 at £21)	252,000	
		372,000
Less supplier credit	52,800	
Corporation tax	8,871	
Unauthorized bank loan[1]	54,845	116,516
Net assets		255,484
Financed by:		
Share capital		100,000
Undistributed profit		35,484
		135,484
Term loan		120,000
		255,484
Note:		
[1] Share capital received		100,000
Term loan received		120,000
Funds available		220,000
Working capital required	271,200	
Interest accrued	3,645	274,845
Unauthorized bank loan		54,845

WORKING CAPITAL RATIOS

There are many ratios designed to measure working capital investment. The major ones are computed from the financial statements of Construction Products plc presented in Chapter 6.

Stockholding ratios

Many analysts compare the stock with the sales. The comparison is not a sensible one as stocks must be valued at cost. Nevertheless, I now present five versions of the Construction Products plc stockholding ratio that are frequently used.

Table 7.7 *Stockholding ratios*

	Stock/sales ratios				
	1998	**1999**	**2000**	**2001**	**Average**
Stock	419.5	575.7	662.3	903	640.1
Sales	4079.6	5034.3	6599.4	8701.8	6103.8
Days	37.53	41.74	36.63	37.88	38.28
Weeks	5.35	5.95	5.22	5.40	5.45
Months	1.23	1.37	1.20	1.25	1.26
Turns	9.72	8.74	9.96	9.64	9.54
Percentage	10.28	11.44	10.04	10.38	10.49

All these ratios say the same thing in slightly different ways. For example, I calculated the days by dividing the sales by 365 to obtain the average daily sales and then divided the result into the stock to get the days of sales in stock. Once you understand how the form of ratio used by your business is constructed you can forget about the four alternative ways of calculating it.

Most UK companies tend to express stock ratios in terms of timeframe (days, weeks or months) whereas many US businesses use turns. To say that the stocks are turned 9.72 times per year means exactly the same as 37.53 days. Only the mode of expression is different.

Comparison of stocks with cost of sales yields more meaningful ratios. This is because you are comparing like with like. I strongly recommend that if your business uses sales-based stockholding ratios, you should encourage a switch to whichever of the cost of sales-based versions shown below suits them.

Table 7.8 _Cost of sales-based stockholding_

	Stock/cost of sales ratios				
	1998	**1999**	**2000**	**2001**	**Average**
Stock	419.5	575.7	662.3	903.0	640.1
Cost of sales	2843.4	3413.4	4511.3	5945.4	4178.4
Days	53.85	61.56	53.59	55.44	55.92
Weeks	7.67	8.77	7.63	7.90	7.97
Months	1.77	2.02	1.76	1.82	1.84
Turns	6.78	5.93	6.81	6.58	6.53
Percentage	14.75	16.87	14.68	15.19	15.32

I strongly favour the weeks stock statistic. Whichever way you choose to view the ratio the table shows substantial consistency with the peak in 1999 and the low in 2000 revealing a variation of 1.14 weeks.

Defects in the cost of sales-based stockholding ratio

There are three problems with the cost of sales-based stockholding ratios:

1. They fail to recognize that a manufacturing business holds stock in four forms: raw materials, work in progress, finished goods, and consumables. An in-house analyst can prepare more appropriate ratios that help to pinpoint areas where stocks may be excessive.
2. In a seasonal business there can be large variations in sales and cost of sales from month to month. To overcome this variability you can use the average actual cost of sales for the last quarter or the budgeted cost of sales for the next quarter.
3. The volume and value of stock can vary enormously during a financial year. For example, one would expect a house builder to have a large volume of work in progress during the summer months and much less in inclement winter conditions. To overcome this volatility you can total the budgeted stock at the end of each month and then divide by 12 to get a more meaningful measure of stock investment.

We will now examine how the stockholding of Model Company Ltd was analysed by its financial controller. She calculated the ratios on a quarterly basis because of the volatility of sales and stockholding. She used the data shown in Table 7.9 (p 180).

Table 7.9 *Budgeted manufacturing accounts*

£'000

Quarter	1	2	3	4	Year
Material consumed	428	355	607	872	2,262
Production labour	280	320	355	332	1,287
Fuel	30	25	24	26	105
Maintenance	20	21	30	25	96
Production other	13	15	17	15	60
Opening work in progress	80	85	70	70	80
Closing work in progress	(85)	(70)	(70)	(80)	(80)
Cost of production	766	751	1,033	1,260	3,810
Opening finished stock	270	286	211	153	270
Cost of production	766	751	1,033	1,260	3,810
	1,036	1,037	1,244	1,413	4,080
Closing finished stock	286	212	152	280	280
Cost of sales	750	825	1,092	1,133	3,800
Sales	1,000	1,100	1,400	1,500	5,000
Gross profit	250	275	308	367	1,200

Summary of stocks

	Q1 Opening	Q2 Opening	Q3 Opening	Q4 Opening	Q4 Closing
Material stock	250	300	200	150	300
Work in progress	80	85	70	70	80
Finished stock	270	286	211	153	280
Fuel	60	65	70	75	80
Maintenance stores	40	44	48	52	60
	700	780	599	500	800

We will now examine the days stock ratios that can be extracted from these detailed figures. Initially we will look at the year-end ratios. Subsequently we will examine how the results vary substantially from quarter to quarter.

Method 1. Raw materials

Weeks material consumed in material stock:

$$\frac{300}{2,262} \times 52 = 6.9 \text{ weeks}$$

This is the most sensible way to evaluate the holding of materials. Comparison is being made between comparable items. I tend to favour the weeks stocks approach and will concentrate on this from now on. If your company measures stockholding in days, months, percentages or turns, you will know how to apply this approach to the subsequent illustrations. Before we proceed to the other elements of the stockholding, let us look at the ratios for material stock on a quarterly basis; see Table 7.10.

Table 7.10 *Ratios for material stock on a quarterly basis*

	Q1	Q2	Q3	Q4	Year
Opening material stock	250	300	200	150	250
Material consumed	428	355	607	872	2,262
Weeks stock	7.6[1]	11.0	4.3	2.2	6.9

Note:
[1] The quarterly figures are based on 13 weeks, eg $250/(428/13) = 7.6$ weeks.

A new approach has been adopted in calculating these ratios. The material stocks are committed to meet future production requirements. At the start of quarter 1 the material stocks are adequate to meet the issue requirements for the next 7.6 weeks. This assumes an average weekly issue to production of $(428/13)$ through the first quarter. The ratios show that material stock has declined substantially by comparison with consumption in the third and fourth quarter.

Method 2. Finished stock

Description   **Calculation**

Weeks cost of sales in finished stock $\dfrac{280}{3,800} \times 52 = 3.8$ weeks

This ratio indicates that the business holds a relatively small finished stock. A strike on the production floor could result in a stock-out, with potentially serious consequences. However, with the cost of stockholding high, businesses try to keep finished goods at a low level. The quarterly figures are:

	Q1	Q2	Q3	Q4	Year
Weeks	4.7[1]	4.5	2.5	1.8	3.8

[1] $270/(750/13)$

The stockholding period declines all the way through the year.

Method 3. Fuel stock

Weeks fuel stocks in fuel consumed $\dfrac{60}{105} \times 52 = 29.7$ weeks

Decisions on the level of fuel stocks are influenced by predicted price movements (stock high if prices expected to rise and low if expected to fall) and the significance or otherwise of a stock-out (disastrous for a transport company but not so serious if used to heat a factory). The quarterly figures are:

	Q1	Q2	Q3	Q4	Year
Weeks	26.0	33.8	37.9	37.5	29.7

In this case we see a build-up of stock through quarter 3 and a decline thereafter.

Method 4. Maintenance stock

Weeks maintenance stock in maintenance cost

$$\frac{40}{96} \times 52 = 21.7 \text{ weeks}$$

Maintenance stocks can vary enormously in size. Some organizations can buy replacements on demand. Others have to hold specialized parts that might not be used for years. The ratio of maintenance stock to maintenance parts is hugely important in the transport business. The quarterly maintenance stock ratios are:

	Q1	Q2	Q3	Q4	Year
Weeks	26.0	27.2	20.8	27.0	21.7

In this case the stockholding period varies significantly from its high at 27.2 weeks in quarter 2, to its low at 20.8 weeks in quarter 3.

Method 5. Work in progress

Weeks work in progress in cost of production $\quad \dfrac{80}{3,810} \times 52 = 1.1$ weeks

This ratio suggests the length of the production cycle. It is a bit misleading. Method 6 is an improved measure of work in progress. It assumes that materials are input at the start, while labour and overheads are applied evenly through the process. On this basis the cost of producing goods to an average level in the work in process phase would be computed as shown in Table 7.11.

Table 7.11   _The cost of producing goods to an average level_

	Q1	Q2	Q3	Q4	Year
Materials consumed	428	355	607	872	2,262
Half labour	140	160	178	166	644
Half other (fuel, maintenance, etc)	31	31	35	33	130
	599	546	820	1,071	3,036

Method 6. Work in progress 2

On the basis of the data above, the average production period is:

Weeks work in progress $\quad \dfrac{80}{3,036} \times 52 = 1.37$ weeks

Work in progress can vary from years in major construction activities to minutes in uncomplicated and highly automated processes. The quarterly ratios for method 6 are:

	Q1	Q2	Q3	Q4	Year
Weeks	1.74	2.02	1.11	0.85	1.37

It looks as if the company concentrated on lines with a long production cycle in quarters 1 and 2 as compared with quarters 3 and 4.

In summary, there are a variety of ways of looking at stockholding. It is wise to be aware of the different approaches. It is important to compare results with the stockholding policy of the company and, where possible, to relate them to competitors.

Debtor ratios

The simplest form of debtor ratio expresses the results in days, weeks, or months of sales. Following our approach to stocks we will concentrate on weeks. The Model Company Ltd debtor ratio at year-end is:

$$\frac{1,042}{5,000} \times 52 = 10.8 \text{ weeks}$$

This analysis is superficial. Many factors can distort it. The following are important issues:

- Cash sales should be excluded in computing the average credit period.
- The turnover figure does not include VAT. The trade debtors figure does. To make a valid comparison you should either gross up the sales to include VAT or net down the debtors to exclude VAT.
- The debtors figure in the balance sheet often includes amounts that relate to staff loans, pre-payments, etc. These tend to distort a ratio designed to establish the average delay in collecting from customers and should be excluded from the calculation. The notes to the accounts should give the trade debtors.
- Annual figures can be misleading, where sales fluctuate substantially in a seasonal business.

The figures in Table 7.12 were obtained from the budget of the Model Company Ltd. They allow us to assess the average customer credit more accurately.

These ratios show significant changes in the average collection period. The low occurs in the third quarter. The pattern of sales growth through the year distorts the average in the annual figure and makes it an unreliable indicator of the effectiveness of credit management. It is wise to calculate the credit taken by major customers as well as looking at the overall figures.

The credit period can vary wildly from one business to another. Among the notorious slow payers are farmers, chemists, vets and builders. Among the fastest payers are people to whom a threat to cut off supplies is disturbing (ie many retail goods, electricity, telephone, etc). It is wise to compare your ratios against the credit period that the industry sector offers.

Table 7.12 _Budget of Model Company Ltd_

	Q1	Q2	Q3	Q4	Year
Cash sales	80	125	70	100	375
Credit sales	920	975	1,330	1,400	4,625
Total sales	1,000	1,100	1,400	1,500	5,000
Add VAT (17.5%)	175	193	245	262	875
Grossed up sales	1,175	1,293	1,645	1,762	5,875
Trade debtors	590	725	790	1,042	1,042
Trade debtor weeks	7.1[1]	8.2	6.6	8.2	10.0[2]

Notes:
[1] 590/(920 × 117.5%/13)
[2] 1,042/(4,625 × 117.5%/52)

The supplier credit ratio

A poor method of measuring supplier credit is often used because no better information is available:

$$\frac{\text{Creditors}}{\text{Average weekly sales}}$$

Ideally the ratio should be calculated by taking the amounts due to suppliers for goods and services supplied on credit, and relating this to the average weekly cost of purchasing goods and services bought on credit. It is essential to ensure that VAT is properly treated, either by grossing up the purchase cost to match creditors, or reducing creditors to match the net of VAT procurement cost.

The information in Table 7.13 (p 186) was taken from the budget of Model Company Ltd.

Table 7.13 *The supplier credit ratio, Model Company Ltd*

	Q1	Q2	Q3	Q4	Year
Purchases on credit (incl. VAT)	930	1,064	1,367	1,499	4,860
Creditors (incl. VAT)	360	403	642	476	476
Weeks credit	5.0[1]	4.9	6.1	4.1	5.1

Note:
[1] 360/(930/13)

These ratios show that the Model Company pays its suppliers reasonably promptly. The third-quarter figure appears high. On investigation a good explanation was found. During the quarter, plant costing £123,000 was bought on credit. It remained unpaid at the end of the quarter. It was included in both the purchases and creditors. This occasional purchase distorted the comparison. The figures were restated as follows:

Quarter 3

Purchases	1,246
Creditors	519
Weeks credit	5.4

Cash ratios

Most businesses need to have some cash available at all times. Some is held in the petty cash float and some is cash receipts that have not yet been lodged. As a business grows, more cash becomes tied up in this way. This type of cash is treated differently from funds on short-term deposit or funds wastefully left lying in current accounts. The simplest way to measure the cash investment is to express it as a percentage or turns of sales.

The Model Company Ltd figures are:

$$\frac{Cash}{Sales}\ \%\quad \frac{25}{5{,}000\%} = 0.5\%$$

or

$$\frac{Sales}{Cash}\quad \frac{5{,}000}{25} = 200 \text{ turns}$$

This ratio is normally calculated annually. Retailers that earn significant interest between point of sale and payment of suppliers should compute the ratio more frequently.

The popular version of the working capital ratio

$$\frac{\text{Net current assets}}{\text{Sales}} \%$$

This ratio is supposed to reveal the amount of additional funds required to support working capital as sales grow or that are capable of being released from working capital as sales decline. It does not do this successfully because not all amounts due and payable in under one year react to changes in sales (ie tax provisions, proposed dividends and short-term bank debt).

A better measure is based on the definition of working capital I used at the start of this chapter. The improved ratio is:

$$\frac{\text{Stock} + \text{trade debtors} - \text{trade creditors}}{\text{Sales}} \% = \frac{800 + 1,042 - 476}{5,000} = 27.32\%$$

Year-end figures can provide an incorrect picture of the cash required to fund the working capital cycle. They reveal an off-season picture of investment and can be further distorted by management decisions to slow down stock purchases and supplier payments and increase customer collection pressure to dress-up the balance sheet for publication.

The ratio can be calculated more meaningfully by averaging the components through the year. First, calculate the average stocks (a simple method is to total the planned stockholding for each of the 12 months and divide by 12). We will assume the average stock is £950,000. Then calculate the average trade debtors and creditors through the year in the same way. We will assume average trade debtors and trade creditors of £1 million and £450,000. The working capital ratio based on these averages is:

$$\frac{950 + 1,000 - 450}{5,000} = 30\%$$

We can conclude that if stockholding and average credit given and taken continue at their current duration, then the Model Company Ltd will require an extra £0.3 million of funds to support a £1 million sales increase next year. A change in stocking policy or a decision to give or take more or less credit would alter the amount required. That said, growth in sales volume or an inflation-driven price increase will result in the need for additional working capital. Note that the £0.3 million calculated above greatly exceeds the profit retained in the previous year. The Model Company will need to arrange additional funds or it will run the risk of over-trading.

EFFECTIVE MANAGEMENT OF WORKING CAPITAL

Stock

There is a fine line between carrying too much and too little stock. There are problems associated with both excessive and inadequate stocks.

Problems with excess stock

Excessive stock damages return on investment, as Table 7.14 shows.

Table 7.14   *The effects of excess stock*

	Efficient Ltd	Less Efficient Ltd
PBIT	16,000	16,000
Stock	60,000	100,000
Other assets	100,000	100,000
Total assets	160,000	200,000
ROI	10%	8%

Excessive stock also leads to deterioration, and a change in customer taste can cause stock losses. Stockholding cost is high. Many organizations fail to realize the true cost, which includes fire insurance, recording and control, interest on borrowings to support stock investment, and space costs (rent, rates, etc). Also, if prices fall then a company with high stocks is poorly placed relative to lower-stocked competitors.

Problems with inadequate stock

Profitable sales may be lost. Our customer, forced to buy from a competitor, may be well treated and not come back to us when our stock shortage is rectified.

Purchasing costs rise as a result of emergency buying decisions, for example 'emergency' airfreight rather than a timely delivery by road or sea freight. With a lengthy set-up time it is cost-effective to produce large batches.

If a supplier increases prices it may place the company in a poor position relative to competitors with large stocks.

The purchasing and stockholding model

To operate this model you need data on sales, stocking policy and stock losses. The stocking plan based on the predictions below is shown in Figure 7.2.

Description	Data
Expected weekly sales	990 units
Standard loss through wastage and pilferage	1% of weekly sales
Delivery delay	5 weeks
Buffer stock to cover demand peaks and unexpected delivery delays	3 weeks

Wk	Opening stock	Order placed	Delivery	Sales	Stock losses	Closing Stock	Buffer	Forward sales
−5	−	8,000	−	−	−	−	−	−
0	−	5,000	8,000	−	−	8,000	3,000	5,000
1	8,000	−	−	990	10	7,000	3,000	4,000
2	7,000	−	−	990	10	6,000	3,000	3,000
3	6,000	−	−	990	10	5,000	3,000	2,000
4	5,000	−	−	990	10	4,000	3,000	1,000
5	4,000	5,000	5,000	990	10	8,000	3,000	5,000
6	8,000	−	−	990	10	7,000	3,000	4,000
7	7,000	−	−	990	10	6,000	3,000	3,000
8	6,000	−	−	990	10	5,000	3,000	2,000
9	5,000	−	−	990	10	4,000	3,000	1,000
10	4,000	5,000	5,000	990	10	8,000	3,000	5,000

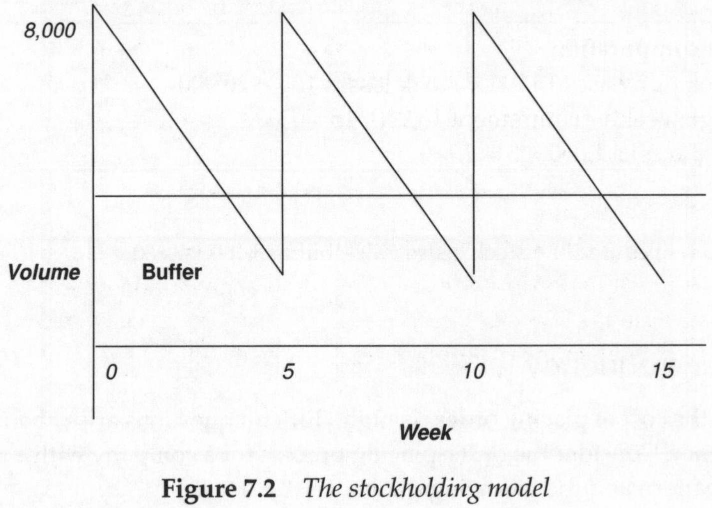

Figure 7.2 *The stockholding model*

A problem with the basic model (erratic sales)

Many organizations experience uneven demand. As a result, purchasing and stock are difficult to plan. In the second example orders are based on budgeted sales; see Table 7.15.

Table 7.15 *Orders based on budgeted sales*

Wk	Opening stock	Order placed	Delivery	Sales	Stock losses	Closing stock	Buffer	Forward sales
–5		7,880[1]						
0		5,200	7,880			7,880	3,180	4,700
1	7,880	–	–	792	8	7,080	3,180	3,900
2	7,080	–	–	891	9	6,180	3,180	3,000
3	6,180	–	–	990	10	5,180	3,180	2,000
4	5,180	–	–	1,089	11	4,080	3,180	900
5	4,080	6,000	5,200	891	9	8,380	3,180	5,200
6	8,380	–	–	1,089	11	7,280	3,180	4,100
7	7,280	–	–	792	8	6,480	3,180	3,300
8	6,480	–	–	1,188	12	5,280	3,180	2,100
9	5,280	–	–	1,287	13	3,980	3,180	800
10	3,980	5,300	6,000	792	8	9,180	3,180	6,000
11	9,180	–	–	1,188	12	7,980	3,180	4,800
12	7,980	–	–	1,089	11	6,880	3,180	3,700
13	6,880	–	–	990	10	5,880	3,180	2,700
14	5,880	–	–	1,287	13	4,580	3,180	1,400
15	4,580	–	5,300	1,386	14	8,480	3,180	5,300
				15,741	159			

Buffer computation
15-week purchases 15,741 + stock losses 159 = 15,900
Average weekly requirement 15,900/15 = 1,060
Buffer 3 weeks 1,060 × 3 = 3,180

Note:
[1] 5-week sales (4,653) + stock losses (47) + buffer 3,180 = 7,880

Order frequency

When the cost of placing orders is high, difficult questions arise about order frequency. Consider the order-placing process for a company with a regular sales pattern and the following data:

Description	Data
Annual sales units	520,000
Budgeted purchase cost per unit	£1
Stockholding cost (per cent of average inventory held per annum)	20 per cent
Cost per order placed	£300

How often should orders be placed? We can see from Table 7.16 that the lowest purchasing cost occurs when orders are based on a four-weekly reorder cycle.

Table 7.16 *Order frequency and stock costs*

Order frequency (weeks)	Orders per annum	Placement cost (£)	Average stock held (£)	Stock holding cost (£)	Total stock cost (£)
1	52.0	15,600	5,000	1,000	16,600
2	26.0	7,800	10,000	2,000	9,800
3	17.3	5,200	15,000	3,000	8,200
4	13.0	3,900	20,000	4,000	7,900
5	10.4	3,120	25,000	5,000	8,120
6	8.7	2,600	30,000	6,000	8,600

Just in time

Just in time (JIT) is an approach to manufacturing developed in Japan. It involves the elimination of buffer stocks and manufacture in small lots. This is contrary to traditional approaches in which the key rules were that long production runs lead to lower unit costs and buffer stocks ensure that direct labour always has a continuous supply of work. Just in time is very suitable for industries where:

- large numbers of standardized units are produced;
- consistent quality is required and the error tolerance is narrow; and
- the manufacturer can arrange rapid delivery of components from suppliers.

It is extensively used in car and computer assembly. Rover claimed to have saved £37 million a year as a result of the introduction of JIT.

The major benefits of JIT are the following:

- Problems become highly visible.
- Weaknesses in the production process are more obvious.
- There is increased awareness of significant problems. In the early stages of using JIT the problems may occur frequently and rapidly.
- Potential problem identification becomes a management priority. This is a dynamic approach as compared to passive problem solving.
- Since the line must stop to resolve any problems, management and staff learn to cure them quickly.
- Removal of buffers results in reduced incidence of breakage and pilferage during production.
- The cost of stockholding is reduced. Lower work in progress reduces the interest cost, releases space for other purposes, and reduces the risk of fires and consequently the cost of insurance.

Trade debtors

The major issues are:

- Too high debtor balances undermine return on investment.
- The greater the level of debtors, the more exposed a business is to the risk of bad debts.
- Money unnecessarily tied up in debtors could have been used to reduce bank borrowings and interest thereon. It also pushes up the gearing.

These issues must be weighed against the consequences of attempts to speed up debt collection:

- depression of demand due to uncompetitive terms of trade;
- high discounts in order to encourage prompt payment;
- heavy expenditure on credit control.

The rules for effective management of customer credit

Rule 1. There should be a defined credit limit for each significant customer. It is good practice to ensure that customer orders are charged to the account on a pro-forma basis before the order is filled. This helps to avoid unauthorized excesses.

Rule 2. Limits should be regularly reviewed to highlight changes in creditworthiness.

Rule 3. When customer purchasing patterns fluctuate, the credit limit should not stay static. The main reason for this is that stocks and trade debtors influence the size of the customer's net assets. This changes the potential liquidation proceeds. Consider the following example: Betty Bradford Ltd has informed us of its planned purchasing pattern:

Quarter	Value of purchases
1	25,000
2	5,000
3	10,000
4	20,000

Betty normally sells the product about one month after purchase and pays us about two months thereafter. All other features of the business remain fairly constant. The seasonal balance sheets are shown in Table 7.17.

Table 7.17 _Seasonal balance sheets, Betty Bradford Ltd_

	Q1	Q2	Q3	Q4
Fixed assets	38,000	38,000	38,000	38,000
Stocks	8,333	1,667	3,333	6,667
	46,333	39,667	41,333	44,667
Capital	15,000	15,000	15,000	15,000
Bank overdraft (secured)	6,333	19,667	16,333	9,667
Creditor	25,000	5,000	10,000	20,000
	46,333	39,667	41,333	44,667

If the company fails and key liquidation forecasts are: a) fixed assets 40% of book value; b) stocks 25% of book value; and c) liquidation costs £5,000 then we will recover:

	Q1	Q2	Q3	Q4
Cash realized				
Fixed assets	15,200	15,200	15,200	15,200
Stocks	2,083	417	833	1,667
	17,283	15,617	16,033	16,867
Liquidation cost	5,000	5,000	5,000	5,000
	12,283	10,617	11,033	11,867
Less bank recovery	6,333	10,617	11,033	9,667
Proceeds for us	5,950	–	–	2,200
Due to us	25,000	5,000	10,000	20,000
Predicted bad debt	19,050	5,000	10,000	17,800

Note:
A fixed credit limit is inappropriate for this customer. If you are prepared to accept a 50% loss in a closedown, then you should set the following floating limits:
Quarter 1 £9,525, Quarter 2 £2,500, Quarter 3 £5,000, Quarter 4 £8,900.

Rule 4. A company that sells at a high profit margin is more likely to be prepared to sell goods to customers that are poor credit risks. Contrast the possible impact of a bad debt on suppliers of goods at various profit margins, shown in Table 7.18.

Table 7.18 *The impact of bad debt on suppliers at various profit margins*

Company	A	B	C	D	E
Monthly sales	10,000	10,000	10,000	10,000	10,000
Margin	60%	50%	25%	20%	10%
Monthly loss if bad debt	4,000	5,000	7,500	8,000	9,000
Gain if collected	6,000	5,000	2,500	2,000	1,000
Payback (months)	0.66	1	3	4	9

If account closed and balance lost after six months of successful trade:

Company	A	B	C	D	E
Takings 5 months	50,000	50,000	50,000	50,000	50,000
Costs 6 months	24,000	30,000	45,000	48,000	54,000
Gain (loss)	26,000	20,000	5,000	2,000	(4,000)

Note:
The bad debt risk is unacceptable for company E, undesirable for companies C and D and may be an acceptable risk for companies A and B.

Rule 5. The Pareto (80:20) rule applies to trade debtors as much as to other statistical distributions. If debtors are listed in order of size, then careful attention to the top 20 per cent will provide an effective shortcut to good credit management. Many companies include a listing of the top 20 debtors in their management accounts in order to highlight their main exposures.

Rule 6. A business should set targets for weekly or monthly collections from customers. The information shown in Table 7.19, taken from a spreadsheet used by Speedy Collections Ltd, shows how it set a collection target and compared it with the actual cash receipts. The forecasts are based on the assumption that 20 per cent of sales will be collected within one month and will take a 2 per cent cash discount, 35 per cent of sales will be collected within two months, and the remaining 45 per cent will be collected in the third month after sale.

Table 7.19 _Comparison of target and actual collections, Speedy Collections Ltd_

	Sales budget	19.6%	35%	45%	Total	Collections actual	Variance month	Variance cumul.
November	36000							
December	58000							
January	22000	4312	20300	16200	40812	39653	–1159	–1159
February	36000	7056	7700	26100	40856	40654	–202	–1361
March	35000	6860	12600	9900	29360	36135	6775	5414
April	38000	7448	12250	16200	35898	30178	–5720	–306
May	37000	7252	13300	15750	36302	37643	1341	1035
June	40000	7840	12950	17100	37890	39835	1945	2980
	302000				221118	224098		

Table 7.19 suggests that collection performance was excellent. In fact, sales in the period were £6,227 above plan. Speedy Collections Ltd should compare the actual collections against a revised target that is based on the actual sales. To do this at the end of each month the actual sales are entered in the spreadsheet in place of the budget. The amended results are shown in Table 7.20.

Table 7.20 _Comparison of revised target and actual collections_

	Actual sales	19.6%	35%	45%	Total	Collections actual	Variance month	Variance cumul.
November	35384							
December	62465							
January	19626	3847	21863	15923	41632	39653	–1979	–1979
February	37809	7411	6869	28109	42389	40654	–1735	–3714
March	34126	6689	13233	8832	28754	36135	7381	3667
April	41245	8084	11944	17014	37042	30178	–6864	–3197
May	36897	7232	14436	15357	37024	37643	619	–2578
June	38675	7580	12914	18560	39055	39835	781	–1798
	306227				225896	224098		

The revised table shows that collections for the January to June period were disappointing. Trade debtors can be a volatile asset. They can escalate unless sensible but demanding collection targets are met. A report similar to that used by Speedy Collections Ltd should be examined at every monthly board meeting in your company.

Rule 7. Discounts for prompt payment are an expensive way of minimizing debtors. See the example in Table 7.21.

Table 7.21 *The effects of prompt payment discounts*

1. Weekly credit sales £4,000
2. Weekly gross margin £1,000.
3. Credit terms are 6 weeks or 2% cash discount for seven-day settlement.
4. Annual running expenses excluding discount £27,000.

		ROI discount		ROI no discount
Gross margin		52,000		52,000
Discounts	4,160		–	
Other running exes.	27,000	31,160	27,000	27,000
PBIT		20,840		25,000
Total assets %		180,000		200,000
ROI		11.58%		12.5%

The conclusions from this example are:

● £4,160 is a high annual cost to reduce debtor investment by £20,000: it is 20.8 per cent pa;
● we get an ROI of 12.5 per cent without discounts: with a 2 per cent discount it falls to 11.58 per cent;
● the maximum discount to advance cash collections by five weeks is £2,500 per annum: this is 12.5 per cent per annum or 1.2 per cent for cash in seven days, as shown in Table 7.22.

Table 7.22 *The impact of advance cash collections*

		ROI no discount		ROI discount
Gross margin		52,000		52,000
Discount	2,500		–	
Other running exes.	27,000	29,500	27,000	27,000
PBIT		22,500		25,000
Total assets		180,000		200,000
ROI		12.5%		12.5%

Each week the settlement discount is £48.08 or 1.2 per cent (ie £2,500/52); 1.2 per cent about the maximum discount that a company can afford sounds too small to act as an incentive to pay promptly.

Rule 8. There is a converse to the discount rule. Any company should consider charging interest on overdue accounts. The attraction is that you can boost profitability without appearing to charge an unreasonable interest rate: 1.5 per cent per month sounds small yet it compounds to 19.56 per cent pa. Interest charges that result in the loss of profitable business are counter-productive. Interest charges only work well in sectors where they are standard business practice.

Rule 9. A business should prepare an aged debtors list. This involves matching payments and credit notes against the outstanding balance plus sales. It provides a breakdown of the amount due on a month-by-month basis. We will examine the ageing of one account and then look at it in the context of an overall aged list. The data in Table 7.23 were extracted from the debtors account for client A.

Table 7.23   *Ageing debtors*

Balance outstanding, Client A, 1 January

October sales	16,325.43
November sales	18,527.26
December sales	17,149.88
	52,002.57

During the next three months the following transactions arose:

	Sales	Credit notes	Cash collections
January	24,659.44	206.94 (Oct)	16,118.49 (for Oct)
		185.27 (Dec)	
February	15,285.67	1,593.17 (Jan)	16,964.61 (for Dec)
			3,600.00 (for Feb)
March	28,755.83	285.42 (Mar)	23,000.00 (for Jan)
	68,700.94	2,270.80	59,683.10

Age analysis, Client A

	March	February	January	December	November	October
Sales	28,755.83	15,285.67	24,659.44	17,149.88	18,527.26	16,325.43
Credit notes	285.42	–	1,593.17	185.27	–	206.94
	28,470.41	15,285.67	23,066.27	16,964.61	18,527.26	16,118.49
Cash	–	3,600.00	23,000.00	16,964.61	–	16,118.49
Balance	28,470.41	11,685.67	66.27	–	18,527.26	–

Table 7.23 *(continued)*

The age analysis suggests a problem with the November balance. This should be investigated.

Example age analysis

Customer	Credit limit	Balance outstanding	Current month	1 month due	2 months due	3 months due	4 months and over
A	60,000	58,749.61	28,470.41	11,685.67	66.27	–	18,527.26
B	8,000	6,495.26	3,581.53	2,913.73			
C	2,000	2,409.67	486.02	430.63	395.77	455.08	642.17
D	500	485.4	245.44	240.00			
E	37,500	40,081.63	21,424.40	18,657.23			
F	12,500	2,049.43	519.16	–	–	–	1,530.27
G	500	367.25	195.25	172.00			
All others	19,000	13,214.15	4,086.10	3,193.16	3,047.44	1,643.17	1,244.28
	140,000	123,852.44	59,008.31	37,292.42	3,509.48	2,098.25	21,943.98

% of limit advanced	88.5	

	Current month	1 month	2 months	3 months	4 months
% of total outstanding	47.6	30.1	2.8	1.7	17.7

Customer	Action taken
A	Sales manager to visit this week.
C	November cheque bounced. In solicitor's hands.
E	Special excess allowed for seasonal peak purchasing.
F	Rep to meet client F.
H–Z	Various recovery actions taken.

This age analysis reveals several key points:

- overall collections are good;
- customer A is a serious problem and action is being taken;
- customer C is dangerous; has a stop been placed on further supplies?
- customer E must be monitored to ensure that the balance is brought back within the limit;
- the debtors' balances are dominated by two customers: customer A 47.4 per cent, customer E 32.4 per cent; all other balances amount to 20.2 per cent.

The fact that the two biggest customers are causing problems is very disturbing.

The rules for management of supplier credit

1. Do not pay too quickly. It will increase your overdraft interest or reduce your deposit interest.
2. Do not pay too slowly. If suppliers place a stop on deliveries it can disrupt production and sales. If they instigate recovery action it can harm your business reputation.
3. Seek discounts for prompt payment. A 2 per cent discount for paying one month early provides a handsome return.
4. Have several suppliers for each product or service. A strike must not affect deliveries.
5. Look for adequate credit limits. If seeking extra credit to cover short-term peaks, ensure that it is properly authorized in writing at a sufficiently senior level in the supplier company. If this is not done, the distribution or credit staff in the supplier might place a stop on deliveries, because they did not know of the additional credit approved.
6. Prepare an aged schedule of supplier indebtedness. It is helpful in planning payments and cash forecasting.

SUMMARY

Working capital is one of the most important issues in finance. The correct definition of working capital is that it is the funds required to pay for the net investment in:

stock + trade debtors – trade creditors

This investment is necessary because of the operating cycle. Most businesses require access to a considerable amount of cash to tide them over from the time when payments to suppliers and staff and for overheads are made, to the point when sale proceeds are collected from customers. This cash should not be diverted to other areas or the business will suffer the dreaded illness of over-trading.

The wise organization will be conscious of the total investment in working capital and will work assiduously to keep it to an optimum level. To do this properly requires the preparation of appropriate ratios and the following of rules laid down to eliminate unnecessary and expensive excess investment.

Part III

Financial planning and control

8

Budgeting

THE PURPOSES OF BUDGETING

The purposes of budgeting are as follows:

1. To prepare a plan of the way that the organization will develop that is attainable and acceptable to institutions assessing it as a basis for funding.
2. To ensure that all sections of the organization are working together. Examples include:
   - purchasing buying what production requires;
   - production making what sales expect to sell;
   - sales only dealing with customers that can be reasonably expected to pay;
   - no department incurring expenditure that the organization cannot afford to pay for.
3. To anticipate points where the 'resources' of the business are inadequate for its requirements in time to enable extra resources to be brought on stream:
   - making for stock at times when production capacity exceeds market demand in order to be able to fill orders when demand subsequently exceeds supply: the scarce resource in this case would be finished stocks;

- commissioning the purchase of extra raw materials in time to meet production requirements, which will exceed the historic pattern: this is particularly important when suppliers are already producing at full capacity;
- arranging the recruitment and training of production workers so that the company will be able to produce enough for sale when demand increases: the scarce resource is skilled labour and is particularly relevant in businesses where training takes a long time;
- arranging the purchase of additional space and equipment for production where the existing facilities are inadequate to service future profitable market demands: the scarce resource in this case is fixed assets (owned or rented);
- arranging for additional funds at times when the company will exceed its spending authority: the scarce resource in this case is cash.

The common feature of these 'resource' examples is that if a scarcity arose next week it would be exceedingly difficult to fill. You cannot buy materials from suppliers who don't have them; sell stock you don't have; train workers to a high quality level overnight; purchase, install and operate machinery instantly. The conclusion from these shortages of resources is that companies must plan at least six months in advance and in many cases a good deal further ahead.

4. To provide a basis for comparison with actual results. You cannot say whether actual results are good, bad or indifferent unless you have previously benchmarked them.
5. To ensure that priorities are set so as to encourage spending that will be beneficial to the organization and discourage spending that will be wasteful.

To satisfy the five purposes a business needs to prepare:

- an operating budget: sales, costs, appropriations;
- a balance sheet budget: assets, liabilities, shareholders funds;
- a cash budget: customer collections, supplier payments, payment of expenses, loans obtained and repaid, asset acquisitions and disposals, dividends, taxes and grants.

LENGTH OF BUDGET PERIOD

The budget period needs to be:

- long enough to identify resources required in time to fill them;
- short enough to enable forecasts to be made with a reasonable degree of confidence;
- compatible with external reporting obligations.

Most businesses find that a one-year budgetary cycle, corresponding with their financial year, is suitable. This can cause problems in anticipating resources, as the timetable in Table 8.1 shows. Planners Ltd budgets in November for its financial year January to December.

Table 8.1 *The budget timetable*

During month	Months planned ahead
December	12
January	11
February	10
March	9
April	8
May	7
June	6
July	5
August	4
September	3
October	2
November	1

Through the second half of the financial year the company is not looking far enough forward. There are many ways of overcoming this problem. These include developing the budget in detail for the financial year and in outline for one or two years further ahead, and developing budgets for 12-month periods but in six-monthly cycles. If this is the process, then as well as the budget in November for January/December there would be a budget in May for July/June. If this process is used it pushes forward the months ahead situation, as shown in Table 8.2 (p 206).

You can still use the original budget to control during the July/December period even though the figures may have been changed at the mid-year review to reflect current and emerging trends.

The third method is to allow the identification of medium-term resource requirements to become part of the corporate planning process and to use a

Table 8.2 *The budget timetable, version 2*

During month	Months planned ahead
June	12
July	11
August	10
September	9
October	8
November	7
December	6

three-year capital budgeting cycle to pick up resource requirements. All of these approaches are used to some degree by organizations committed to quality planning. Which one (or combination) is most suitable for your organization may have been decided long ago. You should, at least once every five years, examine the planning process. Is it still the most appropriate for the company? If not, change it.

KEY ELEMENTS OF A GOOD BUDGETING PROCESS

The people charged with achieving the income and expenditure budgets must feel stretched to achieve the planned performance, but the following should be borne in mind.

They must regard the targets as sensible, otherwise they may become totally demotivated. Consider the situation where the estimated market this year for a product is 100,000 units. The market is expected to grow by 10 per cent next year and the company doing the planning currently has a 40 per cent market share. To set a budget of 66,000 units (without concrete marketing plans to secure a 60 per cent market share) would be ludicrous. Sales staff would ignore it. When unfavourable comparisons between budget and actual emerged, they would feel no motivation to try to recover lost ground. They might define satisfactory performance as beating last year's volume by 1 or 2 per cent, whereas 20 per cent might have been possible if everyone had been committed to trying for a challenging but attainable target.

It is best to request the 'experts' in each field to set themselves targets (against an organization climate that presses people to challenge themselves). The specialists should be in possession of greater knowledge of the way the particular area is developing than some non-specialist handing down the budget, and most people strive harder to recover lost ground where they set themselves the targets.

The sequence of planning must be arranged so those departments that depend on the volume of activities in other areas should have the plans for those areas before they develop their budgets. To illustrate this point, we will examine the relationship between sales, purchasing and production in Planners Ltd:

1. The sales target is 100,000 units.
2. Production cannot plan manufacturing volume without knowing the following:
   - the estimated stock level: 5,000 units at the start of the budget period;
   - the required stock level: 8,000 units at the end of the budget period;
   - the expected level of spoilage during production (2,000 units).
3. On receipt of these data they can compute the production plan:

	Units
Expected sales	100,000
Spoilage	2,000
Increase in stocks (8,000 – 5,000)	3,000
Production required	105,000

4. When the production target has been set they can determine the hours needed to achieve an output of 103,000 good units and the expected 2,000 spoiled units.
5. The purchasing manager must wait until the production level of 105,000 units is set, and combine this knowledge with the raw material stock targets of 10,000 units at the start and 6,000 units at the end of the budget period to compute the purchasing plan.

		Units
Purchased for issue to production		101,000
Add reduction in material stock	-	4,000
		105,000

The plan that emerges from this sequential treatment of sales, production and purchasing is now presented in Table 8.3 (p 208).

The company must avoid the standard pitfall 'If it is not in the budget, you cannot do it.' Attractive opportunities, not envisaged at the budget stage, should be taken if they arise. However, in this flexible environment it is essential that if significant non-budgeted developments are approved, they must not allow the existing profit target to be missed, and cash should be

Table 8.3 *The purchasing, stockholding and production budget*

	Units
Opening raw materials	10,000
Bought in materials	101,000
	111,000
Held in material stock	6,000
Issues to production	105,000
Opening finished stock	5,000
Production	110,000
Less spoiled	2,000
Closing finished stock	8,000	10,000
For sale	100,000

available to fund the expenditure involved rather than trying to divert funds from areas to which they are already committed. Consider Table 8.4.

Table 8.4 *The effects of taking on a non-budgeted initiative*

	Original budget	New initiative	New target
	A	B	A + B
Sales	500	150	650
Running costs	400	100	500
Profit	100	50	150

Note:

If sales of 150 from the new initiative are achieved and only 350 on the original product, then the original target is met but the result is disastrous. The company wants sales of 650; it expects to incur 500 of running costs. If only 400 are available to pay these costs there will be a funding crisis.

Another pitfall that can affect budgets is the attitude 'If it is in the budget, you must spend it (you won't get it next year).' If the time is not right for a particular expenditure, then managers should feel that they can postpone it and have it restored at a later date. This is difficult to arrange where budgets tend to be extrapolative. The state system worldwide is frequently caricatured in this way.

The key elements of an excellent budget are:

- It is challenging.
- It is sensible.
- Managers are committed to it.
- Departments are working together;
- It is adaptable to changing circumstances.

THE SEQUENCE OF BUDGETING

Define an appropriate start time

Strangely enough, the only way to do this satisfactorily is to work back from the date when the budget must be approved. The sequence is as follows:

1. Final approval should come at a board meeting, say two weeks before the end of the financial year.
2. Before the budget is presented to the board, the operating team must have time to assess it. You normally need to allow four to six weeks for this. There are hard-nosed negotiations involved in changing unsatisfactory areas.
3. The finance section needs about a week to prepare the overall budget from departmental plans.
4. Departments need time to involve staff in budget preparation and to combine the figures from various sections. Since some budgets cannot start until they receive detailed plans for other functions, this can take four to six weeks.

A count-back will show when the budgeting should start; see Table 8.5.

Table 8.5 *Count-back and the timetable for starting the budgeting process*

	Longest	**Shortest**
A. After board approval	4 weeks	2 weeks
B. Operating team approval	6 weeks	4 weeks
C. Accounting consolidation	1 week	1 week
D. Detailed departmental budgeting	6 weeks	4 weeks
	17 weeks	11 weeks

If the budget has to be passed through one or more parent company consolidation processes, it will add more time. Extremes would be four weeks for inclusion in the European budget and four weeks for inclusion in the world budget, resulting in lead times of 25 weeks at longest to 15 weeks at best.

Define the expected position at the end of the current financial year

This is necessary for two reasons: if you are using the previous year's financial results as a forecasting base, your starting point can be up to six months out of date; and key data relating to stocks, debtors and creditors will be required.

Define an acceptable profit target

You need a benchmark against which to compare the proposed budget. If the proposed budget promises an inadequate ROI it may be necessary to seek amendments. If managers are already committed to unacceptable targets it may be divisive to seek to increase such targets. I believe it is fairer to set out broad parameters initially, debate the parameters with senior staff, hopefully have them accepted, and request the development of budgets against the background of the agreed parameters. Setting challenging but reasonable profit targets is difficult. You will need the following information:

- three-year historical statements, and market share and growth statistics;
- estimated actual financial statements;
- projected movements in size of market, share of market, assets and funding;
- products being launched and discontinued.

Table 8.6 illustrates how to set an appropriate profit target.

Planners Ltd will have £2.25 million of total assets. Since it certainly needs a profit before interest of 12 per cent, the minimum acceptable profit target would be £270,000 before interest. While 12 per cent is a sensible target, it would be modified in the following cases. First, the return on investment has averaged 5 per cent in recent years and is expected to be 6 per cent this year. It is unrealistic to expect a jump to the minimum economic return in one year. The company might settle for 8 per cent, leading to a target of £180,000, but with the expectation that this would move to 10 per cent and 12 per cent in the next two years.

Second, the return on investment has averaged 16 per cent in recent years and is projected to be 17.5 per cent this year. Market conditions are encourag-

Table 8.6 *Setting an appropriate profit target*

	Estimated total assets end this year	Assets to be acquired	Depreciation	Estimated total assets end next year
Fixed	1,200	108	(141)	1,167
Stocks	300	113		413
Debtors	500	170		670
	2,000	391	(141)	2,250

	Stock	Debtors
In balance sheet at end of this year	300	500
Volume growth (20% of projection)	60	100
Price growth		
8% of projection + volume increase 360 × 8%	29	
5% of projection + volume increase		30
New product (budget sales 200)		
Stock 12% of sales, debtors 20% of sales	24	40
	113	170

ing. We should seek an ROI of at least 18 per cent (even with a new product launch that will be lucky to break even next year). The minimum acceptable profit target is £405,000.

It is important to communicate the volume change and profit expectations to senior management. Try to get their agreement that the target is sensible. If cogent arguments are advanced as to why it is too high, it may be necessary to reduce it, otherwise you will wind up with over-optimistic budgets and a lack of managerial commitment to them. It is to be hoped that this will not happen and the profit target will provide a sensible framework for the detailed budgets. Also, let the departments work through the detail of their budgets in sequence and in line with the deadlines.

In preparing the detailed budgets it is important for managers to consider what factors will help and hinder future development; see Table 8.7 (p 212).

If this is not done, there is a danger of bland assumptions such as 'since the market has grown by 10 per cent per annum on average over the last five years, it will continue to do so and we will maintain our market share'. The right way to budget is to examine all the factors that will influence the market growth and our share:

Table 8.7 *Considering future development*

Plus Points	Minus Points
An old competitor is getting out of the industry. He held a 10% share. We should sell an extra 4,536 units. *Adjustment 2.*	An alternative to this product is being introduced. Though not good, it may initially take 5% of the market as customers try it. *Adjustment 3.*
A top-class salesman we recruited last year is now well used to his customer portfolio. This should lead to a 2% extra market penetration. *Adjustment 4.*	Our promotional approach will be similar to the current year. A competitor is expected to launch a TV advertising campaign. This may boost his market share by 2%, of which we may lose our proportion. *Adjustment 5.*
If recent sterling weakness continues, foreign competitors will have to increase selling prices in the UK by 8%, thus reducing their competitiveness. We hope to gain an extra 5,000 units. *Adjustment 6.*	A new six-month credit scheme for large customers launched by a competitor is attracting business from other suppliers. It is expected to cost us 4,000 units. *Adjustment 7.*
An improved delivery system will allow same-day supplies rather than next day. This should give us an extra 2% market share. *Adjustment 8.*	Our product is a semi-luxury. The projected market growth may not be achieved owing to the impact of inflation on discretionary spending. This will cost us 840 units. *Adjustment 1.*

- Projected market total units this year: 100,000.
- Our share was 40 per cent and has grown fairly steadily from 30 per cent five years ago.
- Market growth averaged 10 per cent in recent years; 8 per cent is expected this year.

A superficial examination of these data might suggest a total market next year of 108,000 and a 42 per cent share, leading to a forecast unit sales of 45,360.

On the basis of these relative marketing advantages, the budget sales are presented in Table 8.8.

Table 8.8 _The sales budget_

	Total market	Our sales	Our share
Expected sales this year	100,000	40,000	40.0
Natural growth	10,000	4,000	–
	110,000	44,000	40.0
Our trend towards improved market share	–	2,200	2.0
	110,000	46,200	42.0
Declining discretionary incomes (1)	2,000	840	–
	108,000	45,360	42.0
Competitor exit (2) (108,000 × 10% × 42%)	–	4,536	4.2
	108,000	49,896	46.2
Product curiosity (3) (108,000 × 5% × 46.2%)	–	2,495	2.3
	108,000	47,401	43.9
Extra penetration by new sales rep (4)	–	2,160	2.0
	108,000	49,561	45.9
TV advertising (5) (108,000 × 2% × 45.9%)	–	991	0.9
	108,000	48,570	45.0
Impact of currency weakness (6)	–	5,000	4.6
	108,000	53,570	49.6
Long-term credit scheme (7)	–	4,000	3.7
	108,000	49,570	45.9
Improved delivery scheme (8)	–	2,160	2.0
	108,000	51,730	47.9

On the basis of these data the marketing staff might forecast sales of 51,500 units. They might offer 46,500 units, to allow room for manoeuvre if the organization is one that always comes back looking for higher sales and reduced costs in the budgeting 'game'. The vital point about this detailed work is that a difficult-to-quantify but sensible analysis leads to a budget 6,370 units or 13 per cent higher than a simple extrapolation might imply. In this case it brings good news of the sales potential. How much more important would it be if the minus points were stronger, resulting in a target significantly below the straight extrapolation of 45,360 units?

The example shows how using expert knowledge of the market place helps to set sensible targets. Before preparing a budget, it is essential to make sure that all factors that may affect the trend have been identified and quantified. Sit down with a blank sheet of paper before getting into detail and ask two questions: what changing factors will affect our sales capability, and how much will they increase or decrease our selling prospects?

THE PURCHASING AND PRODUCTION BUDGET

Some aspects of purchasing and production budgeting are now illustrated:

a. Sales target 100,000 units.
b. Opening stock 5,000 units.
c. Closing stock 8,000 units.
d. Products stolen during throughput: 2 per cent of annual quantities on production line.
e. Products damaged during production but recycled: 3 per cent of throughput net of pilferage.
f. Products damaged in production: 2.5 per cent of throughput net of pilferage.

The percentages in d, e and f are based on previous experience. Production management believes they will continue.

The purchases volume budget

Table 8.9 *The purchases volume budget*

Units	Units	
Sales target	100,000	
Add stock increase (8,000 – 5,000)	3,000	103,000
Gross up to include scrap		
Scrap (103,000/97.5%)	105,641	
Scrap 105,641 × 2.5%		2,641
Gross up to include recycle (103,000/97%)	106,186	
Recycle 106,186 × 3%		3,186
Circulating in production		108,827
Gross up to include pilferage (108,827/98%)	111,048	
Pilferage 111,048 × 2%		2,221
Net issues to production		111,048
Returned to stores		3,186
Issues from stores		107,862

Purchase cost budget

Table 8.10   *The purchase cost budget*

---

1. The current price of materials is £100 per unit.
2. 40,000 units will be bought at this price and issued to production before a price increase.
3. The balance will be bought and issued to production at £105 per unit.

The cost of issues from stores will be:

40,000 units at £100	4,000,000
67,862 units at £105	7,125,510
	11,125,510

With material stocks valued at £100 and £105 the material cost of sales is:

Opening stock 5,000 × £100	500,000
Material issues	11,125,510
	11,625,510
Closing stock 8,000 × £105	840,000
Material cost of sales	10,785,510

The direct labour budget

We will use the data in the materials budget. We will also assume that the items rejected at quality control have been fully processed, and (see Table 8.11, p 216)

- a worker takes 20 hours to produce a unit, accepted or rejected;
- allowing for absenteeism, that is expected to be 5 per cent of normal working hours; each worker would produce for 1,748 hours in the budget year;
- 1,000 is the maximum number of production workers and any extra production will be at overtime (1.5 times basic);
- basic rates will average £10,400 per annum;
- social security costs to the employer: 9 per cent of basic;
- fringe costs (pensions, food subsidies, protective clothing): 15 per cent of basic.

A standard approach is used to budget for overheads whether they are related to establishment, administration, marketing, production or elsewhere. You start by asking the following questions:

Table 8.11 *The budgeted direct labour cost*

Items circulating multiplied by hours per item (108,827 x 20)	2,176,540
Labour hours at basic 1,000 × 1,748	1,748,000
Labour hours at 1.5 times	428,540
Production hours at basic	1,748,000
Gross up for public holidays and annual leave	
(24 days x 1,000 staff)	240,000
Normal hours paid	1,988,000
Labour hours at overtime 428,540 at 1.5 times equivalent to	
642,810 at normal rate	642,810
Total equivalent hours at normal rate	2,630,810

Hourly rate	**£**
£10,400 pa/52 weeks/5 days/8 hours =	5.00
Add employment taxes £5 × 9%	0.45
Fringe costs £5 × 15%	0.75
Cost per hour	6.20
Budgeted direct labour 2,630,810 x £6.20 = £16,311,022	

- What will be the estimated actual cost this year (to bring the forecasting base up to date)?
- Will this function be done in the same way next year? This year's cost would be a useless forecasting base if a different quality level were planned:
  - shift from contracted to own transport
  - shift from bought-in power to own generator
  - shift from computer bureau accounting to in-house, etc.
- Will this function be performed on a similar, greater or lesser scale next year? Some costs rise and fall as volume changes. This can affect the budget size (as is examined in detail in Chapter 11).
- When (if at all) will prices change for each unit of service and by how much?
- Could a similar level of service be obtained at a lower cost?

Three examples, in Table 8.12, show how the answers to these questions help to compute an appropriate budget.

Table 8.12   *Budgeting for overheads*

Example 1. Power

Estimated actual this year	860,000
Add consumption for two additional machines to meet volume	120,000
growth	980,000
Add 2% inefficiency for existing machines (due to ageing)	17,200
860,000 × 2%	997,200
Add impact of price increase 5% expected at month 4	
(a) raising cost to 7% over present year	
average levels (860,000 + 17,200) × 7%	61,404
(b) additional cost of power consumption	
new machines 120,000 × 7% for nine months	6,300
Budgeted power cost	1,064,904

There is believed to be no genuine alternative. Question 5 is ignored in this case.

Example 2. Fire insurance

Estimated actual current year	240,000
Uplift value to be covered by 10% to reflect index of value	
of industrial buildings	24,000
	264,000
Value of additional building to be covered at premium rate	12,000
Original revised budget	276,000

Reduction in premiums arising from installation of fire detection and prevention systems 10%. (The finance manager estimates that the capital cost of this system £84,000 is worthwhile.)

Revised budget 276,000 × 90%	£248,400

Note:

Be sure to include maintenance, depreciation, etc in the fire prevention/detection budget and the capital cost £84,000 in the capital and cash budgets.

Example 3. Telephone

Estimated actual current year	525,000
Add 6% (impact of extra staff)	31,500
	556,500
Deduct 10% (new call monitoring system recently installed)	55,650
	500,850

Table 8.12 *(continued)*

Add 8% expected average price increase	40,068
	540,918

Reduced to allow for savings from a) transfer of some long-distance calls that must in future use e-mail, and b) better night rate utilization for long-distance calls.

Final budget	£500,000

Normal explanations for shortfall

When the data have been assembled, they will be put in the detailed operating budget. It is probable that the budgeted operating profit is lower than the target set initially. There are three reasons why this is likely to be so.

First, experienced managers quickly come to terms with the fact that whatever they offer, the organization will demand more. Managers offer less than they want. For instance, the sales manager expects to sell 100,000 units. She offers a budget of 91,000, expecting to be pressed to increase it by 10 per cent and knowing that if she offered 100,000 a 10 per cent increase would still be demanded in spite of the fact that 100,000 is a challenging target. A cost centre manager needs a budget of £200,000. He may ask for £222,222 expecting to be pressured to reduce it by 10 per cent. If he asked for £200,000, he might get only £180,000.

Second, some managers rebel against the never-ending chase for growth. They offer budgets which, even after the padding is removed, leave undemanding targets. The sales manager might offer 85,000 units, expecting a 10 per cent uplift. If she gets away with this she can make life easier for her staff. She will avoid the overt criticism that unfavourable variances in management accounting reports represent.

Third, in developing budgets, many managers slip in new initiatives they wish to implement. Many of these provide inadequate short-term pay-offs even where the long-term return is attractive. These initiatives come from many sources. Usually some have to be deferred or eliminated, but it is dangerous to remove too many. Some new initiatives are necessary to secure the long-term development of the organization. They are frequently ignored in the chase for profit and leave a business in danger of becoming old-fashioned.

We now look at a summarized budget (see Table 8.13) and examine approaches to bridging the gap between it and the profit target of £2 million that the managing director and board are seeking.

Table 8.13 *Draft budget*

Sales revenue		10,000,000
Materials	5,160,000	
Production labour	1,890,000	
Production overhead	450,000	7,500,000
Administration		518,000
Selling and distribution		344,000
Research and development		238,000
Total cost		8,600,000
Profit		1,400,000

Additional profit of £600,000 must be found. A popular but highly dangerous method of finding it is across-the-board surgery. This assumes comparable padding everywhere. A simplistic approach would be to seek a 3.25 per cent increase in sales and a 3.25 per cent reduction in costs. This would ignore three facts:

1. Some costs will rise if sales are increased.
2. Some managers budgeted honestly and are being punished for doing so.
3. Some managers padded their budgets in the expectation of more severe changes and are being rewarded for doing so.

A better approach is to go through the budgets systematically and try to find the padding, then to negotiate its removal while leaving the genuine plans untouched. The negotiations must be carefully done and accepted by the budget holders or they will disclaim responsibility for any failure to attain targets in the control phase.

ZERO-BASED BUDGETING

In zero-based budgeting (ZBB) a company allows each cost area to plead for positions of importance in the spending power of the organization. If they come into the rank above the spending limit, the budget will be sanctioned. If they do not, the proposal will be shelved until the next ZBB analysis.

In the following example costs may be incurred at two levels: the minimum viable level and the quality image level. The company has a spending limit of £1 million for the current year. It is distributing books. The budget bids are presented in Table 8.14 (p 220).

Table 8.14 *The ZBB budget bids and options*

	Minimum level	Quality level
Purchase 200,000 paperbacks	500,000	500,000
Post to customers 2nd class/1st class	150,000	200,000
Telephone orders 4 hours a day/8 hours a day	8,000	15,000
Delivery Jiffy bags/boxes	20,000	240,000
Accounting manual/computerized	35,000	95,000
Display in showrooms only	100,000	
Use brochures and showrooms		150,000
Full customer collection service		30,000
Premises tatty/regularly painted	–	25,000
	813,000	1,255,000

The company will make an adequate profit if £1 million is spent. It can offer more than the minimum viable level of service in some areas but not in all. The decision on priorities might be as shown in Table 8.15.

Table 8.15 *Decisions on priorities*

Cost type	Rank	Rationale	Cost	Approved
Paperbacks	1	We must have stock	500,000	500,000
Four-hour order taking	2	We must take orders	8,000	508,000
2nd class mail	3	Critical for deliveries	150,000	658,000
Packing in envelopes	4	Critical for deliveries	20,000	678,000
Showroom display	5	To stimulate demand	100,000	778,000
Manual accounting	6	For adequate control	35,000	813,000
Extra order taking	7	To promote extra sales	7,000	820,000
Improved packing	8	Minimize transit damage and improve reputation	220,000	1,040,000
Promotional brochures	9	Attract profitable business	50,000	1,090,000
Regular painting	10	Attractive premises needed	25,000	1,115,000
Customer collection	11	Improve demand and save on expensive post and packing	30,000	1,145,000
1st class mail	12	Could speed up deliveries	50,000	1,195,000
Computerized accounting	13	Better record keeping	60,000	1,255,000

The owner might decide to allocate £180,000 to improved packaging and not accept any spending on items 9–13. By examining the alternatives in decision packages 8–13, it might be possible to improve on this. The owner might decide to reduce the quality of improved packing so as to allow some allocation for items 9 and/or 10. To assess this the owner might consider these options:

a) Packing cost   130,000
Promotional brochures   50,000
Total   180,000 or
Packing costing   180,000

If the brochure option is favoured, then:

b) Packing cost   105,000
Regular painting   25,000
Total   130,000 or
Packing costing   130,000

The revised ZBB ranking might now be as shown in Table 8.16.

Table 8.16   *Revised ZBB ranking*

Cost head	Rank	Rationale	Item cost	Cumulative cost
Items 1–7	1	Core service	820,000	820,000
Improved packaging (lowest standard)	8	Improve customer service and reduce transit damage	105,000	925,000
Promotional brochures	9	As previously	50,000	975,000
Improved packaging (medium standard)	10	Deemed more important than painting	25,000	1,000,000

COST REDUCTION

Most organizations have some cost waste. The reasons are usually historical and include:

- decisions by senior managers to spend on items that boost their personal profile;
- decisions to spend that made good sense at the time but no longer make sense owing to changing circumstances. 'That is the way we always did it' is an excellent route to cost waste;
- decisions to provide a standard of service without testing whether customers would be satisfied with a lower-quality, less expensive option;
- absence of a climate that deplores waste. This develops in organizations that are so profitable that they do not need good cost control, or so unprofitable that the difference to the results from control of spending is insignificant. (This often results in managers trying to crack big and insoluble problems while totally ignoring small and easily reduced cost waste.)

How can an organization go about identifying cost reduction opportunities? If cost reduction is sufficiently important it is necessary to identify a manager with the following qualities:

- imagination (to conceive of alternative ways of achieving results through lower spending);
- analytical skills (to identify attractive areas and quantify the consequences of change);
- colleague acceptability (to be able to discuss possibilities with people at all levels in the organization). The major elements of this are to be a good listener, to not be biased in favour of or against specific departments, and to be perceived as fair and influential;
- power (to ensure that realistic cost reductions are implemented even when strongly opposed by managers of departments that are afraid of adverse effects on their section).

If this sounds like a corporate Clark Kent, it is. Worse still, getting this person to take this on is difficult: someone else may do their job, often for a long period (and might do it better), and it is a sure way to make enemies. You have to break eggs to make the cost reduction omelette.

If you have managed to get someone to take the job, they will need a sound methodology. I suggest the following approach:

Step 1

Ask each employee to tell you their opinion of the single biggest cost waste in the company. In doing so, guarantee that the suggestion will not be attributed to the individual. Many ideas will relate to spending of their immediate bosses or other departments. If this confidentiality is not respected, then there is a danger of boss–subordinate or interdepartmental warfare. In examining the data from this fact-finding mission, you will tend to find a range of different views emerges. A large proportion of suggestions will cross departmental boundaries. Don't worry if some of the ideas are nit-picking. Look for consistency.

Step 2

Obtain a detailed breakdown of the cost structure from the annual budget. Armed with this cost structure, the ideas generated at Step 1, and your own perceptions of cost waste, proceed to slot each cost heading into the cost reduction matrix, which I adapted from the Boston Consulting Group product portfolio matrix (see Figure 8.1).

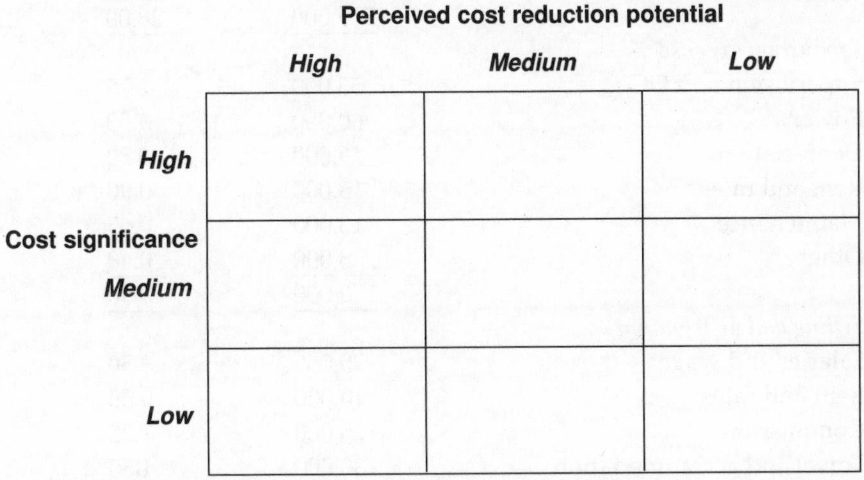

Perceived cost reduction potential

	High	Medium	Low
High			
Cost significance **Medium**			
Low			

Figure 8.1 *The cost reduction matrix*

The classification of perceived cost reduction potential into high, medium and low is done as follows: high = saving exceeding 10 per cent of budget, medium = saving in range 5–10 per cent of budget, and low = saving less than 5 per cent of budget. The size of the savings is based on employee ideas and your own judgements.

Examining the percentages (Table 8.7, pp 224 and 225), we find that only two items (cost of efficient production, and production labour basic pay)

Table 8.17 *Overall cost significance*

	£	% of budget
Raw material		
Cost of efficient production	714,000	35.70
Pilferage	42,000	2.10
Wastage not recovered	24,000	1.20
	780,000	39.00
Production labour		
Basic pay	320,000	16.00
Overtime on production	90,000	4.50
Rework	30,000	1.50
Employment taxes	44,000	2.20
Pensions	48,000	2.40
Other	28,000	1.40
	560,000	28.00
Production expense		
Supervision and QC	55,000	2.75
Power	60,000	3.00
Depreciation	16,000	0.80
Rent and rates	18,000	0.90
Maintenance	13,000	0.65
Other	8,000	0.40
	170,000	8.50
Selling and distribution		
Salaries and wages	70,000	3.50
Rent and rates	10,000	0.50
Commission	25,000	1.25
Travel and accommodation	30,000	1.50
Other	5,000	0.25
	140,000	7.00
Administration		
Salaries and wages	85,000	4.25
Telephone	20,000	1.00
Rent and rates	18,000	0.90
Light and heat	11,000	0.55
Stationery	9,000	0.45
Audit fee	15,000	0.75
Depreciation	12,000	0.60

Table 8.17   _(continued)_

Other	10,000	0.50
	180,000	9.00
Research and development		
Salaries and wages	56,000	2.80
Material	24,000	1.20
Other	20,000	1.00
	100,000	5.00
Interest		
Long-term loans	40,000	2.00
Short-term loans	5,000	0.25
Leases, etc	25,000	1.25
	70,000	3.50
Total cost	2,000,000	100.00

exceed 5 per cent of the total cost structure. This blurs the true position. As a first step to unmasking the real situation we recalculate the cost headings as a percentage of the total cost excluding the dominant items: material; cost of efficient production; production basic pay; and departmental salaries and wages; see Table 8.18 (p 226).

From this analysis it emerges that overtime production at 12.86 per cent has a high cost significance, while pilferage, power, employment taxes, long interest and pensions have medium cost significance. The analysis can be done at a departmental level where appropriate. Combining this objective analysis with informed views about potential savings, we get the picture shown in Figures 8.2 (p 227) and 8.3 (p 228).

Making cost reduction happen

- Prove that it is in the best interests of the organization. This will be difficult. Many of the people controlling budgets will raise spurious arguments to defend the status quo because they fear change. Concerns that arise in proving it is worthwhile are:
  - you may have to buy fixed assets to save costs;
  - sometimes employees are so opposed to an idea that even if demonstrably good, it may lower morale seriously, or in some extreme cases lead to sabotage of the initiative;
  - if it affects third parties, we may be afraid of an unfavourable reaction.

225

Table 8.18 *Cost significance (excluding dominant costs)*

	£	% Remaining budget
Pilferage	42,000	6.00 Medium
Wastage	24,000	3.43
Overtime production	90,000	12.86 High
Overtime rework	30,000	4.29
Employment taxes	44,000	6.29 Medium
Pensions	48,000	6.86 Medium
Other direct labour	28,000	4.00
Power	60,000	8.57 Medium
Depreciation	16,000	2.28
Rent and rates	18,000	2.57
Maintenance	13,000	1.86
Other production	8,000	1.14
Rent and rates (S&D)	10,000	1.43
Commission	25,000	3.57
Travel and accommodation	30,000	4.28
Other (S&D)	5,000	0.71
Telephone	20,000	2.86
Rent and rates	18,000	2.57
Light and heat	11,000	1.57
Stationery	9,000	1.29
Audit fees	15,000	2.14
Depreciation	12,000	1.71
Other (admin)	10,000	1.43
Materials (R&D)	24,000	3.43
Other (R&D)	20,000	2.86
Long interest	40,000	5.71 Medium
Short interest	5,000	0.71
Leases	25,000	3.59
	700,000	100.00

- Ensure that managers controlling cost areas believe the reductions can be achieved and are committed to making them happen.
- Provide regular feedback of planned against actual savings in the control reports.
- Identify some quick wins. Make them happen. Publicize the success. Show the sceptics it works and that they should find savings too. Many

	High	Medium	Low
H I G H	Overtime Telephone	Efficient materials Power	Basic pay Supervision and QC Salaries, etc Sales Salaries, etc Admin Salaries, etc R&D Interest, long loans
M E D	Pilferage Light and heat Unrecovered waste Rework	Travel and accommodation R&D materials Interest/leases	Employment taxes Pensions Commission Admin rent and rates
L O W	Audit Stationery	Maintenance Other (admin) Interest, short loans	Other production Production Depreciation Production rent and rates Production other Sales rent and rates Sales other Depreciation R&D other

Figure 8.2 _The cost reduction priorities_

cost reduction ideas involve fixed asset expenditure. These initiatives should be evaluated, using the procedures described in Chapter 12. Examples of this type include mechanized stock control, random telephone monitoring and burglary/fire protection systems.

THE FINAL ELEMENTS OF THE BUDGETING PROCESS

- Divide the budget into accounting periods for use in the control process.
- Convert the budget into cash flows.
- Include the costs and revenues that arise from approval of capital expenditure proposals. These are dealt with in Chapter 12.

High	Medium	Low
Category 1 Emergency Action required	**Category 4** Urgent Attention needed	**Category 7** Hard-nosed What can we get away with?
Category 2 Urgent Attention needed	**Category 5** Hard-nosed What can we get away with?	**Category 8** Implement obvious ideas immediately
Category 3 Hard-nosed What can we get away with?	**Category 6** Implement obvious ideas immediately	**Category 9** Implement obvious ideas immediately

Figure 8.3 *Cost reduction search strategy*

SUMMARY

The first step to effective financial control is an excellent budget. It will help to pinpoint problems that will occur in the future, in time to tackle them. It will also provide a benchmark against which actual performance can be measured.

Most organizations waste a lot of money on things that provide poor value. Part of the problem is the 'that is the way we always did it' culture. The wise organization will constantly seek suggestions on how to save money without damaging organization effectiveness. The use of a cost reduction matrix helps to pinpoint major areas of waste that need to be attacked if an organization is to survive and thrive.

9

Financial control

Of all the job titles used in business, it seems to me that 'financial controller' is the least appropriate. Certainly the chief financial officer must put in place systems and reports that help to ensure that the funds of the organization are under control. Nevertheless, the real financial controllers are the budget holders. They are responsible for operating within the plans that they set themselves. To do this they must receive prompt, comprehensible and reliable information from the management accountant that compares actual performance with their budgets. It is when they receive this information that the real work of financial control starts. On receipt of the management accounts, budget holders must ask themselves three major questions:

1. Why did variance(s) occur?
2. What action can be taken to compensate for adverse variances?
3. What implications do the variances have for future performance? This is the core of effective control. The actual results reflect the changing market place and help to pinpoint weaknesses in the budget for forthcoming periods.

VARIANCES

To do their diagnostic work, budget holders must recognize that there are four types of variance: efficiency, price, volume and policy. Each type of variance may be:

- One-off. Such variances affected performance in the latest accounting period.
- Ongoing. Such variances will affect performance in future periods as well as in the latest accounting period.
- Reversing. A variance that is reversing is one that affected performance in the latest accounting period but the effect of which is expected to be reversed in a future period. A simple example is the late arrival of a regular monthly order from a customer. This means no sales to that customer in the latest accounting period and two months' sales in the following period. The expectation that an adverse variance will reverse in a subsequent accounting period is comforting to a budget holder and the organization.

The key skill of control is to diagnose the cause of variance(s) and their expected impact on future performance. We will now consider each of the four types of variance.

Efficiency variances

Efficiency variances usually occur only on the cost side of the business. In setting the budget the operations manager will frequently depend on predictions from the engineering department. For example, the standard time for making one widget is 2.5 hours. Therefore a worker should be able to make 16 widgets in a 40-hour week. The worst types of efficiency variance occur when operatives fail to live up to the standard set in the budget. The consequences of such failure are overtime payments to complete the budgeted volume; scrapping of materials rejected by quality control; and rework where extra time and cost have to be incurred to bring the product to the quality standard expected by customers. Efficiency variances are usually encountered in the material usage budget; the operative pay budget; and the power consumption budget.

Price variances

Price variances occur on both the cost and the revenue sides of an organization. If the marketing department decides to sell at a price that is higher or lower than budget, a sales price variance results. Selling at a price that is below budget will be bad for an organization unless it results in an increase in volume. If the purchasing department has to buy materials or services at prices that are different from budget then a price variance also occurs.

Volume variances

Volume variances are driven by sales. If the quantity sold is higher than budget then both the sales and cost of sales will exceed budget. It may seem strange that a cost of sales figure that exceeds budget can be good news. What makes it good is the fact that the favourable sales variance should be greater than the cost of sales variance. Conversely, if the quantity sold falls short of budget then both the sales and cost of sales will be lower than budget. In this situation the reduction in cost of sales will not be sufficient to compensate for the fall in sales.

Policy variances

Organizations frequently incur costs that were not envisaged when the budget was being framed. Such additional costs arise as a result of a change in policy. They usually affect all future periods as well as the latest period.

Figure 9.1 (p 232) shows the four types of variances linked to the ongoing consequences. It is unusual to find an efficiency variance that is reversing.

A company that is in control of its finances will consistently:

- know whether there were significant variances from budget in the previous month;
- know the reasons for such variances and the action(s) being taken to capitalize on favourable and overcome adverse developments;
- know the sales, costs and profits that are likely to emerge in the financial year, given the results for the year to date and the projections for the rest of the year. The projections will be based on knowledge of changes experienced and likely to arise, and actions to be taken that were not included in the budget but will affect future revenues and costs;
- be aware of all significant payments that it will have to make in the next six months and be confident that there will be sufficient cash available to cover them.

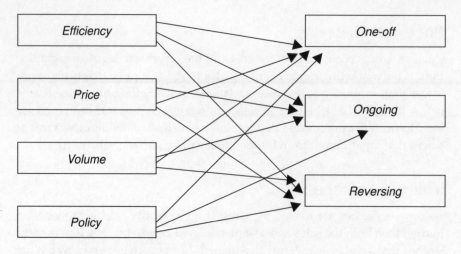

Figure 9.1 *The variance diagnosis model*

The full management team must be involved in the job of control. If they are, then the stakeholders can expect that sensibly formulated plans will be achieved. We will now examine these key elements of financial control in detail.

The four-part financial control process

1. Preparation of management accounts.
2. Diagnosis of the cause and ongoing consequences of variances. Budget holders carry out this task.
3. Feedback to management accounting of the causes and ongoing consequences of variances. The feedback is presented by the budget holders, often at a management meeting.
4. Preparation of revised forecasts of sales, costs, profits and cash requirements. The management accountant does this final phase of the control cycle.

DEPARTURES FROM BUDGET

There are three major elements in assessing departures from budget:

1. Knowing variances exist. This is a management accounting responsibility.
2. Ascertaining the causes and ongoing consequences. While the primary responsibility for identifying the causes lies with the budget holder, the

management accountant can often help in the process, particularly where a standard costing system is in place.

3. Identifying responsibility. This is frequently the most difficult part of the process. For example, a slowdown in production may be instigated because of sluggish sales or inefficiencies in the process.

Knowing variances exist

The first step is to quantify the actual results and extract the variances from the budget. This is straightforward. One line from the management accounts might be:

£'000	Budget	Actual	£ variance	% variance
Raw material	630	676	(46)	(7.3)

The company has overspent by £46,000 or 7.3 per cent of its raw material budget. The £ variance is important because £46,000 is significant in this business. The percentage variance is also worth disclosing. There may be a need for corrective action in areas where the overall planned and actual spending is relatively low but the variance percentage is high:

	Budget	Actual	£ variance	% variance
Power	50,000	62,385	(12,385)	(24.8)

Comparing these two cost lines, we see that if the company regards all variances below £20,000 as insignificant, it might lose sight of the 24.8 per cent overrun on power costs. A variance of this magnitude suggests poor budgeting. Can some of it be recovered? What will happen in subsequent periods?

Ascertaining the causes and ongoing consequences

The second step in the control process involves trying to establish the reason(s) why a variance has occurred. The use of standard costing can help to establish the cause. A standard cost can be defined as the cost of a specific volume of activity, at a specific level of efficiency, and at a specific cost per unit. Standard costing helps the management accountant to divide a variance into its volume, efficiency and price elements.

We will look behind the budgeted and actual figures for raw materials, shown previously, and try to find reasons for the variances. Three standards were used in preparing the budget:

1. The volume budget: 180,000 units.
2. The consumption budget: 3.5 grams per unit.
3. The price budget: £1 per gram.

Variances will arise if the volume we produce is different from budget, the grams of input are different from the budget, or the price per gram is different from the budget. The actual results revealed:

1. Volume produced 130,000 units.
2. Grams of input per unit 4.
3. Cost per gram £1.30.

Having these details we can prepare the part of the operating statement that deals with materials, shown in Table 9.1.

Table 9.1 *Operating statement for materials*

	£'000
Budget cost (180,000 × 3.5 grams × £1 per gram)	630
Volume variance (50,000 × 3.5 grams × £1 per gram)	175
Standard cost (130,000 × 3.5 grams × £1 per gram)[1]	455
Efficiency variance (130,000 units × 0.5 grams × £1 per gram)[2]	65 (A)
	520
Price variance (520,000 grams at 30p per gram)[3]	156 (A)
Actual cost	676

Notes:
[1] If we knew that 130,000 items would be produced we would have set the budget at £455,000. It is against this standard cost that the actual cost should be benchmarked. An analysis that simply compares the budget and actual results conceals the size and importance of inefficiency (using a higher input per unit than we expected) and price (paying more per gram than we expected) variances. Overlaying the standard cost enables us to uncover the efficiency and price variances.
[2] The fact that the average input per unit was 4 grams caused an adverse efficiency variance of £65,000.
[3] The fact that each gram used cost £1.30 caused an adverse price variance of £156,000.

Having identified the volume variance, we try to ascertain the cause. Was it a deliberate slowdown in production to avoid stockpiling in the face of sluggish customer demand? Was it a forced reduction in production because inadequate materials were available, skilled labour hours fell owing to absenteeism, or production machine hours fell owing to unexpected breakdowns? The answers to these questions will need to be obtained. The variance could be caused by the marketing/sales department (sluggish sales); the purchasing department (inadequate supplies); the production or personnel department (inadequate labour hours); or the maintenance department (unscheduled maintenance). One or more departments will have to take the blame.

Identifying responsibility

On investigation, the primary responsibility for the variances may be identified as:

- A decline in efficiency. Each unit of volume required an actual input of 4 grams. Did this lead to material wastage? Was it the responsibility of the production or personnel department to ensure that production line workers have the experience, skill and enthusiasm to work at the standard input of 3.5 grams per unit? Was it the result of poor supervision that allowed sloppy work by production staff whose training justifies an expectation of standard performance? This would clearly be a production control problem.
- An excessive purchase cost. Purchasing will be blamed for the 30 per cent price increase relative to standard and will be put under pressure to find ways of overcoming the cost overrun already experienced and to avoid similar cost overruns in future.
- A slowdown in response to slack demand. Marketing will be blamed for the shortfall.

Revising expectations for future performance

The identification of ongoing consequences of the variances must now be examined; see Table 9.2 (p 236).

Whichever the explanation for a variance, it will be necessary to carry out a detailed examination of the ongoing consequences. These could have a major impact on the expected profit for the year and the cash required at various times in the year.

Preparing the revised forecast should be done by the management accountant some time after the identification of variances. Departmental managers need time to think about the causes, corrective actions and the sometimes insoluble difficulties that uncorrectable variances can cause.

Table 9.2 *Identifying ongoing consequences*

Variance type and possible explanation	Consequences
1. The input standard was set incorrectly. Experience this year suggests that 4 grams per unit is a realistic input estimate for the rest of the year.	1. The variance is ongoing. It implies that if no compensating action can be taken: a) The costs for the rest of the year will exceed plan; b) there will be a profit shortfall for the year; and c) we will need more cash to pay the extra costs.
2. The standard was set correctly but due to inadequate control was not matched by actual performance.	2. The variance is defined as a one-off. It implies that unless compensating action can be located: a) once corrective action has been put in place it will not affect performance in future periods; and b) we will need more cash to cover the one-off cost overrun.
3. The standard was set correctly. The report is incorrect (ie the wrong volume of production was recorded).	3. If this is so, it is good news for the company. Some or all of the variance relates to incorrect transaction recording.
4. The budget was correctly set but a problem arose in spreading it over accounting periods. I once saw a sales budget for Xmas trees divided by 12 for comparison with monthly results.	4. The variance in this case is timing. Of itself this is good news because if for example there were only 15 working days in this period then the volume variance may be picked up in later periods when the working days are higher.

We will now return to the business that Larry Leeds set up in Chapter 5 to illustrate effective financial control. To be in control, any business needs to compare budgeted and actual performance every month. However, Larry, a novice businessman, foolishly waits three months before having his first comparison between budget and actual prepared; see Table 9.3.

When Larry saw the results he was shocked. When preparing the budget he had not drawn up a quarterly profit and loss account. Consequently, the

Table 9.3 _Operating statement, three months to 31 March, Larry Leeds_

	Budget	**Actual**	**Variance £**	**Variance %**
Sales volume	1,500	1,605	105(F)	7.0(F)
Sales revenue	30,000	31,163	1,163(F)	3.9(F)
Purchases	38,783	39,167	384(U)	1.0(U)
Less stock	9,600	9,600		
Material consumed	29,183	29,567	384(U)	1.3(U)
Closing fin stock	(33,000)	(32,000)	1,000(U)	3.0(U)
Payroll	37,950	39,950	2,000(U)	5.3(U)
Pensions	5,693	5,993	300(U)	5.3(U)
Power	450	400	50(F)	11.1(F)
Light	210	225	15(U)	7.1(U)
Telephone	150	150		
Insurance	2,700	2,700		
Rent and rates	4,750	4,750		
Leases	900	900		
Post and packing	156	180	24(U)	15.4(U)
Advertising	525	750	225(U)	42.9(U)
Other	225	256	31(U)	13.8(U)
Bad debts	332	–	332(F)	100.0(F)
Depreciation	1,951	1,951		
Interest	1,410	1,404	7(F)	0.3(U)
	53,585	57,176	3,591(U)	6.7(U)
Loss	23,585	26,013	2,428(U)	10.3(U)

quarterly results were the first time that he realized that the low sales and high costs would lead to a budgeted loss. He had monitored sales very carefully and knew they were ahead of budget. He was even more disturbed to find that the extra sales that he had achieved were not enough to compensate for the extra costs he had incurred. When he got over the initial panic, he started to examine where things had gone wrong and to try to forecast the results for the rest of the year; see Table 9.4 (p 238).

Larry decided to reduce his selling price to £19 in the UK market. He believes that home sales will exceed his original monthly forecast by 10 per cent through the remainder of the year. Export sales will be as forecast.

Orders for materials have been placed at a rate of 1,600 items per month. This will continue until such time as Larry finds he is short of stock to feed his revised sales target. Stock losses have run at 2 per cent of purchases. Larry fears that they will continue at this level.

237

Table 9.4 *Balance sheet as at 31 March, Larry Leeds*

	Budget	Actual	Variance
Fixed assets			
Cost	44,000	44,000	
Depreciation	2,305	2,305	
Book value	41,695	41,695	
Current assets			
Stock of materials	9,600	9,600	
Stock of finished goods	33,000	32,000	1,000(F)
VAT	122	52	70(F)
Insurance	8,100	8,100	
Grant	7,080	7,080	
Trade debtors	17,957	15,747	2,210(F)
	75,859	72,579	3,280(F)
Amounts due under one year			
Trade creditors	11,393	11,505	112(F)
Accruals	9,113	9,413	300(F)
Overdraft	34,736	33,471	1,265(U)
	(55,242)	(54,389)	853(U)
Net assets	62,312	59,885	2,427(F)
Financed by:			
Share capital	40,000	40,000	
Less loss	24,414	26,841	2,427(U)
	15,586	13,159	
Term loan	40,000	40,000	
Capital grant	6,726	6,726	
	62,312	59,885	2,427(U)

Rework cost the company £2,000 in the first quarter. With good quality control he expects it to cost £1,000 in subsequent quarters. Larry did not have an allowance for rework in his original budget.

With the exception of interest charges, which will be affected by changes in cash flows, Larry expects that his overheads will correspond with budget through the rest of the year.

Export customers will continue to settle their accounts on confirmed irrevocable letters of credit. Half will be received in the month of sale and the balance in the following month. Larry is pleased that this arrangement has left his overdraft position lower than he budgeted at the end of March.

On 1 October Larry now plans to buy a machine for £12,000 plus 17.5 per cent VAT. This will allow him to add 600 units to his output each month with his existing production staff. The machine will have a five-year life and no terminal value.

On the basis of these forecasts, Larry prepared a revised profit projection for the year; see Table 9.5 (pp 240–42).

Larry was pleased with the revised balance sheet forecast. The picture looked sound. The reduction in export debtors would finance the extra machine. He looked forward to a five-year saving in overtime costs as a result.

Comments on Larry Leeds' control system

- The budget against actual comparison was prepared in the first week of April. This allowed Larry to quickly address the major issues facing his business.
- Informed estimates were used to speed up the reporting process.
- Larry found the report easy to understand. The report contained two pages (operating statement to 31 March and balance sheet at 31 March). Larry used it to revise his estimates for the following nine months. The revised forecast involved a three-page report (operating statement for the year to 31 December, balance sheet at 31 December, and nine-month cash projection).

Flexible budgets for control

If the costs have been correctly divided into fixed and variable components, you can do a comparison of budget against actual based on the throughput achieved. This makes the variances more meaningful. The following is an illustration of flexible budgeting. The company expects to produce an output of between 90,000 and 110,000 units. The budgeted cost based on an output of 100,000 units is:

Materials per unit (Variable)	6.00
Labour per unit (Variable)	2.50
Overhead per unit (Variable)	1.50
Overhead per unit (Fixed)	1.98
Total cost	11.98
Unit selling price	15.00
Unit profit	3.02

Table 9.5 *Revised forecast operating statement year ended 31 December, Larry Leeds*

	3 Months actual	9 Months estimate	Annual estimate	Original budget
Sales revenue	31,163	374,854	406,017	395,000
Opening stock		9,600		
Purchases	39,167	89,105	128,272	119,404
Less stock	(9,600)	(11,440)	(11,440)	(10,400)
Material consumed	29,567	87,265	116,832	109,004
Opening fin stock	–	32,000	–	
Closing fin stock	(32,000)	(506)	(506)	
Payroll	39,950	116,850	156,800	154,550
Pensions	5,993	17,527	23,520	23,183
Power	400	1,350	1,750	1,800
Light	225	630	855	840
Telephone	150	450	600	600
Insurance	2,700	8,100	10,800	10,800
Rent and rates	4,750	14,250	19,000	19,000
Leases	900	2,700	3,600	3,600
Post and packing	180	1,044	1,224	1,200
Advertising	750	975	1,725	1,500
Other	256	675	931	900
Bad debts		2,912	2,912	4,365
Depreciation	1,951	6,453	8,404	7,804
Interest	1,404	3,057	4,461	4,821
	57,176	295,732	352,908	343,967
Profit/(loss)	(26,013)	79,123	53,111	51,033
Corporation tax			10,327[1]	12,427
Retained			42,784	38,606

Note:
[1] Corporation tax

Profit per accounts		53,111
Add depreciation		8,404
		61,515
Less writing down allowances		
Original	9,130	
new machine	750	9,880
Taxable profit		51,635
Corporation tax at 20%		10,327

Table 9.5 (continued)

	Apr	May	Jun	Jul	Aug	Sep	Oct	Nov	Dec	Total
					Updated cash forecast April to December					
Cash inflows										
Collections home sales[1]	10761	14288	20481	27775	34700	37941	32378	29175	29911	237410
Collections export sales[1]	7000	10000	14000	18000	21000	19000	16000	16000	18000	139000
Capital grant	7080									7080
	24841	24288	34481	45775	55700	56941	48378	45175	47911	383490
Cash outflows										
Suppliers (2)	11505	9971	9972	9971	9972	9971	13711	13711	13711	102495
VAT (3)	-52			5421			8798			14167
Payroll (4)	12983	12983	12984	12983	12983	12984	12983	12983	12984	116850
Overhead (5)	3986	783	4645	3744	872	846	3836	696	27669	47077
Plant							14100			14100
Total before interest	28422	23737	27601	32119	23827	23801	53428	27390	54364	294689
Monthly balance	-3581	551	6880	13656	31873	33140	-5050	17785	-6453	88801
Cumulative monthly balance	-3581	-3030	3850	17506	49379	82519	77469	95254	88801	88801
Bank interest (6)						719				719
Monthly balance including interest	-3581	551	6880	13656	31873	32421	-5050	17785	-6453	88082
Opening cash	-33471	-37052	-36501	-29621	-15965	15908	48329	43279	61064	-33471
Closing cash	-37052	-36501	-29621	-15965	15908	48329	43279	61064	54611	54611

Notes:

In this updated cash forecast Larry concentrated on four major factors:

1. The actual bank overdraft at 31 March £33,471.
2. The implications of actual purchases and sales in the first quarter on cash collections in subsequent quarters.
3. The implications of revised production and sales forecasts for the following nine months on the payments to suppliers, payroll and collections from customers.
4. The decision to purchase additional plant at a cost of £14,100 including VAT.

Table 9.5 *(continued)*

Forecast balance sheet as at 31 December

	Revised budget	**Latest estimate**
Fixed assets		
Plant	18,880	30,280
Truck	9,600	9,600
Car	6,300	6,300
	34,780	46,180
Current assets		
Stock materials	10,400	11,440
Stock finished goods	–	506
Trade debtors	61,990	51,331
Cash	53,555	54,274
	125,945	117,551
Payable in under one year		
Suppliers	12,342	10,327
VAT	8,365	8,138
Bank interest	3,321	3,107
Corporation tax	12,427	12,909
	(36,455)	(35,283)
Net assets	124,270	128,448
Financed by:		
Share capital	40,000	40,000
Revenue reserve	38,606	42,784
	78,606	82,784
Government grant	5,664	5,664
Bank term loan	40,000	40,000
	124,270	128,448

Actual output was 94,000 units. Comparison between the flexible budget at this output and the actual is shown in Table 9.6. This comparison discloses an overall variance of £7,860. It is more revealing than the variance of £37,860 that would have been shown if compared with the target of 100,000 units.

Table 9.6 _Comparison of the flexible budget and the actual_

Flexible budget at 94,000 units

	Per unit	Total £'000	Per unit	Actual £'000	Variance £'000
Output	94,000			94,000	
Revenue	15.000	1,410	14.95	1,405.30	–4.70
Materials	6.000	564	5.80	545.20	+18.80
Labour	2.500	235	2.63	247.22	–12.22
Overhead variable	1.500	141	1.51	141.94	–0.94
Overhead fixed	2.106	198	2.20	206.80	–8.80
Total cost	12.106	1,138	12.14	1,141.16	–3.16
Profit	2.894	272	2.81	264.14	–7.86

The reason for the difference is:

	£
Variance based on budgeted output	37,860
Lost through volume decline 6,000 × £3.02	18,120
	19,740
Fixed costs not recovered 6,000 × £1.98	11,880
Actual profit	7,860

Fixed and variable costs are examined in detail in Chapter 10.

Controlling a large product range

Control tends to be relatively easy when an organization is providing only one product or service. When a range of items is sold problems can arise. First, a wide variation can exist in the margins for individual items. The sales revenue can provide a large profit if concentrated into high contribution lines, or a low profit if concentrated into low contribution lines. Second, a wide variation in the working capital deployed to support individual products exists, resulting in a greater or lesser working capital requirement, depending on the mix of sales.

We now examine a business with three product lines to illustrate the control problem; see Table 9.7.

Table 9.7 *A business with three products*

	Product A Budget	Actual	Product B Budget	Actual	Product C Budget	Actual	Total Budget	Actual	Variance
Sales volume	100000	113765	50000	47965	20000	19125			
Sales revenue	100000	113765	120000	115116	180000	172125	400000	401006	1006
Variable cost	70000	79180	75000	72907	100000	96008	245000	248095	3095
Contribution	30000	34585	45000	42209	80000	76118	155000	152911	−2089
Fixed cost							46000	45663	−337
Profit							109000	107248	−1752
C/S ratio	30.00	30.40	37.50	36.67	44.44	44.22	38.75	38.13	

In this three-product business, sales are slightly ahead of budget but the profit for the month is below budget. This was mainly caused by the fact that the sales of the low-margin product A were ahead of budget, whereas sales of the higher-margin products B and C were below budget. This example points to the need for budgeted and actual contribution to be measured in a multi-product business. For the purposes of this chapter, contribution is similar to gross profit and C/S ratio is the contribution as a percentage of sales (this is similar to the gross margin). A more detailed treatment of contribution is presented in Chapter 11.

Many trading businesses have a wide range of products that offer substantially different C/S ratios. The profitability of such businesses is heavily influenced by product mix. The greater the proportion of high contribution sales in the mix the higher the profit. Conversely, the greater the proportion of low contribution sales in the mix the lower the profit. Such businesses need to link contribution analysis to bar code scanning at point of sale if they wish to obtain prompt and reliable product profitability information.

THE QUALITIES OF AN EFFECTIVE FINANCIAL CONTROL SYSTEM

- Even in a small firm, management accounts should be prepared and interpreted at least quarterly. Variances need to be computed and investigated.

- The accounts must be prepared quickly. If something is wrong, prompt corrective action is needed. The results should be ready for circulation five days after the end of the accounting period. Organizations that take a long time to prepare reports miss opportunities to take swift and appropriate corrective actions.
- It is sometimes necessary to use estimates to produce prompt results. As an example, many businesses find that a full count and valuation of stock takes too long and disrupts production and sales. In these cases the use of book stocks, supported by sampling, can overcome the need for lengthy stock count and valuation procedures. Similarly, since many overheads are billed only from time to time it is necessary to introduce reliable accruals.
- The essence of a good financial control report is that it is easy to read and understand, and that important variances are highlighted.

Two problems arise in trying to meet these criteria. The first is that many reports are too long. Managers find it difficult to identify the critical issues from lengthy reports. Departmental reports can be an effective way of achieving brevity. Consider a company with a large number of products and the following marketing structure:

- Representatives (60). Analysis of his or her sales, budget against actual by product and customer, to help in preparing for the regional meeting. Analysis of debtor accounts requiring attention.
- Regional managers (5). Analysis of sales budget against actual by representative within the region, followed by a meeting with the sales representatives to discuss actions required.
- Brand managers (8). Analysis of brand sales budget against actual by region for discussion with marketing, sales and production.
- Directors. Analysis of sales budget against actual by region, followed by a meeting with the area managers to discuss action required.

This outline shows how more than 70 people get appropriate reports. If all staff are given the full information for each product and customer it is unlikely to be as effective. Reports of this kind are not used often enough.

The second problem is that there is a case for a lot of comparative data. Where the reports are not designed on responsibility lines as outlined above, there can be too much information to interpret. The column headings that are sometimes encountered include:

1. Budget this period
2. Actual this period
3. £ variance this period
4. Per cent variance this period
5. Budget year to date
6. Actual year to date
7. £ variance year to date
8. Per cent variance year to date
9. Actual last period
10. Variance against last period
11. Actual this period last year
12. Variance against this period last year

This list is not exhaustive. If 12 items are reported, you wind up with a page composed of 144 numbers. It becomes difficult to establish which are important and which are not. Table 9.8 shows the reasons people want these column heads included and the possible methods of reducing their number to manageable proportions.

Table 9.8 *Reasons given for including certain headings in reports*

Heading	Rationale	Options for reducing columns
1–4	These give a full analysis of current performance. Column 4 is required because large % variances can occur in small budgets.	Budget, actual and £ variances are derived by addition and subtraction. You only need three of these columns. Possible combinations include: a) budget £ and % variance; and b) actual £ and % variance.
5–8	Year to date results must be monitored. They identify recovery of previous adverse variances.	As with the current period, you may only need the three chosen columns.
9–10	This helps to track progress since the last period.	This is vital in a seasonal business. Are these columns better than 11 and 12?
11–12	Progress may best be measured by comparison with last year.	Variances are driven by changes in volume and price. Percentages are often the best measure of progress.

It may be possible to produce a meaningful report with only eight columns. To achieve this the management team must decide which columns can be sacrificed.

A good report is one that is tailored to meet the needs of budget holders. Frequently this is forgotten when those who prepare the reports design them to meet the needs of group accounting and to suit software designers. Complicated terminology is one major reason why non-accounting managers find budget reports difficult to understand. Excellent reports are ones that recognize that to be in control a manager needs more than just budget actual and variance numbers. Some of the key control data are best expressed in non-monetary terms:

- planned versus actual market share data;
- comparison of promotion costs per unit with major competitors;
- comparison of relative product quality;
- state of the order book;
- comparison of planned and actual rejects and rework;
- overtime hours as a percentage of normal hours;
- absenteeism statistics;
- capital expenditure reports.

All budget holders should see the receipt of the management accounts as the first step in an effective control process. The really effective part of the control process can then start. Dialogue can begin about what has happened, why it happened and what will happen next.

I frequently see management accounting reports of client companies. Some contain a column that shows the revised estimate for the financial year. Asking the management accountant to complete such a forecast without first discussing the causes and ongoing consequences of variances with the budget holders is ridiculous. Revised estimates can only be sensibly prepared when feedback has been received on the causes and ongoing consequences of variances.

SUMMARY

To be in control any business needs a prompt and reliable comparison between budgeted and actual performance. The world of business is changing so rapidly that no business can be said to be in control unless monthly management accounts are prepared. The real financial controllers in a business are the budget holders. They are the people who are in a position to identify the causes and ongoing consequences of variances. They analyse the management accounts and ask three questions:

1. Why did a variance occur?
2. What if anything can be done about adverse variances?
3. What are the implications of variances for subsequent accounting periods?

When they have answered these questions they feed their conclusions back to the management accountant who can then prepare a revised forecast for the financial year. Such forecasts should be top of the agenda for management and board meetings.

A company that goes through the cycle shown in Figure 9.2 at the end of each accounting period should be able to meet its profit goal unless the market has collapsed.

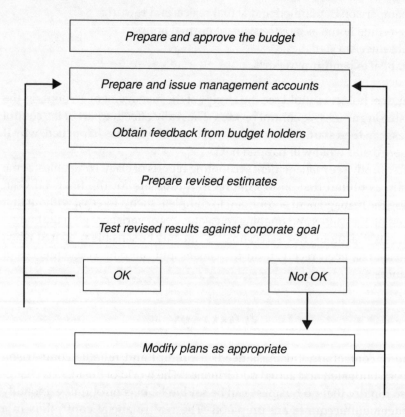

Figure 9.2 *A model of an effective control process*

10

Total costing

Some products or services are more profitable than others. Indeed, some products and services may even be loss making. Equally, selling to some customers is more profitable than to others. Costing systems are designed to attribute the expenses of a business to its products or services and its customers so that management can see:

- the products or services that are most profitable and should be promoted;
- the customers and markets that are most profitable and should be developed;
- the products or services that offer inadequate profits and need to be re-engineered;
- the customers and markets that are marginal (mainly because of small order sizes and expensive transport costs). Sales to such customers and markets can sometimes be reorganized so that they become more profitable;
- the products or services that are loss making and need drastic cost reduction or removal from the range;
- the customers and markets that are loss making and also need drastic cost reduction or to have orders refused.

In order to pinpoint the strategic necessities that emerge from the above list it is necessary to prepare a number of mini profit and loss accounts that aggregate into the overall operating budget. To prepare these accounts it is necessary to break down the revenues and costs to products, services, customers and markets. These will reveal the profitable, marginal and loss-making areas. Mini profit and loss accounts help management to make correct promotional, cost reduction and order refusal decisions. The process is called 'costing'.

There are two distinct approaches to costing: establishing what the cost was in the past (called historic cost), and forecasting future costs (budgeted costs). There are often significant differences between the budgeted unit cost and what it proves to be when the historic cost is calculated. Differences are caused by forecasting errors. Incorrect costs can lead to poor management decisions.

Most organizations find that, with the aid of computers, sales budgets and invoices can easily be broken down by product, service, customer or market. The difficult problems arise on the cost side. This is because many of the costs have only a tenuous relationship with the products, services, customers and markets that they are applied to.

Costing is straightforward in a one-product business. It becomes complicated and subjective when more than one product or service is involved; see Table 10.1.

We will now look at the results when some of the budgeted costs turn out to be incorrect. There are four cases. In each case only one item turns out to be incorrect; see Table 10.2 (p 252).

PRINCIPLES OF COST ATTRIBUTION WITH MORE THAN ONE PRODUCT OR SERVICE

It can be difficult to attribute costs reliably in a multi-product business. To understand how to attribute the costs we can classify them in three types:

1. Costs that can be directly and accurately attributed to a product or service. Examples include direct materials (booked from the stores to the specific product), and direct labour (booked to the product by 'swipe cards').
2. Costs that could be directly and accurately attributed to a product or service but the cost of measuring and attributing them exceeds the benefit from attribution. For example, power costs could be directly attributed if meters were used to measure output to products or machines. The cost of doing so would be prohibitive in many small businesses.

Table 10.1 *Steps in predicting the product cost in a one-product business*

Cost category and relevant data	Calculation data	Cost £
Direct materials (excl VAT)		
Price per unit	£10	
+ +		
Allowance for spoilage, offcuts and pilferage	10%	11.00
Labour hours per unit	2	
×	×	
Standard labour hour rate	£3	
×	+	
Allowance for rework, scrap, etc	6%	6.36
Prime cost		17.36
Period overheads (£10,000) divided by units to be sold (5,000)		2.00
Total cost		19.36
Selling price per unit		22.50
Profit per unit (13.96% of selling price)		3.14
Forecast sales volume	5,000 units	
Forecast profit		£15,700.00

3. Costs that have no specific connection with the products or services of an organization. Such costs (usually called indirect costs) may be attributed using some fairly arbitrary basis.

Cost attribution systems

Method	Features
Direct allocation	Relevant for direct material, direct labour and some sizeable production costs. Allocation in proportion to spending on dominant cost
	Often suitable where the cost of more 'scientific' methods exceeds the benefits from their use. Accumulation in an area (called a cost centre) for transfer to products in proportion to time in process.

Table 10.2 *Four cases of incorrect budget costs*

	Case A Material £12.10 each		Case B Labour £7 each		Case C Overhead £11,000		Case D Sales volume 4,000 units	
	Per unit	Total	Per unit	Total	Per unit	Total	Per unit	Total
Material	12.10	60,500	11.00	55,000	11.00	55,000	11.00	44,000
Labour	6.36	31,800	7.00	35,000	6.36	31,800	6.36	25,440
Overhead	2.00	10,000	2.00	10,000	2.20	11,000	2.50	10,000
Total cost	20.46	102,300	20.00	100,000	19.56	97,800	19.86	79,440
Sales	22.50	112,500	22.50	112,500	22.50	112,500	22.50	90,000
Profit	2.04	10,200	2.50	12,500	2.94	14,700	2.64	10,560
Margin (%)		9.1		11.1		13.1		11.7

Reason for change from budget

	Case A	Case B	Case C	Case D
Units sold	5,000	5,000	5,000	
Units not sold				1,000
Change in margin	£1.10	£0.64	£0.20	
Margin lost				£3.14
Overheads not recovered				£2,000
Profit lost	£5,500	£3,200	£1,000	£5,140

Cost centres may be people, departments or machines.

This approach is used to attribute a wide range of costs in a similar way. The traditional approach was to use machine hour rates or direct labour hour rates. Modern systems use cost drivers and activity-based costing.

To attribute costs to products, services, customers and markets we must also find out whether they will be incurred if a product or service is not produced. This question relates to the fact that costs behave in three different ways:

1. Those that rise and fall in direct proportion to output. These costs are called _variable_ costs. Examples are: a) raw materials – if output falls we should buy less of them or carry more stock, if output rises we should buy more or carry less stock; and b) piecework labour – if people are not making product they are not paid. In many textbooks all direct labour is treated as a variable cost. In times of falling demand this often proves unreliable. Companies cannot afford redundancy costs. They also fear the cost of recruitment and training when demand picks up.
2. Those that will be incurred on a similar scale regardless of output. These are called _fixed_ costs. Examples include: rent and rates, based on the occupation not the volume of activity taking place; and administration salaries, based on employment costs rather than production activity.
3. Those that are partly fixed and partly variable. These are called _semi-fixed, semi-variable, or mixed_ costs. Examples of semi-variable costs include: a) machine maintenance, which could include an annual overhaul regardless of output (fixed) and a replacement of parts after each 10,000 units (variable); and b) a sales incentive scheme based on a flat rate up to a specific level with a percentage commission for each £1 of sales in excess of quota.

Semi-variable costs. Example 1. Fuel

Is distribution cost fixed or variable? We must look at the various components of this cost; see Table 10.3 (p 254).

Why are the fuel and maintenance costs semi-variable? The distribution manager has extracted reliable statistics that provide the following information about a vehicle:

Table 10.3 *Distribution costs*

Cost type	Fixed	Semi-variable
Driver's wages	/	
Vehicle tax and insurance	/	
Fuel		/
Maintenance		/
Depreciation		/

- Weight of product transported when fully laden: 5 tonnes.
- Fuel cost fully laden: 20p per mile.
- Each 20 per cent reduction in load will result in a 10 per cent decrease in fuel consumption (non-cumulative).

Table 10.4 *Vehicle statistics*

Weight (tonnes)	Fixed cost per mile	Variable cost per mile	Cost per tonne/mile
5	12p	8.0p	20.0p
4	12p	7.2p	19.2p
3	12p	6.4p	18.4p
2	12p	5.6p	17.6p
1	12p	4.8p	16.8p

The budget is developed by predicting the miles to be travelled at each load factor:

Tonnes carried	Miles this load	Fixed cost	Variable cost	Total cost
5.0	3,000	360	240	600
4.5	4,000	480	304	784
4.0	5,000	600	360	960
3.5	2,000	240	136	376
3.0	1,000	120	64	184
		1,800	1,104	2,904

Semi-variable costs. Example 2. Sales remuneration

Basic salary is £15,000 regardless of sales volume.

Each 5,000 units sold in excess of quota will attract the following commission: 5 per cent for each 5,000 units in excess of 50,000 up to 75,000, and 10 per cent for each 5,000 units in excess of 75,000. The total cost at various volumes is shown in Table 10.5.

Table 10.5 *The total cost at various volumes*

Sales volume	Base fixed	Low variable	High variable	Total
50,000	15,000	–	–	15,000
55,000	15,000	250	–	15,250
60,000	15,000	500	–	15,500
65,000	15,000	750	–	15,750
70,000	15,000	1,000	–	16,000
75,000	15,000	1,250	–	16,250
80,000	15,000	1,250	500	16,750
85,000	15,000	1,250	1,000	17,250
90,000	15,000	1,250	1,500	17,750
95,000	15,000	1,250	2,000	18,250
100,000	15,000	1,250	2,500	18,750

Dominant cost allocations

Many organizations attribute indirect costs to products or services in proportion to the spending on their dominant cost. To illustrate how this is done we will examine a business about which the following information has been obtained:

● A product is made in two sizes. The large version is twice as big as the small one.
● Material content is in direct proportion to size.
● Labour content is 25 per cent greater for the large version.
● Machine running cost is the same for each product.
● Total direct cost is £400,000 and total overhead to be allocated is £50,000.

Table 10.6 *Dominant costs allocations*

Cost type	Small product	Large product	Total
Material	65,000	130,000	195,000
Labour	60,000	75,000	135,000
Machine running	35,000	35,000	70,000
Total direct	160,000	240,000	400,000
Indirect cost	?	?	50,000
Total cost	?	?	450,000
Sales	200,000	320,000	520,000
Product profits	?	?	70,000

The challenge is to fill in the question marks in a defensible way. There are five possible methods. Unfortunately, each method leads to a different indirect cost allocation and consequently different product profits. Method 1 requires the indirect costs to be apportioned in proportion to direct material cost. In methods 2, 3, 4 and 5 the indirect apportionment will be based on direct labour, machine running, sales and total direct costs respectively; see Table 10.7.

Table 10.7 *Different methods of indirect cost allocation*

Method	Apportionment	Indirect small	Indirect large	Profit small	Profit large
1 Material	1:2	16,667	33,333	23,333	46,667
2 Labour	4:5	22,222	27,778	17,778	52,222
3 Machining	1:1	25,000	25,000	15,000	55,000
4 Sales	10:16	19,231	30,769	20,769	49,231
5 Total direct	2:3	20,000	30,000	20,000	50,000

This table shows that the profit for the small product could be as high as £23,333 or as low as £15,000 depending on the attribution method used. The challenge is to decide which of the five methods provides the most reliable indicator of product profitability. Many retail organizations use method 1. The justification for this is that in retailing the material cost tends to dominate all costs, and the bigger the hook you hang the indirect costs on, the more reliable the resulting product cost. Many manufacturing organizations use method 5. Some do so for the simple reason that no single cost is dominant in their industry but the combination of direct materials and direct labour (called 'prime cost') is dominant. Method 2 would be chosen in craft industries and in many service industries where direct labour costs tend to dominate.

Which method is suitable in your industry? Before I try to help you answer this question we will examine ways to convert costs from indirect into direct. There are two major approaches: the cost centre approach and activity-based costing.

THE COST CENTRE APPROACH

The cost centre approach can be used to make indirect costs product-specific. The approach has been widely used in jobbing engineering and printing for many years. The factors that link these two types of industry are, first, that machines do the bulk of the work. Costs such as depreciation, space, maintenance, operative time and power that might otherwise be labelled as indirect can be reliably attributed to the machines used to do the work. Second, each job has its own individual characteristics that make it unique. Once the cost of using a machine can be reliably determined it can be converted into an hourly rate. This hourly rate can then be charged to products 'buying' time on the machines.

Consider a factory that uses four machines. The management accountant has attributed the cost of using the machines utilizing a variety of sensible mechanisms. The results are shown in Table 10.8.

Table 10.8 *An example of attribution to machines*

Cost type	Allocation method	Total ratio	Machine cost	A	B	C	D
Space	Square feet	4:3:2:1	90,000	36,000	27,000	18,000	9,000
Power	Consumption	3:2:1:1	35,000	15,000	10,000	5,000	5,000
Depreciation	Machine cost	5:3:2:1	44,000	20,000	12,000	8,000	4,000
Maintenance	Machine cost	5:3:2:1	33,000	15,000	9,000	6,000	3,000
Operative	Machine specific		60,000	15,000	15,000	15,000	15,000
Total cost			262,000	101,000	73,000	52,000	36,000
Productive hours per period				5,000	4,000	3,000	6,000
Charge rate per hour				£20.20	£18.25	£17.33	£6.00

The first step in preparing the analysis was the collection of relevant costs. For example, the space cost was extracted from the following cost budgets:

- light and heat;
- rent and rates;
- insurance;
- maintenance of premises; and
- security.

The space cost for the whole business was budgeted at £360,000. Since the factory space was 25 per cent of the total, £90,000 was to be spread over the four machines. The factory space was 6,000 square feet, which was being used in the proportions shown in Table 10.9.

Table 10.9 *Factory space usage per machine*

Machine	A		B	C		D
Sq ft	2,400		1,800	1,200		600
Space ratio	4	:	3	2	:	1

On the basis of this analysis, machine A was charged with £36,000 (40 per cent of the space cost). The other machine costs were aggregated and spread in appropriate ways. The analysis leads to a budgeted cost of £101,000 for machine A. With the machine expected to run for 5,000 hours in the accounting year this led to a charge-out rate of £20.20 per hour. Any product that would 'buy' time on machine A would be charged this rate. Similar rates based on expected usage were struck for the other three machines. The charge-out rates could be used for both estimating and product costing. All that was needed was correct estimates of material, labour and machine times for the job.

Costing a job that uses all four machines is shown in Table 10.10. The important issue in this example is that £262,000 of indirect costs were spread reliably and as a result the residue of indirect costs to be spread had become much smaller.

Total cost absorption: the snags

In previous illustrations we looked at budgeted product costs. If actual costs or operating hours are different, problems arise.

Table 10.10 *Costing a job that uses all four machines*

	£
Direct material 1,000 grams at 50p	500
Direct labour 240 hours at £3.50 per hour	840
Machine A 25 hours at £20.20	505
Machine B 16 hours at £18.25	292
Machine C 12 hours at £17.33	208
Machine D 18 hours at £6.00	108
Total cost	2,453
Add mark up to cover indirect costs and obtain a profit (40%)	981
Price to be quoted	3,434

If costs exceed budget, or volume targets are underachieved, the unit overhead allocation is too small and the expected unit profit is not realized. For example, if only 4,000 hours of the machine A capacity are sold, then on the basis of the actual output, products using that machine should be charged £25.25 per hour.

If the costs are below budget, or volume exceeds budget, the overhead allocation is too big and the unit profit exceeds budget.

The cost-driven price spiral

Any business that fails to sell to capacity can find itself in a frightening price spiral. We will use the hourly rate for machine A to illustrate the problem. Suppose that after setting the budget it was recognized that only 4,000 hours could be expected to be sold. The quotation shown previously was modified at the suggestion of the finance director; see Table 10.11 (p 260).

Based on the new costing, the price to be quoted rose from £3,434 to £3,611. Now suppose that this and several other jobs were lost owing to the price increase. As a result:

● The volume expected to be used by all four machines declined.
● The charge-out rates had to be increased, leading to even less competitive quotations.
● With each unsuccessful quotation, the machine utilization declined further, the charge-out rate increased, the mark-up to cover indirect costs had to be increased, and the company succeeded in attracting less and less business until its losses became unsustainable and it closed.

Table 10.11 *Modified quotation*

	£
Direct material 1,000 grams at 50p	500
Direct labour 240 hours at £3.50 per hour	840
Machine A 25 hours at £25.25	631
Machine B 16 hours at £18.25	292
Machine C 12 hours at £17.33	208
Machine D 18 hours at £6.00	108
Total cost	2,579
Add mark-up to cover indirect costs and obtain a profit (40%)	1,032
Price to be quoted	3,611

This story is painfully true. This kind of disaster has affected numerous businesses. At the core of the problem is a failure to understand pricing in a competitive market. Accountants sometimes mistakenly think that prices are determined by costs. In the long run this is certainly true. In the short run, however, a business that is experiencing a decline in demand will survive only if it can cut its costs (particularly the indirect ones) to a level that the volume can support.

To sell or not to sell (unprofitable products or services)?

It may sound strange, but sometimes a business does better to persist with a loss-making product or service than to discontinue it. The reason for this is that the loss-maker is helping to cover some of the indirect costs of the organization. If such a product or service is discontinued and the indirect costs remain the same, then the products or services that remain will be burdened with an increased share of the indirect costs. Suppose that the additional costs turn a product that was previously profitable into another loss-maker. The company finds itself once again in a cost-driven spiral that will kill the organization unless it is properly addressed.

The data in Table 10.12 were taken from the costing records of a business. The proprietor felt that the overall profit £100 was unacceptable, and that if Product A were discontinued the total profit would rise to £500. Do you agree?

The conclusion is faulty. If Product A is discontinued, its material, labour and avoidable overhead will no longer be incurred. The product has been

Table 10.12 *Product costing*

	Products			
	A	**B**	**C**	**Total**
Sales revenue	5,000	4,000	4,000	13,000
Direct materials	1,900	1,600	1,700	5,200
Direct labour	2,000	1,200	1,200	4,400
Avoidable overheads	1,000	600	600	2,200
Unavoidable overheads[1]	500	300	300	1,100
Total cost	5,400	3,700	3,800	12,900
Profit/(loss)	(400)	300	200	100

Note:
[1] 25% of direct labour

allocated £500 of unavoidable costs. These will remain and must now be attributed to Products B and C, and the product costing changes to that shown in Table 10.13.

Table 10.13 *Product costings after Product A is discontinued*

	Products		
	B	**C**	**Total**
Sales revenue	4,000	4,000	8,000
Direct materials	1,600	1,700	3,300
Direct labour	1,200	1,200	2,400
Avoidable overheads	600	600	1,200
Unavoidable overheads [1]	550	550	1,100
Total cost	3,950	4,050	8,000
Profit/(loss)	50	(50)	–

Note:
[1] 45.8% of direct labour

The £100 profit has vanished. Should he now decide to discontinue Product C? If he does, then Product B will be burdened with a further £550 of unavoidable overhead. It will be a loss-maker. Does this mean that the whole analysis is faulty? No, it shows that Product A is a poor performer. Since it

261

sells above direct cost, it is recovering some overhead. A range of options is available to try to improve it:

- increase the selling price;
- increase the volume;
- negotiate a lower material cost;
- reduce the labour cost (lower overtime, improved efficiency, wage freeze, etc);
- reduce avoidable and unavoidable overheads.

If none of these options is feasible, then the business must search for an alternative product that can cover the Product A overheads and yield a profit. Product A should certainly not be discontinued until a replacement product comes on stream or the situation has deteriorated to a level where the selling price falls below direct cost. When a replacement product is paying the unavoidable costs, it is time to take action on Product A. Initially increase the price to make sales profitable; if sales collapse then discontinue it. A hopeful scenario is shown in Table 10.14.

Table 10.14 *The effect of increasing Product A's price by 10 per cent and adding Product D*

| | Products | | | | |
	A	B	C	D	Total
Sales revenue	2,200	4,000	4,000	3,840	14,040
Direct material	760	1,600	1,700	1,260	5,320
Direct labour	800	1,200	1,200	1,400	4,600
Avoidable overheads	400	600	600	700	2,300
Unavoidable overheads	191	287	287	335	1,100
Total cost	2,151	3,687	3,787	3,695	13,320
Profit	49	313	213	145	720

Product A has been increased in price by 10 per cent and declines in volume by 60 per cent. It will generate a profit of 49 after bearing a share of the unavoidable overheads. The inclusion of Product D is vital. Without it Product A would be loss making and the overall profit would be lower, as the three-product forecast in Table 10.15 shows.

Table 10.15 *The effect of not including Product D*

	Products			
	A	**B**	**C**	**Total**
Sales revenue	2,200	4,000	4,000	10,200
Direct material	760	1,600	1,700	4,060
Direct labour	800	1,200	1,200	3,200
Avoidable overheads	400	600	600	1,600
Unavoidable overheads	275	413	412	1,100
Total cost	2,235	3,813	3,912	9,960
Profit/(loss)	(35)	187	88	240

The changing perspective on product costs

In recent years disenchantment with traditional indirect cost attribution methods has been growing. There are four main reasons:

1. It has become widely accepted that such attribution systems penalize high-volume, low-hassle products and subsidize low-volume, high-hassle products. The reason for this is that costs such as product engineering and set-up have been included in indirect costs. If such indirect costs are attributed in proportion to direct labour or some similar method, it fails to recognize that high-volume, low-hassle products 'buy' very little of such services whereas low-volume, high-hassle products 'buy' large amounts of such services.
2. Many large organizations have become assembly and marketing oriented. As a result, most components are being outsourced, leading to a decrease in direct labour, an increase in direct materials, and significant additional indirect costs in areas of supplier support. In such an environment, attribution of indirect costs in proportion to direct labour becomes more and more inaccurate as higher amounts of indirect costs are piggybacked on a smaller amount of direct labour cost. Computer hardware and car manufacturing are major examples of this changing cost structure. In both industries most components are bought in and direct labour represents less than 5 per cent of total cost.
3. Increasingly, automation has replaced direct labour. This automation increases machine costs and makes the use of machine hour rates more relevant than traditional attribution mechanisms.

4.   Customer service and quality control have become among the most important business priorities. These costs were usually classified as indirect. Increases in indirect costs once again magnify the error of piggybacking.

In this environment, as support costs rise, traditional attribution methods have become more and more inaccurate and less and less acceptable. In recent years activity-based costing (ABC) has come to the forefront as it tends to attribute indirect costs to products, services, customers and markets more accurately.

ACTIVITY-BASED COSTING

Most companies tend to budget and record costs by type of expenditure. For example, if you want to know how much your company has spent on rent or electricity in the last quarter, the management accountant should be able to answer your question quickly by referring to the appropriate computer file. If you were to ask what was the cost of quality control or customer service in the last quarter, the management accountant might not be able to tell you. The major reason for this is that the cost of such activities is spread over a number of types of expenditure. For example, the cost of quality control would include:

Type of expenditure	Included in expenditure type
Operative time	Direct labour and fringe costs
Test materials	Direct materials
Space costs	Light, heat, insurance, depreciation, rent, rates, maintenance, etc
Test equipment	Depreciation and maintenance

Only when the costs are structured to answer such questions is it possible to prepare reliable activity-based costings. There are four key issues in the preparation of activity-based costs.

1. The use of a computer spreadsheet makes it possible to re-sort costs so that they can be reported by activity as well as by expenditure type.

2. There is a hierarchy of costs that is helpful in downloading them to products, services, markets or customers. To do so, the costs must be aggregated in the following groups: staff costs, facility costs and technology costs. When the costs have been aggregated in these groups it becomes possible to

download them to products, services, customers and markets using appropriate attribution mechanisms.

The following approach is recommended. The first step involves the correct collection of the costs; see Table 10.16.

Table 10.16 _Collecting costs_

Staff	Facilities	Technology
Salaries and wages	Light and heat	Power
National insurance	Rent and rates	Depreciation of machines
Employer pension contributions	Insurance	Maintenance of machines
Protective clothing	Depreciation of premises	Space costs (from facilities)
Fringe benefits	Maintenance of premises	Operative costs (from staff)
Workmen's compensation	Security	

The second step is to attribute the costs. Staff costs are attributed in line with the way that employees spend their time. Facilities costs are attributed in line with the space occupied by the users of facilities. Technology costs are attributed using machine hour rates. Note that in this complex analysis costs must be transferred from one group to another. For example, the staff are users of facilities and technology; equally, technology is a user of staff and facilities.

3. Cost drivers are identified and used to attribute costs to activities. Cost drivers include time, space, weight and distance.

4. One of the most controversial aspects of activity-based costing is that it seeks to isolate idle capacity. There are three major reasons for this. First, every organization has some idle capacity. This is because it is practically impossible to have a supply of services that exactly equals demand. Second, it is only when the cost of idle capacity has been correctly quantified that management will be provoked to attack it by vigorously marketing the surplus or shrinking it to meet the demand. The most effective way to match supply and demand is often through outsourcing. Third, and arguably most important, in a highly competitive market customers are not prepared to pay for your unused capacity.

The problem with idle capacity is that some costs are time based and have no connection with volume. For example, suppose that the budgeted depreciation cost for a machine is £9,600 and that in theory the machine could be used for eight hours per day on each of the 240 days that the factory will be open. On the basis of these facts the company might decide to include a charge of £1 per hour for depreciation in the machine hour rate. Now suppose that the demand for time on the machine is budgeted to be 8,000 hours. If the demand were used as the cost driver then the charge for depreciation should be increased to £1.20 per hour. This would not be fair to buyers of time. It is not their fault that the machine will be idle for 1,600 hours in the budget year. The cost of idle capacity is £1,600. This is money being 'burned' when the machine lies idle. As the machine sells the expected usable hours, 'buyers' should be charged £1 per hour for depreciation. By the end of the year the machine should have charged out £8,000 as these hours are sold. The remaining £1,600 must be shown separately from the product costs in the budgeted profit and loss account. In this way the management will be made aware of the cost of failing to stimulate adequate demand and hopefully encouraged to tackle the mismatch between supply and demand.

In some cases the measurement of practical capacity can be difficult to compute. For example, in the depreciation illustration above the theoretical maximum operating hours is 14,600. This is irrelevant if the business operates an eight-hour working day and is closed at weekends and bank holidays. However, management should recognize that as depreciation is calculated as a time-based cost, it is possible to use the machine on a second and third shift and at weekends and bank holidays without adding to the depreciation cost if obsolescence is the determinant of the operating life.

A set-up illustration

Set-up is an important cost in many manufacturing industries. Traditional costing systems would not answer the question as to what set-up is expected to cost. Furthermore, the cost would be included in the indirect cost budget and attributed using a mechanism such as direct labour. This would have the effect of penalizing high-volume products that require long production runs and subsidizing low-volume products that require only short production runs. The following illustration shows how the attribution of set-up costs using direct labour as the cost driver leads to a serious error in product costs.

To change from one product to another has been costed at £200. The product is manufactured in three sizes. The 'midi' is the most popular size. It is expected to be set up four times next year. The 'mini' is less popular. It is expected to be set up five times next year. The 'maxi' is least popular. It is predicted to be set up nine times next year. Consider the allocation of the £3,600 set-up costs using traditional and activity-based costing methods shown in Table 10.17.

Table 10.17 *Traditional and ABC-based overhead attribution*

	Midi	**Mini**	**Maxi**	**Total**
Traditional attribution				
Volume produced and sold	10,000	1,000	750	
Direct labour budget	100,000	5,000	15,000	120,000
Set-up attributed (3% of direct labour)	3,000	150	450	3,600
Set-up cost per unit	30p	15p	60p	
ABC based attribution				
Volume produced and sold	10,000	1,000	750	
Set-up times	4	5	9	18
Set-up costs (times × £200)	800	1,000	1,800	3,600
Set-up cost per unit	8p	£1	£2.40	

The different attribution methods have a significant effect on product profitability. The ABC attribution correctly adds 22p per unit to the profit of the midi. The traditional cost attribution punishes the high-volume midi by failing to recognize that the large throughput has a beneficial impact on unit cost. Equally, the unit profit of the mini and maxi is overstated by 85p and £1.80 respectively because the high set-up cost per unit of low-throughput products is not recognized. Once the manufacturer becomes aware of this, it is sensible to consider a pricing policy that encourages customers to buy the high-volume midi and not to buy the low-volume mini and maxi.

The logic of this leads me to conclude that large manufacturers will attempt to eliminate demand for low-volume, high-hassle products by dramatic increases in the prices they quote. Happily, this will create interesting 'niche' opportunities for small companies that will be able to make good profits by selling low-volume, high-hassle products at high prices.

Set-up is a tiny proportion of total indirect cost. If the effect of attributing it on an activity basis is so great, it is easy to believe that attributing other indirect costs using such a methodology could substantially change product profitability

To compute reliable activity-based costs, you must budget for each activity correctly, define the cost driver, and define the idle capacity. Activities and possible cost drivers include:

Activities   **Suggested driver**
Procurement   Number of purchase transactions

Material handling	Product requisitions
Machining	Machine hours
Supervision	Time studies
Quality control	Time studies
Packaging	Packing hours
Shipping	Product specific
Product marketing	Product specific
Interest	Product capital employed
Credit control	Time studies

The important challenge is to recognize that some costs are not driven by either production or time and to identify the appropriate driver for cost attribution. Identifying logical drivers frequently involves detailed consultation with the staff who provide the service.

Some cost types are difficult to attribute to specific products or services. Such costs are driven by the entity rather than its products or services. Even in activity-based costing they are often attributed to products using variations on traditional overhead recovery mechanisms. Examples include:

Cost type	Suggested attribution
Corporate marketing	Budgeted product sales
Research	Budgeted product sales
Personnel	Budgeted head count
Staff training	Budgeted departmental usage

An activity-based costing illustration

This activity-based costing analysis (Table 10.18) shows that all products are making a significant contribution to the overall profit even though product B offers a much lower margin than the other two products.

The use of a traditional labour-based attribution shown in Table 10.19 suggests that product C is loss making. This is not correct. The reality is that as a 'low-hassle' product it is being asked to unfairly subsidize the true costs of products A and B.

Product C, which appeared to be loss making, is quite profitable. Product A is the most profitable, compared to the total costing conclusion that it was a small contributor. Product B, the shining star under traditional costing, earns the smallest profit when activity-based costing is used.

Table 10.18 *An activity-based costing illustration*

£'000	Product A	Product B	Product C	Total
Sales	10,000	16,000	9,000	35,000
Direct material	3,600	5,000	3,000	11,600
Direct labour	2,500	2,900	2,600	8,000
Total direct	6,100	7,900	5,600	19,600
Procurement	20	30	50	100
Material handling	100	340	60	500
Set-up	10	70	20	100
Machining	300	850	250	1,400
Supervision	150	450	200	800
Quality control	50	550	100	700
Packaging	120	440	40	600
Shipping	200	775	125	1,100
Marketing	500	1,840	810	3,150
Interest	250	600	150	1,000
Central costs	300	1,260	540	2,100
Total attributed	2,000	7,205	2,345	11,550
Total cost	8,100	15,105	7,945	31,150
Operating profit/(loss)	1,900	895	1,055	3,850
Unutilized capacity				450
Profit before tax				3,400

Table 10.19 *The application of labour-based overheads to the same products*

	Product A	Product B	Product C	Total
Sales	10,000	16,000	9,000	35,000
Direct material	3,600	5,000	3,000	11,600
Direct labour	2,500	2,900	2,600	8,000
Overhead 150%				
of direct labour	3,750	4,350	3,900	12,000
Total cost	10,250	12,250	9,500	31,600
Profit before tax	150	3,750	(500)	3,400
Contrast of profits reported				
ABC	1,900	895	1,055	
Traditional	150	3,750	(500)	
Error in traditional	1,750	2,855	1,555	

Customer and market profitability

As we have seen, good costing systems help to pinpoint profitable, marginal and unprofitable products and services. It is also true that some customers and markets are profitable, unprofitable and marginal. In the United States a major piece of research led to the identification of the rule of 20:225 in service industries. This rule states that 225 per cent of the profit of such an industry is earned from the top 20 per cent of customers. This means that if a business expects to earn a profit of £10 million, then it will earn a profit of £22.5 million from the top 20 per cent of customers and lose £12.5 million on the remaining 80 per cent. While I am not aware of similar research in the UK, I can confidently state that it is widely accepted that a similar situation exists. What drives the rule of 20:225? It is these facts: customer service is very expensive; labour tends to be the dominant cost in service industries; and this cost is a much higher proportion of a small transaction than a large one. Recognition of these facts has led to the development of computerized interfaces with customers through, for example, the use of ATMs.

It may not be practical to prepare a mini profit and loss account for each one of the thousands of small customers that buy from you. If it is not then you should decide to examine the profitability of customers in groups. For example, an insurance company would look at the profitability of selling motor insurance to individuals. On doing so it would almost certainly find that the people cost was a very high proportion of the premium as compared with fleet insurance. This should lead it to search for ways to make individual policies more profitable. A twofold attack leading to higher premiums and lower people costs (through the use of increased computerization) has emerged as the way to try to alter the 20:225 effect in the insurance industry.

The fact that customer service costs are high in service companies necessitates a change in the sequence of managing the hierarchy of costs. The facilities and technology costs need to be channelled into the staff costs. This is the opposite of the normal sequence in manufacturing companies.

TRANSFER PRICING

Transfer pricing is a system designed to charge for products or services created by one section of a business and supplied to another. This system has been used in jobbing industries such as printing and engineering for many years.

In recent times transfer pricing has been more extensively used for two reasons. First, companies designing activity-based costing systems have used transfer pricing as one of the methods intended to improve their attribution methods. Second, multinational businesses have found that they need to set prices for products or services created in one country and sold to a fellow subsidiary in another country. The price is often designed to ensure that the bulk of the profits are 'earned' in the country with the lowest corporation tax regime. Such prices must be carefully designed and not too greedy, as the tax authorities in many countries have realized that such schemes are depriving them of large amounts of tax revenue.

The fundamentals of an effective transfer pricing system

Earlier in this chapter I gave you an example of how costs that would have been indirect in an overall organization context could be made direct by collecting them in a cost centre. For example, in the printing business costs are attributed to a machine and charged out as products 'buy' time on the machine. This methodology has been widely applied in calculating the cost of activities for activity-based costing purposes.

There are four variations in the calculation of transfer prices:

1. the cost centre approach;
2. the profit centre approach;
3. the investment centre approach;
4. the market value approach.

Before we examine how transfer prices are computed in these approaches, some general comments need to be made. It has become widely recognized that the cost centre approach has a severe limitation. This is that the cost centre manager is effectively responsible for living within budget and is not really challenged to reduce costs or to search for value for money. When the transfer price includes a profit element, the centre manager realizes that the achievement of the profit goal can be aided by cost consciousness and value-for-money initiatives. Therefore it is reasonable to argue that the profit centre approach is superior to the cost centre one. However, it still has a drawback. This is that the centre manager is not challenged to try to optimize asset utilization. This ability to squeeze sales out of assets is an important aspect of centre effectiveness. The investment centre helps to focus on this by including a capital charge in the computation of the transfer price.

Examples of cost-, profit- and investment centre-based transfer prices

The following data have been budgeted for a key service centre in a business:

Volume (hours)	5,600	
Operating assets	£28,000	
Staff costs		£14,850
Space costs		£8,350
Technology costs		£21,600
		£44,800

A cost centre-based transfer price would be £8 per hour. This is derived by dividing the centre costs of £44,800 by the 5,600 hours that the centre is expected to produce and sell. The challenge for the centre manager is to live within the £44,800 budget and to produce and sell the 5,600 hours of output.

A profit centre-based transfer price where the unit was required to earn a margin of 20 per cent on its sales would be £10 per hour. This would yield a profit of £11,200 if the volume target were achieved while living within the cost budget. If demand for the output were falling below budget, the manager of the profit centre should be motivated to find cost reductions to compensate for the shortfall.

An investment centre transfer price would require the inclusion of a capital charge (say 10 per cent of the centre assets) in the charge-out rate. This would add £2,800 to the cost base and require a transfer price of £10.625 per hour if a 20 per cent profit were to be earned in the investment centre.

Setting sensible transfer prices

Once a section of a business decides to charge internal customers for the products or services that it creates, some difficult problems can occur. For example, the internal customer might find that the product or service could be bought more cheaply from a third party. If this is the case then the policy makers must decide whether the internal customer will be permitted to outsource. The problem with permitting outsourcing is unused internal capacity that results in idle but expensive fixed costs. A decision to permit outsourcing could result in the service centre asking to be permitted to sell to third parties. A decision to permit this leads to the difficult question as to who gets priority when there are internal and external emergency orders.

The transfer price must be designed to encourage actions that will optimize results for the business as a whole. In the language of finance this is called 'goal congruence'. To ensure this congruence organizations sometimes place an embargo on third party purchases and sales. Such a decision can lead to interdepartmental bitterness, particularly when internal customers believe they are being overcharged. The solution is to find a transfer price that assures goal congruence. The textbook solution is to set the transfer price at market value. To do so is sensible. However, two difficulties may be encountered. First, there is rarely a market price available for products that are at an intermediate stage of production. Second, sometimes a small service provider may be quoting an unsustainably low price in order to attract business.

Lack of goal congruence: an illustration

Door to Door Ltd delivers its products to customers all over England. The company has just decided to set up its delivery wing as an investment centre and to allow it to charge the sales and marketing unit for transport to customers. The budgeted data for next month are shown in Table 10.20.

Table 10.20 *Budgeted data for Door to Door Ltd*

	£
Drivers' and helpers' wages and fringe costs	85,624
Fuel, maintenance and depreciation	16,240
Space costs	22,400
Technology costs	15,736
Capital charge	20,000
	160,000
Mark-up 25%	40,000
Charges to be recovered	200,000

Of the cost budget, £32,000 is variable; it varies with the number of tonne/miles driven. The remaining £128,000 will remain constant, in the short term, regardless of the number of tonne/miles driven. The budgeted tonne/miles of deliveries for the month is 12,500. Consequently, a transfer price of £16 per tonne/mile has been set.

The marketing wing is divided into four regions that collectively account for the 12,500 tonne/miles. Of this total, 3,000 tonne/miles are budgeted for the northern division, also an investment centre, with a high profit target. The manager of the northern division has received a quote from a business acquaintance of £14.50 per tonne/mile. She decided to outsource her deliveries. The consequences for Door to Door overall are shown in Table 10.21.

Table 10.21   *The consequences of outsourcing deliveries for Door to Door Ltd*

	Outsource	**Insource**
Fixed	128,000	128,000
Variable (in house)	24,320[1]	32,000
Sub-contract cost	43,500[2]	–
	195,820	160,000

Notes:
[1] $9,500 \times £2.56 = 24,320$
[2] $3,000 \times £14.50 = 43,500$

This table shows that the total cost of deliveries rises by £35,820 if the northern division is allowed to outsource. At the same time the cost for the northern division will fall by £4,500. The transfer price is encouraging the northern division to take an action that is not consistent with the overall good of the organization. What is causing this lack of goal congruence? The root of the problem is that in the short term the fixed costs will be much the same whether the unit does 9,500 or 12,500 tonne/miles of deliveries. This means that with the northern division outsourcing its deliveries there will be 3,000 tonne/miles of unutilized capacity and consequent idle fixed costs. If Door to Door wishes to persist with the deliveries investment centre, then the only viable solution is to set the transfer price at £14.50. If this keeps the northern division deliveries in-house then goal congruence will be achieved. However, the transport investment centre will only earn a profit of £21,250.

This issue opens up the very important question of whether to insource or outsource the deliveries. There is really no middle ground in this case. If she wants to defend in-house deliveries the manager will have to find ways to reduce costs and to improve asset utilization. Possible options are:

- Impose the proposed price of £16 per tonne/mile.
- Use a market value-based transfer price of £14.50.
- Scrap the idea. Continue to treat transport as a central overhead. This effectively makes it 'free' to user departments.

International transfer pricing

The creation of production units charged with supplying overseas subsidiaries has led to special pricing considerations:

- The country where profits are taken can have a significant impact on the overall corporate tax bill. Tax rates vary considerably from country to country or even within countries such as the United States. To minimize group tax liabilities, organizations may sell part-manufactured goods to sister companies in tax havens at low prices. Their customers based in tax havens then finish the products and sell them to third parties at high prices. Artificial tax-based transfer pricing can have the following adverse consequences:
  - pressure for enormous wage settlements because of the 'paper' profits earned;
  - inadequate attention to cost control. Cost-saving initiatives may seem insignificant relative to profitability; and.
  - expensive litigation where tax authorities/governments feel the transfer pricing system is unfairly designed to dilute their tax collection potential.
- Subsidiaries in various countries bidding against each other for the right to make new corporate products paying scant attention to the real cost structure involved.
- Lack of contact with end users can cause a manufacturing department to lose sight of changing consumer requirements. Such contact helps to sharpen awareness of product needs and to encourage them to take a role in new product development.
- The network of marketing and overhead costs in other countries is often transferred to the production units through complicated cost or profit centre mechanisms. The danger of divisiveness arising from transfer pricing within a company multiplies when the costs are transferred from relatively invisible units abroad.

An international transfer pricing policy must be carefully designed to address the needs and expectations of various stakeholders. The key stakeholders in this case are managers, operatives, tax authorities and shareholders.

Illustrations of international transfer pricing systems are usually closely guarded secrets, particularly where their primary purpose is tax minimization.

SUMMARY

To be in control any business needs to understand that not all products, services, customers and markets yield equal profitability. Positive steps can be taken to improve profits or eliminate losses if the management team recognizes that problems exist in parts of their business. If the problems are to be correctly identified the business must prepare a series of mini profit and loss accounts that feed into the overall operating budget. As we have seen, traditional cost attribution systems are no longer reliable. Activity-based cost attributions need to be used. At the core of an effective activity-based costing system are the aggregation of data by activity as well as by type of expenditure; the identification and isolation of idle capacity; and the correct use of cost drivers to help in the attribution of costs to products, services, markets and customers.

If the aim of this chapter were to enable you to handle every complication that can arise in cost collection and attribution, it would have to run to hundreds of pages. My duty is to make you aware of the need for an excellent costing system in a modern competitive business. The installation of such a system will take months of work by a highly skilled management accountant or consultant.

There are many different types of costing systems in use in industry in the UK. These include: process costing, joint product costing, by-product costing, batch costing, standard costing, etc. Systems must be finely tuned to meet the specific conditions in the organization. To do justice to such systems would need a full book in itself. If you wish to develop an appropriate system for your company you will need to refer to one of the many excellent specialized texts on costing.

Large and diversified companies need to test the effectiveness of performance in small, manageable units. They do so by setting up sections of the group as performance centres. These can be cost centres, profit centres or investment centres. It is often difficult to set up such performance centres because their customer is often a related division and no market price exists. The key goal of a transfer pricing system must be to motivate buyer and seller sections to take actions that are consistent with optimizing group profitability. Failure to achieve this goal congruence leads to cost waste as expenditures are duplicated.

11

Contribution costing

Contribution costing is the key to setting sales targets. To apply it, the first step is to divide the budgeted costs of a business into their variable and fixed components. Variable costs are those that rise and fall in direct response to changes in volume. The classic example of a variable cost is direct materials. To understand why materials are a variable cost, consider the following.

Bert Barnsley bought 5,000 pairs of shoes at £15 each. In his first month of trading he sold 2,000 pairs at £20 each. How much gross profit did he earn, given that he still has 3,000 pairs to sell and that all of these are in saleable condition?

Common sense tells us that he made a gross profit of £5 per pair and a total gross profit of £10,000. The profit and loss account computes the same answer, as shown in Table 11.1.

Table 11.1 *Profit and loss account, version 1, Bert Barnsley*

		£
Sales		40,000
Purchases	75,000	
Less stock	45,000	
Cost of sales		30,000
Gross profit		10,000

The materials used (cost of sales) are 75 per cent of sales and the gross profit is 25 per cent of sales. If Bert had sold 3,000 pairs of shoes the profit and loss account would show the data in Table 11.2.

Table 11.2   *Profit and loss account, version 2, Bert Barnsley*

		£
Sales		60,000
Purchases	75,000	
Less stock	30,000	
Cost of sales		45,000
Gross profit		15,000

Once again the materials used are 75 per cent of sales and the gross profit is 25 per cent of sales. For as long as Bert can buy shoes at £15 per pair and sell them at £20 per pair, materials used will be 75 per cent of sales regardless of the number of pairs of shoes that he sells.

Other variable costs include piecework labour, royalties calculated as a percentage of sales, and commission paid to sales staff.

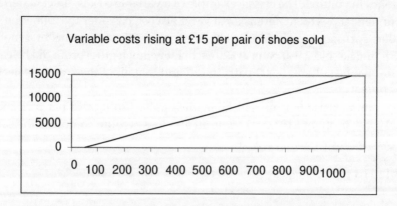

Figure 11.1   *Variable costs rising at the rate of £15 per pair of shoes*

Fixed costs are ones that remain the same regardless of volume. The classic example of a fixed cost is rent. The landlord does not care what quantity the tenant produces or sells; the rent remains the same. Other fixed costs include depreciation, rates, fire insurance and telephone rental.

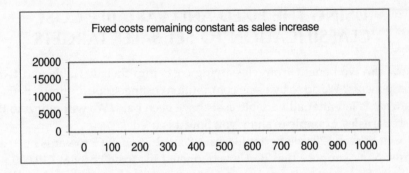

Figure 11.2 _Constant fixed costs as sales increase_

To use the contribution costing approach to set sales targets, all costs must be classified into fixed and variable components. In practice this is not as simple as it sounds. The major snag is that some fixed costs are constrained by a capacity ceiling.

Consider this problem. A manufacturing company uses a machine to make gadgets to sell to its customers. The machine can make 4,000 gadgets per week. The annual depreciation charge is a fixed cost. A problem would arise if the customers wanted to buy 5,000 gadgets per week. The company would have to buy another machine and this would result in a second depreciation charge. Does this nullify our classification of depreciation as a fixed cost? No. However, it points to the fact that some resources have a limited capacity and that if this capacity is breached it will be necessary to take on additional fixed costs. We will examine how the breaching of capacity is handled later in the chapter.

Interest charges are notoriously difficult to classify. It helps if you determine the reason why the borrowings were arranged. For example, interest on money borrowed to buy a truck is not influenced by sales volume and is a fixed cost. Interest rates rise and fall in response to supply and demand for cash, and government policy. Does this mean that interest on money borrowed to buy a machine should be classified as a variable cost? Certainly not. The variability of interest costs is driven by economic factors and not by the rises and falls in output that would make it a variable cost. Interest on money borrowed to fund investment in working capital is a variable cost. When sales are high the investment in stocks and debtors and the consequent borrowings and interest charges are high. When sales decline the stocks, debtors, borrowings and interest charges fall in response.

USING THE FIXED AND VARIABLE COST CLASSIFICATION TO SET SALES TARGETS

How can we benefit from classifying costs into their variable and fixed components? We do so by using contribution costing. Contribution is defined as what is left after all variable costs have been paid. We will return to the Bert Barnsley example to show you how it is used.

Out of each £20 sale Bert will earn a contribution of £5 towards his fixed costs. Now suppose that Bert has budgeted his fixed costs at £10,000 per month. He wants to know how many pairs of shoes he will need to sell to break even. Contribution costing tells us it is 2,000. We use the equation: contribution = fixed costs + profit. Applying this equation, we find that Bert needs to sell 2,000 pairs of shoes to break even:

$$\frac{\text{Contribution required}}{\text{Contribution per unit}} \qquad \frac{10,000 + 0}{5} = 2,000$$

Once he has sold 2,000 pairs of shoes Bert will earn a profit of £5 on each additional pair he sells. He wants to make a profit of £5,000 per month and has asked us how many pairs of shoes he will need to sell to achieve this. Contribution costing tells us it is a further 1,000 pairs in addition to the 2,000 required to break even. In this case the contribution required is £15,000:

$$\frac{\text{Contribution required}}{\text{Contribution per unit}} \qquad \frac{10,000 + 5,000}{5} = 3,000$$

The profit or loss that Bert would achieve at various volumes is shown in Table 11.3. Dividing the fixed costs by the £5 contribution per unit yields volume answers. These can readily be converted into money answers by multiplying the volume by the £20 sales price. This method can only be used when a company sells one product or service at one price. If two or more products are sold we must use a different method to calculate the break-even point and the sales required to yield the target profit. This method is based on the contribution sales ratio.

The contribution sales ratio

The contribution sales (CS) ratio is the percentage that the contribution is of the sales revenue. In the Bert Barnsley example it is 25 per cent. We can use this ratio to answer the two questions posed earlier in the chapter. First, Bert

Table 11.3 _Profit or loss at various volumes, Bert Barnsley_

Sales volume	1,000	2,000	3,000	4,000	5,000
Sales revenue	20,000	40,000	60,000	80,000	100,000
Variable cost	15,000	30,000	45,000	60,000	75,000
Contribution	5,000	10,000	15,000	20,000	25,000
Fixed cost	10,000	10,000	10,000	10,000	10,000
Profit/(loss)	(5,000)	–	5,000	10,000	15,000

asked how much he would need to sell to break even. The CS ratio answers this question using the following equation: 25 per cent of sales = £10,000 + 0. Bert solves this equation to find the break-even sales. It is £40,000 and corresponds with the 2,000 pairs found using the £5 contribution per unit method.

Second, Bert asked for the value of sales required to earn him a profit of £5,000. The CS ratio answers this question using the following equation: 25 per cent of sales = £10,000 + £5,000 (£10,000 for fixed costs and £5,000 for profit). Solving this equation, Bert finds he needs £60,000 of sales. Again this is the same answer as the contribution per unit method yielded, as it must be.

The CS ratio method is the only satisfactory way to compute the target sales when two or more products are sold. In his original plan Bert was selling only men's shoes. He has decided to diversify into ladies' shoes. He will buy them at £24 per pair and will sell them for £40 per pair. The CS ratio for ladies' shoes is 40 per cent. Since Bert will need additional selling space and staff he has recomputed the fixed costs and now expects them to be £22,750. Once again Bert wishes to calculate the break-even sales. This cannot be reliably computed without first forecasting the proportions of men's and ladies' shoes in the sales mix. The greater the proportion of men's shoes in the mix, the higher will be the break-even point. The greater the proportion of ladies' shoes in the mix, the lower will be the break-even point. Bert predicted that he would sell equal quantities of men's and ladies' shoes. He then worked out the contribution he would earn by selling 2,000 pairs of shoes in the forecast mix; see Table 11.4 (p 282).

The weighted average contribution sales ratio is 35 per cent. This is £21,000 expressed as a percentage of sales of £60,000. Using this, Bert can apply the formula: 35 per cent of sales = £22,750 + 0. Solving this equation, Bert finds that he needs to sell £65,000 worth of shoes to break even. Note that if Bert had used 4,000 pairs of shoes or 500 pairs of shoes he would still get a

Table 11.4 *Contribution from selling 2,000 pairs of shoes, Bert Barnsley*

	Men's	Ladies'	Total
Sales volume	1,000	1,000	2,000
Sales revenue	20,000	40,000	60,000
Variable cost	15,000	24,000	39,000
Contribution	5,000	16,000	21,000

contribution sales ratio of 35 per cent provided that he expected to sell equal quantities.

If Bert required a profit of £7,000 per month from his enlarged business he would use the formula: 35 per cent of sales = £22,750 + £7,000. Solving this, he finds a sales target of £85,000 per month. This is verified in Figure 11.3, where I have graphed the results for Bert Barnsley for volumes up to 5,000 pairs of men's and 5,000 pairs of ladies' shoes in equal quantities. The fixed cost line is set at £22,750 per month. The variable cost line is set at the average cost of £19.50 per pair of shoes. The total cost line is set at £22,750 per month plus £19.50 per pair. The sales line is set at £30 per pair. This is the average price when equal quantities are sold. The break-even point is 2,167 pairs of shoes where the sales and total cost lines intersect. Below this volume a loss of £10.50 will occur for each pair of shoes not sold. Above this volume the £10.50 contribution per pair of shoes sold is clear profit.

If Bert had predicted that sales would be in the proportion of two pairs of men's for each pair of ladies' shoes he would have had to recompute the weighted average CS ratio. Before reading on, pause for a moment and try to decide whether the break-even point will rise or fall as a result of this change in product mix.

I hope you decided that the break-even point will rise. This is because there is a higher proportion of lower-margin men's shoes in the new mix. We must now calculate the new weighted average CS ratio. For convenience of calculation we will use a sample of 3,000 pairs of shoes and calculate the break-even sales given fixed costs of £22,750.

Based on the new mix, the contribution sales ratio falls to 32.5 per cent. This is £26,000 expressed as a percentage of sales of £80,000; see Table 11.5.

Using the contribution formula Bert calculates the break-even sale as 32.5 per cent of sales = £22,750. Solving this equation, Bert finds that he needs to sell £70,000 worth of shoes to break even.

In Figure 11.4 (p 284) I graphed the results for volumes up to 12,000 pairs of shoes in the proportion two pairs of men's to one pair of ladies' shoes. The

	Men's	Ladies'	Total
Sales revenue	28,333	56,667	85,000
Variable cost	21,250	34,000	55,250
Contribution	7,083	22,667	29,750
Fixed costs			22,750
Profit			7,000

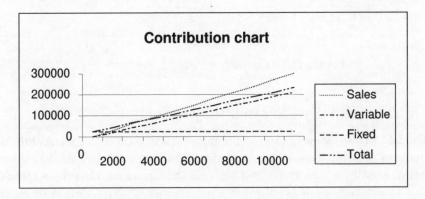

Figure 11.3   *Contribution chart, Bert Barnsley*

Table 11.5   *Contribution from selling 3,000 pairs of shoes, Bert Barnsley*

	Men's	**Ladies'**	**Total**
Sales volume	2,000	1,000	3,000
Sales revenue	40,000	40,000	80,000
Variable cost	30,000	24,000	54,000
Contribution	10,000	16,000	26,000

fixed cost line is set at £22,750 per month. The variable cost line is set at £18 per pair. The total cost line is set at £22,750 per month plus £18 per pair of shoes sold. The sales line is set at £26.67 per pair. This is the average price per pair taking into account the mix of 2:1 in favour of men's shoes. The break-even point is 2,625 pairs of shoes where the sales and total cost lines intersect. Below this volume a loss of £8.67 will occur for each pair of shoes not sold. Above this volume the £8.67 contribution per pair of shoes sold is clear profit.

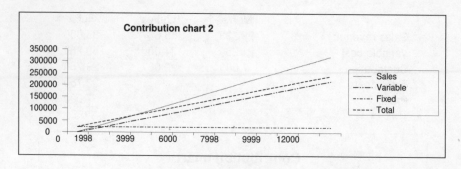

Figure 11.4 *Contribution chart 2, Bert Barnsley*

Dealing with a wide range of products

The last two examples pinpoint the importance of product mix. A shift in demand towards the low-margin product leads to a rise in the break-even point. Equally, a shift in demand towards the higher margin product leads to a fall in the break-even point. Product mix is so important in most businesses that their management accounts must monitor it and the contribution earned as a result.

The public house business is an interesting example of the importance of product mix. Many public houses serve food as well as drink. Product mix can be divided into five broad categories: beers, spirits, mixers, food and wines. The problem in planning and control is that each category contains a variety of products that offer different margins. For example, a number of brands of ale, stout and lager will be on sale. Some of these will be priced to suit the pocket of ordinary working people. Others are high-margin 'designer' labels. Control of such product ranges can be done using a spreadsheet. The size of the spreadsheet would be enormous if every single brand and food item were calculated separately down to the contribution line. For this reason publicans and many other businesses that offer a wide range of products plan and control using product groups that offer similar margins.

The sampling technique we used earlier in the chapter to calculate the weighted average contribution sales ratio becomes awkward when assessing a large number of products. For this reason we will examine a different way to calculate it.

The first step is to express the sales of each product group as a percentage of total sales. For example, if Bert expects to sell equal quantities then men's shoes will represent 33.33 per cent of turnover and ladies' shoes 66.67 per cent. If Bert expects to sell twice as many men's shoes as ladies' then each product group represents 50 per cent of turnover.

The second step is to calculate the contribution sales ratio for each product group. As we have seen, Bert forecasts 25 per cent for men's shoes and 40 per cent for ladies' shoes.

The final step is to multiply the CS ratio for each product group by the turnover percentage. When these results are totalled you get the weighted average contribution sales ratio; see Table 11.6.

Table 11.6 *Weighted average CS ratio, Bert Barnsley*

	Equal quantities			**2:1**		
	Men's	*Ladies'*	*Total*	*Men's*	*Ladies'*	*Total*
Turnover (%)	33.33	66.67		50	50	
	×	×		×	×	
CS ratio	25%	40%		25%	40%	
Weighted CS input	8.33% + 26.67% = 35%			12.5% + 20% = 32.5%		

We will now apply this method to the budgeted sales and the contribution sales ratios for the product groups to be sold in a public house; see Table 11.7.

Table 11.7 *Weighted average CS ratio for a public house*

Product group	CS range	Average CS ratio	% Total sales	Weighted contribution
Beers	36%–48%	40%	36%	14.40%
Spirits	45%–56%	48%	32%	15.36%
Mixers	50%–56%	52%	8%	4.16%
Food	44%–66%	56%	15%	8.40%
Wines	67%	67%	9%	6.03%
			100%	48.35%

The weighted average contribution sales ratio is 48.35 per cent. If the fixed cost budget is £580,200 then the break-even sales target is £1.2 million. To earn a profit of £200,000 will require a turnover of £1.61 million.

The calculations become cumbersome if each brand is handled separately. To keep the calculations to a minimum the publican had estimated the contribution margin for each product group. For example, the CS ratio for beers was estimated for a range of brands that would yield margins from 36 per cent for the lowest to 48 per cent for the highest. In computing the average he took into account that in his pub the bulk of the beer sales were in the lower-margin brands.

The margin of safety

Bert Barnsley set the sales budget at £90,000 per month. He had predicted that:

- The quantity of men's shoes would be twice that of ladies'.
- The selling prices would be £20 per pair of men's shoes and £40 per pair of ladies' shoes.
- The variable costs would be £15 per pair of men's shoes and £24 per pair of ladies' shoes.
- The fixed costs would be £22,750 per month.

On the basis of these data he prepared his overall budget, as shown in Table 11.8.

Table 11.8 *Overall budget, Bert Barnsley*

	Men's	Ladies'	Total
Sales volume	2,250	1,125	3,375
Sales revenue	45,000	45,000	90,000
Variable cost	33,750	27,000	60,750
Contribution	11,250	18,000	29,250
Fixed cost			22,750
Profit forecast			6,500

Bert needs to be aware of the margin of safety contained in his budget. This is calculated by dividing the excess of budgeted sales over break-even sales by the budget sales. In this case the margin of safety is just over 22 per cent. The calculation is:

$$\frac{\text{Budget excess}}{\text{Budget}} \quad \frac{90,000 - 70,000}{90,000} \quad \text{per cent} = 22.2 \text{ per cent}$$

It should be comforting to Bert to know that sales could fall by 22.2 per cent before his business would become loss making.

CAPACITY COSTS AND THEIR EFFECT ON A PROFIT FORECAST

As mentioned earlier in the chapter some fixed costs are subject to a capacity ceiling. If the business needs to produce and sell more than this ceiling it will be necessary to take on additional fixed costs. In this situation there can be more than one break-even point and the business could make a profit by operating at a lower capacity but a loss by operating at a higher capacity.

Consider the following. Bert is trying to decide whether to rent a larger shop or not. If he does not do so he considers that space will limit him to selling £90,000 worth of shoes. The larger shop will add £11,375 per month to his fixed costs. He believes the product mix will continue to be two pairs of men's shoes for each one pair of ladies' shoes. Compare the results of the smaller and larger shops; see Table 11.9.

Table 11.9 *Comparative costs of a small and large shop, Bert Barnsley*

Sales	Contribution	Small shop Profit/(loss)	Large shop Profit/(loss)
50,000	16,250	(6,500)	(17,875)
60,000	19,500	(3,250)	(14,625)
70,000	22,750	–	(11,375)
80,000	26,000	3,250	(8,125)
90,000	29,250	6,500	(4,875)
100,000	32,500		(1,625)
105,000	34,125		–
110,000	35,750		1,625
120,000	39,000		4,875
125,000	40,625		6,500

This table shows that the larger shop is much more risky:

- The break-even sales will rise to £105,000 per month, a 50 per cent increase.

- To earn a profit of £6,500 per month will require sales of £125,000.
- He would be unwise to move to the bigger shop unless he was confident that sales would exceed £125,000 per month, as he would otherwise be taking on substantial extra risk without earning a commensurate increase in reward.

Examples of fixed costs that can be affected by capacity limitations include:

- Area costs (essentially fixed). They grow if you need a greater area.
- Fixed production costs: supervision, quality control, production management, machine costs, depreciation, maintenance contracts and insurance.
- Administration costs: additional accounting and human resources staff.
- Fixed selling and distribution costs: warehouse and display space, transport fixed costs depreciation (more vehicles), tax and insurance (more vehicles) and more drivers.

Limiting factors

A limiting factor is the item that places a ceiling on growth. In the Bert Barnsley example it was the shortage of space that limited the sales capacity to £90,000 with a single shop. The limiting factor can be a shortage of:

- customer demand;
- supply of raw material;
- skilled labour;
- production machinery/space;
- working capital finance.

If the limiting factor is not customer demand then the contribution sales ratio may encourage a business to adopt an inappropriate marketing strategy. The ratio can be adapted to reflect the limiting factor, so as to overcome this defect.
   Consider a business that sells four products; see Table 11.10.

Contribution per £1 of sales

If the limiting factor is customer demand of £100,000, then sales staff should try to encourage customers towards product 1. It offers the highest contribution per £1 of sales; see Table 11.11.

Table 11.10 _Limiting factors for a company selling four products_

Product	1	2	3	4
Unit selling price	1.00	2.00	5.00	10.00
Unit material	0.60	0.50	3.75	4.50
Unit labour	0.10	1.00	0.25	4.00
Unit contribution	0.30	0.50	1.00	1.50
Production hours	2	3	4	3.6
Working capital/sales (%)	40	20	25	10

Table 11.11 _Contribution per £ of sales of the four products_

Product	1	2	3	4
Sales	100,000	100,000	100,000	100,000
CS ratio (%)	30	25	20	15
Contribution	**30,000**	25,000	20,000	15,000
Promotional sequence	(a)	(b)	(c)	(d)

Contribution per £1 of materials

If the same material is used in all four products and only £47,250 of this material is expected to be available, then sales staff should try to encourage customers towards product 2. It maximizes contribution per £1 of materials; see Table 11.12.

Table 11.12 _Contribution per £ of materials of the four products_

Product	1	2	3	4
Material	47,250	47,250	47,250	47,250
Contribution/material ratio (%)[1]	50	100	26.7	33.3
Contribution	23,625	**47,250**	12,600	15,750
Promotional sequence	(b)	(a)	(d)	(c)
[1] Unit contribution	£0.30	£0.50	£1	£1.50
Unit material	£0.60	£0.50	£3.75	£4.50
Contribution per £ materials	50%	100%	26.7%	33.3%

Contribution per £1 of labour

If the same production staff make all four products and only £19,500 of work can be produced, then sales staff should try to encourage customers towards product 3 because it maximizes contribution per £1 of labour; see Table 11.13.

Table 11.13 *Contribution per £ of labour for the four products*

Product	1	2	3	4
Skilled labour	19,500	19,500	19,500	19,500
Contribution/labour ratio (%)[2]	300	50	400	37.5
Contribution	58,500	9,750	**78,000**	7,313
Promotional sequence	(b)	(c)	(a)	(d)
[2] Unit contribution	£0.30	£0.50	£1	£1.50
Unit labour	£0.10	£1.00	£0.25	£4.00
Contribution per £ labour	300%	50%	400%	37.5%

Contribution per machine hour

If the four products are made on the same machine and 120,000 machine hours are available, then sales staff should try to encourage customers towards product 4 because it maximizes contribution per machine hour; see Table 11.14.

Table 11.14 *Contribution per machine hour for the four products*

Product	1	2	3	4
Production hours	120,000	120,000	120,000	120,000
Contribution per hour [3]	15p	16.7p	25p	41.7p
Contribution	18,000	20,000	30,000	**50,000**
Promotional sequence	(d)	(c)	(b)	(a)
[3] Unit contribution	£0.30	£0.50	£1	£1.50
Hours per unit	2	3	4	3.6
Contribution per hour	15p	16.7p	25p	41.7p

Contribution per £1 of working capital investment

If only £25,000 of working capital finance is available, then sales staff should try to encourage customers towards product 4. It maximizes contribution per £1 of working capital invested; see Table 11.15.

Table 11.15 _Contribution per £ of working capital for the four products_

Product	1	2	3	4
Working capital	25,000	25,000	25,000	25,000
Contribution per £ capital[4]	75%	125%	80%	150%
Contribution	18,750	31,250	20,000	**37,500**
Promotional sequence	(d)	(b)	(c)	(a)
[4] Unit contribution	£0.30	£0.50	£1	£1.50
Working capital per unit	£0.40	£0.40	£1.25	£1
Contribution per £ of working capital	0.75	1.25	0.80	1.50

You will find that the display strategy in good retailers follows the principles outlined above. High-contribution lines are given a lot of display space. Low-contribution lines get little display space. Items in short supply also get little display space.

In spite of the implications of maximizing contribution per £1 of limiting factor, a prudent business will try to sell a variety of products. If only one line is sold, a collapse in demand or an increase in variable costs could reduce earnings drastically. A portfolio of products offers protection against this danger. Also, customers get annoyed if a full range of products is not available, and customers who intend to buy low-contribution items often also make impulse purchases of high-margin items. This is particularly important in retailing.

OPERATING LEVERAGE

Operating leverage is the relationship between contribution and profit. Consider the budget for two companies shown in Table 11.16 (p 292).

291

Table 11.16 *Budgets for Company A and Company B*

£'000	Company A		Company B	
Sales		100		100
Variable costs		80		20
Contribution	⟶	20	⟶	80
Fixed costs		10		70
Profit	⟶	10	⟶	10

Company A has a low CS ratio and low fixed costs. The operating leverage is 2:1. Company B has a high CS ratio and high fixed costs. Its operating leverage is 8:1. Company B will be much more grievously damaged by depressed economic conditions.

Table 11.17 *The effect of a 20 per cent reduction in sales, Company A and Company B*

£'000	Company A	Company B
Sales	80	80
Variable costs	64	16
Contribution	16	64
Fixed costs	10	70
Profit/(loss)	6	(6)

Note:
Company B makes a loss whereas Company A still makes a profit.

Table 11.18 *The effect of a 25 per cent increase in sales, Company A and Company B*

£'000	Company A	Company B
Sales	125	125
Variable costs	100	25
Contribution	25	100
Fixed costs	10	70
Profit/(loss)	15	30

Note:
The profit of company A rises by 50% whereas the profit of company B rises by 200%.

Consider the effect of a 20 per cent reduction in sales on both companies, shown in Table 11.17, and the effect of a 25 per cent increase in sales on both companies, shown in Table 11.18. We can conclude that company B will be severely damaged by a recession but will benefit greatly from a boom. Company A is much better placed to cope with a recession but the potential for growth in boom conditions is more limited.

Operating leverage is heavily influenced by the nature of the industry. Capital-intensive industries nearly always have high fixed costs and operating leverage. Nuclear power generation is an industry with enormous fixed costs. It needs a very high CS ratio. Other examples of capital-intensive highly leveraged industries include cement manufacturing, telecommunications and railways. At the other extreme we find craft industries with low contribution sales ratios and low fixed costs. An extreme example of low operating leverage is a car boot sale.

Can a company protect itself against the worst ravages of recession? It can to some extent by reducing the fixed costs and consequently the operating leverage. It is a good generalization that in-house services tend to be fixed costs while outsourced services tend to be variable costs. Consider distribution. The cost of postal deliveries rises and falls in response to the volume transported. Conversely, many of the costs of running a company's own delivery van (driver's wages, depreciation, road tax) are fixed. The increasing trend towards outsourcing helps to reduce operating leverage, smooth profit expectations and solve the problem of idle capacity. This strategic initiative becomes very attractive when the outlook for sales is discouraging. Another action that will reduce operating leverage is a move from debt towards equity financing. There is no better time to arrange a rights issue (sell more shares for cash) and use the cash to reduce bank borrowings and interest charges than when a recession is looming. The equity will then only have to be rewarded in line with performance, whereas the debt would have to be rewarded regardless of performance.

Should operating leverage have important implications for investment strategy? Companies with high operating leverage tend to produce very disappointing results in the depths of recession. If an investor feels confident that economic conditions are about to improve then this is the ideal time to invest in such companies. Profits will take off as sales grow. This is because there is a multiplier effect in operating leverage. The effect is that any percentage change in sales will result in a change in profits that is the change in sales multiplied by the operating leverage. We will return to companies A and B to show you how it works; see Table 11.19 (p 294).

Table 11.19 *The multiplier effect in operating leverage, Company A and Company B*

	Budget		
£'000	Company A	Sales –20%	Sales +25%
Sales	100	80	125
Variable costs	80	64	100
Contribution	20	16	25
Fixed costs	10	10	10
Profit	10	6	15
Decrease in profits (20% × 2)		40%	
Increase in profits (25% × 2)			50%

	Budget		
£'000	Company A	Sales–20%	Sales +25%
Sales	100	80	125
Variable costs	20	16	25
Contribution	80	64	100
Fixed costs	70	70	70
Profit	10	(6)	30
Decrease in profits (20% × 8)		160%	
Increase in profits (25% × 8)			200%

Once the break-even point is passed, the profits of a highly leveraged business will grow rapidly. Astute investors will buy such shares, as the share price should follow the profit growth. The converse also applies. If an investor thinks the economic outlook is discouraging, a speedy exit from investment in industries that are fixed cost-intensive is indicated.

SUMMARY

A vital piece of information for any company is its break-even point. This is easily calculated for a company with only one product. You simply divide the contribution per unit by the fixed cost budget and this tells you the quantity you must sell to break even. When a variety of products are for sale, particularly at different contribution margins, this method will not work. The

CS ratio method examined in this chapter shows how the break-even point is calculated in a multi-product business. However, if the sales mix turns out to be different from what was predicted, the break-even point will change. For this reason, any business that offers a variety of products or services needs to prepare control information down to the contribution level. Once the break-even point has been passed, the contribution from each additional £1 of sales is pure profit.

Marketing effort should be focused on products and services that offer the highest contribution margins even though retailers often use 'loss leaders' to attract customers with the intention of tempting them to buy higher-margin lines.

Capital-intensive industries have a high break-even point. If the break-even sales target is not reached, large losses are incurred. Once the break-even point is passed, profits will grow rapidly in such industries. If the economic outlook is discouraging then investors are advised to sell any shares they hold in such industries immediately. If the economic outlook is encouraging then investors are advised to consider buying shares in such industries, as share prices should rise very rapidly as volumes recover.

Part IV

Finance techniques for developing the organization

12

Capital investment
decisions

Capital investment decisions are among the most important items on the
agenda for board meetings. A decision to accept a major proposal that
subsequently turns sour can wreck a healthy organization. Directors and
managers need to be skilled at assessing the risks and rewards promised by
investment proposals and the results of the appraisal tools applied to them.

The calculations involved in a substantial project can be lengthy and
complicated. For this reason projects are normally evaluated using computer
spreadsheets. Managers and board members will not normally be involved
in the application of the evaluation tools. However, they must understand
what the tools set out to test and know how to interpret the results. To help
you to this understanding I have included a number of examples in this
chapter. It will be hard work but you can console yourself that it will enhance
your interpretative skills and could even help you to reject a potentially
disastrous investment proposal.

The chapter helps you to understand how a capital investment proposal
is analysed and whether you should accept or reject it. It is divided into five
main sections:

1. Shows you how to test the adequacy of the returns promised.
2. Examines errors and risks associated with such cash forecasts.
3. Shows you how to assess the cost of capital.
4. Looks at the barriers that can be erected to stop projects that:
   - do not promise an adequate return;
   - are being commissioned without passing through the test and approval phase;
   - although promising a good return, cannot be funded because all the cash available has been committed to better projects.
5. Summarizes the rules required to create an excellent investment appraisal policy.

THE APPRAISAL TOOLS

Six tools can be applied to the cash flows to help a board to assess an investment proposal:

1. return on investment (ROI);
2. payback;
3. net present value (NPV);
4. internal rate of return (IRR);
5. modified internal rate of return (MIRR);
6. economic value (EVA).

I will demonstrate the use of each tool by applying it to the cash flow forecasts for an investment proposal submitted to the board of the Model Company. The key data for the project are:

- The cost of the plant and machinery will be £400,000.
- The expected selling cycle is four years.
- Sales quantities and prices; see Table 12.1.

Table 12.1 *Forecast sales, Model Company*

Year	Units	Per unit
1	1,000	£300
2	1,600	£300
3	2,500	£250
4	1,500	£250

- The machine capacity is 3,000 units per annum.
- Forecast operating costs (£'000) are as shown in Table 12.2.

Table 12.2 *Forecast operating costs, Model Company*

Year	Materials	Labour	Overheads	Total
1	60	40	50	150
2	96	64	60	220
3	150	100	80	330
4	90	60	50	200

Should the board approve the proposal? They will need the appraisal tools to be applied to the project cash flows in order to help them decide whether to accept or reject it.

Method 1. Return on investment

You will remember from Chapter 6 that ROI is measured by expressing profit before interest and tax as a percentage of total assets. To measure the ROI we must prepare project profit and loss account forecasts. These and the ROI calculations are shown in Table 12.3.

Table 12.3 *The forecast profit and loss accounts and ROI for the Model Company project (£'000)*

Years	1	2	3	4	Total
Sales	300	480	625	375	1,780
Materials	60	96	150	90	396
Labour	40	64	100	60	264
Other	50	60	80	50	240
Depreciation	100	100	100	100	400
Cost excluding interest	250	320	430	300	1,300
Profit before interest	50%	160%	195%	75%	480
Total assets[1]	400	400	400	400	
ROI	12.5%	40%	48.75%	18.75%	

Note:
[1] Based on the original investment cost.

In Chapter 6 I suggested that ROI is an excellent test of management effectiveness. It is frequently applied to investment proposals. As an appraisal tool it suffers from two serious problems. These problems are such that ROI should only be used to eliminate proposals that do not merit more detailed investigation. In Table 12.4 you will see that average ROI fails to indicate that project B is better than project A. This is because a premium is not placed on the front-end loading of its cash flows

In Table 12.5, I compare projects with different lives and conclude that ROI will not tell you whether 15 per cent over three years or 14 per cent over four years is better.

Table 12.4 *The problem of front and back loading of cash flows using ROI*

Year	£'000	A	B	Change in profit if B preferred
0	Total investment	500	500	
1	Profit before interest	80	140	+60
2	Profit before interest	90	110	+20
3	Profit before interest	110	90	−20
4	Profit before interest	140	80	−60
	Average annual profit	105	105	
	Average annual return on investment	21%	21%	

Table 12.5 *The problem with comparing projects with different lives*

Year	£'000	C	D	Project C preferred
0	Investment	400	400	
1	Profit before interest	50	30	+20
2	Profit before interest	55	50	+5
3	Profit before interest	75	80	−5
4	Profit before interest	–	64	−64
	Average annual profit	60	56	
	Average return on investment	15%	14%	

These examples point to the need for a more searching test of the timing of project cash flows. Return on investment cannot handle timing properly.

Method 2. Payback

Payback is used to test how quickly you recover your investment. In calculating it we will assume that all cash flows occur at year end. The payback is calculated in Table 12.6.

Table 12.6 _The payback from the Model Company project_

Year		£'000
0	Capital investment	−400
1	Net cash flow	150
	Balance outstanding	−250
2	Net cash flow	260
	Project surplus	10

To calculate the payback from a project you deduct the future cash inflows year by year until the cost of the investment has been recouped. In the Model Company project £250,000 remains invested in the project after one year, but £260,000 of cash is recovered in the second year. If the forecast cash flows are correct the investment will be repaid in less than two years. Note that since depreciation is not a cash cost it is not taken into account in a payback analysis. The financing cost is also ignored in payback evaluation. It can be handled more satisfactorily by the methods examined later.

Payback also has defects as an investment appraisal tool. In Table 12.7 (p 304) we compare two further projects. Since both have a three-year payback period it might appear to be a toss-up as to which to support. Payback ignores two important factors that relate to these projects: the front-end loading of the cash flows in project F, and the fact that project E offers a bigger cash flow beyond the payback period. More sophisticated appraisal tools will show that project E is very attractive and project F is quite unattractive.

Payback is a good screening tool. It eliminates projects that depend too much on long-term cash flows. This is desirable in cases where products or services are exposed to rapid changes in demand or technology. For example, a computer software designer would need to recover its investment before imitators bring 'me-too' projects on stream.

The timing defects of payback were recognized in the 1960s and it went out of fashion as an appraisal tool. In the 1970s it came back into fashion as inflation accelerated dramatically and changes in technology and customer demand increased. These changes made it far more difficult to predict long-

Table 12.7 *The failure of payback to identify the fact that project E is more attractive*

Year		Project E £	Project F £
0	Total investment	20,000	20,000
1	Cash return	3,000	10,000
2	Cash return	7,000	7,000
3	Cash return	10,000	3,000
4	Cash return	15,000	1,000

Note:
Each project recovers the investment of £20,000 in exactly three years.

term cash flows with confidence and rightly restored the emphasis on early recovery of the amount invested. Payback is now widely used but only as a part of the investment decision process. It focuses on the fact that the more quickly you can recover your investment, the lower will be the risk. A good rule of thumb is that projects other than infrastructure development should not be undertaken if the payback period is longer than four years. Many businesses that created capacity based on forecasts of long-term sales growth still regret that they ignored payback. A classic example is Burmah Oil. In the 1970s it commissioned giant tankers in the expectation of increasing oil consumption. As a result of the oil crises the demand fell, leading to disastrous utilization and operating losses.

The timing aspect of project cash flows

The key element of my criticism of both ROI and payback is their inability to adequately reflect the timing of cash flows. To do so you need to be able to calculate the present value of future cash flows. This is done using discounting. The first step to understanding discounting is the related issue of compounding. Remember your early days at school. The teacher asks: if you deposited £100 in a bank deposit account at a fixed interest rate of 10 per cent pa and did not withdraw the interest, how much would be on deposit at the end of three years? In answering this question you may assume there is no withholding tax. Most adults would use what I call a mental ladder to answer this question. They would say:

£100 plus 10%   = £110
£110 plus 10%   = £121
£121 plus 10%   = £133.10

The mental arithmetic involved is not too difficult. Suppose that the next question involved a deposit of £100 for eight years at 7.5 per cent per annum. Most people would find the mental arithmetic too difficult. You could solve it using a spreadsheet or a calculator. The answer is £178.35.

At school we learnt a formula that helped us to answer compounding questions. It was:

$A = P \times (1.0R)^n$

where A = future amount, P = principal, R = rate of interest and n = number of years.

A compounding table at an interest rate of 7.5 per cent could also be used. I built Table 12.8 on a spreadsheet using logic similar to the mental ladder discussed above.

Table 12.8   *Compounding factors at 7.5 per cent per annum*

Year	Cell	Value	Logic
1	E6	1.0750	1 × 1.075
2	E7	1.1556	E6 × 1.075
3	E8	1.2423	E7 × 1.075
4	E9	1.3355	E8 × 1.075
5	E10	1.4356	E9 × 1.075
6	E11	1.5433	E10 × 1.075
7	E12	1.6590	E11 × 1.075
8	E13	1.7835	E12 × 1.075
9	E14	1.9172	E13 × 1.075
10	E15	2.0610	E14 × 1.075

When we multiply the deposit of £100 by the compound factor for eight years at 7.5 per cent we get £178.35.

Discounting

Now that you remember the mathematics of compounding we can examine the related issue of discounting. Suppose that a financial institution offered to pay you £133.10 in three years' time, what is the most you would be prepared to invest to pay for this promise? The answer depends on what you consider to be an acceptable return. Suppose that you require a return of 10 per cent pa from your investments. You should be prepared to pay up to £100 for the promised future cash flow. In the language of project appraisal the promise of £133.10 in three years' time is said to have a present value of £100. This is based on a restructuring of the compounding formula:

$$P = \frac{A}{(1.0R)^n}$$

We get an NPV of £100 when we solve this equation using:

A discount factor of 10% pa ($R = 0.1$)
A future amount of £133.10 ($A = 133.10$)
A period of three years ($n = 3$)

Put another way, £133.10 in three years' time is just as attractive as £100 now provided that we require a 10 per cent return on our deposit.

We use the principles of compounding to convert promised future cash flows into their present value. The best way to do this is to use a spreadsheet. In order to explain how the spreadsheet carries out the discounting process we will now consider a discounting table similar to the compounding table presented in Table 12.8.

Table 12.9 *A discounting table at 7.5 per cent pa*

Year	Cell	Value	Logic
1	E6	0.9302	1/1.075
2	E7	0.8653	E6/1.075
3	E8	0.8050	E7/1.075
4	E9	0.7488	E8/1.075
5	E10	0.6966	E9 x 1.075
6	E11	0.6480	E10/1.075
7	E12	0.6028	E11/1.075
8	E13	0.5607	E12/1.075
9	E14	0.5216	E13/1.075
10	E15	0.4852	E14/1.075
11	E16	0.4513	E15/1.075
12	E17	0.4199	E16/1.075

To use Table 12.9 to find the present value of a future cash flow at a discount rate of 7.5 per cent, you multiply the promised cash flow by the relevant discount rate. For example, if you expect a cash flow of £10,000 in five years time then you multiply this by 0.6966 and get a present value of £6,966. To verify that you will get a 7.5 per cent return on the money invested we will examine a deposit account that earns an interest rate of 7.5 per cent for five years; see Table 12.10.

Table 12.10   _Using a deposit table to verify the present value of £10,000_

Deposit of £6965.58 for 5 years at 7.5% pa

Year		
0	Deposit	6965.58
1	Interest	522.42
	Balance	7488.00
2	Interest	561.60
	Balance	8049.60
3	Interest	603.72
	Balance	8653.32
4	Interest	649.00
	Balance	9302.32
5	Interest	697.67
	Balance	10000.00

Discounting solves the problem of timing that was at the heart of my criticism of ROI and payback. Discounting is used in the remaining four investment appraisal tools.

Method 3. Net Present Value (NPV)

NPV is used to discount future cash flows to their value today. When there are substantial calculations involved it is best to use discount tables or a spreadsheet. Both methods are now used to calculate the NPV of the Model Company project. In Table 12.11 (p 308) the calculations were done manually. In Table 12.13 the calculations were done on my Microsoft Excel spreadsheet.

Before you read on, I have two tasks for you. These will make sure that you understand the computation of NPV. The first task is to prepare discount

Table 12.11 *The NPV of the Model Company project at 10% using discount tables*

Year	Cash flows[1]	Discount factor 10%[2]	Present Value
1	150,000	0.90909	136,364
2	260,000	0.82645	214,876
3	295,000	0.75131	221,638
4	175,000	0.68301	119,527
			692,405
Less investment			400,000
Net present value			292,405

Notes:

[1] The cash flows are taken from the project profit and loss accounts at the start of the chapter.

[2] The discount factors are: a) Year 1, $1/1.1 = 0.90909$; b) Year 2, $0.90909/1.1 = 0.82645$. The logic behind the NPV of £292,405 is that if you attended an auction and were considering your bid for a job lot offering:

    a) £150,000 in one year's time   b) £260,000 in two years' time

    c) £295,000 in three years' time   d) £175,000 in four years' time

and you required a return of 10% on the cost of your investment then you should be prepared to bid up to £692,405 for it. If you are lucky enough to buy the lot for £400,000 then you will receive a premium, expressed in money of today, of £292,405 over the 10% return you require.

factors based on an assumption that the Model Company requires a return of 15 per cent on investments. The second task is to compute the NPV of the Model Company project using the discount factors you created.

The discount factors are: a) year one $1/1.15 = 0.86957$; b) year two $0.86957/1.15 = 0.75614$; c) year three $0.75614/1.15 = 0.65752$; and d) year four $0.65752/1.1 = 0.57175$. The NPV of the Model Company project at 15 per cent is shown in Table 12.12.

Using an Excel spreadsheet to calculate NPV

A spreadsheet helps to take the drudgery out of NPV calculations and reduces the risk of mathematical error. You enter the project cash flows into a series of cells and use the =NPV command to instruct the spreadsheet to calculate the net present value. Using the =NPV command you do not see the discount factors being applied to the cash flows but the cell in which the command is entered shows the result of the discounting process. The NPV of the Model Company project reproduced from my spreadsheet is shown in Table 12.13.

Table 12.12 _The NPV of the Model Company project if a 15 per cent return is required_

Year	Cash flow	Discount factor 15%	NPV
1	150	0.86957	130,435
2	260	0.75614	196,597
3	295	0.65742	193,967
4	175	0.57175	100,057
			621,056
Less investment			400,000
Net present value			221,056

Table 12.13 _The NPV of the Model Company project when a return of at least 10 per cent is required_

Year	Cash flow	Cell
1	150000	E22
2	260000	E23
3	295000	E24
4	175000	E25
	692405	E26
Invested	400000	E27
NPV	292405	E28

In cell E26 I entered the command =NPV(0.1,E22..E25). The 0.1 told the spreadsheet to use a 10 per cent discount rate. The E22..E25 told it to apply this discount rate to the cash flows in these cells and to add the results together. When this instruction was entered, the spreadsheet showed a value of £692,405. The capital cost was then deducted in cell E27 to leave the NPV in cell E28.

If your company requires a higher or lower return you simply change the interest rate in the command. For example, if you require a 15 per cent return you change the formula in cell C26 to =NPV(0.15,E22..E25). The result is shown in Table 12.14 (p 310). In cell E26 I entered the command =NPV(0.15,E22..E25). The answer is as calculated manually earlier.

Table 12.14 *The NPV of the Model Company project when a return of at least 15 per cent is required*

Year	Cash flow	Cell
1	150000	E22
2	260000	E23
3	295000	E24
4	175000	E25
	621056	E26
Invested	400000	E27
NPV	221056	E28

The project bank account

To really understand NPV you need to visualize the cash flowing out of and into the project bank account. We will use the Model Company project to illustrate it. If the board approves the project then the corporate treasurer will lend it £400,000 at 15 per cent pa. The cash flows generated by the project will be used to repay the loan and interest. When the loan has been repaid, any surpluses will be credited with interest at 15 per cent pa. If the cash flow forecasts are realized the project bank account will be as in Table 12.15.

Table 12.15 *The bank account for the Model Company project*

		£
Borrow		400,000
Cash flow year 1	150,000	
Less interest (400,000 × 15%)	60,000	90,000
Balance outstanding		310,000
Cash flow year 2	260,000	
Less interest (310,000 × 15%)	46,500	213,500
Balance outstanding		96,500
Cash flow year 3	295,000	
Less interest (96,500 × 15%)	14,475	280,525
Balance on deposit		184,025
Cash flow year 4	175,000	
Add interest (184,025 × 15%)	27,604	202,604
Balance on deposit		386,629

Table 12.15 shows the total profit, including interest that will be earned from the Model Company project. The balance on deposit at the end of the project life, £386,629, is the profit. The accounting name for this is future value (FV). This appraisal tool is of limited value because it is difficult to interpret and is seldom used in practice. However, it helps to provide a clearer picture of the real meaning of NPV. You have to ask yourself how much this profit is worth in terms of today's money given that you require a return of at least 15 per cent pa from your investments. To answer this question you have to discount the profit in four years' time to its present value:

$$P = \frac{386,629}{(1.15)^4} = 221,056$$

NPV questions

I now want you to practise computing NPV by calculating it for projects A and B. You can write discount tables or use a spreadsheet. This time we will assume that the investor requires a return in excess of 14 per cent. The forecast cash flows for these two projects are shown in Table 12.16. The NPVs are presented in the Appendix at the back of the book.

Table 12.16 *Forecast cash flow for projects A and B*

Year	Project A	Project B
0	−300,000	−300,000
1	80,000	140,000
2	90,000	110,000
3	110,000	90,000
4	140,000	80,000

Method 4: Internal Rate of Return (IRR)

The next appraisal tool is IRR. This is the maximum rate of interest that the corporate treasurer could charge and still recover the full loan to the project and interest thereon. Earlier in the chapter we saw that the Model Company project would be able to repay the loan and interest at 15 per cent pa and still earn a substantial profit. You should conclude that the project could afford a higher interest rate. IRR sets out to establish the highest rate affordable. Calculating IRR manually has to be done by trial and error and can take a lot of time. Fortunately, computer spreadsheets can calculate the IRR quickly and accurately. The IRR for the Model Company project reproduced from my spreadsheet is shown in Table 12.17.

Table 12.17 *The IRR of the Model Company project*

IR Year	Cell	Cash flow
0	F32	−400000
1	F33	150000
2	F34	260000
3	F35	295000
4	F36	175000
	F38	38.8767%

I entered the cash flow forecasts in cells F32 to F36. In cell F38 I entered the command =IRR(F32..F36). This instructed the computer to find the maximum rate of interest that the project could afford. When entered and formatted to four decimal places cell F38 read 38.8767 per cent. IRR tells us that this is a superb project. The return is nearly 40 per cent per annum. Note how the cash flows are laid out in a different order from that used to calculate NPV. To help you to understand IRR, Table 12.18 shows the loan being repaid with interest at 38.8767 per cent pa.

Many commentators have been critical of IRR as an evaluation tool. They rightly claim that the implicit assumption about earning power is not justifiable. To understand the problem we will assume that the positive cash flows generated by the Model Company project are kept in a deposit account separate from the funds borrowed to pay for the project. The deposit account plus interest will be used at the end of the project life to repay the loan and accrued interest. Table 12.19 shows the deposit and borrowing pools.

After four years the deposit pool will be used to clear the loan and accrued interest. The snag is that it is very rare for an organization to be able to invest surplus cash at such a high rate. Failure to do so would mean that the deposit pool would not be sufficient to repay the loan and interest. Modified Internal Rate of Return (MIRR) overcomes this defect, as we will see in method 5.

Table 12.18 *The Model Company project repaying the £400,000 loan and interest at 38.8767 per cent*

Year			
0	Borrow		400,000
1	Repay	150,000	
	Interest at 38.8767%	155,507	5,507
			405,507
2	Repay	260,000	
	Interest at 38.8767%	157,648	102,352
			303,155
3	Repay	295,000	
	Interest at 38.8767%	117,856	177,144
			126,011
4	Repay	175,000	
	Interest at 38.8767%	48,989	126,011

Table 12.19 *IRR: the deposit and borrowing pools*

Year	Deposit pool		Year	Borrowing pool	
1	Deposit	150,000	0	Borrow	400,000
	Interest	58,315	1	Interest	155,507
2	Deposit	260,000			555,507
		468,315	2	Interest	215,963
	Interest	182,065			771,470
3	Deposit	295,000	3	Interest	299,922
		945,380			1,071,392
	Interest	367,533	4	Interest	416,521
4	Deposit	175,000			1,487,913
		1,487,91			

Method 5. Modified Internal Rate of Return (MIRR)

This appraisal tool was developed to overcome the defect in IRR described above. It does so by finding the maximum interest rate that a project can afford to pay given a defined earning power in the deposit pool. We will assume that surplus cash can be invested at 15 per cent pa and ask our spreadsheet to calculate the MIRR. This is reproduced in Table 12.20.

Table 12.20   *The MIRR of the Model Company project*

Surplus funds invested at 15% pa

Year	Cell	Cash flow
0	C5	−400000
1	C6	150000
2	C7	260000
3	C8	295000
4	C9	175000
	C10	28.3706%

In cell C10 I entered the command =MIRR(C5..C9,0.1,0.15)*100. The structure of the command is made up of three facets:

a.   The instruction to use cells C5 to C9 as the range of project cash flows.
b.   The 0.1 to tell the computer to start searching for the MIRR using an interest rate of 10 per cent pa. You could use a different start point – for example, 0.12 to tell the computer to start at 12 per cent – and the MIRR would still be 28.3706 per cent.
c.   The 0.15 to tell the computer that the deposit pool will earn interest at 15 per cent pa. If the company only expected to earn 12 per cent it would use 0.12.

When the command is entered and the result is formatted to four decimal places the spreadsheet reports that the project could afford an interest rate of 28.3706 per cent given that surplus cash would earn 15 per cent pa. In Table 12.21, I prove this using the deposit pool and borrowing pool format.

IRR is usually quoted in the board papers in support of investment proposals. As we have seen, it is defective. The MIRR should be quoted instead. As many busy company accountants are not familiar with this improved measure it is incumbent on the board to suggest that it be quoted in place of IRR.

Before proceeding I want you to compute the MIRR of the Model Company project given that surplus cash is deposited at an interest rate of 12 per

Table 12.21 *Verification of the MIRR for the Model Company project*

Year	Deposit pool		Year	Borrowing pool	
1	Deposit	150,000	0	Borrow	400,000
	Interest at 15%	22,500	1	Interest at 28.37%	113,482
2	Deposit	260,000			513,482
		432,500	2	Interest at 28.37%	145,678
	Interest at 15%	64,875			659,160
3	Deposit	295,000	3	Interest at 28.37%	187,008
		792,375			846,168
	Interest at 15%	118,856	4	Interest at 28.37%	240,063
4	Deposit	175,000			1,086,231
		1,086,231			

cent pa. You will need to use your spreadsheet to get the answer and modify the command to reflect the 12 per cent deposit rate. The MIRR with a deposit rate of 12 per cent pa is shown in Table 12.22.

Table 12.22 *The MIRR of the Model Company project with deposits earning 12 per cent pa*

Surplus funds invested at 12% pa

Year	Cell	Cash flow
0	C5	−400000
1	C6	150000
2	C7	260000
3	C8	295000
4	C9	175000
	C10	27.0520%

The project can now afford an interest rate of just over 27 per cent. As you would expect, the affordable interest rate falls when the earnings from deposits decline from 15 per cent to 12 per cent.

Method 6. Economic Value Analysis (EVA)

A major goal for any commercial enterprise must be to enhance shareholder value. It is the paramount goal for quoted businesses. In Chapter 13 we will explore how to assess whether the financial strategy of a business will enhance or destroy shareholder value.

Decisions to invest should also be exposed to shareholder value tests. The test of whether a capital investment will enhance shareholder value is Economic Value Analysis (EVA). EVA is similar to NPV except that the project cash flows are charged for the average value of net assets invested. We will now examine how the EVA of the Model Company project is calculated. We will assume that 10 per cent is the capital charge on the average value of net assets. The first step is to find the average value of net assets and the consequent capital charge; see Table 12.23.

Table 12.23 *The average value of net assets and the capital charge, the Model Company*

Year	Opening assets	Closing assets	Average assets	Capital charge 10%
1	400,000	300,000	350,000	35,000
2	300,000	200,000	250,000	25,000
3	200,000	100,000	150,000	15,000
4	100,000	–	50,000	5,000

The second step is to deduct the capital charges from the project cash flows and calculate the EVA using the NPV methodology. The EVA is reproduced from my spreadsheet in Table 12.24.

In cell E26 I entered the formula =NPV(0.1,E22..E25). When entered, the present value of the future cash flows £625,241 was reported. When the investment cost of £400,000 was deducted, the project provided an EVA of £225,241. In calculating EVA it is wise to use a capital charge rate and a discount factor that are not too high. This is because there is some overlap between the two levies. In this case the EVA using a 10 per cent discount rate and a 10 per cent capital charge is very similar to the NPV using a 15 per cent discount rate.

I am not keen on EVA as an evaluation tool but it is important that you understand it. Local subsidiaries of US companies are likely to use it as a key measure of project attractiveness.

Table 12.24 *The EVA of the Model Company project at 10 per cent*

Year	Cash flow	Capital charge	Net flow	Cell
1	150000	−35000	115000	E22
2	260000	−25000	235000	E23
3	295000	−15000	280000	E24
4	175000	−5000	170000	E25
			625241	E26
		Invested	400000	
		EV	225241	

ERRORS IN FORECASTING PROJECT CASH FLOWS

There are two significant errors in the cash forecasts used to assess the Model Company project. If these were not identified and corrected the board might approve an inappropriate project because the appraisal tools promise excellent results. I wonder if you can spot the problems. Think about this before reading on.

The two major errors in the cash flow forecasts are: a) the finance for the stock and debtor investment has been overlooked; and b) corporation tax on the profits earned by the project has not been included.

In addition to demanding that these errors be corrected, the wise board member will be aware of the possibility that other cash flows have been estimated too optimistically. The exposure of the project to optimistic cash flows should be calculated using a technique called sensitivity analysis. This helps to pinpoint the most critical cash flow assumptions.

Correction for the omission of working capital investment

The investment of working capital to support a project is frequently overlooked or underestimated. It should not be. It increases the initial funding required. Even if the company can recover the working capital when the project ends, the application of discount rates to the working capital cash flows lowers the NPV significantly.

We will now include working capital in the Model Company project. We will assume that:

- Stocks will represent 25 per cent of next year's material and labour cost. These will require additional funding at the outset and as sales grow.
- Debtors will represent 20 per cent of next year's sales (this means that on average cash will start to be collected from customers 2.4 months after sales commence and collections will continue for 2.4 months after sales cease). The debtor investment is approximated by assuming a cash outflow at the start of each year to reflect the strain on cash resources imposed by allowing credit to customers.
- Funds invested in working capital will be recovered at the end of the project.

To allow for the working capital invested through the project life and recovered at the end of its life we need to make two groups of calculations. In the first set of calculations the investment in stocks and debtors is computed. In the second set of calculations the project cash flows are adjusted to reflect this investment. The impact of working capital on the Model Company project is shown in Table 12.25.

Table 12.25 *The working capital investment in the Model Company project*

Year	0	1	2	3	4
Materials and labour	100,000	160,000	250,000	150,000	
Total stocks (25%)	25,000	40,000	62,500	37,500	
Incremental stocks	−25,000	−15,000	−22,500	25,000	37,500
Sales	300,000	480,000	625,000	375,000	
Debtors (20%)	60,000	96,000	125,000	75,000	
Incremental debtors	−60,000	-36,000	−29,000	50,000	75,000
Total (invested) recovered	(85,000)	(51,000)	(41,500)	75,000	112,500

In order to start the project, £485,000 of funds will be required rather than the £400,000 erroneously reported at the original board meeting. The investment continues to rise as sales grow in the second and third year of the project. Subsequently working capital investment is recovered as sales decline; see Table 12.26.

The working capital adjustment reduces the NPV by £47,093. In addition it recognizes that an additional £85,000 is required to commence the project. If this is overlooked, the company might overstretch its borrowing facilities.

Table 12.26 *The corrected NPV of the Model Company project including working capital*

Year	Original cash flow	Working capital	Net cash flow	Discount 15%	NPV
1	150,000	(51,000)	99,000	0.86956	86,086
2	260,000	(41,500)	218,500	0.75614	165,217
3	295,000	75,000	370,000	0.65752	243,282
4	175,000	112,500	287,500	0.57175	164,378
	880,000	95,000	975.000		658,963
Less initial investment including working capital					485,000
Revised present value					173,963

Taxation and the Model Company project

Corporation tax is a significant drain on the net cash resources of a project. It would be foolish to ignore it. To adjust for corporation tax we will use the following additional information:

- The corporation tax rate will be 25 per cent.
- A writing down allowance of 25 per cent for corporation tax purposes is available. This allowance is calculated in the same way as reducing balance depreciation (ie allowance is based on the remaining undepreciated value).
- Corporation tax is payable about six months after the end of the accounting period in which a profit is earned. We will treat it as payable one year in arrears. This simplifies the calculations and is consistent with the implicit assumption that cash flows occur at year-end.
- The company depreciates the plant over four years straight line for accounting purposes. This assumes no proceeds will be realized on disposal. Since the writing down allowance will not fully shelter the loss of value to be experienced, a balancing allowance will be available at the end of the final year of the project.

We will adjust the NPV of the Model Company project for corporation tax in two stages. In the first stage the corporation tax charges are computed. In the second stage these cash outflows are included in the revised NPV calculation. This is done in Table 12.27 (p 320).

Table 12.27 *The NPV of the Model Company project after deducting corporation tax*

Computation of corporation tax liabilities

Year	Pre-tax profit	Add depreciation	Deduct WDA[(a)]	Taxable profit	Tax at 25%
1	50,000	100,000	−100,000	50,000	12,500
2	160,000	100,000	−75,000	185,000	46,250
3	195,000	100,000	−56,250	238,750	59,688
4	75,000	100,000	−168,750	6,250	1,562
	480,000	400,000	−400,000	480,000	120,000

Note:

	£
[(a)]Cost of plant	400,000
WDA year 1 at 25%	100,000
Written down value	300,000
WDA year 2 at 25%	75,000
Written down value	225,000
WDA year 3 at 25%	56,250
Written down value	168,750
Disposal proceeds	0
Balancing allowance year 4	168,750

The NPV of the Model Company project after tax

Year	Previous cash flow	Corporation tax	Net flow	Discount 15%	NPV
1	99,000	–	99,000	0.86957	86,087
2	218,500	−12,500	206,000	0.75614	155,765
3	370,000	−46,250	323,750	0.65752	212,872
4	287,500	−59,688	227,812	0.57175	130,252
5	–	−1,562	−1,562	0.49718	−777
	975,000	−120,000	855,000		584,199
Less investment					485,000
Net present value					99,199

Impact of the project on future financial statements

Because large capital investments cause major cash outflows they have a detrimental effect on financial stability. For example, if all the funds are borrowed then gearing will rise and interest cover will fall. It is wise to prepare financial statements for major projects so as to check the effect on corporate health of a decision to invest. To do this you must view major projects as separate strategic business units and prepare forecasts of their profit and loss accounts and balance sheets. In the preparation of these forecasts it is important to remember that the taxable profits will be earned in a slightly different pattern from the accounting profits and that as a consequence deferred tax adjustments will be required. The financial statements for the Model Company project are shown in Tables 12.28 (below) and 12.29 (p 322).

Table 12.28 *The profit and loss account forecasts for the Model Company project*

Year	1	2	3	4	Total
Sales	300,000	480,000	625,000	375,000	1,780,000
Cash costs	150,000	220,000	330,000	200,000	900,000
Depreciation	100,000	100,000	100,000	100,000	400,000
	250,000	320,000	430,000	300,000	1,300,000
Profit before tax	50,000	160,000	195,000	75,000	480,000
Corporation tax	−12,500	−46,250	−59,688	−1,562	−120,000
Deferred tax[a]	0	6,250	10,938	−17,188	0
Profit after tax	37,500	120,000	146,250	56,250	360,000
Cumulative profit	37,500	157,500	303,750	360,000	

Note:
[a] Deferred tax arises because accounting depreciation exceeds writing down allowances:

Year	2	3	4
Depreciation	100,000	100,000	100,000
WDA	75,000	56,250	168,750
Deferrable	25,000	43,750	(68,750)
Deferred at 25%	6,250	10,938	(17,188)

In the second and third year of the project, because of the reducing balance nature of the writing down allowance, the profit for tax purposes will exceed

321

the profit for accounting purposes. In the fourth year of the project the balancing allowance corrects for the shortfall of previous tax depreciation and the accounting profit is higher than the taxable profit. Note how the deferred tax cancels out over the three-year period.

Table 12.29 *The balance sheet forecasts for the Model Company project*

Year	0	1	2	3	4
Plant at cost	400,000	400,000	400,000	400,000	400,000
Less depreciation	–	100,000	200,000	300,000	400,000
	400,000	300,000	200,000	100,000	–
Stocks	25,000	40,000	62,500	37,500	
Debtors	60,000	96,000	125,000	75,000	
Deferred tax			6,250	17,188	
Project surplus[a]	–	–	–	133,750	361,562
	485,000	436,000	393,750	363,438	361,562
Project borrowings[a]	485,000	386,000	190,000		
Corporation tax		12,500	46,250	59,688	1,562
Cumulative profit	–	37,500	157,500	303,750	360,000
	485,000	436,000	393,750	363,438	361,562

Note:
[a]

Year	Change Loan	Change stock	Operating debtors	Cash flow	Tax	Loan
1	485,000	15,000	36,000	(150,000)	–	386,000
2	386,000	22,500	29,000	(260,000)	12,500	190,000
3	190,000	(25,000)	(50,000)	(295,000)	46,250	(133,750)
4	(133,750)	(37,500)	(75,000)	(175,000)	59,688	(361,562)

THE IMPACT OF FORECASTING ERRORS ON PROJECT VIABILITY

Sensitivity analysis helps to pinpoint the importance of the various cash flow assumptions that are made in assessing a capital investment. We will use it to check the impact of a 10 per cent disimprovement in each of the major cash flow assumptions. There are four key assumptions:

1. The price at which the output will be sold.
2. The quantity that will be sold.

3. The operating costs of the project.
4. The cost of the plant.

To test the significance of each major cash flow assumption we will make a 10 per cent unfavourable adjustment while holding the other cash flows constant. We will just measure the change in NPV. We could equally revise the total appraisal. This would have the same impact on NPV.

Sensitivity analysis 1. Sales price falls by 10 per cent

If the sales price falls by 10 per cent then it will affect the following areas:

- The project sales and operating profits will decline.
- As a result of the decline in operating profits the corporation tax bill will fall.
- As a result of the reduction in sales a lower investment in debtors will be required.

The increments of change in NPV are shown in Table 12.30.

Table 12.30 *The impact of a 10 per cent fall in selling price on the Model Company project NPV*

Year	Reduced operating cash flow	Reduced debtors	Corp. tax 25%	Incremental net cash flow	Discount factor 15%	NPV
1	–30,000	3,600	–	–26,400	0.86956	–22,956
2	–48,000	2,900	7,500	–37,600	0.75614	–28,341
3	–62,500	–5,000	12,000	–55,500	0.65752	–36,492
4	–37,500	–7,500	15,625	–29,375	0.57175	–16,795
5	–	–	9,375	9,375	0.49718	4,661
	–178,000	–6,000	44,500	–139,500		–100,013
Less reduction in initial debtors						6,000
Decline in NPV						94,013

Sensitivity analysis 2. Sales volume falls by 10 per cent

If the quantity of goods sold falls the following changes must be made to the project cash flows:

1. The project sales and variable costs will decline by 10 per cent.
2. As a result of the decline in operating profits the corporation tax bill will fall.
3. As a result of the reduction in sales the investment in debtors will fall by 10 per cent.
4. As a result of the change in variable costs the investment in stocks will fall by 10 per cent.

The effect of a 10 per cent decline in the volumes sold is shown in Table 12.31.

Table 12.31 *The impact of a 10 per cent fall in sales volume on the Model Company project NPV*

Year	Reduced sales	Reduced costs	Reduced stocks	Reduced debtors	Corp. tax	Cash flow	Discount factor 15%	NPV
1	−30,000	10,000	1,500	3,600	–	−14,900	0.86956	−12,956
2	−48,000	16,000	2,250	2,900	5,000	−21,850	0.75614	−16,522
3	−62,500	25,000	−2,500	−5,000	8,000	−37,000	0.65752	−24,328
4	−37,500	15,000	−3,750	−7,500	9,375	−24,375	0.57175	−13,936
5	–	–	–	–	5,625	5,625	0.49718	2,797
	−178,000	66,000	−2,500	−6,000	28,000	−92,500		−64,945
Less reduction in initial stocks and debtors								8,500
Change in NPV								−56,445

Sensitivity analysis 3. Operating costs rise by 10 per cent

As operating costs rise the following changes must be made to the project cash flows:

1. The project variable and fixed costs will rise by 10 per cent.
2. As a result of the change in variable costs the investment in stocks will rise by 10 per cent.
3. As a result of the decline in operating profits the corporation tax bill will fall.

The impact of the increases in costs is shown in Table 12.32.

Table 12.32 *The impact of a 10 per cent increase in costs on the NPV of the Model Company project*

Year	Extra variable costs	Extra fixed costs	Impact on stocks	Corp. tax	Cash flow	Discount factor 15%	NPV
1	−10,000	−5,000	−1,500		−16,500	0.86956	−14,348
2	−16,000	−6,000	−2,250	3,750	−20,500	0.75614	−15,501
3	−25,000	−8,000	2,500	5,500	−25,000	0.65752	−16,438
4	−15,000	−5,000	3,750	8,250	−8,000	0.57175	−4,574
5	–	–	–	5,000	5,000	0.49718	2,486
	−66,000	−24,000	2,500	−22,500	−65,000		−48,375
Less initial reduction in stocks							2,500
NPV relevant flows only							−45,875

Sensitivity analysis 4. Plant cost increases by 10 per cent

If the plant cost rises by 10 per cent so will the writing down allowances and balancing allowance. The impact on the Model Company project NPV is shown in Table 12.33.

Table 12.33 *The impact of a 10 per cent increase in the cost of plant on the project NPV*

Year	Reduced tax	Discount factor	NPV
2	2,500	0.75614	1,890
3	1,875	0.65752	1,233
4	1,406	0.57175	804
5	4,219	0.49718	2,098
	10,000		6,025
Less 10% increase in plant cost			−40,000
NPV relevant flows only			−33,975

The corrected NPV (after inclusion of working capital and corporation tax) was £99,199. Table 12.34 (p 326) shows the relative importance of the various project forecasts.

Table 12.34 *The relative significance of the four key project forecasts*

Variable adjusted	NPV change	% of original	% change to break-even[1]	Rank
Sales price	−94,013	95	10.5	1
Sales volume	−56,445	57	17.6	2
Operating costs	−45,875	46	21.6	3
Plant cost	−33,975	34	29.2	4

Notes:

[1] This table shows us that the project is disturbingly sensitive to a fall in selling price. The margin for error is dangerously small. It can be calculated as follows: Sales price (10% × £99,199/£94,013) = 10.5%. The margin for error for the other variables is:

Sales volume	17.6% (10% × £99,199/£56,445)
Operating costs	21.6% (10% × £99,199/£45,875)
Plant cost	29.2% (10% × £99,199/£33,975)

NPV: the most important appraisal tool

In the chapter so far we have examined how the six major appraisal tools can be applied to a project. It is reasonable for you to ask which of these tools should be given the most attention when the board is considering an investment proposal. In my opinion NPV is by far and away the most important tool. If you have defined the minimum return that you require from investments you can use it to discount the cash flows. Good projects will promise a positive NPV at this discount rate. Projects that do not offer a positive NPV should be rejected.

There is one exception to this general rule. Projects that are required to meet social and environmental obligations are frequently imposed on an organization even though they will not provide a commercial return.

THE WEIGHTED AVERAGE COST OF CAPITAL (WACC)

How do you decide the minimum return that you require? You should base it on the rewards that you will have to give to the providers of funds that you will use to pay for capital investments. When the total rewards are expressed as a percentage of the total funds to be invested, this will provide the discount rate that you should use. This discount rate is called the weighted average cost of capital. The funds to be raised to pay for capital investment come from two main sources: the shareholders' investment – shareholders invest by forgoing dividends and by subscribing to 'rights' issues; and the additional bank loans that can be raised, without damaging the gearing, on the back of the additional shareholder investment.

What return will the bankers and shareholders require for providing the investment funds? The cost of the bank funds is easier to predict. It is determined by the interest rates charged on the loans less a deduction to reflect the fact that interest is allowed as a cost in computing corporation tax liabilities. The effect of this is that to service a loan at an interest rate of 10 per cent will really cost you a net 7.5 per cent as it saves you tax at 25 per cent. The cost of shareholders' funds is more difficult to predict. It is determined by the shareholders' expectation for a growing dividend income and for capital appreciation. The literature of business finance is laden with complex models designed to help you to calculate the service cost of shareholders' funds. For most businesses these models are of little practical benefit. There are four important issues that must be taken into account in calculating the cost of shareholders' funds:

1. If a business becomes bankrupt, the shareholders will be last in the queue for repayment of the funds provided. Indeed, the shareholders often receive nothing when the assets are realized in a liquidation. This is because preferential, secured and unsecured creditors rank higher in the queue. To compensate for the risk of share ownership the return that the shareholders require is significantly higher than the cost of servicing other funds providers.
2. Unlike interest, dividends are not allowed as a deduction for corporation tax purposes. As a result, the 25 per cent deduction that we used in the interest cost calculation must not be made.
3. Some businesses are much more risky than others. Obviously, if the risk of failure is greater then the reward for success must be higher. For example, exploration for oil in the seas is a high-risk venture. Equally, a business such as a high street bank should have little risk of failure and should be able to attract funds in exchange for a much lower return.
4. The return that is earned for shareholders is not all given to them in cash. Most shareholders make a decision to buy shares on the grounds that future growth in profits and dividends will lead to capital appreciation. The owners' share in this expected appreciation must be taken into account in calculating the service cost of shareholders' funds.

When these four factors have been taken into account the service cost of shareholder investment lies between 12 per cent for safe investments and 20

327

per cent for high-risk investment. Readers are warned that these figures will rise if the rate of inflation increases substantially.

It is tempting to identify the type of funds used to pay for a specific project (called the marginal cost of capital) and to use the cost of servicing these funds as the discount rate in calculating NPV. However, this approach can lead to an inappropriate portfolio of capital investments. The problem arises because the cost of servicing bank debt is lower than the cost of servicing shareholder investment. It would be a pity if an organization accepted a project offering a moderate return because it was proposed when lower cost bank debt was being raised and rejected a better project later because it had to be funded by equity after the debt-raising capacity had been exhausted. The solution is to rightly assume that all projects will be financed from a basket of funds to be raised from investors and lenders. The cost of servicing this basket of funds expressed as a percentage of the total funds is called the weighted average cost of capital (WACC).

We will now examine how two companies computed their WACC. The first example in Table 12.35 is a low-risk business; the second example in Table 12.36 is a high-risk business.

Table 12.35 *The weighted average cost of capital in a low-risk business*

Type	Funds to be raised A £'000%	Return required B £'000	WACC B/A %
Bank	800	60 (7.5%)	
Owners	1,200	144 (12.%)	
Total	2,000	204	10.2%

Note:
It would be sensible but not essential to round the WACC down to 10% for discounting purposes.

There are five steps involved in calculating the WACC:

1. Assess the amount of funds available to finance capital investments (the capital budget).
2. Assess the proportion of these funds that will be raised from shareholders' and from interest bearing loans.

Table 12.36 *The weighted average cost of capital in a high-risk business*

Type	Funds to be raised A £'000%	Return required B £'000	WACC B/A %
Bank	1,000	90 (9%)	
Owners	1,000	200 (20%)	
Total	2,000	290	14.5%

Note:
In this case I would discount at 15%. I used an interest rate of 12% (9% after tax) owing to the higher gearing. Because of the additional risk the owners require a return of 20%

3. Establish the return(s) required by the funds providers.
4. Calculate the WACC from the data assembled in steps 1 to 3.
5. Discount all proposed investments at the weighted average cost of capital. Accept projects that provide the best positive NPV until the available funds are exhausted. Reject projects that offer a negative NPV.

PROFITABILITY INDEX

A business may have capital investment proposals that have a higher aggregate cost than the company can fund. In order to decide which projects to accept and which to reject the company should compile a profitability index. This is done by expressing the NPV for each project as a percentage of the capital cost. Projects with high profitability indices should be accepted. Once the investment funds have been committed, projects with lower profitability indices should be rejected or deferred until additional funds become available.

The use of profitability indices is illustrated in Table 12.37 (p 330). Growth plc is considering some capital investment proposals. It has £4.5 million to spend.

Table 12.37 *Selecting the best portfolio of projects*

£'000 Proposal	Capital Cost	NPV	Profitability Index	Rank
1	2,000	1,000	50%	5
2	1,500	900	60%	3
3	1,800	990	55%	4
4	2,500	1,200	48%	6
5	1,000	800	80%	2
6	200	180	90%	1
	9,000			

Note:

If you simply approved the projects with the highest NPV you would select projects 1 and 4. This would consume the total capital budget but would not maximize the potential return. A closer inspection reveals that an NPV of £2.87 million is available from the other four projects. The profitability index steers you to the best portfolio:

Choice	Proposal	Cost	Balance uncommitted	NPV	Cumulative NPV
1	6	200	4,300	180	180
2	5	1,000	3,300	800	980
3	2	1,500	1,800	900	1,880
4	3	1,800	–	990	2,870

ACCEPT/REJECT CRITERIA IN PROJECT EVALUATION

Every business should develop criteria upon which projects are accepted and rejected. It is difficult to generalize about such criteria. The major problem is that projects have very different characteristics and risk profiles. The guidelines in Table 12.38 should help you to formulate your accept/reject criteria.

Setting payback limits can help to avoid time-consuming studies of unattractive projects. If a project passes the payback test then more detailed discounted cash flow techniques should be applied. This chapter stresses the application of discounting based on the cost of capital. In general, projects that do not produce a positive NPV should be rejected. An exception is where ability to remain in business depends on modernizing the asset base. In such

Table 12.38 *Guidelines for project accept/reject criteria*

Project type	Risk profile	Maximum payback
1. Replacement of out of date assets	Medium	5 years
2. Value engineering or cost reduction	High	2 years
3. Infrastructure development	Low	10+ years
4. Project to acquire long-term secure returns (eg an assurance company seeking a long-term return to underpin bonuses)	Low	10+ years
5. Projects of a social or environmental nature	Not for commercial purposes	

cases a capital investment might be undertaken even though the NPV is negative.

Buying your own shares as a capital investment

Sometimes the board of directors think that the stock market has failed to recognize the true value of the company's shares. In such circumstances they may decide that to buy its own shares is the best investment available and commit part of the capital budget to this. If it does so, then the board may decide at some future time to sell the shares back to the market, particularly where the shares have appreciated to a more sensible level.

THE 10 PRIORITIES OF AN EXCELLENT APPROACH TO CAPITAL INVESTMENT

1. Define how much you are prepared to spend on capital projects (the capital budget). This will help to protect your business from over-trading.
2. Never assume that historic demand patterns will continue indefinitely. Remember my comments on the Burmah Oil tanker fleet.
3. Never spend money on capital investments that is needed for and committed to other organizational uses.
4. Define appropriate payback and NPV criteria. They will help you to make correct accept/reject decisions. The values vary from business to business. They are related to changes in production technology and consumer taste. Criteria should be regularly reviewed as conditions change.

5. Don't waste a lot of time on complicated cost of capital calculations. Pragmatic discount rates are the sensible approach for most UK businesses.

6. Avoid funding capital investments from short-term sources. Remember our conclusions from the cash flow matrix in Chapter 4.

7. When computing project cash flows, remember to charge an appropriate amount for R&D. The best projects are ones that provide margins adequate to cover the cost of a search for even better ones.

8. Think long and hard before investing in a project that adds more than 25 per cent to sales, assets or staff. If it goes sour it could seriously damage your business.

9. Remember the mnemonic GIGO (Garbage In Garbage Out). Time spent on improving the accuracy of cash forecasts is the secret of winning in the capital investment race.

10. Carefully consider the impact of major new investments on the overhead structure of the business. An investment that imposes a small additional strain on the establishment should not significantly affect the fixed costs. A major new investment will cause extra fixed costs unless the business is operating below its establishment cost capacity.

SUMMARY

In this chapter we examined the six major appraisal techniques that can be applied to capital investment proposals. We saw that ROI and payback help us to quickly identify projects too risky to warrant the deeper investigation involved in discounted cash flow techniques. We found that the best appraisal techniques were those that reflected the time value of money. We concluded that NPV and payback were the two most important appraisal techniques. We realized that you could not get sensible answers from incorrect cash flow forecasts and learnt how to use sensitivity analysis to pinpoint the relative risk of each key forecast. We examined a pragmatic approach to assessing the weighted average cost of capital. We saw how a profitability index helps to identify the most suitable investments in a capital-rationing situation.

13

Financial strategy and shareholder value

If a business is to thrive it needs to have a strategy that will confer a competitive advantage. Such a strategy allows a business to generate a greater free cash flow than its competitors. Shareholder value analysis can then be applied to identify those businesses that are capitalizing on their competitive advantage and enhancing value and those without a competitive advantage that are frequently destroying value.

COMPETITIVE ADVANTAGE

The competitive position of an organization has a huge influence on the type of strategy that it should adopt. As a general guide the competitive position is somewhere on the scale:

Competition scale		
None Few	Many	

Usually when a business is on the left side of this scale there is a significant barrier to new entrants. The most common barrier is the need for very large asset investment to create and supply the products and services to customers. It is for this reason that there are very few telecommunications businesses in the UK and huge numbers of retailers. In many countries the size of the entry cost is such that major industries remain nationalized. Privatization initiatives in the UK and EU have resulted in a move from monopoly conditions to oligopoly conditions (a small number of high-volume competitors). Again the telecommunications industry provides a good example, having moved from the virtual monopoly of BT to a situation where the vast bulk of the market is controlled by a small number of high-volume competitors.

The Harvard guru Michael Porter is the definitive author of thinking on competitive advantage. He defines how this advantage should determine how businesses should compete. He suggests two possible approaches: a) product differentiation; and b) lowest cost producer.

A product differentiation strategy

A business whose strategy is designed to compete by differentiation is usually able to charge premium prices for its products or services. The differentiation may be real (achieved by superior product design and quality) or imagined (achieved by marketing initiatives) or a combination of both.

How can a business afford the additional costs that are the inevitable consequences of a product differentiation strategy? It can do so only when the extra cash inflows derived from the premium price exceed the extra outflows incurred to create the basis for differentiation and make customers aware of it. A product differentiation strategy challenges competitors to catch up and surpass it. For this reason, the sensible differentiator can expect only a short-term competitive advantage. However, the fact that they can generate premium cash flows will permit them to invest in finding and marketing further differentiation.

Methods of differentiation

The following methods of differentiation may be used:

- *Branding.* The pharmaceutical industry offers numerous examples of businesses selling an undifferentiated product at a premium price. For example, consider the price of the world-leading pain relief tablet. Most people seem to realize that it is exactly the same as the generic competitor yet most customers ask for the brand leader.
- *Product development.* In many industries the level of investment in product development is very high. To fund this development a business needs a

substantial price premium that generates enough additional cash flow to pay for expensive and frequently unsuccessful research.

- _Advertising._ Some would argue that marketing is the most cynical aspect of business. For example, the marketeer conjures up an image of a product that is superior to the offerings of competitors. The differentiation is often more imaginary than real. For example, the world leader in the vodka market has long argued that charcoal filtering makes its product smoother. A chemist friend assures me that you could filter until you were blue in the face and it would not affect smoothness.

Lowest cost producer strategy

As the name suggests, any business can strive to create and deliver its product or service to its customers at a lower cost than its competitors. A lowest cost strategy is most often found where there are a large number of suppliers and little opportunity for product differentiation. Such a strategy should also generate a cash flow premium as acceptance of the market price is accompanied by lower costs than competitors. The cost advantage is also quite often short lived as competitors strive to compete and surpass it.

A combined differentiation and lowest cost strategy

The majority of businesses have a strategy that is not totally focused on differentiation or on lowest cost but on a combination of the two. There is a serious danger that by not setting one or the other as the top priority, a business will not be able to generate a cash flow premium. Failure to do so leaves a business 'stuck in the middle' and without the cash to switch to a differentiation strategy (fund product design and development, marketing, etc) or a lowest cost strategy (major capital expenditure is often required to enhance cost competitiveness). Organizations that fail to decide on which type of strategy to adopt frequently fail to compete effectively with their better-focused peers.

Computing the financial strategy

Once a business has decided how it will compete it should prepare financial statements for a period four to five years ahead based on its strategy. As usual, profit and loss accounts, balance sheets and cash flow statements are required. These projected statements will pinpoint whether the business can fund the strategy and will indicate whether an adequate cash flow premium will be generated. The key ratios should be computed from the projections to help in assessing profitability, financial stability and working capital requirements. We will examine the projections later in the chapter when we look at shareholder value models.

SHAREHOLDER VALUE

What should be the primary objective of any business enterprise? It may seem extraordinary but the objective of enhancing shareholder value was not fully recognized or enunciated until recent years. In 1986 Alfred Rappaport in his book *Creating Shareholder Value* first brought this goal centre-stage. It should always have been there for quoted companies. Their shareholders are taking the major risk and should be rewarded by the board and management setting a strategy that will increase the underlying worth of the business and consequently the price of its shares. Any company that has a business strategy that is likely to enhance shareholder value more quickly than its peers deserves an above average PE and PBITDA multiple and, as a consequence, share price. A business strategy that is likely to destroy shareholder value deserves to be given a below average multiple and a depressed share price.

In current stock market conditions it is a good generalization that the average business will be valued at about ten times its profit after tax and seven times its PBITDA unless it operates in a sector that is totally out of favour. If the market perceives that the financial strategy and prospects for a business are better than average then the price will move up and the multiples rise. The converse is also true. A company that has a strategy and business outlook that are not as good as average will trade down to a lower multiple. How does the market judge the strategy and business prospects? It does so by assessing whether the business plan will enhance or destroy shareholder value. The judgement is normally made as a result of a briefing by the company.

The enhancement of shareholder value may not be the primary objective of an owner-managed private company. Such businesses, sheltered from the hunger of stock market investors and analysts, frequently adopt a more altruistic primary goal. For example, many owner-managers see the provision of managerial positions to the next generation as a primary objective.

Earnings measurement

The investing community has until recent years placed their primary focus on earnings per share (EPS). Rappaport and his imitators have rightly pointed to the fact that since earnings are an accrual-based concept, growth in earnings is not necessarily accompanied by an increase in the real value of an enterprise. The defects in profit-based measures as a means of assessing the economic value of an enterprise are as follows:

- Accounting adjustments used in determining profits include accruals, prepayments and depreciation. These adjustments mean that there is unlikely to be the same amount of cash left to pay to shareholders as dividends or retain to contribute towards expansion as the profit after tax indicates.
- The profit and loss account, by measuring and reporting sales and cost of sales, fails to recognize that, particularly in a business that is growing, some of the profits are left behind in cash used to support additional working capital investment.
- The use of depreciation charges in the profit and loss account reflects the loss of value of tangible fixed assets rather than the level of capital investment undertaken in the current year. This capital investment is of four major types: a) expenditure to replace worn-out assets (usually for more than the cost of the previous assets); b) legislative investments, eg pollution control, safety at work and other social priorities; c) expenditure incurred to increase production capacity and logistics capability; and d) expenditure incurred to create new products or services as an organization diversifies its product portfolio or markets. These investments normally result in the use of a far greater amount of cash than the depreciation charges might imply.
- The fact that traditional profit measurement techniques fail to take into account two major forms of business risk. First, there is operating risk. This reflects the products or services supplied in the business sector in which the organization is competing. For example, it is fascinating to see how the fortunes of computer hardware and software suppliers fluctuate at the stages where their products are ahead of and behind those of competitors. Second, there is financial risk. This reflects the level of debt in the funding mix. The greater the level of debt in the mix, the more the business will be affected by a downturn in economic conditions. It is certainly fair to say that the effects of operational and financial risk are observable in past performance. However, predicting future trends is more difficult.
- The fact that predicted strategic cash flows should be adjusted to their present value is not taken into account in conventional business plans.

As a consequence of these observations there is no doubt that the amount of free cash that a business plan promises to generate, discounted to reflect the time value of money, is a far superior determinant of whether a strategy will create or destroy shareholder value than the change in earnings per share implicit in such plans.

Free cash flow as compared to ROI and ROE

In addition to the arguments presented above as to why free cash flow is superior to earnings growth there is a further problem that affects the reliability of ROI and ROE as a measure of shareholder value. This relates to the fact that depreciation charges are normally applied evenly over the useful life of assets. This has the effect of depressing the returns in organizations that have relatively youthful assets and flattering the returns of organizations that have older assets. For example, consider two organizations that hold a fixed asset that cost £1 million and generate operating profits of £100,000. The assets of both companies are depreciated on a straight-line basis over their useful life of five years. The asset of company A is one year old; the asset of company B is three years old. The ROIs of the two companies are shown in Table 13.1.

Table 13.1 *The effect of the age of assets on performance*

	Company A	Company B
Operating profit	100,000	100,000
Net asset	800,000	400,000
ROI	12.5%	25%

Company B appears to be performing twice as well as company A. However, it only appears to be so because its assets are older. In a subsequent year when company B has to replace its worn-out assets it will generate an ROI of 10 per cent (100,000/1,000,000 per cent) whereas company A with its ageing asset will generate an ROI of 50 per cent (100,000/200,000 per cent).

Examples of the impact of the age of assets on ROI and ROE should not be taken to suggest that they are not valuable tools. They certainly are, but the failure to reflect future capital investment obligations make them unsuitable for assessing shareholder value.

Growth in sales: the cornerstone of shareholder value

The essence of an above-par strategy is growth in sales. In the past the valuation of a strategy was largely based on prospects for growth in earnings per share. In recent years the focus has turned towards ability to generate a free cash flow premium. Why has the emphasis shifted? It is because such surplus cash can be paid to shareholders as dividends or retained to contribute towards organic or acquisition-led growth. The problem with growth in EPS as a goal is that it fails to take cash into consideration. Many businesses have a strategy that promises substantial growth in EPS but are trapped in a spiral of ever-increasing investment that leads to a negative cash flow.

The shareholder value literature focuses on four main ways that sales growth affects free cash flow. These are called value drivers. They are:

1. The inevitable increase in cost that is associated with additional sales. These costs affect the margin that will be derived from the extra sales.
2. The fact that an increase in profits will be accompanied by additional corporation tax payments.
3. The need for working capital investment to support the additional sales. We met this investment before in two contexts. First, we saw it in the context of the cash flow statement where it was necessary to convert the operating profit into the operating cash flow through the working capital adjustments. Exactly the same logic is used in the measurement of free cash flow. Second, we saw it in the context of ratio analysis where the working capital ratio was used to diagnose the additional investment required to support growth in sales. It is important to remember that business sectors such as retailing can release additional free cash flow as sales grow because they usually operate with relatively low stocks and generally do not give credit to customers. Indeed, the strategy of many multinational retailers is clearly focused on opening new outlets. Each opening creates surplus cash, as a) the premises are generally rented and the fixtures leased; b) no credit is given to customers; and c) substantial supplier credit more than pays for the stock investment. Equally, other sectors, particularly in manufacturing, must make large investments in working capital in order to support growth in sales. World stock markets seemed to totally ignore the working capital issue in the 'dotcoms' share price explosion that took place in 2000 and early 2001.
4. The need for fixed asset investment to support the additional sales. In particular, extra investment in plant and machinery is required as production increases in a manufacturing business. Equally, investment in the additional distribution required to support extra sales through

339

the growing use of contract distribution means that this is a margin rather than a fixed asset issue.

THE STANDARD SHAREHOLDER VALUE MODEL

This is derived using the seven recognized drivers of value. These are:

1. sales;
2. operating margin;
3. effective tax rate;
4. incremental fixed capital investment;
5. incremental working capital investment;
6. cost of capital;
7. life of the financial strategy.

These drivers will now be examined.

Sales projection

Sales are the key input in determining the free cash flow, if any, that will be generated by a business or business unit over the period of its strategic plan. In the example that follows, Smart plc predicts that sales will grow at 20 per cent per annum.

Operating margin

The inevitable consequence of selling products or services is the costs. The bulk of the cash flow associated with the sales will be spent to pay the operating costs. In the Smart plc example an operating margin of 12 per cent is predicted.

Effective tax rate

Shortly after a business earns a profit it becomes liable to pay a significant portion of the profit as tax. The percentage that will be paid is usually higher than the nominal tax rate because some of the expenses are not allowed as deductions in calculating the corporation tax bill. Smart plc predicts an effective corporation tax rate of 28 per cent.

Incremental fixed asset investment

As a business develops it incurs fixed asset expenditure of two main types. First, there is replacement expenditure as existing fixed assets wear out or become obsolete. Second, there is fixed asset expenditure that will create the additional capacity required to support the growth in sales. Smart plc predicts total fixed asset investment of 1.5 times the depreciation charge.

Incremental working capital investment

In Chapter 6 we examined the working capital/sales ratio. We pointed out that as a business grows it requires additional investment in stocks and debtors less a reduction for growth in creditors. Smart plc predicts an investment of 6.2 per cent of the additional sales.

Cost of capital

In Chapter 12 I showed you how a business calculates its weighted average cost of capital. This will be needed to discount the free cash flow that the business will generate and to assess the terminal value of the business at the end of the strategic plan period. Smart plc calculated a WACC of 10 per cent. This was rounded up from the 9.75 per cent that it predicted.

Life of the strategy

Smart plc decided that it was appropriate to assess its competitive advantage over a period of five years. It also predicted that it would be able at least to maintain the level of free cash flow achieved in year 5 thereafter, owing to continuing differentiation-focused investment. The corporate value of £205.98 million is shown in Table 13.2 (p 342).

The finance director prepared this shareholder value analysis on an Excel spreadsheet. As with many other forms of financial analysis I recommend the use of a spreadsheet. It simplifies the calculations involved. You should be able to follow the workings because of the data I gave you when explaining the value drivers. Nevertheless, the following explanations of the corporate value are provided:

- The sales in year 1 are predicted to be £132.78 million + 20 per cent = £159.34 million.
- The operating margin in year 1 is predicted to be £159.34 million × 12 per cent = £19.12 million.

Table 13.2 *The corporate value of Smart plc*

	Current	Year 1	Year 2	Year 3	Year 4	Year 5	Total
Sales (£ million)	132.78	159.34	191.20	229.44	275.33	330.40	
Operating margin	15.93	19.12	22.94	27.53	33.04	39.65	
Depreciation		1.88	2.22	2.62	3.07	3.61	
Effective tax rate		−5.35	−6.42	−7.71	−9.25	−11.10	
Incremental fixed asset		−2.82	−3.33	−3.93	−4.61	−5.42	
Incremental working capital		−1.65	−1.98	−2.37	−2.85	−3.41	
Free cash flow		11.18	13.43	16.14	19.41	23.33	
Discount factor 10%		0.909	0.826	0.751	0.683	0.621	
PV of free cash flow		10.16	11.10	12.13	13.26	14.48	61.14
Terminal value							144.84
							205.98

- Depreciation is added back as a non-cash cost.
- The tax liability in year 1 is £19.12 million × 28 per cent = £5.35 million.
- The incremental fixed assets in year 1 is £1.88 million × 1.5 = £2.82 million. The 1.5 factor is the reinvestment rate.
- The incremental working capital is (£159.34 − £132.78) × 6.2 per cent = £1.65 million.
- The free cash flow in year 1 is £19.12 million + £1.88 − £5.35 million − £2.82 million − £1.65 million = £11.18 million.
- The free cash flow in each of the five years is then discounted at 10 per cent pa. For example, in year 3, £16.14 million is multiplied by 0.751 to give a present value of £12.13 million.
- The five years of present value are then added together to give the total of £61.14 million for the strategy.
- Finally, the NPV of the terminal value of the strategy is calculated and added to the NPV of the total free cash flow to provide the corporate value. The calculation was done in four stages:
  - the free cash flow in year 5, £23.33 million, was divided by the cost of capital to yield a terminal value of £233.3 million at the end of year 5;
  - the present value of the terminal value was obtained by applying the five-year discount factor, £233.3 million × 0.6209 = £144.84 million;
  - the PV of the terminal value is then added to the PV of the free cash flows to provide the corporate value of £205.98 million.

The final step is to convert the corporate value into a share price prediction. We do this in two stages. First, the net bank borrowings of £45.25 million must be deducted from the corporate value to provide the value of the total business from a shareholder perspective: £160.73 million. Second, this value is divided by the 50 million shares in issue to provide a share price prediction of £3.21.

When compared with the current profit after tax we find that the predicted share price implies a multiple of 14 times current EPS. This is £3.21/(£15.93 million × 0.72/50 million) where tax at 28 per cent (the 0.72 factor) is deducted from the operating profit and the result is then divided by the 50 million shares in issue to provide EPS of 22.93p. This is then divided into the predicted share price to give the PE 14.

I have serious reservations about the terminal value aspect of corporate and shareholder value methodology: 70.3 per cent of the corporate value of Smart plc is composed of the terminal value of £144.84 million. This very significant part of the value depends on the ability of Smart plc to generate this level of free cash flow indefinitely. It is certainly true that Smart plc is investing heavily in the real drivers of growth. Nevertheless, investors would be foolish to buy shares at £3.21 if this was the market price when this price is so dependent on market conditions far into the future.

A suggested alternative to the methodology outlined above

It would only be fair to criticize the terminal value approach if one were prepared to offer a viable alternative. I believe that a workable alternative exists. To understand how this works requires one to consider why some businesses trade on a higher PE than others. There are two reasons: a) the industry sector is likely to be viewed as less risky than the average for all quoted companies; and b) the competitive advantage offers a free cash flow premium. Taking these factors into account, I will show you how to approximate what the share price of Smart plc should be.

First, we will assume that the appropriate PE for the sector is 12, having taken into account the perception of risk in the sector. With EPS of 22.93p this would justify a share price of £2.75 if Smart plc did not have a strategy that promised a free cash flow premium. Since the strategy of Smart plc promises a discounted free cash flow of £1.22 per share this should be added to the 'par' value to provide an indicated price of £3.97 and a PE of 17.3. I believe this provides a simple and far superior indication of what the share price of Smart plc ought to be.

In the same way, the share price of a business in a more risky sector or having a dangerous level of gearing would be estimated using a lower PE and adjusting this for the free cash flow premium promised by the strategy.

Finally, where the strategy will destroy value the negative free cash flow per share should be deducted from the share price to indicate the appropriate market price.

THE REAL DRIVERS OF GROWTH

The predicted share price of £3.21 and the PE 14 are not very exciting for a company that plans to grow its sales at a compound rate of 20 per cent pa. Smart plc is investing heavily in the drivers of growth in order to generate its predicted sales. These drivers, which should generate a free cash flow premium, are product development, market development, customer care and staff development. These investments have a major influence on sales growth. They have been largely overlooked in shareholder value models, possibly because they are included in the normal costs of running a business and charged as expenses in the profit and loss account. Nevertheless, I believe that excellent products or services, excellent staff and excellent customer care are fundamental to the generation of a free cash flow premium. Consequently, the development drivers should be recognized, as laid out in Figure 13.1.

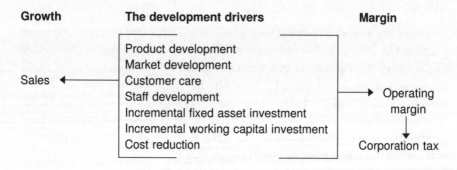

Figure 13.1 *The development drivers*

Product development and shareholder value

It is generally accepted that in five years' time progressive businesses will derive at least one-third of their sales and profits from products not currently sold. As a consequence, a prudent business will invest heavily in new product development. Leading-edge industries such as pharmaceuticals and electronics are committing between 10 and 15 per cent of sales to new product development. If your business wants to create and sustain a competitive advantage it is necessary to have an R&D budget that commits at least as much funds to product development as your competitors, and a high-quality product development function that spends its cash resources wisely.

Product research can be highly speculative, and as a consequence megamergers have taken place, notably in the pharmaceutical industry, where the merger of Glaxo with SmithKline Beecham was undoubtedly motivated by the need for excellent research and the elimination of overlap.

Market development and shareholder value

Until recent years the sales of most businesses were mainly achieved in local markets. It is interesting to look at the geographic breakdown of sales, profits and assets in the segmental analysis of successful multinationals. In many cases they derive more than half of their sales and profits from export markets.

The development of new markets is difficult and expensive. This is because promotional strategies must be tailored to meet local conditions. Advertising and local language labelling are two obvious examples of such tailoring. Many businesses approach the development of new markets through joint ventures and acquisitions. The advantage of such initiatives is that you can import a ready-made presence in the new market and staff that are already tuned in to local conditions.

Unfortunately, there is very little information disclosed in published accounts on market development expenditure, and this makes benchmarking difficult. Nevertheless, to achieve significant growth in free cash flow many businesses have defined the world as their marketplace and are prepared to commit the funds necessary to enable them to create competitive advantage in virtually every country. Perhaps the longest-established and best examples of the world as their market place come from the soft drinks industry (Coca-Cola and Pepsi).

Customer care and shareholder value

Experts in marketing have recognized that it costs five times as much to recruit a new customer as it does to retain an existing one. As a consequence, expenditure needed to protect existing customers is strongly focused on quality and care. This is necessary because any customers lost will increase the stretch required to achieve growth in sales and free cash flow. Quality control is a cornerstone of customer care. Many assembly functions will allow zero tolerance of defects in components they acquire. To survive in this climate suppliers must invest in excellent and expensive QC.

Once again, very little information is disclosed in published accounts on customer care expenditure and this makes benchmarking difficult. Nevertheless, the wise business accepts that customer care is paramount and will have correctly identified what it costs through their activity-based costing system.

Staff development and shareholder value

Expenditure on staff development is an integral part of creating and sustaining competitive advantage. Companies like IBM are prepared to spend in excess of 10 per cent of salaries and wages on staff development. Some staff development expenditure is linked to the other value drivers such as product and market development and customer care. A wise business requires that staff spend at least two weeks on management and technical training each year. The commitment of this time is built into their job descriptions and appraisals. Benchmarking staff development costs in your sector is once again difficult. Nevertheless, the wise business will commit large sums in the pursuit of excellence.

STRATEGIC INITIATIVES THAT HELP TO ENHANCE SHAREHOLDER VALUE

In constructing its financial strategy and shareholder value analysis, Smart plc placed the emphasis on sales growth and differentiation. As we saw at the start of this chapter, a lowest cost strategy is the way to compete in a market where substantial differentiation is not possible. Any organization can achieve improvements in shareholder value by locating and implementing more effective management practices. Cost reduction, process re-engineering and asset utilization all provide routes to enhanced shareholder value. Market, customer and product profitability analyses, particularly using activity-based costing techniques, also provide insights into ways that value can be enhanced.

An example of shareholder value for a lowest cost producer

Slim plc operates in markets where there are many competitors and little opportunity for differentiation. It expects sales to grow at 5 per cent pa over the next four years. The corporate and shareholder value computations are shown in Table 13.3.

Table 13.3 _Corporate and shareholder value computations, Slim plc_

Corporate value, Slim plc	Current	Year 1	Year 2	Year 3	Year 4	Year 5	Total
Sales £ million	145.24	152.50	160.13	168.13	176.54	185.37	
Operating margin	17.43	18.68	20.02	21.44	22.95	24.56	
Depreciation		1.50	1.80	2.10	2.46	2.89	
Effective tax rate		−5.51	−5.90	−6.32	−6.77	−7.25	
Incremental fixed asset		−1.80	−2.16	−2.52	−2.95	−3.47	
Incremental working capital		−0.62	−0.65	−0.68	−0.71	−0.75	
Free cash flow		12.25	13.10	14.01	14.97	15.99	
Discount factor 11%		0.901	0.812	0.731	0.659	0.593	
PV of free cash flow		11.04	10.63	10.25	9.86	9.49	51.27
Terminal value							86.25
							137.52

Shareholder value, Slim plc

Corporate value	137.52
Deduct net debt	46.75
Shareholder value	90.77
Shares in issue	40 million
Predicted price	2.27

Notes:

The sales in year 1 are predicted to be £145.24 million + 5% = £152.5 million.

The operating margin in year 1 is predicted to be £152.5 million × 12.25% = £18.68 million. In each subsequent year the margin will improve by a further 0.25%.

Depreciation is added back as a non-cash cost.

The tax liability in year 1 is £18.68 million × 29.5% = £5.51 million. The effective rate of tax is predicted to remain at 29.5% in the four subsequent years.

The incremental fixed assets in year 1 are £1.5 million × 1.2 = £1.8 million. The 1.2 factor is the reinvestment rate and will continue at this level for the remaining years.

The incremental working capital is (£152.5 − £145.24) × 8.5% = £0.62 million. The 8.5% investment will continue to be needed to support growth in subsequent years.

The free cash flow in year 1 is £18.68 million + £1.5 − £5.51 million − £1.8 million − £0.62 or £12.25 million.

The free cash flow in each year is then discounted at 11% pa, the cost of capital of Slim Plc; for example, in year 1, £12.25 million is multiplied by 0.901 to give a present value of £11.04 million.

The five years of present value are then added to give the total of £51.27 million for the strategy.

Finally the terminal value of the strategy is calculated and added to the total free cash flow to provide the corporate value. The calculation was done in four stages:

1. The free cash flow in year 5, £15.99 million, was divided by the cost of capital to yield an assumed value of £145.36 million at the end of year 5.
2. The present value of the terminal value was obtained by applying the five-year discount factor: £145.36 million × 0.6209 = £86.25 million
3. The PV of the terminal value is then added to the PV of the free cash flows to provide the corporate value of £137.52 million.
4. The net bank borrowings of £46.75 million is deducted to give a value for shareholders of £90.77 million.

This is divided by the 40 million shares in issue to give a predicted share price of £2.27.

The predicted share price yields a PE of 7.4. This is so low that it is clear that the proposed strategy is not generating enough value and should be rejected by the board of directors. The board instructed the finance director to prepare a second version of the strategy in which sales were targeted to rise by 7 per cent pa and margin to improve by 0.4 per cent pa. The revised valuation is shown in Table 13.4.

Table 13.4 *Revised corporate and shareholder value, Slim plc*

Corporate value, Slim plc	Current	Year 1	Year 2	Year 3	Year 4	Year 5	Total
Sales (£ million)	145.24	155.41	166.29	177.93	190.38	203.71	
Operating margin	17.43	19.27	21.28	23.49	25.89	28.52	
Depreciation		1.50	1.80	2.10	2.46	2.89	
Effective tax rate		−5.68	−6.28	−6.93	−7.64	−8.41	
Incremental fixed asset		−1.80	−2.16	−2.52	−2.95	−3.47	
Incremental working capital		−0.86	−0.92	−0.99	−1.06	−1.13	
Free cash flow		12.42	13.72	15.15	16.70	18.40	
Discount factor 11%		0.901	0.812	0.731	0.659	0.593	
PV of free cash flow		11.19	11.14	11.08	11.00	10.92	55.32
Terminal value							99.24
							154.56
Shareholder value, Slim plc							
Corporate value	154.56						
Deduct net debt	46.75						
Shareholder value	107.81						
Shares in issue	40 million						
Predicted price	2.70						

This revised corporate and shareholder value computation helps us to understand that a lowest cost producer strategy tends to lead to an unexciting share price. If the price rises to the £2.70 indicated by the shareholder value computation, the PE remains an undemanding 8.8. This is consistent with the view that a differentiation strategy will lead to a higher multiple than a lowest cost strategy.

My valuation of Slim plc

As the sector is highly competitive and offers little scope for differentiation, I will assume that a 'par' PE of 8 is appropriate for the sector. With earnings per share of 30.72p this would justify a share price of £2.46 if Slim plc did not have a strategy that promised a free cash flow premium. Since the strategy of Slim plc promises a discounted free cash flow of £1.38 per share, this should be added to the 'par' value to provide an indicated price of £3.84 and a PE of 12.5.

LINKING VALUE ENHANCEMENT TO REMUNERATION

When shareholder value has been recognized as the key goal of an organization, it is now widely accepted that the remuneration of key employees should be linked to their ability to devise and implement value-enhancing strategies. Such bonuses should ideally be in the form of share options rather than cash because this part of the remuneration package is then firmly linked to stock market judgements of the success of the strategy.

Nevertheless, it is true that many quoted companies trade at share prices wildly different from those that the shareholder value model suggests. This causes much frustration for directors and managers who hold options to buy shares that have not been traded up to the value implied by the model. The fundamental problem is that the market has a different view of prospects from that of management. The challenge implicit in the price gap is that management must persuade the market that it can deliver its strategy. Success in these persuasive and delivery roles justifies the giving of share options.

SHAREHOLDER VALUE IN A DIVERSIFIED BUSINESS

It is inevitable that when a business operates in a variety of markets and product sectors that the free cash flow will vary dramatically in different parts of the group. In such cases it is necessary to break down the shareholder value analysis into smaller, discrete sections. It is normal for a business that makes such a breakdown to discover that some sections of the business are destroying value. Such findings lead to initiatives to re-engineer or 'unbundle' poor performers. ('Unbundling' will be examined in Chapter 15.) The analysis is complicated by the fact that many of the assets and costs are central rather than product or market related. Activity-based costing techniques (examined in Chapter 10) help to apportion the costs reliably.

SUMMARY

The enhancement of shareholder value has now been accepted as the primary goal of publicly quoted companies. It is measured by computing the PV of the free cash flows promised by the financial strategy and the terminal value. As with most aspects of finance, sales are the core. However, the projected growth in sales must be offset by additional overheads, development drivers and projected corporation tax liabilities in order to assess whether the strategy will enhance or destroy value. In all cases where the strategy indicates a destruction of value the relevant sector should be re-engineered or sold.

The shareholder value methodology is much more scientific than the crude traditional PE-based valuation mechanisms. In my opinion, as explained in this chapter, the value of any business should be estimated starting from a PE appropriate to the risk profile of the industry and adjusted for the free cash flow that the strategy indicates will be created or destroyed. Estimating the appropriate share price in this way removes the questionable estimation of terminal value.

14

Foreign currency transactions and translations

Most companies have some foreign currency transactions. Such transactions expose a business to additional risks and rewards as rates of exchange can vary dramatically even in short periods of time. The problem for businesses is that even the exchange rate experts frequently predict movements incorrectly. In saying this I am not being over-critical of such experts. They can only predict trends on the basis of their current knowledge and experience. Nevertheless, readers should understand that significant movements in exchange rates can wreak havoc on profitability and financial stability. Furthermore, active treasury management can reduce or remove the risk of adverse exchange rate movements.

Writing illustrations of exchange rate issues and treasury management techniques is also a hazardous occupation. The problem is the time that will elapse between writing about it and when you read it. Even the daily financial press are exposed to this problem. Their reports of exchange rates are based on the close of business on the previous day. Overnight news and supply and demand for currencies in US and Asian markets sometimes result in significant changes in exchange rates. Nevertheless, let me assure you that though exchange rates may be different at the time of reading, the risks of unfavourable movements and the ways of insulating against them will remain valid.

RISKS ASSOCIATED WITH FOREIGN CURRENCY TRANSACTIONS

When a business carries out transactions denominated in foreign currencies it becomes exposed to six major types of additional penalties, as shown in Table 14.1.

Table 14.1 *The six major additional penalties in foreign currency transactions*

Transaction type	Exchange rate movement	Impact
Credit sale	Local currency strengthens	Exchange rate loss
Credit purchase	Local currency weakens	Exchange rate loss
Future credit sale	Local currency strengthens	Reduced sales revenue
Future credit purchase	Local currency weakens	Increased cost
Monetary asset	Local currency strengthens	Loss on translation (asset value declines)
Monetary liability	Local currency weakens	Loss on translation (liability increases)

The first and second types of penalty are based on actual transactions. The loss will affect the profit and loss account of the business. The third and fourth types of penalty affect expected future transactions. The movements in exchange rates will reduce future revenue or increase future cost that will be included in future profit and loss accounts and will damage the competitive position of the seller or buyer. The fifth and sixth types of penalty have nothing to do with day-to-day operations, but the paper losses will have to be included in the statement of total recognized gains and losses and will reduce the value of assets or increase the scale of liabilities on future balance sheets.

What should a business do in the face of these potential losses? It can decide to ignore them or to actively manage them. If it decides to ignore them it takes a gamble that is not normally part of its mandate from shareholders. It might try to justify the gamble on the grounds that it is possible that it could gain from a favourable movement in exchange rates. For example, if its local currency weakens then the amount collected from an export credit sale increases and provides a gain on the transaction. This gain will be included in the profit and loss account. The potential to gain exists in each of the six types of currency exposure. Any business can actively manage its foreign currency exposures. The fact that there must always be an equal and opposite exposure provides the basis for all exchange risk management techniques.

Table 14.2 _The effect of exchange rate movements on sales, liabilities, costs and assets_

	Sales	Liabilities	Costs	Assets
Local currency strength	Lose	Lose	Gain	Gain
Local currency weakness	Gain	Gain	Lose	Lose

The impact of movements in exchange rates provides the foundations upon which exposures can be eliminated. An exporter that fears local currency strength can be matched with an importer that fears local currency weakness. A holder of a foreign currency asset that fears currency weakness can be matched with a holder of a foreign currency liability that fears local currency strength.

Equal and opposite exposure within a business

The cheapest and most effective way to manage exchange rate exposure is to do it in-house. To do so requires that the organization has equal amounts of exposure to currency strength and currency weakness. For example, if a UK company has equal values of US dollar purchases and US dollar sales it will not care whether the dollar strengthens or weakens. This is because if the dollar strengthens then gains from exporting in dollars will cancel losses from importing in dollars, and if the dollar weakens then gains from importing in dollars will cancel losses from exporting in dollars.

The operation of this exchange rate management can be done in two ways. First, the company can maintain a bank account denominated in US dollars and pass all dollar receipts and payments through this account. Second, it can synchronize the receipts and payments denominated in dollars using 'leading' and 'lagging'. To 'lead' involves making a payment before the agreed settlement date. To 'lag' involves delaying a payment beyond the agreed settlement date. The foreign currency bank account is by far the better approach. It avoids the cost of the spread involved in buying and selling foreign currencies. For example, today a Welsh company will receive and pay $1,124,800. The bank quotes £1 = $1.48–1.52. The bank is prepared to buy the dollars at £1 = $1.52 and to sell the dollars at £1 = $1.48. If the company sells its dollars it will receive £740,000. If it buys its dollars it will cost £760,000. The spread will cost the organization £20,000.

These examples relate to profit and loss account items. Assets and liabilities denominated in foreign currencies also leave a business exposed to exchange rate risk. This is because when the financial statements are being prepared, SSAP 20 requires that monetary assets and liabilities should be translated to local currency at the rate prevailing on the balance sheet date. Once again the simplest and cheapest form of balance sheet exchange rate management is for a business to have equal amounts of monetary assets and monetary liabilities denominated in the foreign currency.

In this chapter we examine how Mundi Ltd manages its foreign currency exposures. The content is divided into three sections: types of transactions, recording transactions, and exchange risks and rewards.

TYPES OF TRANSACTIONS

Mundi Ltd is involved in the following types of foreign currency exposures. It:

- sells goods priced in foreign currencies;
- collects from customers in foreign currencies;
- purchases goods priced in foreign currencies;
- pays suppliers in foreign currencies;
- borrows money in foreign currencies;
- owns assets denominated in foreign currencies;
- tenders for contracts in foreign currencies;
- has a wholly owned subsidiary in the United States that keeps its accounts in US dollars.

In each case Mundi Ltd must record the transactions correctly, must decide how to treat them in its sterling financial statements and should take steps to minimize the impact of unfavourable movements in exchange rates.

RECORDING TRANSACTIONS

The eight types of exposure can be divided into four categories for accounting purposes:

1. Purchases and sales denominated in foreign currencies.
2. Assets and liabilities denominated in foreign currencies.
3. Investment in companies that maintain their accounts in foreign currencies.
4. Actions that may or may not create a foreign currency exposure. Tendering is the normal source of such uncertainty.

Category 1. Purchases and sales

Purchases and sales denominated in foreign currencies are converted into local currency at the rate prevailing on the date when the transaction takes place. This provides the data for inclusion in the profit and loss account. When the transaction is on credit it also creates a group 2 exposure. The settlement cost or proceeds may turn out to be different from the recorded value due to local currency strength or weakness. When the settlement is different, the value of the purchases or sales is not changed. The difference between the recorded figure and the settlement cost or proceeds are included in the profit and loss account as an exchange rate gain or loss.

Recording category 1 transactions

Example 1. A cash sale to a US customer denominated in dollars

On 9 August Mundi Ltd sold goods to a US customer for $1 million cash. The most favourable exchange rate quotation from three London banks was £1 = $1.6090–1.630. This quotation was accepted. How should the transaction be recorded?

Mundi Ltd will wish to sell the dollar proceeds. The rule is that the bank buys the dollars high (right-hand quote). It will credit Mundi with £613,497 ($1 million/1.63). This will be recorded as a sale and as a cash receipt.

Example 2. A cash purchase from a German supplier denominated in euros

Mundi Ltd bought goods from a German supplier for €2.4 million cash. The most favourable exchange rate quotation was £1 = €1.6129–1.6389. The quotation was accepted. How should the transaction be recorded?

355

Mundi Ltd will need to buy euros. The rule is that the bank sells euros low (left-hand quote). It will charge Mundi Ltd £1,488,003 (€2.4 million/ 1.6129). This will be recorded as a purchase and as a cash payment.

To simplify subsequent illustrations I will use a single exchange rate for buying and selling foreign currencies. The cost of the spread between bid and offer price is nevertheless significant.

Category 2. Assets and liabilities

Assets and liabilities denominated in foreign currencies are also converted into local currency at the rate prevailing on the date when the transaction takes place. The assets and liabilities can be divided into two major groupings: monetary assets and liabilities, and non-monetary assets and liabilities.

Monetary assets and liabilities expose an organization to potential future currency gains and losses. This is because in preparing subsequent balance sheets the assets or liabilities must be translated into local currency at the rate prevailing on that date. When a monetary asset is realized (for example, by collection of a debt from a customer or repatriation of funds previously held in a foreign currency bank account) any difference between the amount realized and the previous carrying value must be recorded as a translation gain or loss. There are two major types of exposure: those that create trade creditors and trade debtors. In these cases any gain or loss between point of purchase or sale and settlement must be recorded in the profit and loss account; and those that create other types of assets or liabilities. These are generally of a long-term nature. Gains or losses on translation are purely 'paper' results. They may be compounded or alleviated by subsequent strength or weakness of the local currency.

Recording category 2 transactions

Example 1. A credit sale to a US customer denominated in dollars

If the $1 million sale by Mundi Ltd is to be paid for on 9 November then the sale and debtor will be recorded at £613,497 as previously. The proceeds at settlement are uncertain at this stage. We will assume two possible exchange rates at 9 November to show how the customer settlement is handled.

In case 1 (Table 14.3) sterling is weak and Mundi Ltd earns an extra profit. In case 2 sterling is strong and Mundi Ltd loses money between sale and settlement. Should Mundi Ltd risk a possible elimination of its margin on the transaction due to sterling strength between sale and settlement? A gambler would take the risk. Sterling might weaken and result in a currency

Table 14.3 _Two possible exchange rates on the date of settlement_

	Case 1	Case 2
	£ = $1.409–1.430	£ = $1.809–1.830
Proceeds	£699,301	£546,448
Debtor balance	£613,497	£613,497
Exchange gain (loss)	£85,804	£(67,049)

gain. Mundi Ltd is not prepared to take the risk. We will see how it can protect itself later.

A further complication can arise. Mundi Ltd prepares a balance sheet as at 31 October. The US debtor was recorded in the books at £613,497. This amount is unlikely to be correct for balance sheet purposes. We will consider two rates of exchange at 31 October; see Table 14.4.

Table 14.4 _Two rates of exchange on the date of preparing the balance sheet_

	Case 1	Case 2
	£ = $1.389–1.410	£ = $1.829–1.850
Correct balance	£709,220	£540,541
Recorded balance	£613,497	£613,497
Exchange gain (loss)	£95,723	£(72,956)

In case 1 the trade debt is adjusted in the balance sheet to £709,220 and an exchange gain of £95,723 is added to the profit as a result of sterling weakness. In case 2 the trade debt is adjusted to £540,541 and an exchange loss of £72,956 will be charged against profits as a result of sterling strength. The settlement figure may be known when the balance sheet is prepared. Any exchange movement subsequent to 31 October is ignored unless a significant loss is involved. A second adjustment is usually required at settlement; see Table 14.5.

Table 14.5 *Adjusting for exchange rate changes*

	Case 1	Case 2
	£ = $1.409–1.430	£ = $1.809–1.830
Proceeds	£699,301	£546,448
Debtor balance (31 October)	£709,220	£540,541
Exchange gain (loss)	£(9,919)	£5,907

The proceeds £699,301 or £546,448 are received. The profit and loss account will be charged with a loss of £9,919 in case 1 or credited with a gain of £5,907 in case 2.

Example 2. A credit purchase from a German supplier denominated in euros

Suppose the €2.4 million purchase from Germany was due to be paid on 9 November; the situation can be summarized assuming the exchange rates shown in Table 14.6.

Table 14.6 *Credit purchases and exchange rates*

	Case 1	Case 2
9 August	£ = €1.6129–1.6389	£ = €1.6129–1.6389
31 October	£ = €1.6429–1.6689	£ = €1.5829–1.6089
9 November	£ = €1.6229–1.6489	£ = €1.6029–1.6229
	£	£
Purchase/creditor	1,488,003	1,488,003
Gain/(loss)	27,172	(28,201)
31 October creditor	1,460,831	1,516,204
Gain/(loss)	(18,003)	18,918
Settlement	1,478,834	1,497,286

The cost £1,488,003 is recorded as a purchase and as a trade creditor on 9 August. In case 1 the creditor is reduced to £1,460,831 as sterling strengthens to 31 October. An exchange gain of £27,172 is credited to the profit and loss account. Part of the gain, £18,003, disappears at settlement when £1,478,834 must be paid to the supplier. This must be charged to the profit and loss account. In case 2 the creditor increases to £1,516,204 at 31 October. An exchange loss of £28,201 is charged to the profit and loss account. Part of the loss, £18,918, is recovered at settlement and is added to the November profit. Should Mundi Ltd risk a possible increase in cost due to a weakness in sterling between purchase and settlement? A gambler would take the risk. Sterling might strengthen and result in a currency gain. Mundi is not prepared to take the risk. We will see how it protects itself later.

Example 3. Foreign currency borrowing/repayments

Foreign currency borrowing can be very attractive. Interest rates on borrowings in some major foreign currencies are currently lower than on sterling loans. Mundi Ltd borrowed $6 million on 9 August at 7 per cent per annum. The loan is repayable in five equal annual instalments of capital and interest. Table 14.7 shows the dollar loan and interest obligations.

Table 14.7 _The dollar loan repayment and interest obligations_

$ Cash flows

Year	Opening loan	Interest at 7%	Total repaid[a]	Capital repaid	Closing loan
1	6,000,000	420,000	1,463,344	1,043,344	4,956,656
2	4,956,656	346,966	1,463,345	1,116,379	3,840,277
3	3,840,277	268,819	1,463,344	1,194,525	2,645,752
4	2,645,752	185,203	1,463,345	1,278,142	1,367,610
5	1,367,610	95,734	1,463,344	1,367,610	–
		1,316,722	7,316,722	6,000,000	

Note:
[a] I calculated the annual payments using the discount factor for the present value of a five-year annuity at 7% pa. This is $6 million/4.1 = $1,463,344.

Sterling equivalent (exchange rate 9 August £ = $1.63)

Year	Opening loan	Interest at 7%	Total repaid	Capital repaid	Closing loan
1	3,680,982	257,669	897,757	640,088	3,040,894
2	3,040,894	212,863	897,758	684,895	2,355,999
3	2,355,999	164,920	897,757	732,837	1,623,162
4	1,623,162	113,621	897,757	784,136	839,026
5	839,026	58,732	897,758	839,026	–
		807,805	4,488,787	3,680,982	

The sterling value of the loan was recorded in the books at the exchange rate prevailing on the date when the loan was received. The liability will usually have to be increased or reduced when subsequent balance sheets are prepared. For example, if sterling were to strengthen to £1 = $1.80 at 31 October then the balance sheet value of the loan would be changed to £3,333,333. The reduction in the liability of £347,647 would be a translation gain. Equally, if sterling were to weaken to £1 = $1.50 at 31 October then the balance sheet value of the loan would be changed to £4 million. The increase in the liability of £319,018 would be a translation loss. Subsequent movements in exchange rates will lead to further translation gains or losses.

If the exchange rate were to remain constant then the total interest cost would be £807,805. This is £275,694 less than for a five-year UK loan at 10 per cent. The possible saving seems attractive, but there is a serious snag. Mundi Ltd will have to buy $1,463,344 each year to make the capital and interest payments. The cost of the dollars will rise if sterling weakens. The exchange rates at the dates of purchase will determine the sterling cost. Consider three possible exchange rates, shown in Table 14.8.

Table 14.8   *The effects of three possible exchange rates*

	Case 1 £ = $1.20	Case 2 £ = $1.30	Case 3 £ = $1.40
Annual repayment[a]	1,219,454	1,125,650	1,045,246
Total repaid[b]	6,097,268	5,628,248	5,226,230
Repaid if rate is constant	4,488,787	4,488,787	4,488,787
Excess cost	1,608,481	1,139,461	737,443

Notes:
[a] Mundi Ltd must buy $1,463,344 at £1 = $1.20, $1.30 and $1.40 respectively.
[b] Assumes a constant but weaker sterling through the five year period (ie £1,219,454 × 5 = £6,097,268, etc).

The repayments on a five-year sterling loan at 10 per cent would be £971,034 pa (3,680,982/3.7908 PV of five-year annuity at 10 per cent). If the exchange rate averages less than £1 = $1.507, the 'cheap' US loan will prove to be a Greek(!) gift. Mundi Ltd should not take the risk of a weakening sterling. Better exchange risk management techniques are available. Nevertheless, if sterling remains stable or strengthens the interest and cash flow savings will be significant.

Example 4. A foreign currency asset

When a business owns an asset overseas that was purchased in a foreign currency, the value for local accounting is determined by the rate of exchange prevailing at the acquisition date. The value of such assets must be recomputed at the exchange rate prevailing on each subsequent balance sheet date. Translation is straightforward. A gain or loss arises when the exchange rate is different from the preceding accounting period. This gain or loss is carried to the statement of total gains and losses and does not affect the profit and loss account.

Category 3. Investments

The day-to-day financial records of overseas subsidiaries and related companies are usually maintained in their local currencies. A UK parent will not need to record such transactions except for planning, control and consolidation purposes. Many UK companies use predetermined exchange rates for planning and control and do not adjust to actual rates unless the predetermined rate has been seriously misjudged. The reason for this is that the rules for conversion of foreign currency assets, liabilities and equity are focused on annual performance. These rules are defined in SSAP 20 and can be summarized as follows.

The financial statements of overseas subsidiaries can be maintained in two different ways. First, the books and accounts may be maintained in sterling. Under this method each transaction is converted to local currency at the rate prevailing at the time. SSAP 20 defines the circumstances in which this form of accounting is appropriate. The affairs of the foreign enterprise must be so closely interlinked with those of the investing company that its results may be regarded as being more dependent on the economic environment of the investing company's currency than its own reporting currency. In such cases the consolidation should be prepared as if all transactions had been entered into by the investing company itself in its own currency. This method of accounting is called the 'temporal rate' method. The rare occasions in which it is appropriate are defined in paragraphs 2, 3 and 4 of SSAP20.

Second, the books and accounts may be maintained in a foreign currency. The conversion of such figures into local currency for consolidation recognizes that the investment is made in the net worth rather than the individual assets and liabilities. Amounts in the balance sheet (other than net worth) should be converted to local currency at the exchange rate prevailing on the balance sheet date. Amounts in the profit and loss account should be converted at the average rate prevailing throughout the financial year or at the closing rate for the financial year. Using this method, exchange gains and losses can be divided into trading (dealt with in the profit and loss account) and non-trading (carried directly to reserves).

The closing rate method is appropriate for the vast majority of overseas investments.

Recording category 3 transactions

The financial results of SubMundi Inc, a US subsidiary of Mundi Ltd, have been received for inclusion in the group accounts. We will examine the impact of translation on the profit and loss account and balance sheet as sterling strengthens and weakens.

Example 1. Profit and loss translation, pound strengthening

Table 14.9 *Profit and loss translation, pound strengthening*

Exchange rates	2001	2002
Average	£ = $1.50	£ = $1.70
Closing	£ = $1.60	£ = $1.80

$ 2001	Closing	Average		$ 2002	Closing	Average
980,000	612,500	653,333	Sales	1,152,000	640,000	677,647
735,000	459,375	490,000	Cost of sales	864,000	480,000	508,235
245,000	153,125	163,333	Gross profit	288,000	160,000	169,412
186,000	116,250	124,000	Other expense	198,000	110,000	116,471
59,000	36,875	39,333	Profit before tax	90,000	50,000	52,941
23,600	14,750	14,750	Tax	36,000	20,000	20,000
35,400	22,125	24,583	Profit after tax	54,000	30,000	32,941
32,000	20,000	20,000	Proposed div.	32,000	17,778	17,778
3,400	2,125	4,583	Profit retained	22,000	12,222	15,163

Sterling strengthened through 2001 and 2002. If the exchange rate remained at £1 = $1.60 at the end of 2000 the sales would have translated into £720,000 and the retained profits into £13,750. As sterling strengthens, the buying power of the translated dollar sales declines to £677,647 on average and £640,000 at the closing rate. Similarly, the buying power of the dollar profit retained becomes £15,163 on average and £12,222 at the closing rate. Mundi Ltd would have preferred a constant exchange rate or weakness in sterling (to increase the buying power of its dollar earnings).

Note that even when using the average rate the tax liability and the proposed dividend must be translated at the closing rate. They are monetary liabilities driven by balance sheet translation rules. Both average and closing rate translations are shown in this example. In most of the subsequent illustrations only the closing rate conversion is shown.

Example 1. Balance sheet translation, pound strengthening

Table 14.10 _Balance sheet translation, £ strengthening_

Exchange rates 2001 £ = $1.60 2002 £ = $1.80

$ 2001	£ 2001		$ 2002	£ 2002
324,000	202,500	Fixed assets	288,000	160,000
300,000	187,500	Current assets	360,000	200,000
Creditors				
160,000	100,000	Trade	144,000	80,000
5,000	3,125	Bank loans	10,600	5,889
23,600	14,750	Tax provision	36,000	20,000
32,000	20,000	Proposed dividend	32,000	17,778
(220,600)	(137,875)		(222,600)	(123,667)
403,400	252,125	Net assets	425,400	236,333
Financed by:				
400,000	285,714	Share capital[1]	400,000	285,714
3,400	2,125	Revenue reserve[2]	25,400	14,347
–	(35,714)	Exchange losses[3]	–	(63,728)[4]
403,400	252,125		425,400	236,333

Notes:

[1] The capital was introduced at start-up in 2000 when the exchange rate was £1 = $1.40. The share capital will always be translated at this rate thereafter.

[2] These are the closing rate profits retained. Average rate translation would have increased the revenue reserve and the translation loss by £5,399 (2001 £2,458).

[3] An exchange loss arose as a result of the strength of sterling. It was computed as follows:

	2001 £	2002 £
Opening net assets	285,714[a]	252,125[c]
Closing net assets	250,000[b]	224,111[d]
Translation loss for year	35,714	28,014
Opening loss		35,714
		63,728

[4] Cumulative translation loss

[a] $400,000/1.4 = £285,714   [b] $400,000/1.6 = £250,000
[c] $403,400/1.6 = £252,125   [d] $403,400/1.8 = £224,111

Closing rate conversion must be used in the balance sheet. Each component of the net assets is translated at the closing rate of £1 = $1.60 in 2001 and £1 = $1.80 in 2002. The exchange losses will be recorded in the statement of total recognized gains and losses.

Sterling strengthened in this example. It had the following serious consequences for Mundi Ltd. The sales, costs, profits, assets and liabilities of SubMundi Inc translate into a lower sterling value than if the exchange rate stayed constant. The starting capital (invested in weakening dollar net assets) causes translation losses.

If the exchange rate strengthened to £1 = $1.60 at the end of 2001 and then remained constant, then the translated value of the dollar net assets would have been £265,875 ($425,400/1.6). The strength of sterling in example 1 reduced their value on translation by £29,542.

Mundi Ltd recognized the risk that losses could occur if sterling strengthened. In the last section of this chapter we will see how it can reduce the translation risk. We will now examine the effect of sterling weakness on the translation of the dollar results.

Example 2. Profit and loss translation, pound weakening

Table 14.11 *Profit and loss translation, £ weakening*

Exchange rates 2001 £ = $1.20 2002 £ = $1.00

$ 2001	£ 2001		$ 2002	£ 2002
980,000	816,667	Sales	1,152,000	1,152,000
735,000	612,500	Cost of sales	864,000	864,000
245,000	204,167	Gross profit	288,000	288,000
186,000	155,000	Other expenses	198,000	198,000
59,000	49,167	Profit before tax	90,000	90,000
23,600	19,667	Tax	36,000	36,000
35,400	29,500	Profit after tax	54,000	54,000
32,000	26,667	Proposed dividend	32,000	32,000
3,400	2,833	Profit retained	22,000	22,000

Example 2 Balance sheet translation, pound weakening

Table 14.12 *Balance sheet translation, £ weakening*

Exchange rates 2001 £ = $1.20 2002 £ = $1

$ 2001	£ 2001		$ 2002	£ 2002
324,000	270,000	Fixed assets	288,000	288,000
300,000	250,000	Current assets	360,000	360,000
Creditors				
160,000	133,333	Trade	144,000	144,000
5,000	4,167	Bank loans	10,600	10,600
23,600	19,667	Tax provision	36,000	36,000
32,000	26,666	Proposed dividend	32,000	32,000
(220,600)	(183,833)		(222,600)	(222,600)
403,400	336,167	Net assets	425,400	425,400
Financed by:				
400,000	285,714	Share capital[1]	400,000	285,714
3,400	2,833	Revenue reserve	25,400	24,833
–	47,620	Exchange gain[2]	–	114,853[3]
403,400	336,167		425,400	425,400

Notes:

If the exchange rate remained at £1 = $1.40 at the end of 2001 the net assets would have translated to £303,857. Weakness of sterling increased the buying power of the dollar assets on translation.

[1] The capital was introduced when the exchange rate stood at £1 = $1.40. The share capital will always be translated at this rate thereafter.

	2001 £	2002 £
Opening net assets	285,714[a]	336,167[c]
Closing net assets	333,334[b]	403,400[d]
[2] Exchange gain year	47,620	67,233
Opening gain		47,620
[3] Exchange gain cumulative		114,853

[a] $400,000/1.4 = £285,714   [b] $400,000/1.2 = £333,334
[c] $403,400/1.2 = £336,167   [d] $403,400/1.0 = £403,400

There are two major issues involved in the translation of SubMundi Inc. First, the assets and liabilities are converted at the rate prevailing on the balance sheet date. If the exchange rate remained at £1 = $1.40 the net assets would have translated to £303,857. A translation loss of £67,524 occurs if sterling strengthens to £1 = $1.80. A translation gain of £121,543 occurs if sterling weakens to £1 = $1. Second, the retained profit is translated as the sum of the closing rate dollar figures for the two years since SubMundi Inc was formed. If the exchange rate remained at £1 = $1.40 the retained profits would have translated into £18,143. A translation loss of £3,796 occurs as sterling strengthens to £1 = $1.80. A translation gain of £6,690 occurs as sterling weakens to £1 = $1.

Translation gains and losses are included in the statement of total recognized gains and losses; see Table 14.13.

Table 14.13 *Statement of total recognized gains and losses*

	Strong	**Weak**
Retained profits	3,796	6,690
Net asset translation	67,524	121,543
Per shareholders' funds	63,728	114,853

Category 4. Contingent exposures

Contingency exposures arise where a business may or may not have an exposure to currency fluctuations. For example, suppose that a UK company quoted US $5 million for a contract in the United States. If the tender is successful then it will be exposed to the risk of fluctuation in the exchange rate between sterling and the dollar. If the tender fails there will be no exposure. Such contingent exposures are best dealt with using foreign currency option contracts, as we will see later in the chapter.

Commercial risks

The risks involved in foreign currency transactions can be substantial. Export credit is most exposed. Assessment of credit risk is more complicated as acquiring and interpreting credit checks and references is difficult. Prudent vendors eliminate the risk using one of the following:

- credit insurance;
- debt factoring;
- confirmed irrevocable letters of credit;
- cash on delivery;
- sight drafts.

In addition, delays in delivery and damage in transit are more likely than with home sales.

EXCHANGE RISKS AND REWARDS

Some businesses ignore exchange risk. They argue that, over a long period, profits and losses on exchange tend to cancel out. Many businesses cannot risk such exposure. They could result in loss of confidence by financial institutions, suppliers, customers and shareholders. The prudent business will seek ways of protecting itself against exchange risks. Management of a business may be able to plead innocence where a company fails for other unforeseen reasons. If the failure is due to currency speculation, stakeholders will be unforgiving.

Exchange rate risk management techniques

To protect against the risk of exchange losses a business must be prepared to sacrifice the chance of exchange profits. The principle that allows the use of exchange rate management techniques is that a business that fears local currency weakness can eliminate the risk of loss by being matched against another business that fears local currency strength. Two protection methods are available: forward rate agreements and foreign currency option contracts.

Forward rate agreements

A forward rate agreement (FRA) is a guaranteed exchange rate offered by a bank whose customer wishes to buy or sell a foreign currency at a future date. The existence of an FRA will be of substantial comfort to the client company. It will enable the client to predict future cash inflows and outflows correctly. Banks offer two types of FRA: a) a forward exchange purchase contract, which guarantees the cost of buying a foreign currency on a defined future date; and b) a forward exchange sale contract, which guarantees the local currency proceeds from an export sale on a defined future date.

FRAs can be used to underpin actual purchase and sale transactions. They can also be used to stabilize the cost of future purchase and sale transactions. For example, a UK exporter wishes to be able to guarantee the dollar price and sterling value of the sales it will make over the next year. It can use a series of FRAs to provide the guarantees.

Forward exchange purchase contracts

Mundi Ltd bought goods costing €2.4 million on 9 August, payable three months later. One way of eliminating the exchange risk would be to buy the euros now, open a German deposit account and lodge the euros in it. A simpler method would be to arrange a forward exchange purchase contract. In theory this uses a UK bank in the creation of a German deposit account. This is how it works. A bank quoted a three-month forward rate of £1 = €1.5970–1.6258. If Mundi Ltd accepts this quote it will commit itself to buy €2.4 million for settlement. The cost would be €2.4 million/1.5970 = £1,502,772. This is £14,769 more than the spot rate would have cost. The extra cost arises because euro interest rates are lower than sterling. In theory this suggests that sterling will weaken, otherwise euro residents would deposit their savings in the UK. Euro interest rates would rise to stem the outflow and British interest rates would fall to reduce the inflow.

How can a bank give a guaranteed quote of £1 = €1.5970–1.6228? The quotation is based on locating another customer with an equal and opposite exposure that is prepared to sacrifice the possibility of a gain as a result of sterling strength to eliminate the possibility of a loss as a result of sterling weakness. In this case it will be a client that wishes to sell euros. It could be either a UK company that is selling in euros or a German company that wishes to buy in sterling.

If Mundi Ltd accepts the quote:

- The bank will deem Mundi Ltd to have opened a deposit account in Germany for three months. Suppose the German inter-bank rate is 3 per cent pa then the deposit required is €2,382,134. Over the next three months this will earn interest of €17,866. The closing balance of €2.4 million will be used to pay the euro bill. The deposit required is calculated as €2.4 million/1.0075.
- The bank will be deemed to buy €2,382,134 on the 'spot' market to make the German deposit. It will cost £1,476,296. This is calculated as 2,382,134/1.6129 (the 'spot' rate).

- The bank will deem Mundi Ltd to have opened a loan account of £1,476,926 for three months at the LIBOR rate of 7 per cent. It will charge Mundi Ltd £25,846 of interest (£1,476,926 × 1.75 per cent).
- At the end of the three-month period Mundi Ltd will pay the bank £1,502,772 to clear the loan.
- The price of the forward exchange purchase contract is quoted as £1 = €1.5970. This is arrived at by dividing €2.4 million by £1,502,772.

The settlement cost £1,502,772 is higher than the spot rate. This is because the deposit account earns interest at 0.75 per cent whereas the loan account is charged interest at 1.75 per cent. This is called an interest rate differential. If Mundi Ltd had bought the euros on 9 September it would have cost £1,488,003 (€2.4 million/1.6129). The three-month settlement delay increases the cost by £14,769.

Forward exchange sale contracts

To illustrate a forward exchange sales contract I will assume that Mundi Ltd sold goods for €2.4 million on 9 August payable in three months. The bank was asked to offer protection against the potential exchange risk. This is how it computed the quotation:

- The bank will deem Mundi Ltd to have borrowed €2,382,134 for three months at the German inter-bank rate of 3 per cent. Interest on this loan will amount to €17,866. The €2.4 million collected from the German customer will be used to repay the loan and interest.
- The amount borrowed in Germany is deemed to be converted into sterling at the 'spot' rate of £1 = €1.6389. This yields £1,453,496 (2,382,134/1.6389).
- This £1,453,496 is deemed to have been placed on deposit at the LIBOR rate of 7 per cent for three months. It earns interest of £25,436.
- At the end of the three months the bank will pay Mundi Ltd £1,478,932.
- The forward sale contract rate is £1 = €1.6228. This is arrived at by dividing €2.4 million by £1,478,932.

Mundi Ltd would only collect £1,464,396 if it could sell the euros on the spot market. It gains £14,536 from the interest rate differential.

The method demonstrated above is used to calculate the price of forward purchase and sale contracts. However, no loan or deposit accounts are opened in practice. The bank locates a business that wishes to sell euros to match the forward purchase agreement or one that wishes to buy euros to match the forward sale agreement.

Foreign currency option contracts

A company tendering for contracts in a foreign currency is in an unclear exchange risk situation. If the tender succeeds, it is exposed. If the tender fails, it is not. Foreign currency option contracts have been developed to cover such unclear situations. The option provides the right, but not the obligation, to buy or sell a foreign currency, at a defined price, on or before a specified date.

A sell ('put') option contract

A 'put' option gives its owner the right but not the obligation to sell a foreign currency at a predetermined price. 'Put' options will be of interest to exporters of goods or services that are denominated in foreign currencies.

Mundi Ltd tendered for a contract that would create net cash of US $15 million if successful. The exchange rate at the time was £1 = US $1.50. The company was concerned about the possible combination of a successful tender and a weakening dollar. It wanted to guarantee the sterling value of the contract if the tender was successful. They asked the bank to quote for an option to sell $15 million at an exercise price £1 = $1.50. The bank quoted a fee of £300,000.

Mundi Ltd accepted the quotation. Four things could occur which will determine whether the option should be exercised or not:

1. The tender might be unsuccessful and the dollar strengthen.
2. The tender might be unsuccessful and the dollar weaken.
3. The tender might be successful and the dollar strengthen.
4. The tender might be successful and the dollar weaken.

In each case Mundi Ltd will have to decide whether it is beneficial to exercise or refuse the option. It may have a substantial value even if the tender is unsuccessful.

Case 1. The tender is unsuccessful and the dollar strengthens to £1 = $1.40. To exercise the option Mundi Ltd would have to buy dollars on the spot market. The option is rejected.

Mundi Ltd would refuse to exercise its option and restrict its loss to £300,000.

Table 14.14   *Case 1*

	£
Cost of currency purchase $15 million/1.4	10,714,285
Option premium	300,000
Cost of option	11,014,285
Proceeds from exercise of option	10,000,000
Loss if the option was exercised	1,014,285

Case 2. The tender is unsuccessful and the dollar weakens to £1 = $1.60. Even though the tender is unsuccessful the company will benefit by exercising the option.

Table 14.15   *Case 2*

	£
It buys $15 million on the spot market at £ = $1.60	9,375,000
It exercises the option and collects	10,000,000
Gross profit from option exercise	625,000
Cost of option	300,000
Net profit from option exercise	325,000

Exercising the option is beneficial if the dollar weakens beyond $1.50. At this exchange rate the holder loses £300,000. The loss declines as the dollar weakens towards the break-even point £1 = $1.5464. The profit on the contract grows as the dollar weakness increases.

Case 3. The tender is successful and the dollar strengthens to £1 = $1.40. The company rejects the option because of the situation shown in Table 14.16 (p 372). The maximum loss that Mundi Ltd can incur is £300,000. If the dollar is stronger than £1 = $1.4563 then Mundi Ltd will make an additional profit by rejecting the option.

Case 4. The tender is successful and the dollar weakens to £1 = $1.60. The option should be exercised; see Table 14.17 (p 372).

Buy ('call') option contracts

A 'call' option gives the buyer the right but not the obligation to buy a foreign currency at a predetermined price. 'Call' options will be of interest to importers of goods or services that are denominated in foreign currencies.

371

Table 14.16 *Case 3*

	£
Proceeds of sale in market $15 million/1.4	10,714,285
Cost of option	300,000
Net received	10,414,285
Proceeds from exercise of option	10,000,000
Extra profit from non-exercise	414,285
The break-even point is £ = US $1.4563.	
Proceeds of sale in market $15 million/1.4563	10,300,000
Cost of option	300,000
Proceeds from exercise of option	10,000,000

Table 14.17 *Case 4 the financial consequences of the option contract*

	£
Sale in market would realize	9,375,000
Cost of option	10,000,000
Gross loss avoided	625,000
Option premium	300,000
Total loss	925,000

Exercising the option restricts the loss to £300,000.

	Dollar strength	Dollar weakness
Tender successful	Reject option Maximum cost £0.3 million	Exercise option Maximum gain unlimited
Tender unsuccessful	Reject option Maximum gain unlimited	Exercise option Maximum cost £0.3 million

Option contracts and trade transactions

It may seem surprising but the use of a forward rate agreement can place a business at a competitive disadvantage. The attraction of a forward sale agreement is that it guarantees a future exchange rate for your foreign currency receipts. The disadvantage is that you sacrifice the potential to benefit from local currency weakness in order to eliminate the disadvantage from local currency strength. This sacrifice of benefit can leave a vendor poorly placed to compete with other suppliers. A 'put' option contract would overcome this potential competitive disadvantage. The beauty of 'put' option contracts is that they allow you to gain from local currency weakness but avoid a loss from local currency strength. This is like entering a coin-tossing competition where the rules are heads you win and tails you don't lose. The only snag is that the entry fee (the cost of the 'put' option) is high. The 'put' option works in exactly the same way as the tender example earlier in the chapter. You will exercise the option if the local currency is strong and reject it if your local currency is weak.

Mundi Ltd sold goods to a French customer at a cost of €1.52 million. It obtained an option to sell the euros at £1 = €1.52. The cost of the option was £10,000. We will now examine whether to accept or ignore the option and the overall gain or loss at various exchange rates; see Table 14.18.

Table 14.18 _A 'put' option example_

Exchange rate at exercise	£ = €1.30	€1.40	€1.60	€1.70
Proceeds if selling spot	1,169,231	1,085,714	950,000	894,118
Option proceeds	1,000,000	1,000,000	1,000,000	1,000,000
Accept	no	no	yes	yes
Gain (loss)	159,231	75,714	(10,000)	(10,000)

Mundi Ltd buys goods for $1.6 million. It buys a 'call' option at £1 = $1.50 at a cost of £25,000. We will now examine whether to accept or ignore the option and the gain or loss at various exchange rates; see Table 14.19.

Table 14.19 _A 'call' option example_

Exchange rate at exercise	£ = $1.30	$1.40	$1.60	$1.70
Cost if buying spot	1,230,789	1,142,857	1,000,000	941,176
Cost if option exercised	1,066,667	1,066,667	1,066,667	1,066,667
Accept	yes	yes	no	no
Gain (loss)	139,122	51,190	(25,000)	(25,000)

Interest rate swaps

Businesses that have large cash reserves fear a reduction in interest rates. Businesses that have large bank debts fear an increase in interest rates. These interest rate exposures offer the opportunity for a swap mechanism that is similar to the matching of equal and opposite foreign currency exposures. The swap can also be used to convert fixed interest rates into variable and variable rates into fixed.

The swap mechanism uses a bank as an intermediary to match a borrower that is prepared to sacrifice the benefit of an interest rate reduction in order to guarantee that its borrowing rate will not increase with a depositor that is prepared to sacrifice the benefit of a rate increase in order to eliminate the risk of an interest rate reduction. The exposures are matched. For example, Mundi Ltd borrowed US $10 million. The interest rate is variable. The company wishes to protect itself against a rate increase. Other Inc has a deposit of US $10 million. The interest rate is variable. The company wishes to protect itself against a rate decline. A bank offers swap agreements to Mundi Ltd at 10 per cent and to Other Inc at 8 per cent. Actual rates are shown in Table 14.20.

Table 14.20   *Rates offered to Mundi Ltd and Other Inc*

Quarter	Loans	Deposits
1	11%	9%
2	13%	11%
3	10.5%	8.5%
4	8%	6%

- In quarter 1 Mundi Ltd incurs excess interest of $25,000 ($10 million × 1 per cent for three months). It recovers the $25,000 excess from the bank. This effectively fixes the interest rate and achieves the target cost. Other Inc earns excess interest of $25,000. It pays the bank the $25,000 excess. This fixes the interest rate and achieves the target return.
- In quarter 2 Mundi Ltd incurs excess interest of $75,000. It recovers the excess from the bank. Other Inc earns excess interest of $75,000. It pays the bank the excess.
- In quarter 3 Mundi Ltd incurs excess interest of $12,500. It recovers the excess from the bank. Other Inc earns excess interest of $12,500. It pays the bank the excess.

- In quarter 4 Mundi Ltd pays the bank the $50,000 it saved in interest. Other Inc recovers the $50,000 it failed to earn. Both companies are charged a fee for the exposure matching.

Financing overseas subsidiaries

In the second part of this chapter we saw how the sterling performance of SubMundi Inc was affected by exchange rates. Had Mundi Ltd used more dollar bank loans to defray part of the set-up cost the scale of the potential exchange loss could have been minimized. This is because the bank debt will be translated at the closing rate. Introducing $200,000 of 8 per cent loan in place of a similar amount of share capital at formation would change the results as follows.

Example 3. Profit and loss translation, pound strengthening

Table 14.21 *Profit and loss translation, £ strengthening, version 2*

Exchange rates 2001 £ = $1.60 2002 £ = $1.80

$ 2001	£ 2001		$ 2002	£ 2002
980,000	612,500	Sales	1,152,000	640,000
735,000	459,375	Cost of sales	864,000	480,000
245,000	153,125	Gross profit	288,000	160,000
186,000	116,250	Operating cost	198,000	110,000
59,000	36,875	PBIT	90,000	50,000
16,000	10,000	Interest	16,000	8,889
43,000	26,875	PBT	74,000	41,111
17,200	10,750	Tax provision	29,600	16,444
25,800	16,125	Profit after tax	44,400	24,667
16,000	10,000	Proposed dividend	16,000	8,889
9,800	6,125	Profit retained	28,400	15,778

Profit and loss items are the same as for example 1 except:

- The $200,000 loan created an interest cost of $16,000.
- The tax provision (tax rate 40 per cent) was reduced by $6,400 as a result of the additional interest cost.
- The same dividend, 8 cents per share, was paid on the $200,000 lower capital base.

Example 3. Balance sheet translation, pound strengthening

Table 14.22 *Balance sheet translation, £ strengthening*

Exchange rates 2001 £ = $1.60 2002 £ = $1.80				
$ 2001	**£ 2001**		**$ 2002**	**£ 2002**
324,000	202,500	Fixed assets	288,000	160,000
300,000	187,500	Current assets	360,000	200,000
		Creditors		
160,000	100,000	Trade	144,000	80,000
21,000	13,125	Bank loan[1]	20,200	11,222
17,200	10,750	Tax provision	29,600	16,444
16,000	10,000	Proposed dividend	16,000	8,889
(214,200)	(133,875)		(209,800)	(116,555)
409,800	256,125	Net assets	438,200	243,445
		Financed by:		
200,000	142,857	Share capital[2]	200,000	142,857
9,800	6,125	Revenue reserve	38,200	21,903
–	(17,857)	Exchange losses[3]	–	32,426[4]
209,800	131,125	Net worth	238,200	132,334
200,000	125,000	Long-term debt	200,000	111,111
409,800	256,125		438,200	243,445

Notes:

[1] Loan 2001 (from example 1)	5,000
Add interest 2001	16,000
Revised loan 2001	21,000
Loan 2002 (from example 1)	10,600
Add interest 2 years	32,000
	42,600

Less reduced dividend paid	16,000	
reduced tax paid	6,400	22,400
Revised loan 2002		20,200

[2] The share capital was introduced at £ = $1.40.

	2001	**2002**
	£	**£**
Opening net assets	142,857[a]	131,125[c]
Closing net assets	125,000[b]	116,556[d]
[3] Exchange loss year	17,857	14,569
Opening loss		17,857
[4] Exchange loss cumulative		32,426

[a] $200,000/1.4 = £142,857   [b] $200,000/1.6 = £125,000
[c] $209,800/1.6 = £131,125   [d] $209,800/1.8 = £116,556

The equity declines in value as the pound strengthens. The $200,000 loan reduces the translation loss. Had SubMundi Inc been financed totally by loans and repatriated all profits, no exchange loss would have been suffered.

Example 4. Profit and loss translation, pound weakening

Table 14.23   _Profit and loss translation, £ weakening, version 2_

Exchange rates 2001 £ = $1.20 2002 £ = $1

$ 2001	£ 2001		$ 2002	£ 2002
980,000	816,667	Sales	1,152,000	1,152,000
735,000	612,500	Cost of sales	864,000	864,000
245,000	204,167	Gross profit	288,000	288,000
186,000	155,000	Operating cost	198,000	198,000
59,000	49,167		90.000	90,000
16,000	13,334	Interest	16,000	16,000
43,000	35,833	Profit before tax	74,000	74,000
17,200	14,333	Tax	29,600	29,600
25,800	21,500	Profit after tax	44,400	44,400
16,000	13,333	Proposed dividend	16,000	16,000
9,800	8,167	Profit retained	28,400	28,400

Interest, tax and dividend are as per example 3.

Example 4. Balance sheet translation, pound weakening

Table 14.24 *Balance sheet translation, £ weakening, version 2*

Exchange rates 2001 £ = $1.20 2002 £ = $1.00

$ 2001	£ 2001		$ 2002	£ 2002
324,000	270,000	Fixed assets	288,000	288,000
300,000	250,000	Current assets	360,000	360,000
Creditors				
160,000	133,333	Trade	144,000	144,000
21,000	17,500	Bank loans	20,200	20,200
17,200	14,333	Tax provision	29,600	29,600
16,000	13,334	Proposed dividends	16,000	16,000
(214,200)	(178,500)		(209,800)	(209,800)
409,800	341,500	Net assets	438,200	438,200
Financed by:				
200,000	142,856	Share capital	200,000	142,856
9,800	8,167	Revenue reserve	38,200	36,567
–	23,810	Exchange gain[1]	–	58,777[2]
209,800	174,833	Net worth	238,200	238,200
200,000	166,667	Long-term debt	200,000	200,000
409,800	341,500		438,200	438,200

Notes:

	2001 £	2002 £
Opening net assets	142,857[a]	174,833[c]
Closing net assets	166,667[b]	209,800[d]
[1] Exchange gain year	23,810	34,967
Opening gain		23,810
[2] Exchange gain cumulative		58,777

[a] $200,000/1.4 = £142,857   [b] $200,000/1.2 = £166,667
[c] $209,800/1.2 = £174,833   [d] $209,800/1.0 = £209,800

Summary of translation issues

- The closing rate method is nearly always used in the balance sheet.
- There is a choice of profit and loss translation methods. Once a method has been selected it must be applied consistently.

- A strengthening pound results in exchange losses on translation of overseas assets. These losses will be abated in so far as foreign currency loans are used to finance the net assets.
- A weakening pound results in exchange gains on translation of overseas assets.
- A strengthening pound results in exchange gains on translation of overseas liabilities.
- A weakening pound results in exchange losses on translation of overseas assets.

Rates of exchange can vary unpredictably. A passive approach to translation risk is to assume that gains and losses will cancel out over a long period. This is a dangerous assumption. The prudent organization seeks to minimize the translation risk. This can be done by using local currency borrowings to finance part of the asset base. Elimination of translation exposure can be achieved by using all local currency borrowings and supporting them by a parent company guarantee. In such a case the UK parent will be indifferent to exchange rate fluctuations.

Mundi Ltd decided that the risk of translation losses was too significant to leave exposed. It was satisfied that the size of US dollar cash inflows would underpin repayment obligations on a high level of dollar borrowings. On formation SubMundi Inc was financed as follows:

	$
Share capital	40,000
8 per cent fixed interest loan	360,000
	400,000

A parent company guarantee was used to support the high gearing.

Example 5. Profit and loss translation, pound strengthening

Table 14.25 *Profit and loss translation, £ strengthening, version 2*

Exchange rates				2001		2002	
Closing				£ = $1.60		£ = $2.00	
Average				£ = $1.50		£ = $1.80	

$ 2001	£ 2001			$ 2002	£ 2002
	Closing	Average		Closing	Average
980,000	612,500	653,333	Sales	1,152,000	576,000	640,000
735,000	459,375	490,000	Cost of sales	864,000	432,000	480,000
245,000	153,125	163,333	Gross profit	288,000	144,000	160,000
186,000	116,250	124,000	Operating cost	198,000	99,000	110,000
59,000	36,875	39,333	PBIT	90,000	45,000	50,000
28,800	18,000	19,200	Interest	28,800	14,400	16,000
30,200	18,875	20,133	PBT	61,200	30,600	34,000
12,080	7,550	7,550	Tax provision	24,480	12,240	12,240
18,120	11,325	12,583	Profit after tax	36,720	18,360	21,760
3,200	2,000	2,000	Proposed dividend	3,200	1,600	1,600
14,920	9,325	10,583	Profit retained	33,520	16,760	20,160

The change in financial structure affects the profit and loss account as follows:

- Interest on the $360,000 loan cost $28,800.
- The tax provision fell by $11,520 (40 per cent of the interest charge).
- The dividend of 8 cents applied to only 40,000 shares.

Example 5. Balance sheet translation, pound strengthening

Table 14.26 _Balance sheet translation, £ strengthening, version 2_

Exchange rates 2001 £ = $1.60 2002 £ = $2

$ 2001	£ 2001		$ 2002	£ 2002
324,000	202,500	Fixed assets	288,000	144,000
300,000	187,500	Current assets	360,000	180,000
Creditors				
160,000	100,000	Trade	144,000	72,000
33,800	21,125	Bank loans[1]	27,880	13,940
12,080	7,550	Tax provision	24,480	12,240
3,200	2,000	Proposed dividend	3,200	1,600
(209,080)	(130,675)		(199,560)	(99,780)
414,920	259,325	Net assets	448,440	224,220
Financed by:				
40,000	28,571	Share capital[2]	40,000	28,571
14,920	9,325	Revenue reserve	48,440	26,085
–	(3,571)	Exchange loss[3]	–	(10,436)[4]
54,920	34,325	Net worth	88,440	44,220
360,000	225,000	Long-term debt	360,000	180,000
414,920	259,325		448,440	224,220

Notes:

[1] Bank loan 2001 (per example 1)   5,000

Add interest 2001   28,800

Revised loan   33,800

Bank loan 2002 (per example 1)	10,600	
Add interest 2 years	57,600	68,200
Reduced dividend paid	28,800	
Reduced tax paid	11,520	40,320
Revised loan 2002		27,880

[2] The share capital was introduced at £1 = $1.40.

	2001 £	2002 £
Opening net assets	28,571 [a]	34,325 [c]
Closing net assets	25,000 [b]	27,460 [d]
[3] Exchange loss year	3,571	6,865
Opening loss		3,571
[4] Exchange loss cumulative		10,436

[a] $40,000/1.40 = £28,571   [b] $40,000/1.6 = £25,000

[c] $54,920/1.6 = £34,325   [d] $54,920/2 = £27,460.

The effect of this high-geared structure was to reduce the potential exchange loss to £10,436 even if sterling strengthened to £1 = $2 by the end of 2002. If Mundi Ltd had used $400,000 of share capital, it would have experienced a translation loss of £136,641. The treasury manager was awarded a handsome bonus for saving the group £126,205.

SUMMARY

Most businesses aspire to play on the world stage. To do so they must involve themselves in transactions that create sales, costs, assets and liabilities denominated in foreign currencies. The value of these transactions can fluctuate dramatically as currencies strengthen and weaken. The board of directors should never have to face an angry shareholders' meeting to explain large currency losses. Such losses occur when a business gambles in the currency market. The management may not even recognize that they are gambling and yet find the profits shrinking and the financial stability disimproving.

Any business can minimize its foreign currency exposures by having equal amounts of sales and costs and equal amounts of assets and liabilities. If such matching cannot be achieved then the use of forward rate agreements and option contracts allows a business to limit its exposures.

Where a UK business borrows money overseas in order to avail itself of lower interest rates and repatriates such funds, it exposes itself to the risk of a substantial increase in the cost of repayments if sterling weakens. Ideally, foreign currency borrowings should only be used to buy assets in that currency or when the borrower expects to generate enough cash flow in that currency to cover capital and interest payments.

15

Mergers and acquisitions

The scale of mergers and acquisitions in recent years has been staggering. A merger is the combination of two similar-sized businesses and is often done in cases where there are opportunities for savings due to overlapping costs. Major examples in recent years were the merger of Guinness and Grand Metropolitan Hotels to form Diageo, and the merger of Glaxo with SmithKline Beecham. An acquisition occurs where a larger business takes over a smaller one. After a combination of businesses the new group will be obliged to present consolidated (group) accounts to shareholders. These accounts will be significantly different if the business combination is deemed to be a merger or an acquisition. The rules of accounting for business combinations are laid down in FRS 6, Mergers and acquisitions.

There are six major elements in this chapter:

1. The reasons for merger and acquisition activity.
2. The valuation of businesses in take-over negotiations.
3. Exchange mechanisms.
4. Preparation of consolidated accounts subsequent to mergers and acquisitions
   - definition of a merger;
   - accounting for a merger;
   - definition of an acquisition;
   - accounting for an acquisition.

5. Special considerations in mergers and acquisitions.
6. 'Unbundling'.

REASONS FOR TAKE-OVER ACTIVITY: THE BUYER PERSPECTIVE

There are two major strategic reasons for M and A activity: to increase profitability or to improve financial stability.

Profit enhancement strategies

1. Increasing earnings per share. The EPS drives the price earnings ratio. It in turn drives the share price, which is a key barometer of shareholder wealth. A take-over, which will increase the expected EPS, is intrinsically attractive. For this reason serious analysts place a major emphasis on the prospective EPS when deciding whether a proposal for businesses to combine is logical and profitable.
2. Reducing the risk profile of the business should earn it a higher PE ratio. A classic example is the tobacco industry. The consistent decline in consumption of tobacco products has lead to the classification of the industry as high risk, in spite of the large positive cash flows it generates. Major diversifications by Imperial Tobacco and BATS, over many years were designed to increase their PE ratios by persuading investors that the acquisitions should be valued at a higher multiple of future profits.
3. Take-over of businesses on a lower PE ratio. This will be very rewarding to shareholders if the stock market applies a higher PE to the new addition to the group earnings. Consider the example shown in Table 15.1.

Table 15.1 *Take-over of a business on a lower PE ratio*

	Company A	Company B
Projected EPS	20p	10p
Share price	£4	£1.20
P/E	20	12
Shares in issue (M)	20	40

Company A offered 12 million of its shares in exchange for the 40 million shares of Company B. In the jargon of take-overs this is three new shares for each 10 held. The board of directors of the buyer decided on the exchange rate by assessing the probable impact of a successful bid on its share price. They did their calculations as shown in Table 15.2.

The application of the multiple of 20 to the earnings to be imported drives

Table 15.2 *Calculating the share exchange rate*

Pro-forma combined earnings (£4 million + £4 million)	£8 million
Shares in issue (20 million + 12 million)	32
Projected EPS	25p
Post-merger PE	20
Post-merger share price	£5

the increase in share price. If the bid succeeds then shares in Company A are expected to increase by 20 per cent. The board of Company B should also assess the attractiveness of the offer by projecting the share price of Company A if a bid were to be accepted. They should conclude that a holder of 1,000 of their shares currently worth £1,200 would receive 300 shares in Company A predicted to be worth £1,500. This is a 25 per cent increase in the value of the investment. Unless the board of Company B believe that they can obtain a higher offer they should recommend that shareholders accept the three for 10 bid.

4. Research worldwide tends to suggest that the higher the market share of a business the greater will be its ROI. This is mainly caused by synergy (combining production, marketing, administration, research, etc). This makes mergers of competitors potentially attractive to both parties. The elimination of overlap in research has been the driving force of a number of mega-mergers in the pharmaceutical industry.

5. A longer-term way of increasing wealth is to acquire a business with under-exploited assets. The introduction of sophisticated management techniques offers the promise of increased sales, reduced costs, and the release of excessive investment in under-utilized assets. This is the corner-stone of the acquisition strategy of many well-managed businesses.

Stability enhancement strategies

1. A company that is over-borrowed may choose to buy one that is cash rich. An extreme example would for a dotcom (voracious consumer of working capital) to acquire a supermarket chain (major cash generator).
2. A company that depends heavily on a key supplier may choose to acquire it to assure quality, quantity and price of key materials.
3. Equally, a company that depends heavily on one customer may choose to acquire it to assure continuity of sales.
4. A company that lacks key management skills may acquire a company that has the required skills (management buy-in). British Aerospace bought a property company during 1989 with a major purpose of acquiring its managerial skills.
5. Eliminate over-dependence on one product. However, the thrust of the diversification strategy is the increased stability of a product portfolio rather than an immediate increase in shareholder value.
6. Buying established businesses tends to be less risky than developing new products or markets from scratch.

Merger and acquisition priorities

A buyer wants to make a take-over at as low a price as possible. A seller will strive to obtain the best possible exit price for its shareholders. Vendors can often get the initial bid improved by emphasizing the reasons why the purchaser needs the take-over more than the seller. Bid negotiations involve a search for a price acceptable to both parties. The arrival of a counter-bid can lead to an auction. In such cases the vendor is likely to obtain an improved price. Management of an organization, faced with an unwanted take-over bid, may try to attract a counter-bid from a more acceptable source (a 'white knight'). Sometimes the white knight is not as acceptable in retrospect as was thought at the time.

Reasons why a business might be for sale

There are seven main reasons why a business may be for sale:

1. A wish to link up with state-of-the-art production, product development or marketing skills.
2. An inability to capitalize on excellent products or customers due to under-capitalization or lack of managerial skills.

3. The owners wishing to retire, not having arranged an effective succession policy. This is often a major problem in family-owned companies where the next generation frequently does not have the ability or enthusiasm to run the business.
4. Some offers are so good that the recipient company simply cashes in.
5. The management may have harvested the business for years by failing to replace obsolete equipment or invest in new product development. Recognition that survival requires major 'catch-up' investment often motivates a decision to offer the business for sale.
6. Overvalued assets, notably stock and debtors.
7. Understated liabilities.

The first four of these situations offer promising bid potential. The remaining three suggest future problems for a successful bidder.

THE VALUATION OF BUSINESSES IN TAKE-OVER NEGOTIATIONS

There are four major factors that vendors should recognize when valuing their business during take-over negotiations:

1. The stock market value of control, if it is quoted. This is not just a simple matter of multiplying the number of shares in issue by the current share price. Factors that need to be considered include:
   - the stock market price tends to reflect the value of small parcels of shares: companies that try to acquire large blocks generally have to pay a premium over the pre-bid price;
   - some quoted shares trade at a discount to their real value. Large blocks of shares may be held for long-term strategic purposes. The supply of shares for sale may be small. You might expect these conditions to artificially boost the share price because demand exceeds supply. In practice, investors tend to avoid such shares because of marketability concerns.
3. The asset value of the business. This is not quite as straightforward as it seems. If no take-over is in prospect, a business may avoid the trouble and expense of revaluing appreciating assets. In defending a bid a company will fight to ensure that the value of properties, brand names, etc are reflected in the bid price.
4. The dividend income of the shareholders. This is particularly important where the vendor tends to pay out a higher proportion of profits as

dividends than a bidder, or where prospects for the business as a separate entity promise substantial dividend growth.

5. Qualitative factors not adequately reflected in the share price, assets and dividends:

    –   the strength of management and their preparedness to work for the new business combination;

    –   the positioning of the product portfolio (stage in the life cycle, quality relative to competitors, market potential for products in development);

    –   the value to the purchaser of synergistic opportunities. A vendor will argue that the purchaser cannot take advantage of these benefits unless a take-over is agreed. They will want part of the benefit reflected in the bid price.

Vendors should take all these factors into account in defending a bid. In the case of a hostile bid they often attack aspects of the potential purchaser's management, products, markets and financial situation. This defensive tactic peaked with the attack on each other's products and past performance when Hanson was bidding for Imperial Tobacco. Bidders, defenders and their financial advisers have been forced to behave in a more civilized way since then.

Valuation methods

The first step in an effective M and A process is to identify a suitable target. It is usually necessary to examine a number of possible targets before a suitable one is selected. The target identification unit in acquisitive companies is usually staffed by a number of highly skilled analysts. Where a business is too small to have its own M and A department it will usually employ a merchant bank to identify suitable targets, carry out business valuations and assess bids. When an interesting target is identified the next step is to estimate an acceptable price. Equally, the board of a company that is in receipt of a bid must be able to assess the attractiveness of an offer.

The valuation of businesses is not an exact science. The valuation process is loosely based on the average PE for quoted companies adjusted to reflect whether the business is in a fast growth, middle of the road or stolid business sector. The growth ratio examined in Chapter 6 helps to adjust the average PE to reflect the shareholder value contained in a business strategy and the potential profits.

Notwithstanding these approaches to business valuation, share prices frequently fail to reflect the underlying fundamentals. The dotcom mania is the most recent example of the lack of science in business valuation. Shares quoted on the Nasdaq traded up to colossal multiples of sales even though some of the businesses had never made a profit. The second half of 2000 saw some semblance of sanity return to the stock market prices of technology businesses. The shareholder value model examined in Chapter 13 is an excellent approach to improving business valuation.

EXCHANGE MECHANISMS

Many business combinations occur as a result of an exchange of shares. There is a useful formula that can be used to calculate an appropriate share exchange proposal when the purchase consideration is to be paper. The formula is:

$$\text{Vendor contribution to merged group} \times \frac{\text{Purchaser shares in issue}}{\text{Purchaser contribution to merged group}}$$

This formula can be adapted to frame a share exchange designed to meet a variety of shareholder expectations. There are four major ways that investors look at shareholding. Some are simply interested in the value of their investment. Others are interested in the earnings created on their behalf. Others are interested in the dividends they will receive. Some focus on the net assets that support their investment. In framing a share exchange offer the valuer must be sensitive to the varied needs and expectations of shareholders in the target company.

We will now examine how the share exchange formula can be adapted to pinpoint the contributions towards a business combination being made by each party and to suggest a share exchange rate.

Analysis of acquisition proposal

The acquisition department of Buyer plc has identified Seller plc as an interesting target; see Table 15.3.

Table 15.3 *Relevant statistics for Buyer plc and Seller plc*

		Buyer plc	Seller plc
Ordinary shares in issue (millions)	(a)	20	6
Profit after tax (£ million)	(b)	4	0.75
Earnings per share (b/a)	(c)	20p	12.5p
Dividend cover	(d)	2.5	2
Proposed dividend per share	(c/d)	8p	6.25p
Net assets (£ million)	(e)	36	9
Asset backing per share (£)	(e/a)	£1.80	£1.50
Latest share price (£)	(f)	£3.00	£1.25
PE ratio	(f/c)	15	10

The analyst recognized that a bid would have no chance of success unless it offered shareholders of Seller plc at least 20 per cent more than its current share price. The proposed share exchange was therefore based on a valuation of £1.50 per share or £9 million in total. On the basis of this valuation the analyst computed the appropriate share exchange as follows:

$$9^{(1)} \times \frac{20^{(2)}}{60^{(3)}} = 3 \text{ million shares}$$

[1] Vendor-revised capitalization.
[2] Buyer plc shares in issue.
[3] Buyer capitalization.

This was then converted into a proposed offer of one Buyer plc share for two Seller plc shares.

The board of Buyer plc is examining a pro-forma analysis of the business combination to discuss whether the offer should be made and the probability of acceptance; see Table 15.4.

Table 15.4 *Pro-forma statistics, B and S Group*

Shares in issue (20 million + 3 million)	(g)	23m
Profit after tax (£4 million + £0.75 million)	(h)	£4.75m
Earnings per share (h/g)	(i)	20.65p
Dividend cover	(j)	2.5
Dividend per share	(i/j)	8.26p
PE	(k)	15
Share price forecast	(i × k)	£3.10
Group net assets (£ million) (36 + 9 + 0.075)	(l)	£45.075m
Asset backing	(l/g)	£1.96

In preparing the pro-forma statistics for the business combination the analyst made the following assumptions:

- Investors would approve of the acquisition and the share price would continue to be 15 times earnings.
- The dividend policy would be that of Buyer plc.
- The reduction in the combined dividend proposed of £75,000 was added to the net assets.
- Any 'fair value adjustments' required would be minimal and were ignored.

Based on this pro-forma table the acquisition analyst compared and contrasted the returns available to shareholders of both organizations before and after a successful take-over. The results are shown in Table 15.5.

Table 15.5 *Shareholder returns before and after a successful bid*

	Buyer plc Before	After	% Change	Seller plc Before	After	% Change
Shares held	1000	1000		1000	500	
Investment value	3000	3100	+3.3	1250	1550	+24.0
Earnings achieved	200	207	+3.5	125	103	−17.6
Dividend earned	80	83	+3.8	63	41	−34.9
Asset backing	1800	1960	+8.9	1500	980	−34.7

The board of Buyer plc concluded that in addition to the modest improvement in returns promised by the business combination, there were substantial opportunities for increased earnings and that the offer was in the best interest of their shareholders. They decided to make the offer to the board of Seller plc. In doing so they were conscious of the fact that the offer represented a substantial decline in earnings, dividends and asset backing for holders of Seller plc shares.

The board meeting of Seller plc

On receipt of the offer the chairman of Seller plc immediately called an emergency board meeting. He asked the finance director to make a comparison between the position of shareholders before the bid with their expected position if the offer were accepted. The finance director prepared an analysis of the proposed business combination similar to Tables 15.3 and 15.4 and presented it to the meeting. She noted that the key reason for the disappointing dividend income and asset backing projections was that Buyer plc was offering only 13 per cent of the enlarged equity (3 million shares out of 23 million) whereas Seller plc was contributing 20 per cent of the combined net assets (£9 million out of £45 million). The chairman asked the finance director to prepare a similar pro-forma based on a share exchange in proportion to the net assets contributed by both parties. The meeting was adjourned briefly while the new pro-forma was prepared. When the meeting reconvened the financial director presented her revised pro-forma, shown in Table 15.6.

Table 15.6 _Pro-forma B and S returns net asset based exchange rate_

Shares in issue (20 million + 5 million)	(a)	25m
Profit after tax (£4 million + £0.75 million)	(b)	£4.75m
Earnings per share (b/a)	(c)	19p
Dividend cover	(d)	2.5
Dividend per share (c/d)		7.6p
PE	(e)	15
Share price forecast (c × e)		£2.85
Group net assets (36 + 9 + 0.075)	(l)	£45.075 million
Asset backing (l/g)		£1.80

	Buyer plc		%	Seller plc		%
	Before	**After**	**Change**	**Before**	**After**	**Change**
Shares held	1000	1000		1200	1000	
Investment value	3000	2850	–5.0	1500	2850	+90.0
Earnings achieved	200	190	–5.0	150	190	+26.7
Dividend earned	80	76	–5.0	75	76	+1.3
Asset backing	1800	1800	N/C	1800	1800	N/C

Share exchange computation

$$9^{(1)} \times \frac{20^{(2)}}{36^{(3)}} = 5 \text{ million shares}$$

[1] Vendor net assets.
[2] Buyer plc shares in issue.
[3] Buyer plc net assets.

This is equivalent to an exchange rate of five Buyer plc shares for each six Seller plc shares held.

Table 15.6 demonstrates that a share exchange based on net assets contributed would solve all the dilution problems caused by the Buyer plc proposal. The board of Seller plc recognized that a bid at this level was very unlikely as it would result in a fall in the share price of Buyer plc. Nevertheless, the board decided to respond to the bid by informing the chairman of Buyer plc that a substantial increase in the offer would have to be made if they wanted the support of the Seller plc board. Battle lines were drawn, with the purchaser offering too little and the vendor asking too much.

The next board meeting of Buyer plc

The Buyer plc board was disappointed but not surprised by the rejection. The financial director explained that the problem was that Seller plc was asset rich while Buyer plc was earnings rich, and this was why three of the pro-forma returns to Seller plc would be significantly diluted. One board member asked whether a bid could be framed that would overcome the structural differences. The finance director said that this could be achieved by an offer that was in cash or one that was a combination of shares and loan stock. He said that, for example, a valuation of £9 million could be offered as a package of either £1.50 per share in cash or a combination such as one Buyer plc share plus £3 of loan stock for each four Seller plc shares. The pro-forma returns for these possible offers are presented in Tables 15.7 and 15.8.

Table 15.7 *Revised pro-forma B and S Group based on a cash offer of £1.50 per share*

Shares in issue	(a)	20m
Profit after tax (£4 million + £0.75 – £0.54 million)	(b)	£4.21
Earnings per share (b/a)	(c)	21.05p
Dividend cover	(d)	2.5
Dividend per share (c/d)		8.42p
PE	(e)	15
Share price forecast (c × e)		£3.16
Group net assets (£m) (36 + 9 – 9.54)	(l)	£35.46m
Asset backing (l/g)		£1.77

Table 15.8 *Pro-forma returns based on a cash offer of £1.50 per share*

	Buyer plc Before	After	% Change	Seller plc Before	After	% Change
Shares held	1000	1000		1200	0	
Investment value	3000	3160	+5.3	1500	1800	+20
Earnings achieved	200	211	+5.5	150	Uncertain	
Dividend earned	80	84	+5.0	75	Uncertain	
Asset backing	1800	1770	–1.7	1800	Uncertain	

Note:

The uncertainty arises because the shares are exchanged for cash and the holders will have to find a suitable new home for their proceeds.

In Table 15.7 the finance director assumed that the £9 million required to fund the take-over would be borrowed at 8 per cent. He deducted the interest net of corporation tax at 33 per cent – £720,000 from the profit after tax. He deducted the loan and interest from the group net assets.

It is quite likely that institutional shareholders in Seller plc would accept this cash offer. Any company that has an asset backing in excess of its share price has performed poorly or is facing a difficult competitive situation. Buyer plc should be aware of this but seems confident that it can institute effective recovery action.

The combined share and loan stock offer shown in Table 15.9 promises a significant improvement in investment value and income but at the expense of reduced earnings and asset backing. As it solves the reinvestment problem

Table 15.9 *Revised pro-forma, B and S group share and loan stock offer*

Shares in issue (20 million + 1.5 million)	(a)	21.5 million
Profit after tax (£4 million + £0.75 million – £0.27)	(b)	£4.48 million
Earnings per share (b/a)	(c)	20.84p
Dividend cover	(d)	2.5
Dividend per share (c/d)		8.33p
PE	(e)	15
Share price forecast (c × e)		£3.13
Group net assets (36 + 9 + 0.75 – 4.77)	(l)	£40.98m
Asset backing (l/g)		£1.91

Interest on the loan stock was calculated at 6% net of corporation tax.

	Buyer plc		%	Seller plc		%
	Before	After	Change	Before	After	Change
Shares held	1000	1000		1200	300	
Investment value	3000	3130	+4.3	1500	1839[1]	+22.6
Earnings achieved	200	208	+4.0	150	135[2]	–10.0
Dividend earned	80	83	+3.8	75	97[3]	+29.3
Asset backing	1800	1910	+6.1	1800	1473[4]	–18.2

The returns of Seller plc assume a rate of 8% net of income tax.

Notes:
[1] ((300 × £3.13) + £900)
[2] ((300 × 20.83p) + (900 × 8%))
[3] ((300 × 8.33p) + (900 × 8%))
[4] ((300 × £1.91) + £900)

posed by acceptance of a cash offer and defers a potential capital gains tax liability, it will be attractive to many Seller plc shareholders. These shareholders are advised to be aware that the loan stock could trade at below par thereby reducing the value of the bid.

When a bidder faces conflicting returns to investors they sometimes solve the problem by offering several exchange options. For example, investors could be offered a share exchange or a cash alternative.

GROUP ACCOUNTS

When businesses combine, they are obliged to prepare group (consolidated) accounts thereafter. The rules for preparation of these accounts depend on whether the business combination is deemed to be an acquisition or a merger. In these group accounts only transactions with third parties are reported. For this reason, transactions between members of the group are eliminated. In the case of a merger the group profit and loss account shows all sales, costs and profits or losses for the financial period. In the case of an acquisition the group profit and loss account shows all the sales, costs, profits or losses of the acquirer but only the sales, costs, profits or losses of the company acquired from the date of acquisition.

Definition of a merger

A merger is defined in paragraph 44 of FRS 6, Acquisitions and mergers:

44 A merger is a rare type of business combination in which two or more parties come together for the mutual sharing of benefits and risks arising from the combined businesses, in what is in substance an equal partnership, each sharing influence in the new entity. No party can be regarded as acquiring control over another, or becoming controlled by another; and the reporting entity formed by the combination must be regarded as a new entity rather than the continuation of one of the combining entities, enlarged by its having obtained control over the others.

A number of criteria must be used to determine whether a business combination is a merger or not. These are presented in paragraphs 6–12 of FRS 6:

6 Criterion 1 – No party to the combination is portrayed as either acquirer or acquired, either by its own board or management or by that of another party to the combination.

7 Criterion 2 – All parties to the combination, as represented by the boards of directors or their appointees, participate in establishing the management structure for the combined entity and in selecting the management personnel, and such decisions are made on the basis of a consensus between the parties to the combination rather than purely by exercise of voting rights.

8 Criterion 3 – The relative sizes of the combining entities are not so disparate that one party dominates the combined entity by virtue of its relative size.

9 Criterion 4 – Under the terms of the combination or related arrangements, the consideration received by equity shareholders of each party to the combination, in relation to their equity shareholding, comprises primarily equity shares in the combined entity; and any non-equity consideration, or equity shares carrying substantially reduced voting or distribution rights, represents an immaterial proportion of the fair value of the consideration received by the equity shareholders of that party. Where one of the combining entities has, within the period of two years before the combination, acquired equity shares in another of the combining entities, the consideration for this acquisition should be taken into account in determining whether this criterion has been met.

10 For the purpose of paragraph 9, the consideration should not be taken to include the distribution to shareholders of:

a) An interest in a peripheral part of the business of the entity in which they were shareholders and which does not form part of the combined entity; or

b) The proceeds of the sale of such a business, or loan stock representing such proceeds.
   A peripheral part of the business is one that can be disposed of without having a material effect on the nature and focus of the entity's operations.

11 Criterion 5 – No equity shareholders of any of the combining entities retain any material interest in the future performance of only part of the combined entity.

12 For the purposes of paragraphs 6–11 above any convertible share or loan stock should be regarded as equity to the extent that it is converted into equity as a result of the business combination.

Accounting for a merger

The key rules of merger accounting are explained in paragraphs 16–19. These are as follows:

16 With merger accounting the carrying values of the assets and liabilities of the parties to the combination are not required to be adjusted to fair value on consolidation, although appropriate adjustments should be made to achieve uniformity of accounting policies in the combining entities (Companies Act 1985 4A Sch 11).

17 The results and cash flows of all the combining entities should be brought into the financial statements of the combined entity from the beginning of the financial year in which the combination occurred, adjusted so as to achieve uniformity of accounting policies. The corresponding figures should be restated by including the results for all the combining entities for the previous period and their balance sheets for the previous balance sheet date, adjusted as necessary to achieve uniformity of accounting policies.

18 The difference, if any, between the nominal value of the shares issued plus the fair value of any other consideration given, and the nominal value of the shares received in exchange should be shown as a movement on other reserves in the consolidated financial statements. Any existing balance on the share premium account or capital redemption reserve of the new subsidiary under- taking should be brought in by being shown as a movement on other reserves. These movements should be shown in the reconciliation of movements in shareholders' funds.

19 Merger expenses are not to be included as part of this adjustment, but should be charged to the profit and loss account of the combined entity at the effective date of the merger, as reorganization or restructuring expenses, in accordance with paragraph 20 of FRS 3, Reporting financial performance.

We will now examine how these rules are applied to the combination of two businesses that is eligible for merger accounting.

The two companies shown in Table 15.10 have agreed to merge. The merger will be effected by creating a holding company, Group C. The nominal value of the shares of Group C is £1 each. The exchange rate is one Group C share for 20 shares in Company A and one Group C share for 12 in Company B. The cost of the merger is £1.5 million. Group C decided to adopt the accounting policies of Company A. Applying these policies to Company B necessitated a reduction in the net assets and in the reserves of £0.8 million. Skeleton financial statements for Group C are as shown in Table 15.11.

Table 15.10 *Company A and Company B, which have agreed to merge*

£M	Company A	Company B
Net assets	<u>60</u>	<u>56</u>
Financed by:		
Share capital[1]	10	12
Reserves	<u>50</u>	<u>44</u>
	<u>60</u>	<u>56</u>

Note:
[1] Nominal value   5p   10p

Table 15.11 *Skeleton balance sheet, Group C*

	£ million
Net assets[1]	<u>113.7</u>
Financed by:	
Share capital[2]	20.0
Consolidation reserve[3]	2.0
Revenue reserve[4]	<u>91.7</u>
	<u>113.7</u>

The footnotes are to explain the figures and are not part of the financial statements.
Notes:

	£ million
[1] Net assets Company A	60.0
Net assets Company B	56.0
Harmonization adjustment	(0.8)
Restructuring expenses	<u>(1.5)</u>
	<u>113.7</u>

	Million
[2] Shares issued to Company A	10
Shares issued to Company B	<u>10</u>
	<u>20</u>

	Company A (million)	Company B (million)
[3] Nominal value of shares given	£10	£10
Nominal value of shares received	<u>£10</u>	<u>£12</u>
Consolidation reserve	–	£2

[4] £50 million + £44 million – £1.5 million – £0.8 million = £91.7 million

Definition of an acquisition

An acquisition is defined in paragraph 45 of FRS 6, Acquisitions and mergers:

45 An acquisition is defined as any business combination that is not a merger. In many acquisitions, the shareholders of the acquired party do not have a continuing interest in the combined entity, but instead sell their shareholdings for cash or other non-equity consideration. Even where all parties in an acquisition retain an interest in the combined entity, the parties do not come together on equal terms; one party has a greater degree of influence than the others, and is seen as acquiring the other entities in exchange for a share in the combined entity. An acquisition is therefore a transaction that is, in substance, the application of resources by the acquiring entity to obtain control of one or more other entities, by the payment of cash, transfer of other assets, the incurring of a liability or the issue of shares.

Accounting for acquisitions

The key rules are contained in paragraph 20 of FRS 6:

20 Business combinations not accounted for by merger accounting should be accounted for by acquisition accounting. Under acquisition accounting, the identifiable assets and liabilities of the companies acquired should be included in the acquirer's consolidated balance sheet at their fair value at the date of acquisition. The results and cash flows of the acquired companies should be brought into the group accounts only from the date of acquisition. The figures for the previous period for the reporting entity should not be adjusted. The difference between the fair value of the net identifiable assets acquired and the fair value of the purchase consideration is goodwill, positive or negative (Companies Act 1985 4A Sch 9).

Application of acquisition rules

In order to compare merger and acquisition accounting we will assume that Company A had acquired Company B. The following data are needed to prepare the group accounts (Table 15.12):

- Company A offered three of its shares for each four Company B shares.
- The value of Company A shares when the offer became unconditional was 70p.
- £1 million of the profits of Company B were earned post-acquisition.
- Fair value adjustments necessitated a reduction in the net assets of Company B of £2.5 million.

Table 15.12 *Comparison of Group C accounts (merger) and Group A accounts (acquisition)*

Skeleton balance sheet, Group A

	£'000
Goodwill [1]	10.5
Other net assets [2]	113.5
	124.0
Financed by:	
Share capital [3]	14.5
Share premium [4]	58.5
Revenue reserve [5]	51.0
	124.0

Notes:

[1] Value of net assets acquired	55.0[6]
Less fair value adjustment	2.5
	52.5
Purchase consideration (90 million × 70p)	63.0
Goodwill	10.5
[2] Net assets Company A	60.0
Net assets Company B at acquisition	55.0
Fair value adjustment company B	(2.5)
Post acquisition profit company B	1.0
	113.5

[3] (200 million × 5p + 90 million × 5p) = £14.5 million
The share capital of company B is cancelled against the purchase consideration.

[4] Market value of shares issued (90 million × 70p)	63.0
Nominal value of shares issued (90 million × 5p)	4.5
Share premium	58.5
[5] Reserves Company A	50.0
Post-acquisition profits company B	1.0
	51.0

[6] £1 million having been earned post acquisition, the value of the net assets before making the fair value adjustment would have been £55 million at the date of acquisition.
  The pre-acquisition profits of company B are cancelled against the purchase consideration.

	Group C	Group A
Goodwill		10.5
Other net assets	113.7	113.5
	113.7	124.0
Financed by:		
Share capital	20.0	14.5
Share premium		58.5
Consolidation reserve	2.0	
Revenue reserve	91.7	51.0
	113.7	124.0

The key difference between these balance sheets is the fact that the revenue reserve from which dividends can be paid is much higher in merger accounts. This is because all of the profits of both merging entities are available for distribution whereas in acquisition accounting only the post-acquisition profits of the subsidiary are available for distribution.

Major factors to be considered by a buyer when approaching an acquisition

When a company is considering an acquisition, the rules of 'Fair value in acquisition accounting' contained in FRS 7 should be considered because they can have substantial implications for subsequent group profit and loss accounts. The key principles are explained in paragraphs 5 and 6 while the application of these principles is explained in paragraphs 7 and 8 of the standard:

5 The identifiable assets and liabilities to be recognized should be those of the acquired entity that *existed at the date of the acquisition.*

6 The recognized assets and liabilities should be *measured at fair values* that reflect the conditions *at the date of the acquisition.*

7 As a consequence of the above principles, *the following do not affect fair values at the date of acquisition and therefore fall to be treated as post-acquisition items:*

a) changes resulting from the acquirer's intentions or future actions;
b) impairments, or other changes, resulting from events subsequent to the acquisition;
c) provisions or accruals for future operating losses or for reorganization and integration costs expected to be incurred as a result of the acquisition, whether they relate to the acquired entity or to the acquirer.

8 The application of these principles to specific classes of asset and liability is detailed in paragraphs 9–22 below. Subject to those paragraphs, fair values should be *determined in accordance with the acquirer's accounting policies for similar assets and liabilities.*

These regulations can have a substantial impact on future performance. First, the application of paragraph 7 is explained in paragraph 39 of the standard:

39 The FRS does not permit provisions for future losses or for reorganization costs expected to be incurred as a result of the acquisition to be included as liabilities acquired: they are not liabilities of the acquired entity as at the date of acquisition. As an example, if the acquirer decides to close a factory of the acquired entity as a measure to integrate the combined operations, this is a post-acquisition event. Only if the acquired entity was already committed to this course of action, and unable realistically to withdraw from it, would it be regarded as pre-acquisition. Similarly, if the acquirer undertakes a reorganization to integrate the acquired operation or to improve its efficiency, this is also a post-acquisition event.

Second, if purchased goodwill results from the inclusion of the acquisition then it will have to be amortized through the profit and loss account as required by FRS 10 and additional write-offs could arise as a result of an impairment review required by FRS 11.

Paragraphs 9–25 of FRS 7 contain guidance on the application rules for determining the fair value of assets and liabilities acquired. These rules are consistent with valuation instructions contained in other standards. The application of the rules is for preparers and auditors of group accounts and for this reason are not reproduced here.

The final important rule relates to expenses connected with the acquisition. Paragraph 28 specifies:

28 Fees and similar incremental costs incurred directly in making an acquisition should, except for the issue costs of shares or other securities that are required by FRS 4 'Capital instruments' to be accounted for as a reduction in the proceeds of a capital instrument, be included in the cost of acquisition. Internal costs, and other expenses that cannot be directly attributed to the acquisition, should be charged to the profit and loss account.

Note the difference between this rule and the one for merger accounting where the merger expenses are charged to the profit and loss account. To help you to understand the application of paragraph 28, the Group A balance sheet is now adjusted to reflect acquisition costs of £1 million; see Table 15.13 (p 404).

Table 15.13 *Skeleton balance sheet, Group A, including acquisition costs*

		£'000
Goodwill[1]		11.5
Other net assets[2]		112.5
		124.0
Financed by:		
Share capital		14.5
Share premium		58.5
Revenue reserve		51.0
		124.0
Notes:		
[1] Value of net assets acquired		55.0
Less fair value adjustment		2.5
		52.5
Purchase consideration (90 million × 70p)	63.0	
Acquisition costs	1.0	64.0
Goodwill		11.5
[2] Net assets Company A (net of acquisition costs)		59.0
Net assets Company B at acquisition		55.0
Fair value adjustment Company B		(2.5)
Post acquisition profit Company B		1.0
		112.5

SSAP 14 requires that, in respect of all material acquisitions during a year, the consolidated financial statements should contain sufficient information about the results of subsidiaries acquired to enable shareholders to appreciate the effect on the consolidated results.

SPECIAL CONSIDERATIONS IN MERGERS AND ACQUISITIONS

1. Investment in businesses listed on the stock exchange can be affected by two important rules:
   - when another business acquires a 30 per cent or greater stake in a company, the buyer is obliged to bid for the remaining equity;
   - the bidder is obliged to offer the highest price paid for any shares acquired in the last six months to all vendor shareholders.

2. The holder of 90 per cent of the shares in a subsidiary may be in a position to acquire compulsorily the remaining shares. The Companies Act 1985 rules that this can only be done within the six months following the offer becoming unconditional.

3. The acquiring company is faced with some major risks in undertaking a take-over:

    -   the cost (money and management time) can be very high. If the bid succeeds, management may neglect normal tasks as time is committed to integration. If the bid fails, there will be a large expenditure on merchant banking advice, 'due diligence' and communications with shareholders. These will have to be charged against the existing business and will reduce the profitability and financial stability;

    -   the valuation of assets being acquired may not be prudent: additional depreciation may be required when accounting policies are harmonized for consolidation; proper deductions may not have been made to reflect the realizable value of slow moving stock; and bad debt provisions may prove to be inadequate;

    -   customers and staff of the company being acquired may be less than happy with the new proprietors. This can result in lost sales, poor productivity and resignations by key staff. Service contracts provide some protection against the problems caused by resignations;

    -   liabilities may be understated;

    -   in a take-over attempt that is bitterly opposed, the vendor company management may create a 'poison pill'. Such techniques include: automatic transfer of attractive assets to third parties; creation of unacceptable levels of debt that are automatically taken up if the bid succeeds; retirement of key managers (with ridiculous 'golden handshakes') etc.

Most of these concerns can be handled in an agreed bid:

-   Warranties can be obtained relating to the realizable value of assets.
-   The buyer may choose not to take on the liabilities or obtain an indemnity against undisclosed items.
-   Part of the consideration can be deferred and made contingent on a defined level of future profit.
-   Indemnity can be requested against 'poison pills'.
-   Study of accounting policies to identify the size of harmonization adjustments can be undertaken.

In a contested bid these protections are difficult to arrange.

In spite of these concerns, take-over is often the most efficient way to expand or diversify a business. There are five basic categories of take-over:

1. Purchase of businesses that supply similar products or services to the same market, eg the merger of two UK newspapers. This type of acquisition is relatively low risk. Understanding of the products and customers and the potential to eliminate duplications in marketing, logistics and product development can make this type of business combination very rewarding.

2. Purchase of businesses that are supplying similar products or services to different markets, eg the acquisition of a UK newspaper by an Australian one. This type of acquisition is medium risk. The problem is that the acquirer has no experience of the market. Continuing involvement of the management of the acquired business helps to limit the risk.

3. Purchase of businesses that supply substantially different products or services to similar customers. The merger between Waterford Crystal and Josiah Wedgwood is a classic example. This type of acquisition is also medium risk. In the Waterford example the challenge arose from the fact that Waterford was strong in the United States and weak in the Far East, whereas Wedgwood was strong in the Far East and weak in the United States.

4. Conglomerate diversification, for example purchase of a clothing retailer by a computer manufacturer. If an acquisition involves a totally different technology and customer base, the risk increases dramatically. Such diversification was very popular in the 1980s. The companies involved and the stock market seemed to forget the huge catalogue of disasters in the history book. Of course, the exception proves the rule. In recent years conglomerates have tended to reverse this trend, leading to 'unbundling', which is dealt with below.

5. Purchase of a key supplier or customer. This type of take-over can be very attractive. Knowledge and experience in the business sector reduce the risk. It suffers from one major drawback: the lead-time from buying or creating products or services for sale to collection from third party customers lengthens. Substantial extra working capital is required. It is widely recognized that manufacturing and retailing are uncomfortable bedfellows.

The risk profile of the first four types of acquisition is presented in Figure 15.1.

Products

	Similar	Different
	Similar	Low risk	Medium risk
Markets			
	Different	Medium risk	High risk

Figure 15.1 *The risk profile of diversification strategies*

'UNBUNDLING'

The managements of many businesses, particularly conglomerates, have come to recognize that the value of the parts is greater than the stock market capitalization of the whole. In such cases it is appropriate to consider 'unbundling'. This is breaking up a group into discrete sections and giving shares in these sections to shareholders. The first major example in the UK was inspired by the Hoylake consortium bid for British American Tobacco. The objective was believed to be:

- to finance the acquisition mainly through 'junk bonds' (they had not yet been totally discredited);
- to sell all the non-tobacco subsidiaries and use the proceeds to repay the borrowings; and
- to wind up with a major tobacco business that cost relatively little.

On 26 September 1989 BAT announced its own demerger proposals. These involved a stock market flotation of the Argos retailing subsidiary and the Wiggins Teape Appleton pulp and paper division. BAT would issue free shares in the divisions to be quoted. Sir James Goldsmith, on behalf of Hoylake, voted in favour of the proposal. The free shares were issued and are now separately quoted. It remains a classic example of the value of the parts exceeding the whole.

A significant recent example is the 'unbundling' of Hanson Group plc. Holders of Hanson shares were given shares in four demerged business sections. Shareholders benefited from this action as the value of the individual investments greatly exceeded the pre-demerger value of their stake in Hanson.

SUMMARY

Successful take-over activity requires a high level of professionalism. A company must assess the potential of a large range of candidates correctly; the number of assessments that turn into bids is usually small. It must also be prepared to back down if the price becomes unrealistic. Megalomania has resulted in many acquisitions at ridiculous prices. Defining your maximum price and sticking to it is a rare and precious skill. If you go down the take-over trail the short-term cost can be high. In the longer term the payoff (for an excellent management team) can be attractive growth in earnings and share price. One of the great skills of companies with exceptional records for successful take-overs is their ability to manage the acquired businesses better than the previous owners. To be able to do this continuously and successfully requires excellent recruitment and training policies.

16

Any other business

You are nearing the end of a long but I hope valuable agenda. My final duty as chairman is to discuss any other business and to summarize our meeting. Six topic areas need to be discussed under 'any other business':

1. corporation tax;
2. group accounts;
3. deferred tax;
4. leased assets;
5. pension funds;
6. the life of a business.

CORPORATION TAX

The (legal) minimization of taxation liabilities is a highly specialized area. Financial directors of most businesses find it impossible to keep up to date with changes in tax legislation. They are prepared to pay significant fees to have the financial structure regularly examined for tax minimization opportunities and to ensure that any possible tax advantages or disadvantages associated with capital investment proposals, leasing, mergers and acquisitions, etc will be optimized.

The alternative is to permit tax planning to form part of the external audit. This can best be described as imprudent. The auditor focuses on what the liability is rather than what it might have been if the business had been structured for greater tax efficiency. Also, it is easier to design a tax-efficient structure in advance than to restructure at a later date. The cost of quality tax planning is high but it can have a significant impact on shareholder wealth. The wise business will be prepared to pay the price.

GROUP ACCOUNTS

Section 150 (1) of the Companies Act 1948 requires the presentation of group accounts to members of a holding company. The only exception is in section 150 (2), where the holding company at the end of its financial year is the wholly owned subsidiary of another body corporate incorporated in the UK. The preparation of group accounts involves the adding together of the financial results for the parent company and the subsidiaries. Rules of consolidation are explained in SSAP 14. These can be summarized as follows:

1. Transactions between group companies are excluded. Only sales, costs, assets and liabilities that relate to third party transactions are included. Items that need to be eliminated include:
    - supply of goods or services to other subsidiaries;
    - purchase of goods or services from other subsidiaries;
    - amounts owed to or from other subsidiary companies; and
    - inter-subsidiary service charges and dividends.
2. Profits legitimately recognized in the accounts of individual subsidiaries, but which have not been realized on sale to third parties, must be eliminated. Stock must be reduced to recognize the lower profit by increasing the cost of sales in the profit and loss account and reducing the value to the group in the balance sheet.
3. The cost of the acquisition (stated in the investing company balance sheet) must be eliminated against the shareholders' funds of the subsidiary in which the investment is made. (This was dealt with in Chapter 15, on accounting for mergers and acquisitions.)
4. Where the subsidiary is not wholly owned:
    - the full assets and liabilities, after adjusting for items 1 to 3 above, will be aggregated in the group balance sheet and the minority interest in the net assets recognized as long-term debt; and
    - the full sales, costs and profits, after adjusting for items 1 to 3 above, will be aggregated in the group profit and loss account. The minority

interest in the profits or losses must be deducted from the profit after tax and added to the minority shareholders' claim on the group net assets in the balance sheet.

5. Any dividends paid by subsidiaries to minority shareholders must be deducted from their share of the profit after tax and from their claim on net assets in the group balance sheet.

6. Accounts for individual group companies may use accounting policies different from the group. In the group accounts the results must be adjusted to ensure uniformity of accounting policies.

7. Wherever practicable, the financial statements of all subsidiaries should be prepared to the same accounting date and for identical accounting periods as the holding company.

Illustration of group accounts Dada plc

One year ago Dada plc acquired a 60 per cent stake in Baba Ltd for £870,000. The revenue reserves of Baba Ltd were £500,000 at that date. The balance sheets and profit and loss accounts of the individual companies and the group are presented in Table 16.1. These show how the above rules are applied in acquisition accounting.

DEFERRED TAX

Frequently the Inland Revenue gives relief for tax-deductible expenses in a way that is different from how these expenses are charged against the profit and loss account. This results in an unevenness in reporting the profit after tax even in cases where the accounting profit before tax is steady. It seems reasonable that when the pre-tax profit is the same from year to year, after making provision for tax the post-tax should also be the same. In order to allow this to happen FRS 19 requires that provision for deferred tax is made in cases where differences in the timing of tax allowances will reverse over time. The most important example arises from the fact that in order to ensure that all businesses are treated equally for corporation tax purposes, the Inland Revenue disallows depreciation and grants a writing down allowance in its place. The writing down allowance is 25 per cent of the reducing balance and this gives rise to the need for a deferred tax provision in most businesses. The following example shows the size of the distortion that would occur if deferred tax were not provided for and the effect that deferred tax provisions have on the profit and loss account and balance sheet.

Table 16.1 *The balance sheet and profit and loss account of the Papa plc group*

Balance sheets (£'000)

	Papa plc	Baba Ltd	Group
Tangible fixed assets at cost	5,000	1,000	6,000
Aggregate depreciation[1]	2,000	300	2,400
	3,000	700	3,600
Investment in Baba Ltd[2]	870		
Current assets			
Stock[3]	1,800	700	2,585
Debtors	2,500	800	3,300
Loan to parent[4]		300	
Cash	800	100	900
	5,100	1,900	6,785
Amounts due and payable in under one year			
Bank overdraft	300	600	900
Trade creditors	1,200	400	1,600
Loan from Baba Ltd[4]	200	–	–
	(1,700)	(1,000)	(2,500)
Net assets	7,270	1,600	7,885
Financed by:			
Share capital[5]	5,000	1,000	5,000
Revenue reserve[5] [6]	2,270	600	2,285
Minority interest[6]	–	–	600
	7,270	1,600	7,885

Notes:

[1] The fixed assets of both companies are two years old. Papa plc and the group use a depreciation policy of 20% straight line. Baba Ltd charges 15% straight line. In the group accounts the aggregate depreciation of Baba Ltd must be increased by £100,000. One half of this relates to last year and must be charged against pre acquisition profits. The balance relates to the current year.

[2] In the group accounts the investment in Baba Ltd is eliminated as follows:

	Papa plc	Minority
Share capital	600	400
Revenue reserve at date of acquisition	300	200
Depreciation adjusted	(30)	(20)
Eliminated	870	
Credited to minority		580[7]

Table 16.1   *(continued)*

[3] Baba Ltd sent goods costing £75,000 to Papa plc. It charged £100,000. The goods have not been received or included in the accounts of Papa plc. The goods sold by Baba Ltd must be taken into stock in Papa plc. The cost is determined by dividing the purchase into two parts:

	Inter-group	Minority	Total
Sale	60	40	100
Unrealized profit	15	–	15[4]
Stock Papa plc	45	40	85[4]

[4] The inter-company accounts must be brought into line for elimination:

	Papa plc	Baba Ltd
Per company accounts	200	300
Add stock [3]	85	
Less unrealized profit		15
Creditor eliminated on consolidation	285	
Debtor eliminated on consolidation		285

[5] The group revenue reserve is:

	Papa plc		Baba Ltd	Group
Per company accounts	2,270		600	
Less pre acquisition			500	
			100	
Less depreciation		50		
unrealized profit		15[3]	65	
			35	
Minority			20[6]	
Per balance sheet	2,270		15	2,285

[6] The minority shareholders are interested in 40% of the profits of Baba Ltd calculated from a group perspective. The £50,000 increase in the depreciation charge to harmonize accounting policies must be recognized in computing the minority interest. Consequently, their 40% claim on the post-acquisition profit net of the additional depreciation charge amounts to £20,000.

[7] The minority interest is:

At acquisition	580[2]
Post-acquisition	20[6]
	600

Table 16.1 *(continued)*

Profit and loss account	£'000		
	Papa plc	**Baba Ltd**	**Group**
Sales	10,000	3,000	12,900[7]
Opening stock	1,600	500	2,100
Purchases	7,100[a]	2,000	9,000[7]
	8,700	2,500	11,100
Closing stock	1,900[a]	700	2,585[3]
Cost of sales	6,800	1,800	8,515
Gross margin	3,200	1,200	4,385
Administration	800	470	1,270
Selling and distribution	750	426	1,176
Depreciation	1,000	150	1,200
	2,550	1,046	3,646
Profit before tax	650	154	739
Corporation tax	228	54	282
Profit after tax	422	100	457
Minority interest	–	–	20
Retained	422	100	437
Opening reserve	1,848	–	1,848
Closing reserve	2,270	100	2,285

[a] The purchases and closing stock of Papa plc are adjusted to reflect the full cost of the goods in transit from Baba Ltd in its own profit and loss account.

[7] The inter-company purchase and sale of £100,000 is not a third-party transaction. It is eliminated from the group purchases and sales. The valuation of stock in transit at £85,000 excludes the inter group profit other than the minority share. The group gross margin is therefore £15,000 less than the sum of the individual companies.

Smoothy Ltd commences business on 1 January. It buys and takes delivery of a machine at a cost of £1 million. The life of the machine is five years, after which the machine will be scrapped. As a consequence, Smoothy Ltd sets a depreciation policy of 20 per cent per annum straight line. Over the life of the machine it is expected to earn a profit of £450,000 pa before depreciation and £250,000 pa after depreciation; see Table 16.2.

At the end of year 5 a balancing allowance will be received when the machine is scrapped. The effect of this is that the full loss of value arising from the use of the machine in the business is allowed for tax purposes; see Table 16.3.

Table 16.2 _Calculation of writing down allowances and balancing allowance_

Year		£
1	Cost	1,000,000
	Writing down allowance (25%)	250,000
2	Written down value	750,000
	Writing down allowance (25%)	187,500
3	Written down value	562,500
	Writing down allowance (25%)	140,625
4	Written down value	421,875
	Writing down allowance (25%)	105,469
5	Written down value	316,406
	Balancing charge	316,406

Table 16.3 _Corporation tax computation, Smoothy plc_

Year	1	2	3	4	5	Total
Profit before depreciation	450,000	450,000	450,000	450,000	450,000	2,250,000
Tax allowance	250,000	187,500	140,625	105,469	316,406	1,000,000
Taxable profit	200,000	262,500	309,375	344,531	133,594	1,250,000
Tax at 25%	50,000	65,625	77,344	86,133	33,398	312,500

Table 16.4 _Profit and loss accounts, Smoothy plc, if deferred tax is ignored_

Year	1	2	3	4	5	Total
Profit before tax	250,000	250,000	250,000	250,000	250,000	1,250,000
Corporation tax	50,000	65,625	77,344	86,133	33,398	312,500
Profit after tax	200,000	184,375	172,656	163,867	216,602	937,500

Table 16.4 shows significant fluctuations in profit after tax that result from the uneven distribution of corporation tax deductions. It is reasonable to argue that the variations in profit after tax are caused by timing differences and that these will be eliminated over the five-year operating life of the asset. Consequently, Smoothy plc should take into account deferred tax. This will result in profits after tax being reported evenly over the five-year period. The

Table 16.5 *Difference between the corporation tax deductions and the depreciation charges*

Year			Depreciation	Difference	Difference at 25%
1	Cost	1,000,000			
	WDA (25%)	250,000	200,000	50,000	12,500
2	WDV	750,000			
	WDA (25%)	187,500	200,000	(12,500)	(3,125)
3	WDV	562,500			
	WDA(25%)	140,625	200,000	(59,375)	(14,844)
4	WDV	421,875			
	WDA (25%)	105,469	200,000	(94,531)	(23,633)
5	WDV	316,406			
	Balancing charge	316,406	200,000	116,406	29,102
				0	0

calculation of the differences and the deferred tax provisions are presented in Table 16.5.

Table 16.5 provides the basis for the deferred tax adjustments required in the profit and loss account. In the first year the accounting profit exceeds the taxable profit by £50,000. In order to provide for the timing difference that will reverse in subsequent years, a deferred tax provision of £12,500 must be made. This will be deducted from the profit before tax and treated as an amount that will become due and payable in beyond one year. In the second year the accounting profit will be lower than the taxable profit by £12,500. As a consequence, part of the timing difference recognized in year 1 will reverse and £3,125 of the deferred tax provision will be released to the profit and loss account. The balance of the deferred tax provision, £9,375 remains in the balance sheet. In the third year the accounting profit will again be lower than the taxable profit, this time by £59,375. The deferred tax adjustment at 25 per cent is £14,844. As this is greater than the balance of the provision remaining from year 1, deferred tax now becomes an asset of £5,469 that will be recovered in year 5. In the fourth year the accounting profit will again be lower than the taxable profit, this time by £94,531. The deferred tax adjustment at 25 per cent is £23,633. This increases the deferred tax asset to £29,102 that will be recovered in year 5. In year 5, as a result of the balancing allowance, the accounting profit will exceed the taxable profit by £116,406. The balance of the deferred tax asset accumulated in years 3 and 4 is then recovered.

The profit and loss accounts, including the deferred tax provisions, are reported in Table 16.6 as required by FRS 19.

Table 16.6 _Profit and loss accounts, Smoothy plc, including deferred tax_

Year	1	2	3	4	5	Total
Profit before tax	250,000	250,000	250,000	250,000	250,000	1,250,000
Corporation tax	(50,000)	(65,625)	(77,344)	(86,133)	(33,398	312,500
Deferred tax	(12,500)	3,125	14,844	23,633	(29,102)	0
Profit after tax	187,500	187,500	187,500	187,500	187,500	937,500

As a result of the deferred tax adjustments, Smoothy plc reports an equal amount of profit after tax in each year. This is consistent with the earning power of the asset and the profile of loss of value represented by the depreciation charge.

Deferred tax and net present value

Paragraph 42 permits but does not require reporting entities to discount deferred tax assets and liabilities to reflect the time value of money. Paragraph 52 advises that the discount rates to be used should be the post-tax yields to maturity that could be obtained at the balance sheet date on government bonds with maturity dates, and in currencies similar to those of the deferred tax assets or liabilities. A complex illustration is presented in Appendix 1 of the standard. We can safely leave it to the finance director and the auditors to decide whether to use discounting or not and to use appropriate discount rates if they decide to do so. For our purposes it is sufficient to note that the present value of the deferred tax adjustments will be lower than those used in the Smoothy plc illustration.

FRS 19 was issued in December 2000. It applies to accounting periods ending on or after 23 January 2002. Earlier adoption is encouraged.

LEASED ASSETS

Finance leases

A finance lease is one in which the user of a leased asset bears substantially all of the risks and rewards consistent with ownership. It should be presumed that this is the case when at the inception of the lease, the present value of the minimum lease payments, including any initial payment, amounts to substantially all (normally 90 per cent or more) of the fair value of the leased asset. This present value should be calculated using the interest rate implicit in the lease. The methodology for calculating present value was described in Chapter 12.

When a finance lease is commenced, the lessee (user of the asset) records the item both as an asset (which will be depreciated in line with normal accounting policy) and as a liability (broken into current and non-current components). This treatment, introduced in August 1984, is interesting. The lessor is the legal owner of the asset. The asset is not recorded in the lessor's balance sheet. What is really owned is a stream of future payments from the lessee. The lessee is not the owner. The leased item is nevertheless recorded as a leased fixed asset. Whether the lease proves profitable or not, the lessee has the use of a depreciating asset, its ongoing earnings potential, and obligations to repay instalments that are very similar to those arising under a term loan or hire purchase agreement.

There are two major reasons for this treatment. First, the balance sheets of financial institutions were becoming silly. They showed many tangible fixed assets suited to lessees' needs rather than banks' needs. SSAP 21 is designed to reflect the 'true' asset, a stream of future cash in the lessor's balance sheet. Second, the balance sheets of lessees did not reveal the scale of future repayment obligations implicit in their finance leases. This was off-balance sheet finance. SSAP 21 was the first step by the Accounting Standards Board to try to cope with the problem.

Tables 16.7 to 16.9 (Table 16.9 is on p 420) show how the profit and loss account and balance sheet of a company using a finance lease compare with those of a term borrower. The data for the tables are as follows:

- Alpha Ltd wishes to acquire a machine at a cost of £1 million.
- Alpha is quoted £437,977 per annum for three years repayable in arrears. It can be arranged as a term loan or a finance lease. An interest rate of 15 per cent is involved in both quotations.
- The machine will have a three-year operating life. It is expected to have a disposal value of £1.
- A profit before interest and depreciation of £700,000 is expected.
- In this first example corporation tax is ignored.

The figures would be exactly the same if the asset were funded by term-loan finance except for the labelling of the debt. Prior to SSAP 21 the asset and

Table 16.7 *Schedule of lease repayments*

£'000 Year	Loan	Interest	Repaid	Loan	Current	Non-current
1	1,000	150	438	712	331	381
2	712	107	438	381	381	
3	381	57	438			

Table 16.8 *Lessee balance sheets*

£'000 Year	0	1	2	3
Machine	1,000	1,000	1,000	1,000
Depreciation	–	333	667	1,000
Book value	1,000	667	333	1
Cash[1]	–	262	524	786
	1,000	929	857	787
Financed by:				
Retained profit	–	217	476	787
Lease current	288	331	381	–
Lease non-current	712	381	–	–
	1,000	929	857	787

Note:
[1] Cash balances:

Year	1	2	3
Opening cash	–	262	524
Profit	700	700	700
	700	962	1,224
Repayment	438	438	438
Closing cash	262	524	786

the underlying borrowings would not have been included in the balance sheet. The figures would have appeared as shown in Table 16.10 (p 420).

Prior to SSAP21 the lease payments were treated as a running expense rather than the underlying depreciation and interest, and the leased asset was not capitalized. This results in a balance sheet that does not show a 'true and fair view' because substantial debt is concealed; see Table 16.11 (p 420).

Table 16.9 *Lessee profit and loss accounts*

£'000 Year	1	2	3
Pre interest and depreciation	700	700	700
Less depreciation	(333)	(333)	(333)
Finance charge	(150)	(107)	(57)
Profit year	217	260	310
Cumulative profit	217	477	787

Table 16.10 *Lessee balance sheets prior to SSAP 21*

£'000 Year	1	2	3
Cash	262	524	786
Financed by:			
Retained profit	262	524	786

Table 16.11 *Lessee profit and loss accounts prior to SSAP 21*

£'000 Year	1	2	3
Profit before lease instalment	700	700	700
Lease instalment	438	438	438
Pre SSAP 21 profit			
	262	262	262
Cumulative profit	262	524	786

Corporation tax and finance leases

Corporation tax complicates accounting for a finance lease. We will now look at the same example including corporation tax. The results are shown in Table 16.12.

Table 16.12 *Lessee accounts including corporation tax and deferred tax*

SSAP 21 Lessee balance sheet including corporation tax and deferred tax

Year	0	1	2	3
Machine	1,000,000	1,000,000	1,000,000	1,000,000
Depreciation	–	333,333	666,667	1,000,000
Book value	1,000,000	666,667	333,333	0
Deferred tax[3]		11,339	11,879	0
Cash[1]	0	262,023	458,540	655,058
	1,000,000	940,029	803,752	655,058
Financed by:				
Retained profit	0	162,500	357,397	589,552
Corporation tax[2]		65,506	65,506	65,506
Debt current	287,977	331,174	380,849	0
Debt non-current	712,023	380,849	0	0
	1,000,000	940,029	803,752	655,058

Lessee profit and loss accounts allowing for deferred tax

Year	1	2	3
Operating profit	700,000	700,000	700,000
Less depreciation	(333,333)	(333,334)	(333,333)
Finance charge	(150,000)	(106,803)	(57,127)
Pre-tax profit	216,667	259,863	309,540
Corporation tax[2]	(65,506)	(65,506)	(65,506)
Deferred tax[3]	11,339	540	(11,879)
Profit for year	162,500	194,897	232,155
Cumulative profit		357,397	589,552

Notes:

[1] Cash balances	Y1	Y2	Y3
Opening cash	0	262,023	458,540
Profit	700,000	700,000	700,000
	700,000	962,023	1,158,540
Corporation tax		(65,506)	(65,506)
Repayment	(437,977)	(437,977)	(437,976)
Closing cash	262,023	458,540	655,058

421

Table 16.12 *(continued)*

(2) Corporation tax	Y1	Y2	Y3
Operating profit	700,000	700,000	700,000
Lease instalment	437,977	437,977	437,976
Taxable profit	262,023	262,023	262,024
Corporation tax (25%)	65,506	65,506	65,506

The tax treatment of finance leases has not changed as the result of the introduction of SSAP 21. The depreciation and finance charge are disallowed in the lessee tax computation. The lease payments are allowed in their place. The lessor is allowed the writing down allowances as a tax deduction and is charged to tax on the lease instalments.

(3) Deferred tax	1	2	3
Finance charge	150,000	106,803	57,127
Depreciation	333,333	333,333	333,334
Accounting expenses	483,333	440,136	390,461
Lease instalment	437,977	437,977	437,976
Difference	45,356	2,159	(47,515)
Deferred tax (25%)	11,339	540	(11,879)
Deferred tax balance	11,339	11,879	0

The fact that the lease instalments are deductible for corporation tax purposes gives rise to the need for deferred tax provisions calculated above. This eliminates the timing difference that will reverse.

A different treatment for operating leases

An operating lease is one that does not transfer substantially all the risks and rewards of ownership of an asset to the lessee. If it is clear that, after netting out the finance charge, less than 90 per cent of the capital cost is repaid through the life of the lease, then it is an operating lease. Operating leases are treated as follows: a) the asset remains on the balance sheet of the lessor and is not included in the balance sheet of the lessee; b) the lease instalments are taxable in the hands of the lessor and are allowed as a deductible expense in computing the tax liability of the lessee.

Because of this treatment, future repayment using an operating lease could conceal major obligations. SSAP 21 makes certain this will not happen. The user of an asset under an operating lease is required to disclose the operating lease rentals in its profit and loss account. The user also has to disclose, in the notes attached to the balance sheet, the payments that it is committed to make in future years, analysed between those in which the commitment expires within that year, in the second to fifth years inclusive, and over five years from the balance sheet date. An intelligent examination of the notes to the balance sheet will enable a reader to understand the scale of operating lease activities and the ongoing repayment obligations involved.

A simple example of an operating lease is a five-year lease on an aeroplane. The lessee could expect to pay far less than 90 per cent of the capital cost over the lease period. The life of an aircraft is perhaps 20 years. The lessor takes most of the risks and rewards consistent with ownership by having to locate a lessee or purchaser for the asset on expiry of the operating lease.

PENSION FUNDS

The publicity that surrounded the pension funds of the Maxwell companies served to highlight the important principles of pension funding:

- The assets are not owned by the employer organization.
- The value of the fund investments should not be inextricably tied to the fortunes of the employer organization.
- Any outstanding contributions to a scheme should be accrued.
- Regular actuarial assessments of solvency should be carried out and reported to fund members and in the case of a deficiency the action, if any, being taken to deal with it in the current and future accounting periods should be specified in the financial accounts. Disclosure requirements for published accounts are documented in FRS 17.

There are two major types of pension funds: defined contribution schemes and defined benefit schemes.

Defined contribution schemes

A defined contribution scheme is one in which an employer commits to pay a specific proportion of salaries and wages into a pension fund. The size of the pension benefits that will be paid to employees depends on the performance of the fund managers. Investment gains will enhance pension benefits while investment losses will reduce them.

Accounting for defined contribution schemes is reasonably straightforward. Paragraph 7 of FRS 17 requires that the contributions payable to the scheme for an accounting period should be recognized within operating profit in the profit and loss account. Where the defined contribution has not

423

been paid to the pension fund by the end of the accounting period, the amount will be accrued and carried in amounts due and payable in under one year in the balance sheet.

Defined benefit schemes

A defined benefit scheme is one in which an employer commits to pay a specific pension to retired former employees. Accounting for such schemes is rather more complicated. The key is to recognize that the pension fund is invested in scheme assets and that these must be sufficient to meet the scheme liabilities, which are future pension payment obligations. Paragraph 14 of the standard requires that the assets of a defined benefit scheme should be measured at fair value on the balance sheet date. The mid-market value of quoted securities is taken as the fair value. The scheme liabilities must be measured on an actuarial basis. This is done by assessing the present value of the pension obligations given the service of the employees to date. Paragraph 35 of the standard requires a full actuarial valuation at intervals not exceeding three years.

The employer should recognize an asset to the extent that it is able to recover a surplus either through reduced contributions in the future or through refunds from the scheme. The employer should recognize a liability to the extent that it reflects its legal or constructive obligation. There are substantial disclosure requirements required by FRS 17 in the case of defined benefit schemes. These are designed so that readers of the financial statements can understand the implications of the scheme for future contribution obligations and scheme assets and liabilities. The preparation and presentation of the disclosures required can best be left to the professionals.

THE LIFE OF A BUSINESS

The last item on the agenda is to summarize the meeting. I have decided to do this by tracing our way through the life of a business as if it were a person. There are five stages.

1. Business infancy

It is a frightening fact that the majority of new businesses in the UK die in infancy. Some of the reasons for the high mortality rate have a strong financial dimension:

- The promoter starts business life with too little capital.
- The sales forecast is too optimistic; product returns and rejects are high; the business is slow to get customer acceptance.
- Necessary tangible fixed assets are overlooked.
- Running expenses are underestimated. For example, a promoter might overlook the cost of scrappage or rework when a product is damaged in production.
- It is unfortunately true that to borrow money is cheaper and easier for a large and stable business than a fledgling. Not only are interest rates higher (which is understandable, because the risk is usually greater) but also some of the cheapest sources are closed to the infant. The most expensive legitimate sources include hire purchase; leasing; debt factoring; bill and invoice discounting; instalment payment schemes, eg insurance; and bridging loans. The most economic sources include:
  - authorized supplier credit. It is well worth the promoter's time to negotiate good supplier credit terms, as John Bermingham did in Chapter 3;
  - customer deposits and cash-with-order or cash-on-delivery sales. The business that can get these starts life with a decided edge; and
  - additional equity capital. Most new business promoters want to own 100 per cent of their infant. This is fine if it can be properly controlled. For many infant businesses the right thing to do is to give away a stake in the company before conception or early in life. There are five major sources:
    - a) an active partner, ideally with different skills and experience from the promoter;
    - b) a sleeping partner, ideally with strong skills in areas where the promoter is deficient;
    - c) a venture capital injection: it is difficult to attract venture capital before start-up even in state-of-the-art technology. The more mundane business must wait until a track record is established. The major advantages are opening doors to cheap sources of finance, strong board representation and conservation of cash. The investor is seeking capital appreciation, not dividends;
    - d) business expansion scheme equity. The advantages are similar to venture capital. The BES may give the promoter more freedom than a venture capitalist; and
    - e) equity investment by a key supplier or customer. They know the industry well and often provide specialized help at little or no cost.

425

- I strongly recommend that the infant business adopts one of these equity sources. It will enable it to grow more rapidly. Growth leads to sturdy adulthood and an opportunity to buy back the equity.
- Failure to provide funds to meet the working capital needs of a fast-growth business. I said much about over-trading in Chapter 7. The partnership can provide the funds for expansion.
- The business cannot afford professional managers. The owner puts financial priorities on the back burner. These include preparation of management accounts; review and revision of cash forecasts; managing suppliers and bankers; and identifying and claiming grants. The partnership can overcome this problem by ensuring that there are two senior staff to perform key tasks.

2. Childhood

If the infant survives to school days it will have to learn to cope with a new set of problems:

- Only one string (product) to its bow. Any business that is totally dependent on one product is likely to be pressured to diversify and spread the risk.
- The child has not been able to save the money it needs for product or market diversification.
- The promoter has been too busy surviving to keep up to date with industry technology and changing customer needs.
- The child has grown big enough to be a thorn in the side of important competitors. They use price wars, extended credit and other dirty tricks to spank it.
- A local financial engineer wants to play with the toys and mounts an unwanted take-over bid. The child neglects the business while protecting itself.
- A major customer knows that the child is too dependent on its orders. It demands large discounts and over-extended credit.
- The business has grown to a size where to manage all the priorities is too much for the child (ambitions to be world champion in five different sports). The wise promoter will bring in the gang (professional managers). The trouble is that they want to play different games and he won't let them. If they are good they leave and play elsewhere. If they are not good they stay and keep the company stuck in a groove.

- The Inland Revenue realizes the child is 'rich'. It takes away 20–25 per cent of its new toys each year. The 'selfish' child wants these toys to play expansion and other games.

The child is so depressed by this treadmill that it wishes it could just go to school and play like other kids. The analogy I used is sadly true for most youthful businesses. A minority manage to break through the clouds to a high-flying and enjoyable teenage period. How do they do it? The answer is two words: planning and people. It sounds simple and obvious, and it is.

Managers can be classified into fire fighters and planners. The fire fighters spend all their time trying to combat the latest problems. The planners try to anticipate problems before they occur and take steps to avoid them.

Planning

Many of the problems that people experience through their lives can be traced back to their formative years. It is the same with young businesses. Top-quality planning from the outset can help to overcome many of the childhood problems outlined above.

The business should plan to retain a substantial part of its earnings. These:

- contribute towards funding the cost of the search for new products or services;
- strengthen the equity base as defence against an unwanted take-over bid;
- help to fight a price or discount war mounted by a larger competitor; and
- permit the recruitment of top-class managers for marketing, finance and other functions.

The promoter must plan for sufficient time to identify problems and find ways of avoiding them rather than waiting until they occur and winding up on a crisis treadmill. This is easier to say than do. The natural instinct of the child is to defend itself against the current crisis and put off planning for tomorrow. It requires a very special kind of experience and dedication to ensure that high-quality planning is not sacrificed on the altar of fire fighting.

People

Friends have a very important role in shaping a child in its formative years. The sensible child recognizes that many things occur in business that are difficult to handle owing to lack of previous experience. One way of coping effectively with this is to identify a mentor to offer advice when important issues arise. The mentor is often a person related to the promoter that is prepared to spend time exploring issues and providing second opinions. The effective mentor has three vital qualities: a wide knowledge of business issues; a network of people who can be tapped for specialized advice on key matters; and a financial independence that will allow him or her to advise the business without charging a lot for the service.

Such people are difficult to find. One must be located and cultivated. If an appropriate mentor is not available within the family, the promoter can use a suitable sleeping partner, venture capitalist or other investor, but they usually expect to be well paid.

If the planning and people issues are properly managed the business can look forward to an enjoyable childhood. Issues on which the mentor can provide important help include capital project appraisal, corporation tax management, stock market flotation and market and product diversification.

3. The teens

It may take less than 13 years for a business to reach its teens. This period usually involves an introduction to courtship. The wise promoter will be anxious to avoid the danger of an undesirable marriage (take-over). The promoter usually uses a merchant bank to advise on a suitable partner. Many of the important issues in planning a suitable marriage were explained in Chapter 15. If the discussions and negotiations lead to a merger or acquisition, then family financial reporting (group accounts) will have arrived. A brief summary of the important issues involved in group accounting was presented earlier in this chapter.

4. Adulthood

The business is now mature. A new set of responsibilities is in place. As a parent it must protect its children (the employees and shareholders). Many of the risks that were taken as a child are no longer acceptable. Strangely, many adult businesses make decisions that are inconsistent with responsible parenthood. These include leveraged buyouts, currency speculation, commodity and interest rate futures, conglomerate diversification and financial engineering.

The responsible parent needs to put two key control mechanisms in place. First, there should be excellent systems to ensure that managers cannot commit the organization to major initiatives that could endanger its very survival if they go wrong. These would involve limitations on authority to undertake capital investment, foreign currency transactions, tax based leasing, etc without approval from the board of directors. Second, there needs to be a board of directors with the skills, experience and authority to stop decisions being made which could put the business at risk. They must be prepared to stop proposals by senior executives where necessary.

5. Old age

An objective of a business should be never to reach old age. The conditions to avoid if the secret of eternal youth is to be found and applied are:

- An ageing management team, set in its ways and resistant to change.
- A portfolio of products that have passed the peak of their life cycle.
- Plant and machinery incapable of competing with the modern equipment of competitors.
- Over-dependence on reputation and lack of attention to quality of product or service.
- A corporate climate that discourages entrepreneurial flair and over-rewards safe behaviour.

The key ways of overcoming the malaise of corporate old age are:

- A planned approach to management succession. This involves training, retraining, recruitment, promotions, etc.
- A target to replace at least 10 per cent in value of group sales with new products or services each year.
- Adherence to the guideline in Chapter 6 that expenditure on tangible fixed assets should average at least 1.4 times the depreciation charge.
- A constant updating of key staff through contact with customers, competitors, development agencies and management training institutions.
- A rewards system (salaries, profit sharing, share options, fringe benefits, etc) that recognizes the contribution of the old stagers whose key role is often defensive and the 'young bloods' whose creative and entrepreneurial spirit will maintain the pace of modernization if constructively controlled.

SUMMARY OF OUR MEETING

- Directors and managers must fully understand the financial consequences of the business decisions in which they are involved.

- It is unlikely that you will remember all the applications we encountered during the book.
- I urge you to keep the book in your office and refer to it when important financial decisions are on the agenda for future management or board meetings.
- Don't forget that no matter how carefully you studied the book, the pressures of business life will allow key issues to slip into oblivion unless you practise applying them.
- The world is changing rapidly. Major developments in accounting and finance will undoubtedly take place in this decade. To keep up with the pace of change you need to read the business page of a quality newspaper every day, keep wide awake for new financial issues mentioned by accountants, bankers, etc at board meetings, and never be afraid to ask questions about things you don't understand. Your colleagues probably don't understand them either!

If you have any queries about applying some of the material in this book you can contact me by e-mail at rfft@eircom.net.

Appendix

SOLUTION TO INCOME CALCULATION TEST IN CHAPTER 2

Table A.1 *Solution to income test in Chapter 2*

Total Income	Units	Sales £	VAT £	Invoiced £
Full price	18	720.00	126.00	846.00
Discount price	2	72.00	12.60	84.60
	20	792.00	138.60	930.60
Less credit note not yet issued	1	40.00	7.00	47.00
	19	752.00	131.60	883.60
Debtors		£		£
Amount invoiced				930.60
Less 11 items settled[1]		512.30		
Credit note due		47.00		
Discount allowed (5 at £47 × 2%)		4.70		
Bad debt		47.00		611.00
Total debtors[2]				319.60

Notes:
[1] $(6 \times £47) + (5 \times £47 \times 98\%)$
[2] $(5 \times £47) + (2 \times £42.30)$

VAT liability	**£**
Amount invoiced	131.60
Less VAT element of returnable item	7.00[1]
Due to Revenue Commissioners	124.60

Notes:

[1] When the defective goods are returned, we will be able to reduce our VAT payable by a further £7.

[2] A bad debt of £40 excluding VAT; and b) A settlement discount of £1.88.

SOLUTION TO JOHN BERMINGHAM'S CURRENT ASSETS IN CHAPTER 3

Table A.2 *Solution to John Bermingham's current assets question in Chapter 3*

Current assets week 10	
Raw material stocks[1]	9,000
Work in progress	220
Finished goods[2]	4,800
Trade debtors[3]	7,520
Cash[4]	1,100
	22,640

Notes:
[1] Material stock

Week	Purchases	Issues	Stock units	Unit cost	Stock value
5			910		9,100
6	100	110	900	10	9,000
7	120	120	900	10	9,000
8	120	120	900	10	9,000
9	120	120	900	10	9,000
10	120	120	900	10	9,000
	580	590			

(2) Finished stock

Week	Units produced	Units sold	Closing units	Unit cost £	Stock value £
5			225		2,700
6	110	55	280	12	3,360
7	120	90	310	12	3,720
8	120	90	340	12	4,080
9	120	90	370	12	4,440
10	120	90	400	12	4,800
	590	415			

(3) Sales and debtors

Week	Units sold	Unit price £	Sales revenue £	Cash collected £	Debtors £
5					3,920
6	55	16	880		4,800
7	90	16	1,440	640	5,600
8	90	16	1,440	640	6,400
9	90	16	1,440	880	6,960
10	90	16	1,440	880	7,520
	415		6,640	3,040	

(4) Cash

Week	Opening cash £	Payments suppliers £	Production £	Customer collections £	Closing cash £
6	5,040	(1,000)		(220)	3,820
7	3,820	(1,200)	(240)	640	3,020
8	3,020	(1,200)	(240)	640	2,220
9	2,220	(1,200)	(240)	880	1,660
10	1,660	(1,200)	(240)	880	1,100

SOLUTION TO NPV QUESTIONS IN CHAPTER 12

Table A.3 *Solution to NPV questions in Chapter 12*

NPV project A at 14%			NPV project B at 14%		
Year	Cell	Cash flow	Year	Cell	Cash flow
1	C6	80000	1	F6	140000
2	C7	90000	2	F7	110000
3	C8	110000	3	F8	90000
4	C9	140000	4	F9	80000
	C10	296566		F10	315562
	Invested	300000		Invested	300000
	NPV	−3434		NPV	15562

Project A will not yield a 14% return. Project B, because of the front-end loading of the cash flows, yields a small positive NPV. The company should consider investing in it unless another project that offers a better return can be found.

AUTHOR'S NOTE

Since I completed this book and passed it to my publisher a number of major accounting scandals have rocked the business world, mainly in the United States. The mechanisms used were all designed to boost the profit and loss account and earnings per share. They involved either the capitalization of expenditure that should have hit the profit and loss or the recognition of income that had not yet been earned. These scandals have sent stock markets tumbling as trust for chief executives, finance directors and auditors collapsed.

I believe that these fraudulent manipulations are examples of a small number of bad eggs in a very large basket. Undoubtedly international stock markets will rebound as trust is rebuilt. The only question for investors is how long it will take.

Ray Fitzgerald
July 2002

Index